The Constitutional Systems of Central-Eastern, Baltic and Balkan Europe

Comparative Public Law Treatise

Founded by Giuseppe Franco Ferrari

The Constitutional Systems of Central-Eastern, Baltic and Balkan Europe

Angela di Gregorio (Ed.)

eleven
international publishing

Published, sold and distributed by Eleven International Publishing
P.O. Box 85576
2508 CG The Hague
The Netherlands
Tel.: +31 70 33 070 33
Fax: +31 70 33 070 30
email: sales@elevenpub.nl
www.elevenpub.com

Sold and distributed in USA and Canada
Independent Publishers Group
814 N. Franklin Street
Chicago, IL 60610, USA
Order Placement: +1 800 888 4741
Fax: +1 312 337 5985
orders@ipgbook.com
www.ipgbook.com

Eleven International Publishing is an imprint of Boom uitgevers Den Haag.

This volume has been published with the contribution of Fondazione Cariplo.
This volume was reviewed through a double-blind peer review procedure.

ISBN 978-94-6236-965-8
ISBN 978-94-6274-493-6 (e-book)

Preface

The Comparative Public Law Treatise results from a desire to publish one single study providing a full panorama of comparative public law. Its aim is in fact to offer the reader – including scholars and students as well as the general reader – an overview, a summary and an original presentation of comparative knowledge in the area of public law, including both an account and summary of the various schools of thought as well as also, where possible, the development of original lines of thinking.

Considering the objective of the Treatise it has been decided that it will extend to more than 50 volumes, in order to ensure a detailed analysis of the issues of greatest interest from a comparative perspective. Whilst the project as a whole will be characterised by a cross-systemic approach, it will include particular monographic studies of the most significant legal systems around the world. In doing so, the aim is to give a voice to the two focuses of comparative study, first the science of comparison *stricto sensu*, and secondly the study of foreign legal systems.

In any case, the unifying characteristic of the study is its broad approach. This is not so much, or in any case not only, due to the number of volumes but rather to the choice that, within a globalised world, comparative law must open itself up to the greatest possible number of legal systems. Starting from this premise the monographic studies will seek to analyse many of the legal systems that have traditionally remained on the margins of comparative law studies.

Finally, the choice to use three languages (Italian, English and Spanish) offers a further demonstration of the broad approach of the Treatise. This is the first time that a study of comparative public law has been conveyed at the same time in three languages. The objective is not only to ensure the wide circulation of the study within the international academic community, but above all to promote and favour a more ample dialogue between different legal cultures.

Milan 2018

Giuseppe Franco Ferrari

Table of Contents

List of Contributors

Authors

Angela Di Gregorio is full Professor of Comparative Public Law at the University of Milan, Italy. Her reasearch interests include constitutionalism and transition to democracy; the dynamics of European integration from the constitutional point of view (i.e. relationships between legal sources and courts); transitional justice.

Jan Sawicki has a PHD in Comparative Public Law at the University of Rome "La Sapienza" and taught Public Law, Comparative Public Law and Constitutional Transitions at "La Sapienza", Università Cattolica di Milano and Università degli Studi di Milano. His current interests involve, on the one hand, democratic transitions – as well as the recent and partial authoritarian backsliding – in Central and Eastern Europe, and constitutional aspects of economic governance, in comparative perspective, on the other.

Arianna Angeli is a Researcher of Comparative Public Law at the University of Milan. Her research interests include territorial decentralization, local self-government, as well as democratization processes and constitutional regressions.

Čarna Pištan is a Postdoctoral Research Fellow in Comparative Public Law at the University of Udine and an Affiliated Researcher at the *Center for Constitutional Studies and Democratic Development* (CCSDD), a partnership between the Johns Hopkins University SAIS Europe in Bologna and the University of Bologna. Her research interests include democratic transitions, constitutional justice, forms of government, and human rights in Central and Eastern Europe and post-Soviet Union sphere.

Editor's Foreword

This volume provides a comparative perspective of the constitutional developments of countries in a specific area of Europe, which is defined as 'Central-Eastern, Baltic and Balkan' (CEBBE).

This is a region whose components came late to state independence following the aftermath of several foreign dominations or other forms of colonization.

The need for a joint analysis of the countries in this region is based on a number of drivers with common historical and constitutional features. In the majority we are dealing with countries that have only recently begun to meet the minimum requirements of liberal-democratic constitutionalism despite having a history of short-lived political phases based on these principles.

The unique historical and cultural heritage, as well as the ethnic and linguistic complexity of these countries demands a deep and detailed constitutional analysis. This approach observes both the first stage of constitutionalism following the seizing of statehood and the later, more complex transitions brought about the succession of different forms of political and state organization.

We start by recognizing that the complexity of constitutional developments is not simply a series of political and state fractures through history (an evolutionary upheaval not found in the rest of Europe), but is also a product of ethnically uneven population compositions. Over the centuries the ethno-national structure of these lands has undergone several transformations, a dynamism that has yet to stabilize.

Their entry into the Council of Europe and, for some of the countries being analysed, also in the European Union has not led to constitutional 'pacification'. Prior to their entry (the 'application' process), the study of constitutional transformations in these countries was the subject of close worldwide scrutiny. However, since their entry attention has wandered if only because of a misplaced confidence in the miraculous ability of democratic conditionality and in the belief that societies with deeply different historical, cultural and social contexts could be shaped so easily by the Euro-Atlantic constitutionalism.

Developments, which began in 2010 marked by the conservative turning point in Hungary, brought the constitutional dynamics of these countries back under the magnifying glass of scholars who have observed, if a little hastily, a marked constitutional backsliding.

The constitutional crisis caused by the rise of populism has called into question many former certainties, in particular respect for and compliance with the European Union values and existing mechanisms to address such challenges. These events in the new members states served as a catalyst to uncover existing weaknesses in the underlying European Union.

The dominant theory in current political and constitutional literature is that there is a failure of constitutionalism in the countries of Central-Eastern, Baltic and Balkan Europe. This volume factors in the need for a long-term observation of the evolution of constitutionalism and does not accept that it has failed. Further, it is necessary to take into account the existing variety of situations and the need for constant and meticulous attention by constitutional scholarship. It is essential to carry out deep scientific analysis and minimize moral judgments based on individual cases, often riding the wave of emotionality. This does not mean to trivialize the constitutional degeneration in progress in Poland and Hungary, but rather to place it in a wider spatial and temporal context.

The countries of Central-Eastern, Baltic and Balkan Europe have constitutional roots going back in history to the beginning of the twentieth century, roots which were expressly or implicitly recovered following the end of the socialist regimes. Because of this fractured path of constitutional development, the democratic institutions of these countries today appear fragile. However, these institutions are still significant and vital despite the continuing opposition of a 'mature' Western perspective that persists on seeing them through its own peculiar lenses. The deviations from Western models are not forgiven in fact are condemned, apparently on a moral basis, to perpetuate the myth of 'Eastern Europe'; a collection of fascinating, chaotic, nationalist and, in recent years, more and more 'sovereignist' countries. In this volume we offer constitutional specialists a starting point for future and alternative observations.

Angela Di Gregorio, April 2019

1 Transition to Democracy in the Countries of Central-Eastern, Baltic and Balkan Europe

Angela Di Gregorio

1.1 Problems of History and Method: The Reason for Focusing on This Particular Geographical Area and Its Many Varied and Complex Differences

Commencing in 1989 and proceeding over a number of years the fall of the socialist system of government involved a large number of Central-Eastern, Baltic and Balkan European countries (CEBBE).[1] This event has great relevance for constitutional law as well as having complex historic, economic and geopolitical significance. It can be regarded as a constitutional laboratory allowing one to analyse, after the fact, the transitions of very complex phenomenon that can only be described with the aid of a multi-structured approach,[2] especially given that the transition occurred on several levels (political, ideological, economic, cultural, national, generational and international), each on different time scales and with varying results.[3]

The traditional scheme used to describe the transition to democracy from the political and institutional point of view is typically composed of several phases such as the political transition with initial free elections,[4] the adoption of a new constitution and the consolidation of democracy.[5] However, in this particular case, this approach is not entirely useful.

1 The necessity to define this area in a geographical manner derives from the need to avoid the use of terms such as 'post-socialist' or 'post-communist' Europe, which seem today to be inappropriate.

2 *See* the more 'holistic' approach to the study of constitutional comparative law by R. Hirschl, 'From Comparative Constitutional Law to Comparative Constitutional Studies: Editorial', *International Journal of Constitutional Law*, Vol. 11, No. 1, 2013, pp. 1-12.

3 *See, e.g.*, M. Ganino, 'Democrazia e diritti umani nelle Costituzioni dei Paesi dell'Europa orientale', *in* M. Ganino & G. Venturini (Eds.), *L'Europa di domani: verso l'allargamento dell'Unione*, Milano, Giuffré, 2002, pp. 113-169. Please refer also to G. de Vergottini, *Le transizioni costituzionali*, Bologna, il Mulino, 1998, pp. 176-192.

4 Here we refer to the transition to democracy *i.e.* to the democratic form of state and to the values of Euro-Atlantic constitutionalism. Technically, transition could be intended as moving from one form of state to another.

5 *See* M. Ganino, 'Democrazia e diritti umani nelle Costituzioni dei Paesi dell'Europa orientale', cit., pp. 115-118, which distinguishes between political scientists' classifications (*i.e.* liberalization without democratiza-

In fact, it is necessary to introduce many exceptions and therefore it would be better to use a series of micro-models or sub-models of more limited significance.[6]

The fall of the socialist system signalled a new era for European constitutionalism. Thanks to the introduction of characteristics of Western constitutionalism in some former socialist countries, particularly those with a certain constitutional heritage and a historically favourable context and following their entry into the Council of Europe and the European Union, we can now observe a clear differentiation between a fully and successfully democratized Europe and a partially transitioned Europe. The latter is comprised of 'European' countries of the former USSR, certain republics of the former Yugoslavia and Albania. However, this classification is provisional and tentative, depending on progress in the acceptance of so-called European standards.

Further, this distinction is an over-simplification because even within the Council of Europe former communist countries are not a homogenous group. In fact, the Council of Europe has confined itself to the role of encouragement towards democracy rather than of the certification of an already existing democratic system.[7]

In any case, old attitudes splitting Europe along certain lines have not completely disappeared. Notwithstanding the fact that European geo-politics underwent very important changes after 1989, one continues to observe old divisive attitudes which are largely remnants of the cold war. Within constitutional studies when considering 'new' democracies in Europe it is common to refer to 'Eastern' Europe (or at best 'Central-Eastern'), as a sort of appendix or receptor of constitutional models elaborated in the 'old' or 'Western' part of the European continent. In making this distinction it is important to appreciate that countries that are geographically and culturally part of Central Europe, though only partially identifiable with *mitteleuropa*, are in fact much wider and culturally richer[8] than the nations of Eastern Europe.

---

tion, free elections, democratization, consolidation of democracy) and ones used by constitutionalists, that point to the adoption of a new constitution and above all on its effectiveness. *See also* J.J. Linz & A. Stepan, *Problems of Democratic Transition and Consolidation. Southern Europe, South America and Post-Communist Europe*, Baltimore, Johns Hopkins University Press, 1996; J.-P. Massias, *Droit constitutionnel des Etats d'Europe de l'Est*, Paris, Puf, 1999 (and the II édition entièrement revue, 2008).

6 On the concept of transition and of its paradigm, and on the demystification of this concept, *see* the original thesis of I. Michel, 'Le paradigme de la transition: chronique d'une fine annonceé. Le cas de l'Europe centrale et orientale', *Revue d'études politiques et constitutionneles Est-Europeennes*, Numéro speciale, 2006, pp. 25-34. *See also* T. Carothers, 'The End of the Transition Paradigm', *Journal of Democracy*, Vol. 13, No. 1, 2002, pp. 5-21.

7 These are members of the Council countries like Russia and Azerbaijan (together with Armenia, Georgia, Moldova and Ukraine), that have regressed in the field of human rights in recent years. The same issues are evident in some countries of the former Yugoslavia.

8 Historically it was the part which major European powers were contesting and therefore not peripheral to Europe. *See* T.G. Masaryk, *La nuova Europa. Il punto di vista slavo*, edited by F. Leoncini, Pordenone-Padova, Studio Tesi, 1997; F. Leoncini, *L'Europa centrale. Conflittualità e progetto. Passato e presente tra Praga, Budapest e Varsavia*, Venezia, Libreria editrice Cafoscarina, 2003. Already Seton-Watson, who also

While past categorizations can be nominally preserved, a historical and cultural analysis will demand a departure from these traditional classifications.

Any study which is focused on the countries of Central-Eastern, Baltic and Balkan Europe is still valid if it is accompanied by a new methodology. In this way one may see an alternative to the old distinction between Western and Eastern Europe, whose origins are comparatively recent especially if we consider that communist regimes lasted for about forty years, as opposed to the centuries long history of the European continent where in past ages we can attest to a different demarcation between geopolitical and cultural spheres.[9]

The element that unifies these countries and justifies their separate study, derives from their common historical experience which is not limited just to the communist period but goes back to the empires of which they were a part before World War I and to the brief but significant constitutional experience between the two World Wars (1918-1939) prior to the imposition of the socialist system.

Historically, the peculiarities of the countries of Central-Eastern, Baltic and Balkan Europe (CEBBE) arise from the much delayed construction of the national state. In Western Europe the building of the state preceded the creation of a national identity, while in other parts of the European continent nationhood had evolved independently from the state that developed later.[10] For this reason, in this part of Europe there is now a rather widespread attraction for a nation-state based on a multinational reality that has its roots in past empires.[11] This is demonstrated by the continuous conflicts, irredentism and the non-recognition of the existing borders (tendencies existing in the rest of Europe in a more

used at the time of writing (between the two World Wars) the term 'Eastern Europe' (for lack of better terms, as he stated), distinguished certain geographical regions, namely the Baltic, the Danube and the Balkans (Russia and Eurasia were excluded from his study). H. Seton-Watson, *Eastern Europe between the Wars, 1918-1941*, Boulder and London, Westview Press, 1986 (1st ed., Cambridge University Press, 1945).

9 For a historical overview, *see* H. Seton-Watson, *Eastern Europe between the Wars, 1918-1941*, cit; L. Valiani, *La dissoluzione dell'Austria-Ungheria*, Milano, Il Saggiatore, 1966; H. Bogdan, *Histoire des pays de l'Est. Des origines à nos jours*, Paris, Perrin, 1990; I. Bibó, *Miseria dei piccoli Stati dell'Europa orientale*, Bologna, il Mulino, 1994; J.-M. Le Breton, *L'Europe centrale et orientale de 1917 à 1990*, Paris, Editions Nathan, 1994; R.J. Crampton, *Eastern Europe in the twentieth century and after*, London and New York, Routledge, 1994; M. Waldenberg, *Le questioni nazionali nell'Europa centro-orientale*, Milano, il Saggiatore, 1994; R.J. Crampton, *Eastern Europe in the Twentieth Century*, London and New York, Routledge, 1995; I.T. Berend, *Central and Eastern Europe, 1944-1993*, Cambridge, Cambridge University Press, 1996; A. Graziosi, *Dai Balcani agli Urali: l'Europa orientale nella storia contemporanea*, Roma, Donzelli, 1999; F. Leoncini, *L'Europa centrale. Conflittualità e progetto. Passato e presente tra Praga, Budapest e Varsavia*, cit. As for the socialist period *see* F. Fejtö, *Histoire des démocraties populaires*, tomo II Après Stalin, Paris, ed. du Seuil, 1969.

10 *See* A. Di Gregorio, 'Stato, nazione e minoranze in Europa centrale: la tutela minoritaria nell'Ungheria post-socialista', *in* D. Amirante & V. Pepe (Eds.), *Stato democratico e società multiculturale*, Torino, Giappichelli, 2011, pp. 131-153.

11 On this point *see* J. Yacoub, 'Les minorités en Europe centrale, orientale, balkanique', *in* S. Milacic (Eds.), *La démocratie constitutionnelle en Europe centrale et orientale. Bilans et perspectives*, Bruxelles, Bruylant, 1998, pp. 344-345.

limited manner).[12] The state, in this part of Europe, seems to have been born twice, the first time after the World War I and the second time after 1989, particularly if we consider the limitations of sovereignty during the socialist period but also the membership of collapsed federations. These countries have experienced many transitions in their history (e.g. in recent times they have been subjected successively to both the Nazi and communist regimes), that were more complex than transitions which occurred in the rest of Europe. Moreover, as regards the dimension of the individual nations, these are generally quite limited.

The area of Central-Eastern, Baltic and Balkan Europe can be split into multiple parts, identifiable on the basis of the level of democratic development within each one. These distinctions coincide not only with old allegiances (based on membership of different empires each with a different economical and cultural development) but also with more recent differences in timing and characteristics of their transition to democracy.[13] Our overview will be based mainly on these latter differences, which influenced the subsequent acceptance in the main supranational organizations (in particular, in the European Union), while also considering both the common and divergent aspects which took place during the transition to and the consolidation of democracy. The areal differences depend on several factors: history and traditions, length of the communist regime, geographic proximity and exchanges with Western Europe, economic prosperity, characteristics of the transition (from above, from below, imposed, apparent), the conditionality of European and international organizations.

From the historical and geographical point of view we can divide the former socialist countries in the following way:

Former USSR satellites

- Poland
- Hungary
- Czechoslovakia
  - Czech Republic

12 On the differences between the Western and Central-Eastern part of Europe from the point of view of the state dynamics, *see* P. Grilli di Cortona, *Stati, nazioni e nazionalismi in Europa*, Bologna, il Mulino, 2003. *See also* N. MacCormick, *La sovranità in discussione. Diritto, Stato e nazione nel «commonwealth» europeo*, Bologna, il Mulino, 2003; P. Häberle, *Costituzione e identità culturale. Tra Europa e Stati nazionali*, Milano, Giuffrè, 2006.

13 Taking for granted a uniformity in the socialist period, which however did not exist. Pre-socialist traditions have influenced the characteristics of the socialist state. There were small but significant differences in the USSR satellite countries which had an impact on the dynamics of the transition (satellite parties of the communist party, a small amount of private property, a monocratic head of state, *etc.*). For a deeper analysis on the differences within the socialist system *see* P. Biscaretti di Ruffia, *Introduzione al diritto costituzionale comparato*, Milano, Giuffrè, 1988.

  - Slovakia

  (the so-called Visegrád group)[14]
- German Democratic Republic
- Bulgaria
- Romania
- Albania

Countries of the former Yugoslavia
- Slovenia
- Croatia
- Serbia
- Montenegro
- Macedonia
- Bosnia-Herzegovina
- Kosovo

Countries of the former USSR, divided in
- *Baltic states*
- Estonia
- Latvia
- Lithuania

Eastern Europe
- Russia
- Ukraine
- Belarus
- Moldova

Caucasus
- Georgia
- Armenia
- Azerbaijan

14 The Visegrád Group was created to combine the democratization path of the neighbouring countries of Central Europe. The relevant documentation and information is available on the Group website www.visegradgroup.eu (last accessed September 2018).

Central Asia[15]

- Kazakhstan
- Kyrgyzstan
- Turkmenistan
- Tajikistan
- Uzbekistan

From the point of view of entry in the European Union and the Council of Europe, events that both have certified a certain level of democratic consolidation, albeit with different characteristics, we can instead make the following distinctions:

1. Countries of Central-Eastern, Baltic and Balkan Europe members of the European Union[16] and of the Council of Europe.
2. Countries of the Balkans and of the former Yugoslavia, candidates for EU membership and members of the Council of Europe.[17]
3. Countries of the former USSR except the Baltics. Some are also members of the Council of Europe and almost all of the CIS.[18]

A more detailed overview will require the introduction of sub-distinctions which is not a simple operation. The inclusion of these countries in a comprehensive scheme is very difficult and symptomatic of the high heterogeneity of the region from the historical and geographical point of view.[19] Compared with the CIS members,[20] countries of the Balkans (mainly of the Western Balkans) are closer to the democratic and economic level of the already stabilized countries who are now members of the European Union and are subject to European 'conditionality' (even if some have yet to start the formal accession proce-

15 Geographically not in Europe but culturally and institutionally related to the post-soviet model, including the participation in the CIS and the Eurasian integration project.

16 Czech Republic, Slovakia, Hungary, Poland, Estonia, Latvia, Lithuania, Slovenia (2004); Romania and Bulgaria (2007); Croatia (2013).

17 Albania, Serbia, Montenegro, the Former Yugoslav Republic of Macedonia, Bosnia-Herzegovina, Kosovo.

18 All the former members of the USSR accept the Baltic countries and Georgia, which left the CIS in August 2008 following the conflict with Russia caused by the secession of South Ossetia and Abkhazia from Georgian territory. Ukraine remains formally part of the CIS despite the deterioration of relations with Russia since 2014 following the conflictual events that led to the annexation of Crimea by Russia and the precarious situation in Eastern Ukraine.

19 M. Lesage (Ed.), *Introduction, Constitutions d'Europe centrale, orientale et balte*, Paris, La documentation française, 1995, distinguishes the following areas from a historical, geographical and cultural point of view: Central Europe (Poland, Hungary, Czech Republic, Slovakia, Slovenia, Croatia), East-Southern Europe (Romania, Bulgaria, former Yugoslav Republic of Macedonia, Bosnia-Herzegovina, Yugoslavia and Albania) and North-Eastern Europe (Baltic states).

20 Not analysed in this volume.

dure).[21] But we must also consider the membership in the Council of Europe, whose conditionality is weaker.

An important difference between the two parts of Europe is revealed also by the recorded history of the last century. By this we mean that while in Western Europe the tragedy of the Holocaust and the Nazi regime prevail alongside that of the partisan's civil war, the memory of the crimes of communism and the subsequent anti-communist culture in Central and Eastern Europe is much fresher and uniquely confined to that area (especially in Poland, Hungary, Czech Republic and the Baltic states).[22]

Thanks to the research done on these countries we can improve our knowledge of the dynamics of transition to democracy and consequently better construct classification patterns (*i.e.* forms of state, forms of government) including the theories about them (do these models set a new paradigm; are the waves of transition to be continued?). A historical and cultural approach is required. In fact, the cultural element (in which culture has a 'normative value')[23] influences the effectiveness of any legal disposition, in particular those regarding fundamental rights, as it is illustrated by the relevance of a particular national heritage (see for example the protection of minorities or the emphasis on social rights in many constitutions in that area).[24] If we want to introduce or impose a particular constitutional model it must take account of this cultural heritage else it will fail. Only a historical knowledge can help to find the origins of legal institutions and interpretations, showing similarities and differences between legal systems. Only a cultural discourse can explain differences between Central-Eastern, Baltic and Balkan Europe on the one hand and the rest of Europe on the other, even in the area of constitutional law.[25]

At the same time a new constitutional framework can be efficient only if mindful of values, ideas and interests of the society to which it is applied.[26] The question of legitimacy

21 For an update of candidacies *see* https://ec.europa.eu/neighbourhood-enlargement (last accessed September 2018).

22 There have been many attempts to approach the question of recorded memory in a global European dimension but the gap between the two parts of Europe in that case is not easy to fill. *See* A. Di Gregorio, *Epurazioni e protezione della democrazia. Esperienze e modelli di "giustizia post-autoritaria"*, Milano, FrancoAngeli, 2012, pp. 450-457. *See* C. Closa, *Dealing with the Past: Memory and European Integration*, Jean Monnet Working Paper 01/11, 2011.

23 *Cf.* L. Pegoraro, *Derecho constitucional comparado. Itinerarios de Investigación*, Querétaro, México, FUNDAp, 2011, pp. 50, 86-87.

24 In particular, in some constitutions of the former Yugoslav republics. *See* C. Ferretto, 'Le nuove Costituzioni balcaniche: paradigma individualistico o paradigma sociale', *federalismi.it*, No. 18, 2009.

25 *Cf.* G. Bognetti, *Introduzione al diritto costituzionale comparato*, Torino, Giappichelli, 1994.

26 "Le Droit démocratique doit être en plus ou moins étroite symbiose avec la culture politique de la société qu'il régit et dont il est censé être le produit légitime. Efficace parce que légitime, mais – aussi – légitime parce qu'efficace". S. Milacic, *De l'âge idéologique à l'âge politique. L'Europe postcommuniste vers la démocratie pluraliste (1989-2009)*, Bruxelles, Bruylant, 2010, p. 431. *See also* K. Kelemen, 'How Should the Legal Systems of Eastern Europe Be Classified Today?', *in* A. Badó *et al.* (Eds.), *International Conference for the 10th*

is strictly connected to the origin of the democratic constitutional model. If it is perceived as an internal product, one that is bought into by those to whom it will apply, it has a better chance of fast implementation, application and success.

1.2 Constitutional Traditions in the Area

Notwithstanding the deep differences existing between countries of Central-Eastern, Baltic and Balkan Europe, we may find many similarities in their constitutional history. First of all, as we have already shown, the birth of statehood – that is of national independence – is relatively recent, and the same can be said of autonomous constitutional pathways. With a few exceptions, we can start to talk about constitutionalism at the end of World War I, after the fall of empires that had trapped the nations in that part of Europe for a long time.

The adoption of the first constitutions was subsequent to the achievement of independence.[27] A very important exception is the 1791 Polish Constitution (the so-called 'May 3rd Constitution'), the first liberal constitution in Europe, preceding the French Constitution of the same year. The May 3rd Constitution was only in force for a very short time, considering the difficult historical context of Poland which was forced to give up its sovereignty until 1918. It was a text that, even though expressing past constitutional traditions (*i.e.* the Republic of Nobles which lasted for more than three centuries), included the revolutionary ideas of that time, particularly in the area of national identity and sovereignty.[28] These are traditional weaknesses in Polish history whose national identity and sovereignty became effective in 1918 and then, after the Nazi and communist domination, have been completely affirmed since 1989. The quest for Polish independence provoked a hostile reaction from neighbouring powers which in turn instigated the rebellion of reactionary nobility. The May 3rd Constitution was subsequently suspended on the 23rd of July 1792.[29]

Anniversary of the Institute of Comparative Law, Lectiones Iuridicae 11, Potsdam, Universitätsverlag, 2014, pp. 197-223.

27 As a historical reminiscence we can recall the constitutional experiences that some of those countries experienced before their national independence. This is particularly true for those nations that were part of the Austro-Hungarian Empire (*see* the liberal charters adopted following the 1848 revolutions). As far as Poland is concerned, *see* those experiences going back to the period of the Polish-Lithuanian Principality, starting from fifteenth century. For further details *see* C. Filippini, *Polonia*, Bologna, il Mulino, 2010; AA.VV., *Poland,* The Netherlands, Wolters Kluwer, 2012.

28 From the social point of view the Constitution expressed a class-conscious approach. The dominant class was obviously the bourgeoisie.

29 On the constitutional history of Poland *see* B. Mirkine-Guetzévitch, *Pologne*, Paris, Delegrave, 1930; J. Wawrzyniak, *La Polonia e le sue Costituzioni dal 1791 ad oggi*, Rimini, Maggioli, 1992; J. Żurawska (Ed.), *La Costituzione polacca del 3 maggio 1791 e il costituzionalismo europeo del XVIII secolo*, Napoli, Istituto Universitario Orientale, 1995; B.M. Palka, 'La Costituzione polacca del 2 maggio 1791: tra tradizione e modernità', *Historia constitucional*, No. 6, 2005; S. Ceccanti, 'Il costituzionalismo polacco dal 1791 ad oggi',

Among the first constitutions of that area that are worth mentioning include the Bulgarian Tărnovo Constitution of April 16th 1879, which was adopted after the achievement of independence from the Ottoman Empire. This was a text not particularly significant from the point of view of liberal constitutionalism and was only applied for a few years. It was suspended many times by the Tsar and then no longer applied after a series of coup d'états (*i.e.* in 1923, 1934 and 1944). Nevertheless, this constitution introduced a form of government with a tentative separation of powers (dualistic parliamentary monarchy) and some of its characteristics, including the procedure of approval, were imitated by the post-socialist Constitution of 1991.[30]

The constitutions of the countries which have obtained or re-obtained their independence since the end of World War I share similar characteristics. We can speak of a special wave of constitutionalism (a special 'constitutional cycle') well documented in the literature and which involved the whole of Europe.[31] The constitutions introduced in the 1920s were substituted in the 1930s by more authoritarian versions (new constitutions or amendments to the constitutional text in force). This was a symptom of the political attitudes of these countries towards the Nazi-fascist powers or a consequence of the imposition of new regimes to the then recently conquered territories by Nazi Germany.

Between the end of the 1920s and the beginning of the 1930s the French constitutionalist of Russian origins, Boris Mirkine-Guetzévitch, was among the most authoritative scholars in the field of constitutionalism of 'new' Europe.[32] He underlined in a series of publications the then recent tendencies of constitutional law in Europe, particularly in Central and Eastern parts.[33] In the new constitutions, he noticed common features. At first

---

federalismi.it, No. 10, 2006; J. Sawicki, 'La Costituzione della Polonia', *in* M. Ganino (Ed.), *Codice delle Costituzioni*, Vol. III, Padova, Cedam, 2013.

30 Among these, the adoption of the constitution by the Great National Assembly, a body especially elected for the approval of the constitution or for amending the basis of the constitutional order (a kind of 'total revision'); the Supreme Administrative Tribunal (suppressed in 1944 and reinstated in 1991). During the socialist regime the parliament, like in the Tărnovo Constitution, exerted a preventive control of the constitutionality of laws (unlike Romania where since 1923 the control was exerted by the Supreme Court). *See* C. Filippini, 'La Costituzione della Bulgaria', *in* M. Ganino (Ed.), *Codice delle Costituzioni*, Vol. III, cit.

31 *See, among others*, P. Biscaretti di Ruffia, *Introduzione al diritto costituzionale comparato*, cit., pp. 601 *et seq.*

32 Other relevant publications of that period were: G. Burdeau, *Le régime parlamentaire dans les constitutions européennes d'après guerre*, Paris, F. Alcan, 1934 and A. Giannini, *Le Costituzioni degli Stati dell'Europa orientale*, Vol. I (Albania, Bulgaria, Cecoslovacchia, Danzica, Estonia, Finlandia, Grecia) and II (Jugoslavia, Lettonia, Lituania, Memel, Polonia, Romania, Ungheria, Urss), Roma, Istituto per l'Europa orientale, 1929.

33 He analyses the following constitutions: Weimar (1919), Finland (1919), the German Länder, Austria (1920), Estonia (1920), Czechoslovakia (1920), Poland (1921), the free town of Danzig (1922), Latvia (1922), Lithuania (1922 and 1928), Greece (1925 and 1927), Romania (1923), Turkey (1924), Kingdom of Serbs, Croatians and Slovenians (1921, suspended in 1929), Ireland (1937). B. Mirkine-Guetzévitch, *Les nouvelles tendances du droit constitutionnel*, Paris, Marcel Giard, 1931. Previous books of the same author are: *Les Constitutions de l'Europe Nouvelle*, Paris, Delagrave, 1928 and 1930; *Le referendum et le parlementarisme dans les nouvelles Constitutions européennes*, Paris, Presses Universitaires de France, 1930. Mirkine did not

glance, the so-called 'rationalization of power', referred not only to the relationships between the legislative and the executive (although on the incongruities of this relationship, which initially saw an unsustainable weakness of the executives, the author lingers a lot, considering them the cause of subsequent degeneration) but also to the introduction of the institutions of direct democracy (the combination of parliamentarianism with direct democracy represented one of the most interesting elements of post-war constitutional law). In a more general way, the rationalization was "the tendency to provide a legal basis for the social dimensions of life", that is "to make subject to law the life of the whole society".[34] He analysed the principles of pluralism, rule of law and the parliamentary system (which was superseded by the power of political parties everywhere), judicial review of legislation (Ireland, Romania and Greece followed the US model, Czechoslovakia and Austria the Kelsenian one), as well as the role of international law and the protection of minorities. The charters of fundamental rights were rich and included social rights. This happened not only in the Weimar Constitution (socialist forces had an active role in the Constituent Assembly) but also in Romania and Yugoslavia, that is in monarchic countries (for fear of social unrest and the risk of communist takeovers), as well as in Poland and Estonia.[35] But notwithstanding the complexity and the extent of these constructs the constitutions failed on practical grounds. They were not properly applied or were significantly amended (in an authoritarian direction), and even ignored in the day-to-day legislation. The main problem was the relationship between the executive and the legislative, generally based on the supremacy of parliament (as a reaction to the past monarchic principle and imitation of the English system of government). Considering the weakness of post-war socially and politically divided societies, this principle became unworkable. The fear of the monarchic executive had become the fear of the executive as such, generating fatal consequences. Fascist forces profited from this situation with no little thanks to the perceived dangers of Bolshevism. As Mirkine wrote

> there was a real gap between aspirations of new men, who in different European countries tried, from 1919 to 1920, to fix new constitutional rules, and the political reality of the following ten years.[36]

In those countries in which the 'new men' had created an 'advanced constitutional regime' this quickly became a dictatorship.

---

analyse the Constitution of Albania of 1928, an expression of the constitutional monarchy in the Balkans, which was ultimately analysed by A. Giannini.

34 B. Mirkine-Guetzévitch, *Les nouvelles tendances du droit constitutionnel*, cit., pp. VIII and 8.

35 Social rights were also be included, following Mirkine, in the general process of rationalization of public life even if they merely expressed an educational function. *Ibidem*, p. 42.

36 B. Mirkine-Guetzévitch, *Les nouvelles tendances du droit constitutionnel*, cit., p. X.

It is not clear, following the author's thesis, if the failure of these attempts had been more serious considering the original constitutional projects, which were very ambitious. Such a kind of democracy was probably too utopian for that time. The countries of the 'new' Europe were not mature enough for such an advanced project and were unable to reach constitutional stability.[37] At the same time we must remember that in the rest of Europe there were not many examples of 'mature' democracies (the transition to a social model of state was in its early beginnings; the universal right to vote had only been introduced in a few countries).

From a formal standpoint, the 1920s constitutions revealed full compliance with democratic principles, even in the Balkans. All these texts proclaimed popular will as the main driving value. The constitutional models taken into consideration were those of the French Third Republic, as the system of government,[38] and the bill of rights of the previous French tradition. In Poland, Baltic states, Germany and Austria, the Swiss constitutional model was also taken into account; in Finland the method of election of the head of state was inspired by the US Constitution. Some of the new constitutions, like those of Weimar, Czechoslovakia and Austria, have themselves been perceived as models and have influenced each other. Among the most important innovations, in addition to the aforementioned introduction of social rights, is the inclusion of new rights and duties, the limitation of property rights, the role of international law in the protection of individual rights and in the limitation of constituent power (considering the constraints of the peace treaties).

Around the mid-1920s a series of constitutional amendments were approved, leading to a strengthening of the role of the executive and to the limitation of the supremacy of the legislative. The first example was the amendments to the Polish Constitution following the *coup d'état* of 12-14 May 1926.[39] Then the Polish system of government was subject to

37 These societies were very complex from the ethnic point of view: *see* the difficulties of building a common state for Serbs, Croatians and Slovenians or the case of Czechoslovakia. In the Baltic states there was a fight between nationalism and bolshevism; Poland and Finland were confronted by an aggressive Soviet Union. In short, there were common problems: territorial changes established by the peace treaties, plebiscites of annexation, forced occupation of the most recalcitrant regions, *etc.*

38 S. Ceccanti, *Il costituzionalismo polacco dal 1791 ad oggi*, cit., underlines the strong influence of the constitutional laws of the French Third Republic on the Polish Constitution of 1921 and on the Austrian Constitution of 1920. Other similarities between Poland and Austria are evidenced in the later strengthening of the executive following the Weimar example (in Poland *see* the constitutional law of 1926 after the march on Warsaw of Pilsudski, inspired by Art. 48 of the Weimar Constitution; in Austria the constitutional amendments of 1929) and in the other authoritarian involutions (in Poland the 1935 Constitution and in Austria 1934 constitutional amendments). The Author considers that "It was impossible to find a viable choice between an assembly-based democracy and decision-efficient non-democratic government, between democracy and autocracy. The Polish 1791 Constitution tried to achieve this but was repeatedly thwarted by neighbouring enemy powers" (ivi, p. 7).

39 We are talking about the amendment of 2 August 1926 which conferred on the President the right to dissolve parliament and at the same time reduced the legislative and budgetary competencies of parliament. The President also acquired the authority to issue emergency decrees.

other modifications confirmed by the new 1935 Constitution. In a similar authoritarian vein we find a series of amendments or newly adopted constitutions of that time (the new Lithuanian Constitution in 1928, the Estonian Constitution of 1934, the acts for the protection of the state in Finland in 1930, etc.). In the monarchic states (constitutional monarchies) the constitution was simply suspended (e.g. Bulgaria, Kingdom of Serbs, Croatians and Slovenians).

At the end of this decade the majority of constitutions formally affirmed the political primacy of the executive thus confirming the political practices developed since the first years of their application. Only Czechoslovakia chose a different and more democratic approach.[40]

The influence of the aforementioned pre-socialist traditions on their constitutions adopted after the fall of the socialist regime is clear throughout the entire area. This is particularly true for the Czech and Slovak Constitutions and for those of the Baltic states (Latvia reintroduced the 1922 Constitution with a series of later amendments; Estonia and Lithuania have utilized many institutions derived from the 1920s and 1930s constitutions).[41] A similar tendency is evident also in Poland, Bulgaria and Romania.[42]

At the end of World War II, following a brief comeback of the pluralist political system, the socialist constitutional model was imposed in 1948. Nevertheless, in this part of Europe there were deep differences from the soviet model of government. This is the reason why many national peculiarities – both economic and cultural – survived until the end of the socialist rule. For example agriculture was predominant, except for East Germany and

40 B. Mirkine-Guetzévitch, A. Tibal, *La Tchécoslovaquie*, Paris, Delagrave, 1930.

41 The 1992 Constitution of Estonia inherits an institution that had existed in the 1938 Constitution with mixed competencies such as the Chancellor of Justice. The Estonian constitutional review model (similar to that of the US) also derives from the inter-war period. In one of the constitutional projects of 1919 this competence had been conferred upon the Estonian Supreme Court. At the time of the adoption of the 1938 Constitution, legislators discussed the possibility of introducing a constitutional court but then decided to refer to the office of the Chancellor of Justice, which exerted constitutional review of the laws before they became valid (*a priori* review). In the 1992 Constitution this control is exerted in a similar manner also by the Chancellor who has additional relevant competencies (such as the defence of citizens' rights against abuses by the public administration and control of the behaviour of senior state officials). *See* M. Mazza, 'La Costituzione dell'Estonia', *in* M. Ganino (Ed.), *Codice delle Costituzioni*, cit., Latvia, as we have already said, reintroduced the 1922 Constitution which needed updating. During the 1990s several amendments were adopted. As for Lithuania, the 1938 Constitution was reintroduced but only for few hours at the time of independence from the USSR; the semi-presidential system of government, which is different from the Latvian and Estonian parliamentary one, is the result of an effort to combine the Constitutions of 1922 and 1928 which expressed respectively an ultra-parliamentarian and an authoritarian system of government.

42 *See* the introductory remarks to the texts of the constitutions *in* M. Ganino (Ed.), *Codice delle Costituzioni*, Vol. III, cit. *See, e.g.*, the Romanian Constitution of 1991 confirmed the legislative Council as an advisory committee of the parliament, with the aim to advise on the legitimacy of the regulations and on the constitutionality of the legislative bills. Such a Council had been introduced in the 1923 Constitution – that conferred *a posteriori* review of legislation on the united sections of the Supreme Court – and continued in some shape during the socialist era. This body provided preventive opinions both of legality (for regulations) and of constitutionality (for draft legislation).

Czechoslovakia. Not all these countries had slavic populations and historically their culture had been more susceptible to the French and German influence than to the Russian one. From the religious point of view Bulgaria, Romania and Serbia had their own orthodox churches that were more accustomed to recognizing the supremacy of the secular state while Croatia, Slovenia, Poland and Hungary had deep rooted catholic traditions that gave the church much greater social prestige especially in Poland.[43]

These differences in context point to why these countries experienced a first transitional phase with a "mixed system" (1944-1948), during which some elements of the previous political system were maintained. Later phases, based on P. Biscaretti di Ruffia's classification, were "strict Stalinian imitation" (1948-1954), in which draconian and undifferentiated uniformity prevailed followed by the "development of particular national socialisms" phase (from 1955 to 1956). In this latter phase, historical and local characteristics emerged. But each nation's search for its own path to socialism (so-called 'socialism with a human face') was universally repressed by the Warsaw Pact Member States (or self-repressed, in the case of Poland in order to pre-empt soviet intervention).

The general characteristics of the socialist constitutions reflected the ideological premises of this form of state since as the premises evolved towards a communist society so the constitutions were amended or completely re-written to fit.[44] We can distinguish three different stages.[45] The first, between 1945 and 1948, was characterized by a series of transitional constitutions which combined elements of old and new political systems (for example, the so-called 'little' Polish Constitution of 1947).[46] In the second stage, between

---

43 P. Biscaretti di Ruffia, *Introduzione al diritto costituzionale comparato*, cit., pp. 456-457.

44 *See* A.Y. Vyshinsky, *The Law of the Soviet State*, New York, Macmillan, 1948; A. Giannini, *Le Costituzioni delle Repubbliche popolari*, Milano, Giuffré, 1955; V. Gsovski & K. Grzybowski (Eds.), *Government, Law and Courts in the Soviet Union and Eastern Europe*, New York, Frederick Praeger, 1959; I. Kovacs, *New Elements in the Evolution of Socialist Constitutions*, Budapest, Akadémiai Kiadó, 1968; R. Charvin, *Les états socialistes européens*, Paris, Cujas, 1975; P. Gélard, *Les systèmes politiques des états socialistes*, Paris, Cujas, 1975; T. Napolitano, *Istitutioni di diritto sovietico. I presupposti e gli ordinamenti*, Torino, Utet, 1975; P. Biscaretti di Ruffia, *Costituzioni straniere contemporanee. Gli Stati socialisti* Vol. II, Milano, Giuffré, 1987. The typical principles of the socialist system related to the structure and the functioning of the state institutions were: the concept of 'organs of state power' directly elected and considered to be above other state organs (administrative, judicial or prosecution); the unity of state power, a principle in contrast to the Western principle of the division of powers; the double dependence and democratic centralism; the socialist legality; the citizens' participation in public activities with the aim of facilitating the building of the communist society and as an alternative to the Western-style rights and liberties; the superiority of social and economic rights and the exercise of rights with the aim of realizing the communist idea; the introduction of the principle of the guiding role of the communist party within the constitution (single or hegemonic party). Please refer also to A. Di Gregorio, 'Uno Stato "nuovo" e un diritto "nuovo": la Rivoluzione Bolscevica e la sua eredità giuridica a cent'anni dall'"Ottobre"', *Diritto pubblico comparato ed europeo*, No. IV, 2017, pp. 993-1030.

45 *See* P Biscaretti di Ruffia, *Introduzione al diritto costituzionale comparato*, cit., p. 618.

46 In some cases in this period the head of state was that of the previous regime: the Tsar Simeon II in Bulgaria (until 1946), King Michael in Romania (until 1947), President Beneš in Czechoslovakia (until 1948). Yet, many anti-fascist political parties participated in the first elections after the war. The position of the President

1948 and 1954, the first socialist constitutions were adopted (like expression of the phase of the 'popular democracies'),[47] following the model of the Stalinist Constitution of 1936 (Albania 1946, Bulgaria 1947, Czechoslovakia 1948,[48] Hungary and GDR 1949, Poland and Romania 1952). The third stage, from 1954 onwards was that of the 'socialist national' constitutions (Czechoslovakia 1960[49] with the federal amendments of 1968, Romania 1965,[50] GDR 1968, Bulgaria 1971, Albania 1976, the 1972 profound constitutional amendments in Hungary and the 1976 amendments in Poland)[51]. A slightly different path was that taken by Yugoslavia, a country that expressed its ideological and ethnic-nationalist peculiarities from the constitutional point of view (Constitutions of 1946, 1953, 1963, 1974).[52]

---

as the head of state was maintained in Czechoslovakia during the entire socialist regime, in Poland until 1952 and in the GDR until 1960. This position was introduced in Romania by Ceausescu in 1974.

47 The 'popular democracy' phase corresponded approximately to that of the USSR during the period of the 'dictatorship of the proletariat', when all the old structures and class divisions of the bourgeois order had not been completely eliminated. In these countries a limited private craft activity remained, and the 'socialization' of the agriculture sector was slow. In addition, several non-communist parties survived, even if they were united in a single National Front at the time of the elections. Then followed the stage of socialist state, in which the opposition parties disappeared (or remained only nominally) and the socialist parties merged with the communist ones into unified workers' parties (like the Polish one).

48 In which there were still 'Western' aspects (a President of the Republic elected by the National Assembly who appointed the ministers responsible to the Assembly and could dissolve the Assembly before the end of the legislature). In 1945 the 1920 Constitution was brought into force temporarily.

49 The first constitution of the region that officially recognized the transition to the socialist form of state.

50 In this constitution it is worth noting the first introduction of a constitutional committee of the Great National Assembly with advisory competences related to the constitutional review of legislation. This committee was composed not only of members of the Assembly but also of external 'experts'.

51 Following P. Biscaretti di Ruffia, *Introduzione al diritto costituzionale comparato*, cit., p. 459, the three stage analysis is not intended in a rigid way considering that the transition from one phase to another was not necessarily accompanied by the adoption of a new constitution but sometimes by a series of amendments to an existing constitution or by a new interpretation of the old text.

52 The peculiarities here refer to constitutional law as well as to economic and social assets (and also to international relations), based on the principles of 'self-management' and social property. There have been four main constitutional phases. The first federal constitution of 1946 – modelled on the 1936 USSR Constitution – in which the state was composed of six republics and two autonomous provinces (in the Serbian republic) made for an extremely complex state structure. This complexity – due both to the complex ethnic composition of the country and the original approach envisaged in the economic-social sphere – had grown in subsequent constitutions or constitutional amendments. Especially after the 1948 political separation from the USSR (stalinism was considered anti-marxist and anti-democratic and the Yugoslav leadership wanted to refer immediately to the state extinction), the originality of Yugoslav constitutions have become evident. The constitutional revision of 1953 (considered a new federal constitution for its amplitude) confirmed the innovations already introduced with ordinary legislation (the transformation of the party into a simple league of communists, the introduction of the principle of self-management, *etc.*). Further transformations were introduced by the 1963 Constitution, which transformed the Federal Assembly into an organ placed at the top both of state power and social self-management being divided into five different Councils. The 1974 Constitution integrated the text of 1963 with the 42 amendments adopted in 1967, 1968 and 1971. The Yugoslav constitutional model was different from the soviet one not only in the field of self-management (as opposed to the centralistic principle in force in other socialist countries) but also in terms of federal relationships. The republics of Yugoslavia (and also the autonomous provinces) had much more autonomy

The socialist world, as we have already said, was not uniform and the transition to democracy started from its inside, by the same communist politicians or widespread protests of their populace. In the third constitutional period some institutional reforms, for example, encouraged the introduction of democratic principles as the basic form of the state.

In Poland and Hungary there were several early signs of such openness. In Poland the constitutional amendments of 13 December 1957 introduced a special Supreme Court of control which was empowered to act as a supervisory board of the administration and which was responsible to the parliament rather than the government. The act of 31 January 1980 introduced a High Court for administrative control over the legality of the decisions of the public administration. After the wave of strikes in 1980 and a series of difficult negotiations, the government recognized the first free trade unions and their right to strike as well as a reduction of censorship (principles later recognized by the party congress in 1981). Consistent with the constitutional amendment of 1982 the Polish parliament introduced the Constitutional Tribunal in 1985 albeit with limited control over statutes passed by parliament. The 1987 constitutional amendments introduced the right to referendum and the office of the Defendant of citizen's rights based on the model of the Swedish ombudsman. In Hungary no more constitutions were adopted after the first socialist one but the text of 1949 was amended several times. In 1967 multiple candidatures for the election in the single-member constituencies were allowed. With the 1972 amendment the centralized economy was partially liberalized and decentralized allowing for the autonomy of enterprises and private initiatives in certain sectors. But the most important amendments were made in 1983. Among these were the introduction of the constitutional law council, a special office composed of members of parliament who were authorized to

than the Federation resulting in a quasi-confederal system which proved to be clumsy and unworkable (constitutional amendments required unanimous vote by the republics, equal participation of republics and autonomous provinces to the federal constitutional bodies, *etc.*). Other institutional differences regarded the electoral system, which in Yugoslavia was mainly indirect and the introduction, since the 1960s of a sophisticated system of constitutional courts (despite the limits due to the characteristics of the socialist state) *See* P. Biscaretti di Ruffia & G. Franchi, *Repubblica socialista federativa di Jugoslavia*, Vol. III of the series *L'amministrazione locale in Europa*, Milano, Giuffré, 1969; S. Bianchini (Ed.), *L'autogestione jugoslava*, Milano, FrancoAngeli, 1982; D. Denkovic, 'Le contrôle de la constitutionnalité et de la légalité des actes réglementaires et des actes autogestionnaires généraux dans le droit yougoslave', *Revue d'études comparatives est-ouest*, Vol. XIII, No.2, juin 1982; P. Nikolic, 'La justice constitutionnelle en Yougoslavie', *in* G. Lombardi (Ed.), *Costituzione e giustizia costituzionale nel diritto comparato*, Rimini, Maggioli, 1985; A. Zorzi Giustiniani, *Norme costituzionali e regolamentari sulla Corte costituzionale jugoslava*, Firenze, Cedeur, 1989; P. Collas, 'Le contrôle de la constitutionnalité en URSS', *Rev. dr. pub. sc. pol.*, 1990; S. Trifunovska (Ed.), *Yugoslavia through documents: from its creation to its dissolution*, Dordrecht, Nijhoff, 1994. For a view of the influence of the old socialist system on the contemporary constitutional review system in the former Yugoslav countries *see* A. Di Gregorio, 'Il modello interno nella configurazione della giustizia costituzionale nei paesi della ex Jugoslavia, ovvero delle ascendenze socialiste', *in* M. Calamo Specchia *et al.* (Eds.), *I Balcani occidentali. Le Costituzioni della transizione*, Torino, Giappichelli, 2008, pp. 257-281.

check the constitutionality of the normative acts. In relation to parliamentary statutes this special office was empowered to ask for a new review by the Assembly and it could suspend certain sublegislative acts. The same constitutional amendment extended the citizen's right of choice in the electoral process. In the Hungarian case we must also consider the relevance of the Academy of Sciences in developing the study of comparative law.[53]

1.3 Time and Path of Transition to the Liberal-Democratic Constitutional System

Many studies are dedicated to the transition from the socialist form of state in the Central-Eastern, Baltic and Balkan Europe examining its many and various aspects.[54] Nevertheless,

53 M. Ganino, 'Introduction to Ungheria', *in* P. Biscaretti di Ruffia in collaboration with M. Ganino, *Le Costituzioni di sette Stati di recente ristrutturazione*, cit., p. 389.

54 *See, e.g.*, P. Grilli di Cortona, *Le crisi politiche nei regimi comunisti. Ungheria, Cecoslovacchia e Polonia da Stalin agli anni ottanta*, Milano, FrancoAngeli, 1989; R. Dahrendorf, *1989. Riflessioni sulla rivoluzione in Europa: lettera immaginaria a un amico di Varsavia*, Bari, Laterza, 1990; Y. Plasseraud, *Les nouvelles démocraties d'Europe centrale*, Paris, Montchrestien, 1991; P. Biscaretti di Ruffia, *1988-1990. Un triennio di profonde trasformazioni costituzionali*, Milano, Giuffré, 1991; S. Bartole, *Riforme costituzionali nell'Europa centro-orientale. Da satelliti comunisti a democrazie sovrane*, Bologna, il Mulino, 1993; S. Bartole & G. Conetti (Eds.), *Federalismo e crisi dei regimi comunisti*, Torino, La Rosa editrice, 1993; V. Knapp & S. Bartole (Eds.), *La dissoluzione della Federazione cecoslovacca*, Torino, La Rosa editrice, 1994; G. Pridham & T. Vanhanen (Eds.), *Democratization in Eastern Europe. Domestic and International Perspectives*, London, Routledge, 1994; M. Lesage, 'Transitions vers la démocratie et l'Etat de droit et changement constitutionnel. Introduction', *in* M. Lesage (Ed.), *Constitutions d'Europe centrale, orientale et balte*, cit.; J.J. Linz & A. Stepan, *Problems of Democratic Transition and Consolidation. Southern Europe, South America and Post-Communist Europe*, cit.; L. Holmes, *Post-Communism. An Introduction*, Cambridge, Polity Press, 1997; S. Bartole & P. Grilli di Cortona (Eds.), *Transizione e consolidamento democratico nell'Europa centro-orientale*, Torino, Giappichelli, 1998; G. de Vergottini, *Le transizioni costituzionali*, cit.; H. Gardner, *Central and Southeastern Europe in Transition*, Westport, Praeger, 2000; E.J. Hobsbawm, *Il secolo breve, 1914-1991. L'epoca più violenta della storia dell'umanità*, Milano, Bur, 2000; L. Mezzetti, *Le democrazie incerte*, Torino, Giappichelli, 2000; Id., *Teoria e prassi delle transizioni costituzionali e del consolidamento democratico*, Padova, Cedam, 2003; S. Saxonberg, *The Fall. A Comparative Study of the End of Communism in Czechoslovakia, East Germany, Hungary and Poland*, Amsterdam, Harwood Academic Publishers, 2001; J. Zielonka (Ed.), *Democratic Consolidation in Eastern Europe*, Vol. I (Institutional Engineering) and II (International and Transnational Factors), Oxford, Oxford University Press, 2001; S. Gambino (Ed.), *Costituzionalismo europeo e transizioni democratiche*, Milano, Giuffré, 2003; G. Gozzi & F. Martelli (Eds.), *Guerre e minoranze. Diritti delle minoranze, conflitti interetnici e giustizia internazionale nella transizione alla democrazia dell'Europa centro-orientale*, Bologna, il Mulino, 2004; H.J. Wiarda & D.R. Herspring & E.M. Skelley, *Development on the periphery: democratic transitions in Southern and Eastern Europe*, Lanham, Rownan & Littlefield, 2006. *See also* the constitutional updates in the countries of the CIS and Eastern Europe edited by P. Gélard on the *Revue française de droit constitutionnel*. Other journals dedicated to these countries are: *Revue d'études compararatives Est-Ouest* (on the transition from socialist rule see in particular 1992, issue 4); *Revue du droit public* (*see* 1994, issues 2 and 6); *Le Courrier des pays de l'Est*; *East European Constitutional Review*; *Review of Central and East European Law*; *Europe-Asia Studies*; *Communist and Post-Communist Studies*; *Post-soviet Affairs*; *"1989" Rivista di diritto pubblico e scienze politiche*; *East European Politics and Societies*; *RFE/RL Research Report* (since 1995 *Transition: News and Analysis of the former USSR and Eastern, Central*

it is appropriate to clarify a number of key concepts. In constitutional law the term transition indicates a transition from a non-democratic (socialist, authoritarian, theocratic, etc.) regime, or 'form of state', to a liberal-democratic one. It is intended to mean a transition to Western-style constitutionalism, which involves the adherence to a set of core values such as the separation of powers and the guarantee of fundamental human rights.[55]

This concept of transition is not neutral because it implies the adherence to a series of constitutional principles and to the democratic standards elaborated by the international organizations within which new democracies were admitted. As for the CEBBE area, the acceptance of these principles and the adaptation to European standards have been easier for some of them. We are talking about the countries with more favourable contexts and with traditions in the area of political pluralism. In other cases we observe many problems from the democratic and economic point of view. But the traditional classification of the 'form of states' does not support many differences and does not provide a proper framework for intermediate situations between democracy and autocracy.

The transition to democracy consists of several stages and aspects. The two most important aspects are in relation to politics and constitutional law. The political transition for its part envisages more than one version depending on the geographical area. Transition to democracy was an early phenomenon in the former satellites of the USSR most culturally predisposed such as Poland and Hungary, where it had a negotiated character but with significant differences (in Poland former communist forces had an almost 'blackmailing' stance at the roundtables with the opposition forces while Hungarian communists maintained a long-held reformist stance). It was swift and with few compromises in Czechoslovakia and the GDR owing largely to the inflexibility of the previous regimes. It was delayed in Bulgaria and Romania, where former communists played an important part. But while in Bulgaria there was a negotiated transition, the regime in Romania met its end in a sort of coup d'état. In the countries of former Yugoslavia the transition was very precarious, with the exception of Slovenia: there had been a transition from communism to post-communist nationalism which led to ethnic conflicts. In Albania the transition was both significantly delayed and incomplete. In the USSR it was brought about from the top-down with little participation from the general population, with the exception of the

and Southeastern Europe); *Slavia*; *Les études de la Documentation française*; *Europa-Europe; Osteuropa Recht*; *Lettre de l'Est*.

55 G. de Vergottini, 'Costituzionalismo europeo e transizioni democratiche', *in* M. Calamo Specchia *et al.* (Eds.), *I Balcani occidentali. Le Costituzioni della transizione*, cit., p. 5, summarizes the characteristics of constitutionalism as follows: "We refer to the liberal ideology which is the basis of the political, social and institutional environment that has characterized the process of development of the West in past centuries. We therefore refer to a set of principles which are considered as a *model* of constitutional orders founded on an articulated system of guarantees, and are interested in ensuring the legitimacy of the ownership and use of power, starting from the classic enunciation of this separation, and at the same time a perfected system of rights and their protection".

Baltic countries where democratization coincided with the struggle for regaining national sovereignty.

As for the paths of transition, some authors focus on a general diagram that involves multiple stages including the crisis of the old leadership, the roundtable discussions between incumbent governments and their opposition, the loss of leadership of the communist party and its subsequent transformation and splintering, the legalization of the opposition forces (in Bulgaria and Hungary the reformist currents of the former communist party prevailed while in Czechoslovakia and East Germany the anti-regime forces were dominant), the change of the name of the state (eliminating adjectives 'socialist' or 'popular'), the first free elections (or semi-free, as in Poland), constitutional amendments or provisional constitutions pending the approval of new constitutions.[56] But this diagram only refers to some of the CEBBE countries (Poland, Hungary, the GDR, Czechoslovakia, Romania, Bulgaria) and only applies with a considerable number of exceptions. One must make some clarifications on the negotiated nature of these transitions, since negotiations for regime change between incumbent politicians and reformist forces or civic opposition is not a phenomenon peculiar to Central-Eastern, Baltic and Balkan Europe. Even the transitions in Spain, South Africa and several Latin American countries were negotiated. Real negotiations occurred only in Hungary and Poland. In most other cases, the bargaining power of incumbent communists forces was predominant (e.g. Romania, Albania, Bulgaria) or alternatively minimized to almost zero (e.g. GDR, Czechoslovakia). In the countries of the former Yugoslavia, the fall of communism was, except for the Slovenian case, quite apparent (the transition was handled by nationalist or socialist forces originating in the communist party) while the Baltic states were the only countries of the former Soviet Union to combine the claim of sovereignty with a genuine democratization of the political system. It should also be noted that the roundtables, where experienced, produced temporary compromises promptly superseded by the results of the first free elections.[57] The transition

56 *See* L. Mezzetti, *Le democrazie incerte*, cit., pp. 45-62. The author summarizes the causes of the collapse of communism thus: the Gorbachev factor, the failure of the economy, the 'external' factor, the role of civil society, pp. 21-41.

57 Following M. Ganino, 'Democrazia e diritti umani nelle Costituzioni dei Paesi dell'Europa orientale', cit., p. 129, "The 'Roundtables' produced 'negotiated Constitutions' ratifying the compromises which had been reached. Such provisions constituted a mutual guarantee for political forces in the subsequent free elections. Parliaments so elected overcame the most compromised contents by approving texts more oriented towards liberal-democratic values and thus hastened the transition".

was truly negotiated only in a very few cases. For the most part it was imposed from above or below.[58] Nevertheless, it was mostly peaceful.[59]

Poland was the first country to embark on the road to negotiations through a series of roundtables between members of the Polish United Workers' Party and the opposition forces. The latter were clearly recognizable as part of the Solidarity trade union movement (a conglomeration of very different political souls who later acquired their own distinct individuality) and in these negotiations representatives of the Catholic Church also participated.[60] Roundtables began on 6 February 1989 and ended on 5 April 1989, giving Solidarność the opportunity to participate in national elections, which were, however, dominated by the still powerful communist party, even if subsequent events collaborated to wipe out its initial advantages.[61]

In Hungary, as mentioned above, the reformist currents of the Hungarian Socialist Workers' Party played a more significant role, such that the internal transformation preceded roundtable discussions between the government, opposition and some social organizations held between June and September 1989. In fact, the Hungarian transformation was faster with truly free elections in which a pluralistic framework of well-structured political parties was shaped from the outset. This is because the first laws in the field of

58 Regime collapsed in Poland following the formation of the Mazowiecki government on 24 August 1989; in Hungary on 23 October 1989; in the GDR on 8 November 1989; in Bulgaria on 10 November 1989; in Czechoslovakia on 24 November 1989; in Romania on 22 December 1989 and in Albania on 20 February 1991. In the Baltic countries the process towards independence was launched after the elections in the spring of 1990 to end in August 1991 (although the USSR formally ceased to exist in December 1991 with the agreements of Minsk and Alma Ata). In Yugoslavia, the process was similar and initially peaceful. On 23 December 1990 Slovenia held a referendum on independence and on 20 February 1991 presented a project on the dissolution of the Federation by mutual consent. On 25 June 1991 Slovenia and Croatia declared their independence. Macedonia organized a referendum on independence on 8 September 1991 and Bosnia-Herzegovina proclaimed its sovereignty on 15 October 1991. In all three socialist federations, although with different dynamics, there have been prior declarations of sovereignty by the internal republics (in Czechoslovakia only by Slovakia) and later real proclamations of independence. With internal sovereignty republics proclaimed the precedence of republican laws over the federal ones in cases of conflict as well as precedence in terms of ownership of natural resources located in republican territory, which was particularly important in areas of the USSR rich in oil and gas.

59 For further details on the development of transition in each country *see* P. Biscaretti di Ruffia, *1988-1990. Un triennio di profonde trasformazioni costituzionali*, cit.; F. Fejtö, *La fine delle democrazie popolari*, cit.; S. Milacic (Ed.), *La démocratie constitutionnelle en Europe centrale et orientale. Bilans et perspectives*, Bruxelles, Bruylant, 1998; J.J. Linz & A. Stepan, *Problems of Democratic Transition and Consolidation. Southern Europe, South America, and Post-Communist Europe*, cit.; J. Zielonka (Ed.), *Democratic consolidation in Eastern Europe*, Vol. I, *Institutional Engineering*, cit.; S. Milacic (Ed.), *La réinvention de l'État. Démocratie politique et ordre juridique en Europe centrale et orientale*, Bruxelles, Bruylant, 2003; M. Lesage, J. Jenger & D. Maus (Eds.), *Constitutions d'Europe centrale, orientale et balte*, cit.

60 M. Ganino, 'Introduction to Polonia', *in* P. Biscaretti di Ruffia, with the collaboration of M. Ganino, *Le Costituzioni di sette Stati di recente ristrutturazione*, cit., pp. 289-312.

61 For the detailed content of the negotiations *see* J.-P. Massias, *Droit constitutionnel des Etats d'Europe de l'Est*, cit. and P. Biscaretti di Ruffia, *1988-1990. Un triennio di profonde trasformazioni costituzionali*, cit.

political and economic liberalization had been adopted in the second half of the 1980s.[62] Hungary was the first country to dismantle its Iron Curtain *i.e.* its border with Austria, in May-June 1989. Transition was so gradual and peaceful that the Hungarians did not even use the term transition but *rendeszerváltás*, which simply means 'system change'.

In the GDR and Czechoslovakia the anti-regime forces prevailed. Rather than negotiations between forces of the same weight and significance the fall of the regime was unilaterally imposed by the opposition without any concession to the old élite. In Czechoslovakia the populace pushed for change, especially during crowd participation related to symbolic events. The regime collapsed in a few days and the subsequent government made no great concessions to the former communists. Nevertheless, Czechoslovakia is the only country among former USSR satellites in which its communist party kept the same ideology and even name (at present in the Czech Republic it is the Communist Party of Bohemia and Moravia; in Slovakia the communist party simply disappeared). It is clear that in this case communism had strong indigenous roots despite attempts to paint it as an external imposition.[63]

18 October 1989 saw the start of the transition in the GDR when the old leader Honecker was replaced by Krenz. Subsequently the government resigned, citizens 'stormed' the Berlin wall, a new government of technicians directed by Modrow was formed and in December Krenz and the members of the Politburo resigned. Immediately after that there was an agreement between the two Germanys and the commencement of a roundtable discussion between communist leaders and the opposition. The various civic movements and citizens played an important role in preserving the memory of the communist regime by, among other acts, attacking the headquarters of the Stasi where officials were destroying secret documents.[64] Here, as in Czechoslovakia, the question of statehood complicated and influenced the transition to democracy, but revolved around reunification rather than division of the country.

---

62 M. Ganino, 'Introduction to Ungheria', *in* P. Biscaretti di Ruffia, with the collaboration of M. Ganino, *Le Costituzioni di sette Stati di recente ristrutturazione*, cit., pp. 385-397.

63 A. Di Gregorio, *Repubblica ceca*, Bologna, il Mulino, 2008. The so-called Velvet Revolution began on 17 November 1989 following a harsh repression by the communist regime of a student's demonstration. Two days later Havel created the Civic Forum, which brought together all the opposition movements in the Czech Republic. In Slovakia, on the other hand, the Public Against Violence movement organized opposition forces in a similar manner. Between 20 and 27 November hundreds of thousands of people demanded the dismantling of the communist regime in a series of public demonstrations. On the third of December the prime minister Adamec presented a 'reconciliation' government though still dominated by the communists and was immediately rejected by the Civic Forum, which declared a general strike for 11 December. After the agreement of 8 December between the Forum and the communist party Gustáv Husák, general secretary of the communist party since 1969 and head of state since 1975, announced his resignation. The communist Marian Čalfa set up a government of 'national reconciliation' with a majority of non-communist ministers. On 28 December, Alexander Dubček was elected President of the Federal Assembly and the day after Havel was elected President of the Republic.

64 A. Di Gregorio, *Epurazioni post-autoritarie e protezione della democrazia*, cit., pp. 214-215.

In Bulgaria, on the contrary, the reformist forces within the communist party played a leading role during the transition. On 3 January 1990, the negotiations between the government and the Union of democratic forces (a coalition of nine of the fifty political forces formed in late 1989) started. Unlike Hungary, however, the Socialist Party, the heir of the Communist Party, had dominated the political arena long after transition but eventually gave way to a coalition of democratic forces in 1997.

In Romania there was a real coup d'état in December 1989 that led to the physical removal of the dictator and his replacement by former communist forces that ruled for several years. The organization of the forces of democratic opposition was therefore slower and more gradual; not dissimilar to the experience in Bulgaria where, while initially, the democratic movement was rife with internal strife and division, it did eventually develop a more even and steady pace.

In other countries, such as Albania and some republics of the former Yugoslavia, the first pluralistic elections took place later, typically between late 1990 and 1991. The transition was therefore limited, and dominated by former communist forces. In addition to this in the former Yugoslavia, with the exception of Slovenia, the transition from communism awakened the spirit of nationalism, particularly in Serbia and Croatia.

In examining the role of civic organizations involved in the transition from communist regimes as well as the reformist forces of the communist parties, we see the appearance of "temporary political organizations based on membership, which tended to concentrate the popular consensus and then assumed power by placing their representatives in control of the constitutional bodies".[65] This organizational model was based on the forum in which different political subjects came together; such as the remains of pre-war political parties, opposition cultural movements, human rights movements, communist reformers or dissidents. The origin of such movements dates back to the 1970s when civic movements began clamouring for humanization rather than a wholesale replacement of the communist system.[66] The forum's pattern, however, only survived briefly and shortly after gaining some visibility during the transition disintegrated leaving behind political entities that were reorganized according to classical party lines.

The first free elections were particularly important for several reasons; to facilitate the identification of new leaders, to consolidate the path towards democratization, to give legitimacy and credibility in the eyes of the international community and to encourage the formation of independent political parties. The movements should therefore be seen as a bridge between one-party and multi-party political systems. In some cases the political traditions and party families of the interwar period were brought back to life.

65 G. De Vergottini, *Le transizioni costituzionali*, cit., pp. 175-176.

66 *Ibidem*.

Not everywhere did the first free (or semi-free) elections lead to the immediate defeat of the communists. In the absence of strong opposition to the former communists, the latter prevailed (in Romania, Bulgaria, Serbia, Montenegro, and in the majority of the countries of the former USSR). In the Baltic countries the first semi-free elections were held in 1990, and pre-dated the dissolution of the USSR.[67]

The First Free Elections
Poland: 4-18 June 1989 (semi-free)
GDR: 18 March 1990
Hungary: 25 March-8 April 1990
Romania: 20 May 1990
Czechoslovakia: 8 June 1990
Bulgaria: 10 June 1990
Albania: 31 March 1991
Slovenia: 5 April 1990 (before independence, which was proclaimed on October 1991)
Croatia: 10 May 1990
Serbia: 9 December 1990[68]
Macedonia (today the Republic of North Macedonia): 10 November 1990
Bosnia-Herzegovina: 18 November 1990
Montenegro: 9 December 1990
Latvia: within the USSR, elections with multiple candidates 18 March 1990[69]; first elections after independence 5 June 1993

67 On the political system please *cf.* G. Wightman (Ed.), *Party Formation in East-Central Europe*, Aldershot, Edward Elgar, 1995; P. Grilli Di Cortona, *Da uno a molti. Democratizzazione e rinascita dei partiti in Europa orientale*, Bologna, il Mulino, 1997; S. Bartole & P. Grilli di Cortona (Eds.), *Transizione e consolidamento democratico nell'Europa Centro-Orientale. Élites, istituzioni e partiti*, cit.; A. Roger (Ed.), *Des parties pour quoi faire? La representation politique en Europe centrale et orientale*, Bruxelles, Bruylant, 2003; S. Berglund & J. Ekman & F. H. Aarebrot (Eds.), *The Handbook of Political change in Eastern Europe*, Cheltenham, Northampton, E. Elgar, 2013.

68 Serbia and Montenegro were the only two of the six former Yugoslav republics to re-elect their former communist leaders in the first multi-party, democratic elections in 1990. Former communists also dominated the Yugoslav federal government during this time as the disintegrating federal union made these elections unimportant for most of the 6-republic Yugoslavia, allowing the former communists to retain power. This gave the former communists great influence over the constitution-writing process.

69 This refers to the elections in the USSR republics held on February-March 1990, following the federal elections held in March 1989 whose purpose was to elect the new 'Congress of People's Deputies of the USSR' (introduced by the constitutional amendments of December 1988). In the 1990 elections several nationalistic candidates were elected, both in the Baltic republics and in Moldova and Ukraine. For the first time multiple candidacies were allowed on the basis of a new federal election law adopted in December 1989. Refer to M. Ganino, 'Introduction to Russia', *in* P. Biscaretti di Ruffia, with the collaboration of M. Ganino, *Le Costituzioni di sette Stati di recente ristrutturazione*, cit.

Estonia: within the USSR, elections with multiple candidates 18 March 1990 then 20 September 1992[70]
Lithuania: within the USSR, elections with multiple candidates 24 February 1990 then 25 October 1992.

In the USSR the form of state had changed since the constitutional reform of March 1990 which included the overturning of two fundamental axioms on which the socialist state was based *i.e.* the single party system and the ban on private ownership of the means of production. So the transition from the communist system of government occurred in the Gorbachev era, long before the collapse of the USSR.

In the territories of the former USSR and Yugoslavia national issues and particularly those related to sovereignty accompanied the political transition leading to the eventual disintegration of the state. The issue of national sovereignty was crucial everywhere during that most critical biennium 1989-1991. It concerns both the re-appropriation of political sovereignty previously limited by soviet domination, and either the conquest or the re-acquisition of statehood following the dissolution of the socialist federations. The long reach of these phenomena extended to the end of the 2000s (cases of Kosovo and Montenegro),[71] without considering the latent hunger for secession across the post-soviet territories, encouraged by the secession of Kosovo.[72]

In the USSR – and earlier in the RSFSR – and in Yugoslavia the federal solution was needed by the complex national structure of the state. In both cases, representation rights and a limited cultural or linguistic autonomy were attributed not so much to the federated

70 The Russian-speaking population and other non-Estonians were not allowed to participate in the elections. The elections took place according to the provisions of the Constitution of 1938, to symbolize the continuity with the pre-war state and to reaffirm the illegitimacy of the soviet occupation.

71 In the USSR the weakening of the party as a result of Gorbachev's reforms of 1988-1990 led to the collapse of the state. In fact, the state organizational structures were totally identified with those of the party (as demonstrated by the combination of state and party offices in the same persons) making it impossible to attempt a separation between state and party in accordance with the leninist model. In Yugoslavia the Serbian hegemony and its disruptive tendencies had begun to grow steadily following the death of Tito. The Yugoslav case is more similar from a constitutional point of view to that of Czechoslovakia, despite the differences in the number of components of the Yugoslav federation relative to Czechoslovakia. In fact, there was very nearly a confederated constitution which provided for the right of secession. The dissolution of Czechoslovakia followed a different path since it was not contemporary with the transition, despite having suffered its dynamics. For further information about the case of Czechoslovakia please refer to A. Di Gregorio, 'Lo scioglimento della Cecoslovacchia: aspetti politico-costituzionali', *in* A. Di Gregorio & A. Vitale (Eds.), *Il ventennale dello scioglimento pacifico della Federazione ceco-slovacca: profili storico-politici, costituzionali, internazionali*, Rimini, Maggioli, 2013, pp. 109-144. For further information on the dissolution of the USSR, please refer to M. Ganino & C. Filippini, *Dall'URSS alla Comunità di Stati indipendenti*, Milano, Cuesp, 1992.

72 We refer to the cases of Transnistria, Nagorno-Karabakh, South Ossetia and Abkhazia. Slightly different is the case of Crimea, which had been 'incorporated' as part of Russia after the self-proclamation of independence via local referendum.

entities as to the peoples and nationalities (to these the Yugoslav constitutions attributed the right of self-determination, which was however considered extinguished when these peoples decided to became part of the federal state). This caused, at the beginning of the reform process that led to the dissolution of the two federations, clear self-determination claims, not only of the titular nations of the respective federated republics, but also of other nationalities, causing secessionist phenomena not yet completed in that area.[73] The declarations of independence were all adopted following procedures which were inconsistent with the constitution then in force (the USSR Constitution provided the right to secession which was however in contrast with the purposes of the socialist form of state and was theoretically possible only after the adoption of a specific act in 1990)[74] and, therefore, challenged by federal authorities, who were forced to recognize *a posteriori* the new states because of the new international scenario.

However, we can notice that in all three cases, there was no question of a real secession of parts of the state but of the state disintegration or dissolution. Only in the case of Kosovo, one could speak of a real secession, while the case of Montenegro is part of long wave of the dissolution of Yugoslavia (although formally it was a 'domesticated' secession procedure governed by the Charter of 2003 strongly influenced by the European Union).

International documents testify to the peculiarity of these phenomena. One of the opinions of the Badinter Commission (No. 1) clearly stated that it was not a matter of secession of the republics[75] and it also referred to the EEC Guidelines of December 1991

73 With reference to the former soviet area, *see* C. De Stefano, 'Dissoluzione e ristrutturazione statuale sullo spazio ex-sovietico', *Diritto pubblico comparato ed europeo*, No. II, 2015, pp. 503-526.

74 Pursuant to Art. 17 of the Soviet Constitution of 1936, to every Union republic was reserved the right freely to secede from the USSR but Art. 18 stated that "the territory of a Union Republic may not be altered without its consent". Pursuant to Art. 72 of the 1977 Constitution "Each Union Republic shall retain the right freely to secede from the USSR" and Art. 76 defined the republic as "a sovereign soviet socialist state that has united with other Soviet Republics in the Union of Soviet Socialist Republics". Art. 1 of the basic principles of the Constitution of Yugoslavia of 1974 referred to the "nations of Yugoslavia, proceeding from the right of every nation to self-determination, including right to secession". In a similar way was the wording of the Art. 1 of the Constitutions of 1946 and 1963. As for Czechoslovakia, while in the 1920 Constitution the principle of national self-determination was mentioned only in the preamble, in the 1960 Constitution, as amended in 1968, it was mentioned twice, in the preamble ("We, the Czech and Slovak nations, ... acknowledging the indefeasibleness of the right of self-determination as far as separation, and respecting the sovereignty of each nation and its right freely to create for itself the way and form of its national and state life, convinced that a voluntary federal union is an appropriate expression of the right of self-determination and equality before the law, ... we have agreed on the creation of the Czechoslovak federation") and in Art. 1, para. 2 ("The Czechoslovak Socialist Republic is founded on the voluntary bond of the equal, national states of the Czech and the Slovak nations, based on the right of each of them to self-determination"). As in the case of Yugoslavia, also in this case the Constitution mentioned the self-determination of the nations and not of the republics.

75 The first ten opinions of the Badinter Commission were published in the *European Journal of International Law*. In particular, opinions 1-3 in the Vol. 1, No. 3, 1992 and opinions 4-10 in the Vol. 4, No. 1, 1993. *See also* L. Caflisch (Ed.), *Règlement pacifique des différends entre États: perspectives universelle et européenne*, avec une préface de R. Badinter, The Hague London Boston, Kluwer, 1998.

on the recognition of the new states in Central and Eastern Europe and the former Soviet Union, which implied the acceptance of the principles of international law and the democratic character of the new form of state (in the case of the former Yugoslavia, the Commission placed particular emphasis on the respect for the rights of ethnic minorities). The opinion n. 2 clearly denied legitimacy to the secession of the Serbian Republic of Bosnia or the Serbian Republic of Krajna.[76]

From the above it is confirmed that the transition to the liberal-democratic form of state and the state restructuring are closely related events. Moreover, both democratization and phenomena of state-building in Central-Eastern, Baltic and Balkan Europe were complex since the birth of the state in the aftermath of World War I, when the multinational structures of some states resulted from the arbitrary division of old empires. We can therefore recognize interesting parallels between the events that led to the collapse of the empires in 1917-1918 and of the socialist federations in 1990-1992.

To coincide with these phenomena ethnic minorities had resumed their claims with muscular force, which in a pluralistic context amounts to an unconditional acknowledgement of their right to autonomy and self-government. In this way tensions and border disputes dating back to the period following the end of World War I were resurrected.

1.3.1 *Constitutional Transition*

From the constitutional point of view the transition also went through several iterations that can be summarized as follows: amendments of the socialist constitutions subsequent to the negotiations of the roundtables or to the loss of legitimacy of the communist party (the form of state had already changed at this point); the adoption of a new constitution, sometimes preceded by a provisional text; the consolidation and effectiveness of the adopted constitution (thanks to the defence of constitutional courts promptly formed) and hence democratic consolidation.

Therefore from the constitutional point of view the transition did not end with the adoption of a new constitution. From the political point of view it is necessary to pass the test of alternation of different governing political forces. In addition, the main levels of change (legal, economic, cultural and national) occurred over different timescales. In each of them, and for the countries considered, we assume that the final destination was the establishment of a genuinely democratic order, or the approximation to it, certified by the

76 It is the opinion No. 2. The concept is reiterated in the *European Parliament Resolution of 30 April 2015 on the 2014 progress report on Bosnia and Herzegovina* (2014/2952 (RSP). But the situation is problematic because Republika Srpska continues to ask for secession.

negotiations with European organizations for a fuller integration within the continent.[77] Following the progressive degeneration of the democratic achievements in Hungary and Poland, the constitutional literature tends to be less optimistic, even if there is no agreement about the interpretation of the phenomenon underway, that is, if it is a degeneration starting from a successful transition to democracy or a failed transition and thus an absence of a true democratic culture in the two countries (and in others of the same area).[78]

Another peculiar feature of this part of Europe is the length of the transformation process and the challenge to the outcomes of the transition even several years after regime change. As evidenced by recent developments, including constitutional, what had happened in 1989 had left indelible scarring in certain political forces, both at the level of the 'management' of the communist past and of the criticism of the manner in which the transition occurred. This is true especially for Poland and Hungary, which lived through the most negotiated and earliest of transitions. The new Hungarian Fundamental Law of 2011 is full of provisions aimed at moving away from the communist past and also from the post-communist past. In this way, we are witnessing a real detachment from the methods and the results of the transition by the main centre-right party that has been in power since 2010. Evidently, a consensus has not yet been reached among political forces about the methods and the results of transition from communist rule, as can be deduced from the vengeful rage against the former communist regime as expressed by the Fidesz party in the 2010-2014 legislature and instituted within the new constitution. In Poland, the remarks made by former prime minister Jarosław Kazcyński in 2006[79] show that the divisions within Solidarity in the context of the roundtable have never been reconciled and continue to resurface periodically causing a re-ignition of the debate between the political forces. We refer in particular to the action to be taken against the remnants of the past. Post-communist reformism is therefore challenged[80] in the name of a new course completely purged from the remnants of the past. This is a position that will become dramatic with the establishment of a nationalist regime with authoritarian traits following the October 2015 general elections.

Several factors have therefore influenced the affirmation of the new form of the post-socialist state: the nature of the transition process, the character of the economic system,

77 For a brief analysis of the various stages of political and constitutional evolution of the countries concerned between 1989 and 2014 please refer to A. Di Gregorio, 'I processi di trasformazione politico-costituzionale ai confini dell'Unione europea: riflessioni sulle pulsioni espansive del modello democratico europeo e sui suoi limiti', *Diritto pubblico comparato ed europeo*, No. III, 2014.

78 There are no organic studies on the subject even if updates on specific aspects are regularly published in the main journals and blogs of Italian or international constitutional law. In addition to the works already cited in other points of this volume, and in a predominantly political perspective, *see also* AA.VV., *Illiberalism in the V4: Pressure points and bright spots*, Political Capital and Friedrich Naumann Stiftung, May 2018, at www.politicalcapital.hu/pc-admin/source/documents/pc_fnf_v4illiberalism_pressure-points_20180605.pdf (last accessed September 2018).

79 A summary in J.-P. Massias, *Droit constitutionnel des États d'Europe de l'Est*, cit., pp. 142-143.

80 And complicit with the new oligarchs recycled from the old *nomenklatura*, following Kaczyński.

the political culture, the chosen constitutional structure (the semi-presidential form of government can easily degenerate into forms of concentration of powers), the presence or absence of policies to purge the political-administrative élite, the role of former communists, the existence of authoritarian or democratic traditions.

In some cases the transition failed, resulting in an authoritarian and nationalist form of state: There are many examples today within the area of the former USSR and there have been for several years in that of the former Yugoslavia. In other cases, the transition had stalled at a certain stage giving rise to hybrids, of unknown nature, whose future evolution cannot be easily predicted. These types of legal systems have some characteristics of the democratic state such as liberal constitutions with frequent and ostensibly free elections, a small niche for the opposition, but also many others at the opposite end of the spectrum (indifference towards the needs and interests of the citizens, a lack of political inclusiveness, corruption, absence of public trust in the authorities).

These limits mainly concern the member countries of the CIS and partly those of the Balkans. However, the institutional dynamics have evolved in a completely different way in the former satellites of the USSR, now fully integrated into the European Union and the Council of Europe (with the recent exception of Hungary and Poland). The reasons are many; the shorter duration of the socialist form of state, the geographical position, the presence of pre-socialist constitutional traditions and the widely accepted circulation of Western constitutional models, a higher level of economic and social development. In addition, these countries have perceived the end of communism as a 'return to Europe', considering that they share a common history with Western Europe, as well as common traditions, and modes of thinking. This consolidates the perception that models circulate better when there are more democratic conditions.[81]

The success of the liberal-democratic constitutional model should be verified by analysing not only the legal but also the political and social context. Such a verification is necessary because the mere consideration of the new constitutional reality is strongly reductive in the absence of established mechanisms of competitive pluralism and the search for consensus by the citizenry.

It becomes necessary to consider two fundamental elements for explaining the post-socialist democratization. The first regards the fact that we should not overestimate the similarities between the countries concerned. There are profound ethnic differences for example as well as other historical, political and social cleavages. The second aspect concerns the particular characteristics of transition from a socialist form of state with a communist ideology, which cannot be compared to previous post-authoritarian transitions, in which

81 W. Sadurski, *Constitutionalism and the Enlargement of Europe*, Oxford, Oxford University Press, 2012.

not all the variables (political, economic, social, cultural, ideological) were invested by the changes.[82]

Over time, the distance between the consolidated democracies and the countries of the former Soviet Union is steadily increasing. In the latter countries, the anti-democratic trends are dominating and we see a regression in contrast to the terminal phase of the soviet period or to the early post-soviet period as evidenced by the failure of the so-called color revolutions in several CIS countries.

1.4 General Considerations on the Influence of External Actors on the Democratization and Consolidation of Democracy

The transition to democracy in the 'other half' of Europe involved, as mentioned above, the whole continent. The international community in general, and more specifically the institutions of the then European Communities, have also faced the question of the recognition of the new states born from the disintegration of socialist federations. In December 1991, the European Community and the Member States in a joint Declaration issued 'Guidelines on the Recognition of New States in Eastern Europe and the Soviet Union' which included five requirements.[83]

For some countries of the former soviet bloc, there was a sort of 'return' to Europe. In any case, it is perceived these new democracies immediately turned their attention to external horizons for a number of reasons. Firstly, there was the desire to be accepted by international organizations and to receive financial support and approval, which drove the need to respect the democratic conditionality required by international institutions. Secondly, there was a deliberate attempt to emulate Western constitutional models, although with significant differences and a return to some previous traditions. In the third place, membership of European organizations was considered as a possible deterrent against a

82 S. Milacic underlines how much easier and immediate is the construction of the 'rule of law' state compared to political democracy, which requires a long run cultural change. *Cf.* S. Milacic, *De l'âge idéologique à l'âge politique. L'Europe postcommuniste vers la démocratie pluraliste (1989-2009)*, cit., pp. 426-427.

83 Declaration on the 'Guidelines on the Recognition of New States in Eastern Europe and in the Soviet Union', adopted by the EC on 16 December 1991; Reproduced in *The European Journal of International Law*, Vol. 4, 1993, pp. 72-73. The purpose of the Declaration was to recognize the new states formed on a democratic basis and to establish a common position on their formal recognition. These states were asked to engage in a number of aspects before obtaining the recognition from the Member States of the EEC: respect for the rule of law, democracy and human rights and the guarantee of the rights of ethnic and national groups; respect for the inviolability of territorial boundaries and commitment to settle all matters concerning the succession of states through international treaties. These are principles that were formally addressed to states born of the dissolution of the Soviet Union and of Yugoslavia. For a comment please refer to J. Charpentier, *La Déclaration des Douze sur la reconnaissance de nouveaux États, R.G.D.I.P.*, No. 96, 1992, pp. 343-355.

return to authoritarian tendencies and a way to consolidate democratic reforms. At the same time, there was a need for their emerging democratic state to be associated with 'civilization' and 'modernization'.[84]

The entry into the Council of Europe and NATO preceded their admission into the European Union, considering that negotiations with the European Union and the conditions for economic and legislative harmonization have been unprecedented compared to previous enlargements.

Apropos the Council of Europe, some countries had applied for admission in 1989. The conditions for membership were articulated in October 1993.[85] The acceptance of the first three countries, Hungary, Czechoslovakia and Poland, had not raised any issues regarding democratic compatibility. For other countries, subsequently accepted (such as some former USSR countries, including Russia, and the former republics of Yugoslavia), the prospect of mutual benefits arising from membership in the Council of Europe was considered more important than the need for compliance with the usual standards for inclusion, which would not have been completely achievable by these states. In some cases the waiving of these usual requirements of entry acted as a spur to the continuing enlightenment and gave rise to the hope that it would eventually lead to democratization.

The requirements for entry into the European Union and the conditions set for the economic and legislative harmonization were much more complex than was the case with the previous enlargements. It was the fifth round of enlargement since the foundation of the European Communities. In the first four rounds, institutions of the Communities only required candidates to meet economic requirements, but commencing with the candidacy of Spain, Greece and Portugal concerns about political and constitutional compliance began to emerge. The European Treaties initially mandated only that "any European state may apply to become a member of the Community" (Art. 205 Euratom Treaty, Art. 237 EEC Treaty) or that "any European state may apply to join this Treaty" (Art. 98 ECSC

84 Synonyms of 'Europeanization'. *See* W. Sadurski, *Constitutionalism and the Enlargement of Europe*, cit., pp. 144-146.

85 With the Vienna Declaration of 9 October 1993, the Council of Europe mandated universal suffrage, the secret ballot and multi-party elections as conditions for the admission of new Member States. It also required to ratify ECHR and to adhere to new conventions, particularly concerning the protection of minorities, a very sensitive issue in former socialist countries. As stated in the Vienna Declaration: "Such accession presupposes that the applicant country has brought its institutions and legal system into line with the basic principles of democracy, the rule of law and respect for human rights. The people's representatives must have been chosen by means of free and fair elections based on universal suffrage. Guaranteed freedom of expression and notably of the media, protection of national minorities and observance of the principles of international law must remain, in our view, decisive criteria for assessing any application for membership. An undertaking to sign the European Convention on Human Rights and accept the Convention's supervisory machinery in its entirety within a short period is also fundamental. We are resolved to ensure full compliance with the commitments accepted by all Member States within the Council of Europe", https://wcd.coe.int/ViewDoc.jsp?id=621771 (last accessed September 2018).

Treaty). At the time of the first enlargement (United Kingdom, Ireland, Denmark, Norway), in the opinion given in 1967 the European Commission noted that the entry of countries whose traditions of political stability and democracy were so deeply rooted would have a beneficial effect for the Community as a whole. For the second enlargement (Greece), the opinion of the Commission in 1976 made entry subject to the consolidation of democracy in that country. For Spain and Portugal (opinions released in 1978) similar expressions were used. For the fourth enlargement (Sweden, Finland, Austria), which followed the adoption of the Maastricht Treaty, the Commission expressly stated that "a state which is a candidate must satisfy the three basic conditions of European identity, democratic status and respect for human rights".[86]

Over time European Union institutions increasingly refined requirements that are the basis of relations with Third Countries, especially in the case of envisaged membership of which some are: democratic clauses included in the association agreements and an insistence on respect for human rights and the rule of law,[87] pre-accession agreements with economic and constitutional parameters as well as a commitment to the acceptance of the *acquis communautaire,* conditions set out in the 1993 Copenhagen European Council followed by the Essen Council of 1994, pre-accession strategy (that is the association agreements subject to verification of some conditions such as rule of law, free elections and market economy; a special white paper underlined measures to be taken to start the association procedures), the new rules approved by the Amsterdam Council in 1997.[88]

The turning point, however, was the Copenhagen Council of 1993, in which the criteria for membership were for the first time expressly set out. Candidate countries seeking membership would have to comply with both political ("stability of institutions guaranteeing democracy, the rule of law, human rights and protection of minorities"), economic ("the existence of a functioning market economy as well as the capacity to cope with competitive pressures and market forces within the Union") and legal conditions ("the applicant countries' capacity to assume the obligations of membership including adherence to the

86 *See* the 1992 opinions on Sweden and Finland. In the opinion on Austria there are only a few references to the 'political criteria'. *See* E. Tucny, *L'Élargissement de l'Unione Européenne aux Pays d'Europe centrale et orientale*, Paris, L'Harmattan, 2000; M. Cremona (Ed.), *The Enlargement of the European Union*, Oxford, Oxford University Press, 2003; T. Cerruti, 'L'adesione della Croazia all'Unione europea e i criteri politici', *federalismi.it*, No. 13, 2013.

87 Apart from economic conditionality (*see* the Phare program), since 1989 the European Parliament has mandated the inclusion of a reference to human rights in association agreements and in the negotiating mandate given to the Commission. Refer to F. Schimmelfennig, S. Engert & H. Knobel, 'The Impact of EU Political Conditionality', *in* F. Schimmelfennig & U. Sedelmeier (Eds.), *The Europeanization of Central and Eastern Europe*, Ithaca, Cornell University Press, 2005, p. 30.

88 European treaties were modified to give legal form to the Copenhagen political requirements (*see* Arts. 6 and 49). On this point, B. Nascimbene, 'La procedura di adesione all'Unione europea' and M. Maresceau, 'From Europe Agreement to Accession Negotiations', both in M. Ganino, G. Venturini (Eds.), *L'Europa di domani: verso l'allargamento dell'Unione*, cit.

aims of political, economic and monetary Union"). European institutions have since adopted a precise notion of political transition in which democracy, rule of law, human rights and minority rights seem different things, despite being included in a common process. The European Council in Madrid in December 1995 added a new requirement viz. administrative capacity, or "the adjustment of administrative structures" of the candidate countries.[89] However, in the period 1993-1997 the main focus was the market *acquis*. Political conditions acquired real meaning after the 1997 European Council of Luxembourg, when the Commission began to assess candidates' progress in annual reports – a real component of the pre-accession strategy – which included sections on 'Democracy and the rule of law' and 'Fundamental rights'.[90]

At the beginning of the monitoring process, some countries already met the criteria of democratic conditionality (Poland, Hungary, the Czech Republic, Estonia, Slovenia) while others only approximated the requirements (Latvia, Lithuania, Bulgaria, Romania). Slovakia failed to meet these criteria and was excluded from the negotiations but was readmitted during the Helsinki European Council in 1999, subsequent to the change in the political landscape brought about by the new prime minister Dzurinda.[91]

Notwithstanding this, early reports identified a series of important limitations (lack of independence of the judiciary and local government, limited independence of the media, discrimination against minorities etc.) thus emphasizing the gap between the letter of the new constitutional provisions and its practice in the political and social context. In particular, the Commission raised concerns about the issue of political rights and minority rights in Romania, Bulgaria and Slovakia.[92]

89 On this point T. Cerruti, 'L'adesione della Croazia all'Unione europea e i criteri politici', cit., and the extensive bibliography on the Copenhagen criteria cited in footnotes 2 and 3. At the Copenhagen Council a fourth criterion was articulated, which has become more important since 2006, namely the Union's ability to grow while maintaining the pace of integration.

90 We are talking about annual evaluation reports and the so-called strategy or composite papers issued every year by the Commission from 1998 to 2003 (for the first ten candidates) and up to 2006 (for Romania and Bulgaria). *See* W. Sadurski, 'Accession's Democracy Dividend: The Impact of the EU Enlargement upon Democracy in the New Member States of Central and Eastern Europe', *European Law Journal*, Vol. 10, No. 4, July 2004, pp. 371-401.

91 *See* G. Pridham, 'The European Union's Democratic Conditionality and Domestic Politics in Slovakia: the Mečiar and Dzurinda Governments compared', *Europe-Asia Studies*, No. 54, 2002.

92 On this point *see* L. Mattina, 'La promozione dei diritti umani', *in* L. Mattina (Ed.), *La sfida dell'allargamento. L'Unione europea e la democratizzazione dell'Europa centro-orientale*, cit., pp. 135-138. Even historical issues, such as the fate of the Sudeten Germans in Czechoslovakia, influenced the accession process in some countries. However, these issues have not been the subject of special attention in the annual reports of the Commission. In relation to minorities, the main instrument at international level were not only bilateral and multilateral treaties but also statements and opinions of a number of organizations. A system of monitoring the implementation of the requirements articulated in the document is part of the Framework Convention for the protection of minority rights, based on reports submitted periodically by Member States. The Council of Europe Committee of Ministers can send to Member recommendations www.coe.int/t/dghl/monitoring/minorities/3_FCNMdocs/Table_en.asp (last accessed September 2018).

Thus, subsequent to the fifth enlargement the political criteria had become far more fundamental to the European Union. This is a product of a certain lack of confidence in the former communist countries, especially the Balkan states. In connection with the enlargement to include the Western Balkans, the EU institutions added to the parameters of Copenhagen other criteria related to political events specific to this area (return of refugees, respect of the peace agreements, non-discrimination against minorities, independent media, good neighbourly relations).[93]

External stresses should necessarily be combined with internal features of post-communist context, which includes any democratic traditions or early institutional reforms. Moreover, if we limit the discussion to the institutional issues (*e.g.* forms of government, constitutional review, regionalization, etc.) the conditionality is limited by its indeterminacy, considering that there are no common standards in these areas among the old Member States of the Union. Conditionality in many cases was applied in a flexible manner and a generic form of 'minimum conditions' was preferred as opposed to the introduction of specific, rigid institutional designs.[94]

European conditionality has not explicitly focused on the drafting of new constitutions (this does not include the opinions of the Venice Commission on the matter), adopted at an earlier stage, even if they were subsequently subjected to adjustment procedures to

93 Since 1999 (*Communication from the Commission to the Council and the European Parliament on the Stabilization and Association Process for Countries of South-Eastern Europe*, 26 May 1999, http://europa.eu/legislation_summaries/enlargement/western_balkans/r18003_en.htm (last accessed September 2018) the EU introduced a program called the *Stabilization and Association Process* (for Western Balkans), which provided various tools such as securing Stabilisation and Association Agreements (the agreement with Croatia envisaged specific regional cooperation, especially with neighbouring states, and cooperation with the Hague Tribunal). Among others, please refer to A.E. Kellermann, J.W. De Zwaan & J. Czuczai (Eds.), *EU Enlargement: The Constitutional Impact at EU and National Level*, The Hague, T.M.C. Asser Press, 2001; A. Ott & K. Inglis (Eds.), *Handbook on European Enlargement: A Commentary on the Enlargement Process*, The Hague, TMC Asser Press, 2002; N. Walker (Ed.), *Sovereignty in Transition*, Oxford, Hart Publishing, 2003; J. Ziller (Ed.), *L'Européanisation des droits constitutionnels à la lumière de la Constitution pour l'Europe*, Paris, L'Harmattan, 2003; L. Mattina (Ed.), *La sfida dell'allargamento, L'Unione europea e la democratizzazione dell'Europa centro-orientale*, cit.; A. Albi, *EU Enlargement and the Constitutions of Central and Eastern Europe*, Cambridge, Cambridge University Press, 2005; H. Grabbe, *The EU's Transformative Power: Europeanization trough Conditionality in Central and Eastern Europe*, Basingstoke, Palgrave Macmillan, 2006; W. Sadurski & A. Czarnota & M. Krygier, *Spreading Democracy and the Rule of Law? The Impact of EU Enlargement on the Rule of Law, Democracy and Constitutionalism in Post-Communist Legal Orders*, The Netherlands, Springer, 2006; P. Levitz & G. Pop-Eleches, 'Why No Backsliding? The European Union's Impact on Democracy and Governance before and after Accession', *Comparative Political Studies*, Vol. 43, No. 4, 2010.

94 This 'minimalism' would make it difficult, according to W. Sadurski, *Constitutionalism and the Enlargment*, cit., p. 153, to determine whether there was or was not imitation. In some areas, where the compliance requirements were more specific, such as the civil service, the transposition was clearer. The opposite was the case for regionalization. Some authors are very critical about the vagueness of the Copenhagen criteria, for instance D. Kochenov, 'Behind the Copenhagen Façade: The Meaning and Structure of the Copenhagen Political Criterion of Democracy and the Rule of Law', *European Integration Online Papers*, http://eiop.or.at/eiop/pdf/2004-010.pdf (last accessed September 2018).

include the so-called European clauses.[95] Nevertheless, in the drafting of these constitutions external influences were present, although using the term 'externally imposed' only applies to a few constitutions.[96]

As for NATO membership, the criteria required for admission, although not as detailed as those of the European Union, were similar, even if the former organization did not have a precise monitoring process. The participation in or candidacy for NATO, however, played a key role in the stabilization of relations between neighbouring countries (as in the case of Hungary and Romania) and improved the protection of the rights of minorities (as for example in the Baltic countries).

Even joining the OSCE had an important influence in the stabilization of democracy in these countries thanks to the Office for Democratic Institutions and Human Rights (ODIHR), which performs the important task of electoral monitoring in the new democracies.

Ultimately the impact of 'external' constraints can be seen at various levels:

1. Acceptance of principles and values of Western legal civilization, within the framework of the liberal-democratic constitutionalism (learning Western models, recovering pre-communist traditions, complying with the opinions of the Venice Commission).
2. Direct influence of international documents (especially the ECHR) and of other European constitutions on the bill of rights and their protection among emerging democracies.
3. Conditionality of the Council of Europe, NATO, OSCE and the European Union; a special positioning of international law among the sources of law of the emerging democracies with the aim of gaining the recognition of major international organizations.

It should however be noted that some of the most important political and institutional innovations (free elections, separation of powers), especially in the initial period, were driven by national public opinion, the democratic opposition participating in the round tables (Poland, Hungary) and the mass demonstrations (Czechoslovakia, Romania).[97]

95 B. de Witte, 'The Impact of Enlargement on the Constitution of the European Union', *in* M. Cremona (Ed.), *The Enlargement of the European Union*, Oxford, Oxford University Press, 2003; A. Albi *et al.*, *The Impact of EU Accession on the Legal Orders of New Member States and (Pre) Candidate Countries: Hopes and Fears*, The Hague, Asser Press, 2006.

96 *See* the cases of Bosnia and Herzegovina; Kosovo in relation to the Constitutional Framework for Provisional Self-Government; the drafting of the Albanian Constitution of 2008; the Constitutional Charter of Serbia and Montenegro of 2003; the amendments of the Macedonian (FYROM) Constitution of 2001 following the civil war.

97 So believes W. Sadurski, *Accession's Democracy Dividend: The Impact of the EU Enlargement upon Democracy in the New Member States of Central and Eastern Europe*, cit. The author insists that internal pressures towards democratization, due to a combination of factors, including the pre-communist traditions and perceptions of the benefits of democracy were pivotal to the transition. Only the combination of

Certain principles were perceived as the minimum standard and therefore a spontaneous emulation of Western models emerged. This emulation was foreshadowed by the dissidents or reformists before the fall of communism and effected immediately after the transition. In some cases, the institutional innovations preceded the transition and were implemented, even if only in a limited way, within the same socialist regime. Some authors have overestimated the impact of the prospect of joining European organizations on the institutional development of these countries, for example with respect to the introduction of strong constitutional courts which was not actually required by European conditionality.[98]

In general, external conditionality had most significant consequences in countries with more developed economic, political and social contexts. On the contrary, where such contexts were less favourable (former USSR, the Balkans) the take-up was either only in form or sluggish. Progress on the path of democratization had been determined, in many cases, by the existence of vibrant civil societies, a favourable geographic position and predominantly anti-communist political cultures. In these cases, the external influence served as a catalyst of an already existing internal transformation.[99]

The degree of influence of external pressures varies not only geographically but also according to the severity of conditionality. The European Union, NATO and the Council of Europe exercised the greatest impact on the process of democratization. The first two because of the high number of stringent requirements for membership (in all spheres of political, economic and social life), and the third because of its technical and legal assistance.[100]

With specific regard to the enlargement of the European Union, the application of the post-socialist countries raised awareness and encouraged debate among the Union members regarding the principles of conditionality which had until then remained in an embryonic state. The so-called democratic conditionality has become an essential element not only for present and future candidates, but also for Third Countries with which the EU has relations in various ways, for example within the European Neighbourhood Policy. There have been countless debates about EU conditionality, especially about whether its transformative power is hugely significant or trivial when we consider countries already advanced

internal and external factors made the democratization a very rapid affair for some countries. We must therefore consider the 'emulation' effect and also the fact that certain institutional innovations – such as the introduction of constitutional courts – preceded the fall of communism.

98 *See, e.g.*, B. Ackerman, 'The rise of World Constitutionalism', *Virginia Law Review*, Vol. 83, No. 4, pp. 771-797.

99 A. Cooley, 'Western Conditions and Domestic Choices: The Influence of External Actors on the Post-Communist Transition', *Nations in Transit 2003: Democratization in East Central Europe and Eurasia*, FreedomHouse, New York, 2003.

100 *See* A. Di Gregorio, 'Il processo di costituzionalizzazione dei paesi dell'Europa centro-orientale', *in* G. Vacca (Ed.), *Dalla Convenzione alla Costituzione. Rapporto 2005 della Fondazione Istituto Gramsci sull'integrazione europea*, Bari, Dedalo, 2005, pp. 143-163.

towards the basic rules of democracy.[101] These debates acquire a significant value not only in rethinking, long after the event, the dynamics of democratic transition, but also in the light of what happened following entry into the Union, with respect to compliance with the standards so rigorously imposed during the entry process.

It should be pointed out that such a 'deployment of forces' in the phase preceding accession is not matched by an equally stringent subsequent monitoring of compliance with the essential requirements of European democratic principles. In this case, the infringement procedure envisaged by the TFEU, and applied in some cases of rule of law crisis, is of limited impact while the application of Article 7 TUE, the so-called 'nuclear option', continues to provoke debates despite the decision of the European Commission to start its activation towards Poland at the end of 2017.[102] Similarly, we point out that for some countries the effectiveness of democratic standards is always at risk. Many authors have in fact criticized the haste with which these countries have been admitted, perhaps motivated by reasons of economic opportunism.

The criteria for joining the EU today are not even remotely comparable to the conditions that applied in the 1970s. In addition, the fifth enlargement has a political implication different from previous ones because of the emphasis placed on the security of Europe.[103] The European institutions require compliance with an increasingly complex system that has at its base the essential elements of constitutionalism *i.e.* the rule of law, respect for human rights and fundamental freedoms. EU membership is expected to dampen nationalist and populist tendencies thanks to the sharing of liberal-democratic values. It is an attempt to harmonize common values across EU states that has failed within the Council of Europe, in spite of the fact that the CoE is based exclusively on the values of democracy.

---

101 For an account, please refer to W. Sadurski, *Constitutionalism and the Enlargement of Europe*, cit. and to F. Schimmelfennig & U. Sedelmeier (Eds.), *The Europeanization of Central and Eastern Europe*, cit.

102 The rule of law crisis literature has already reached a considerable amount of contributions, starting from 2011-2012. *See, e.g.*, A. von Bogdandy & P. Sonnevend (Eds.), *Constitutional Crisis in the European Constitutional Area. Theory, Law and Politics in Hungary and Romania*, Oxford, Hart Publishing, 2015; D. Kochenov & L. Pech, 'Monitoring and Enforcement of the Rule of Law in the EU: Rethoric and Reality', *European Constitutional Law Review*, Vol. 11, Issue 3, 2015; C. Closa & D. Kochenov (Eds.), *Reinforcing Rule of Law Oversight in the European Union*, Cambridge, Cambridge University Press, 2016; A. Di Gregorio, 'Lo stato di salute della rule of law in Europa: c'è un regresso generalizzato nei nuovi Stati membri dell'Unione?', *DPCE on-line*, No. 4, 2016; D. Kochenov & L. Pech, 'Better Late than Never? On the Commission's Rule of Law Framework and Its First Activation', *Journal of Common Market Studies*, Vol. 54, No. 5, 2016; D. Kochenov & M. van Wolferen, *The dialogical rule of law and the breakdown of dialogue in the EU*, EUI Working Paper Law 2018/01. For updates on the debate on the topic, *see* the posts published on *Verfassungsblog on matter constitutional*, http://verfassungsblog.de (last accessed September 2018).

103 S. Bartole, 'Considerazioni conclusive', *in* M. Ganino & G. Venturini (Eds.), *L'Europa di domani: verso l'allargamento dell'Unione*, cit. *See also* W. Sadurski, *Accession's Democracy Dividend: The Impact of the EU Enlargement upon Democracy in the New Member States of Central and Eastern Europe*, cit.

Once the process of entry has been successfully completed there is the risk that new Member States regress in respect of the rule of law and human rights[104] when they apply to areas of competence not completely standardized at European level.[105] However, despite a certain political fragility in some countries there has not been a general decay of democratic standards.[106] This is because there are several control mechanisms, albeit less stringent and less visible than those of the pre-accession conditionality. Apart from the soft law of the Council of Europe and the case law of the Strasbourg Court, and not including here the extreme case of the mechanisms under Article 7 TEU (included in the Treaty to preclude authoritarian resurgence in new Member States),[107] there are other measures that EU institutions can invoke.[108] Firstly, there is the obligation to comply with EU legislation in the fields of competence of the Union. Then there is the action of the Court of Justice, which, however, in regard to respect for fundamental rights is limited to those areas in which Member States apply EU law. Further, there are reports of the European Parliament on the respect of fundamental rights within the EU, seen as a kind of control and soft monitoring. In general the emulation effect and the desire for integration continues even subsequent to entry. There are also economic levers such as financial incentives, with commensurate sanctions, which may be applied against countries failing to respect fundamental principles, like was the case with Romania and Bulgaria.[109]

---

104 D. Kochenov, *EU Enlargement and the Failure of Conditionality*, The Hague, Wolters Kluwer International, 2008.

105 B. de Witte, *The Impact of Enlargement on the Constitution of the European Union*, cit., p. 240, mentions, *e.g.*, children's rights, prison conditions, protection of minorities.

106 Despite the constitutional crises of Hungary and Poland, other new members of the Union seems to continue to express solid democratic institutions, despite the growth of nationalism and populism that characterizes most European countries as a reaction to the economic crisis (and therefore to the crisis of the welfare state) and to the migrant emergency.

107 So W. Sadurski, *Constitutionalism and the Enlargement of Europe*, cit., which maintains that the application and subsequent entry of Central and Eastern European countries within the EU has triggered a self-sustaining process of mutual influence. This has prompted the EU towards a greater 'constitutionalization' and concern for the requirements of democracy and on how best to preserve them. Even the old Member States have benefited from this. The conditionality based on democratic requirements has also helped to configure the EU not only as a community of interests, but also of common values. The entry of new members has prompted the European Union to formulate its own catalogue of rights complete with commensurate control mechanisms. It is a circular process of conditioning and synergies, which also involves the courts both national and European. The same observation applies to the Council of Europe and the Strasbourg Court which has gradually become an European constitutional court (the practice of 'pilot' judgments was inaugurated just after the entrance of the countries of Central and Eastern Europe and the Balkans). *See also* O. Pollicino, *L'allargamento ad est dell'Europa e rapporti tra Corti costituzionali e Corti europee. Verso una teoria generale dell'impatto interordinamentale del diritto sovranazionale?*, Milano, Giuffrè, 2010.

108 Refer to U. Sedelmeier, 'After Conditionality: Post-Accession Compliance with EU Law in East-Central Europe', *Journal of European Public Policy*, Vol. 15, No. 6, 2008.

109 For Romania and Bulgaria the post-admission monitoring focused mainly on issues such as corruption and organized crime, with the possibility of sanctions such as cuts in subsidies. In the case of Romania, in December 2006 the Commission considered that it was necessary to activate this mechanism because there was not sufficient progress after joining the EU in relation to the accountability and efficiency of the judiciary.

However, the new EU Framework to Strengthen the Rule of Law of 11 March 2014,[110] applied to Poland and adopted as a consequence of the failure of other types of intervention against Hungary, is turning out to be unsuitable for its purpose. The escalation of the confrontation between the European institutions and the Polish government has led the European Commission to initiate the procedure for the activation of Article 7 of the TEU in December 2017. Despite the difficulties that these institutions have experienced in combating the crisis of the founding values of the Union, the debate that has taken place at different levels is avoiding similar degenerations in other Member States while keeping alive the attention on the protection of fundamental values.

Clearly, European institutions have a continuing concern about these issues, as evidenced by the constant reference to European constitutional heritage. Democracy and human rights are values in themselves. They are not goals whose attainment is specifically targeted by EU legislation for implementation by the market but are crucial to the process of European unification regardless of their economic role.

See Commission Decision of 13 December 2006 *Establishing a mechanism for cooperation and verification of progress in Romania to address specific benchmarks in the areas of judicial reform and the fight against corruption* at https://eur-lex.europa.eu/legal-content/EN/TXT/PDF/?uri=CELEX:32006D0928&from=EN (last accessed September 2018). The link to the mechanism is the following: https://ec.europa.eu/info/strategy/justice-and-fundamental-rights/effective-justice/rule-law/assistance-bulgaria-and-romania-under-cvm/reports-progress-bulgaria-and-romania_en (last accessed September 2018).

110 *Communication from the Commission to the European Parliament and the Council of 11 March 2014: A new EU Framework to strengthen the Rule of Law.*

2 Constitutions

Angela Di Gregorio

2.1 Introduction

As aforementioned in the previous chapter, with the collapse of the socialist state we witness the origin of a new concept of Europe, also from a constitutional perspective. Indeed, since the moment the former USSR satellites and some of the former soviet republics started adopting the features of the liberal-democratic constitutionalism, Europe can be divided into two different spaces, one almost completely democratic and another that is still in the process of democratization.[1]

There are two main reasons to consider countries which 'came back to Europe'[2] as constitutional laboratories: firstly, because they are receptors of Western constitutional models,[3] and then because they are innovators, thanks to their unique identity and to their cultural characteristics. Our research aims, therefore, to discover if – in addition to the European constitutionalism's heritage – these new constitutions include also innovative aspects and remnants of their historical past.

It is easy to understand, in the light of what have just been explained, why it is in these countries that the most wide-ranging constitutional developments in the last thirty years occurred. However, this constitutional dynamism cannot be always considered positive. In some cases, the legislative and constitutional changes that took place after the entry into the European Union (as well as into the Council of Europe and OSCE) caused constitutional

---

1 Lights and shadows have been highlighted by the papers published on the special issue of the *International Journal of Constitutional Law*, Vol. 13, No. 1, 2015 dedicated to the *Constitutionalism in Central and Eastern Europe*. Please refer also to the special issue of the *Revista General de Derecho Público Comparado*, No. 16, 2014 titled *2004-2014: Diez años desde la ampliación hacia el Este de la Unión Europea: un balance multidisciplinar* (2004-2014 Ten Years since the Eastward Enlargement of the European Union: A Multidisciplinary Balance) edited by Carlos Flores Juberías. *See also* Ph. Claret (Ed.), *L'Europe centrale et orientale, 25 ans après la chute du Mur de Berlin. Retour sur "l'expérience post-communiste"*, Numero spéciale de *Est Europa*, No. 2, 2016. Quite old but very interesting: S. Milacic (Ed.), *La démocratie constitutionnelle en Europe centrale et orientale. Bilans et perspectives*, Bruxelles, Bruylant, 1998.

2 On the 'return' to Europe of some of these countries *see* M. Kundera, 'Un Occidente sequestrato, ovvero la tragedia dell'Europa centrale' (original *Únos západu aneb Tragédie střední Evropy*, 1983), *Nuovi Argomenti*, No. 9, 1984; J. Rupnik, *L'autre Europe. Crise et fin du Communisme*, Paris, Odile Jacob, 1990.

3 A. Stanger, 'How Important Are New Constitutions for Democratic Consolidation? Lessons from the Post-communist States', *Democratization*, Vol. 11, No. 3, June 2004, pp. 1-26.

backslidings[4] which have alerted the EU institutions. The reference/confrontation with the EU and Council of Europe's institutions is a staple in the constitutional development in these countries. However, democratic conditionality mechanisms have not always been successful, considering that they are based on standards that do not take into account the traditions and national context of the candidate countries.

The overlapping of different cultural layers makes the study of post-communist constitutionalism rather complex. The early impression of a general reception of the classical and established constitutional models is followed by a more complex evaluation. It is necessary to 'rediscover' some constitutional roots (that have already been highlighted in the first chapter of this volume), deriving from the constitutions written in the period between the two World Wars. Secondly, it is to be considered that these 'borrowings' or influences are often adapted to fit the new context, and this may lead to large discrepancies with the original model. Thirdly, residues of socialist constitutionalism may be found.

For what concerns the autochthonous elements of constitutionalism, we can say that they have been diluted as a result of the constant comparison with European constitutionalism, and that they are often hidden behind the rhetoric these countries use to distance themselves from their past. If the distancing from the communist past can be generically seen as a positive trend, we should not forget it could also lead to lose even the positive aspects of the socialist constitutionalism (social rights, civic participation, the role of the prosecution organs in the citizens' protection, the public debate on the adoption of laws and constitutions, workers' participation in the management of enterprises,[5] etc.). A greater focus on social rights and civic participation in a pluralist context would have had a new significance. In addition, the most recent constitutions have not taken the opportunity to experience new forms of civic participation – which have been under discussion for years in Europe – such as electronic consultations, regulation of lobbyism, transparency of the decision-making process.[6] Likewise, they did not introduce innovations in terms of political participation, which was once again tied to the 'party model', despite the initial push towards civic and environmental organizations, or trade unions.

Focusing the observation on countries where the transition to constitutionalism has been more successful (the Baltic countries, Slovenia, the Czech Republic, and since April 2010 and October 2015 also Hungary and Poland), it is possible to notice how the distance

4 B. Bugarič, 'A Crisis of Constitutional Democracy in Post-communist Europe: "Lands in-Between" Democracy and Authoritarianism', *International Journal of Constitutional Law*, Vol. 13, No.1, 2015, pp. 219-245.

5 Although some of these constitutions, especially in the former Yugoslav countries, are rich of remnants of the socialist constitutionalism.

6 Even if, thanks to the pressures of GRECO, the Group of States Against Corruption of the Council of Europe, these countries are currently taking care of these problems through amendments of legislation or of the parliamentary standing orders.

in time makes it easier to assess their constitutional and political history, in which the socialist form of state represented only an interlude – though a significative one, in terms of systemic transformations. However, differences among the different regions of Central-Eastern, Baltic and Balkan Europe are macroscopic and even the equalizing communist factor could not produce a total levelling.

As reported in the first chapter, the 1920s and 1930s are two essential decades in which the roots of constitutionalism were set in that area. Constitutional patterns predominating in the first post-war period were those of the French Third Republic and of the Weimar Republic (as well as those of Switzerland, for some institutions). These patterns were used as references by Czechoslovakia, Poland and the Baltic states. In Bulgaria, Romania and Serbia (which were monarchies) the constitutional law was less developed. In any case, with the exception of Czechoslovakia, societies to which those constitutional engineering – influenced by Western models – had to be applied were weak, divided and heterogeneous from a social and ethnic point of view. These weaknesses, along with a deeply fragmented political framework, favoured the rise of authoritarian systems of government founded upon the fascist or Nazi model.[7]

The existence of these constitutional traditions, though, is not to be overlooked. In fact, although with all the limitations deriving from the lack of lasting or effective implementation of constitutional provisions which were very advanced for that time – far more advanced than the societies to which they had to apply: social rights, primacy of international law, protection of minority rights, constitutional justice – they had an influence on post-socialist constitutionalism. It is thanks to those traditions that – when the socialist system of government was imposed in this part of Europe – there were profound differences from the soviet prototype, that lead to national variations survived until the end of the socialist period, which affected the way the transition to democracy occurred.[8]

2.2 Constitutional 'Seasons' in Central-Eastern, Baltic and Balkan Europe

The political and constitutional developments subsequent to 1989 can be differentiated into three main phases.

7 Please refer to P. Fornaro, 'L'Europa orientale tra passato, presente e futuro: Hugh Seton-Watson e il suo posto nella storiografia sull'Est europeo', Introduction to the Italian version of H. Seton-Watson, *Le democrazie impossibili. L'Europa orientale tra le due guerre mondiali*, cit., pp. 9-10.

8 *Cf.* P. Biscaretti di Ruffia, *Introduzione al diritto costituzionale comparato*, cit., pp. 456-457.

2.2.1 1989-1999

The first decade was characterized by the discovering or rediscovering of the democratic system. An extreme political pluralism was the effect of the formation of new parties and of the reconstitution of historical ones, along with the disintegration of civic and labour movements that were protagonists of the transition. Other features of this period were the instability of governments and the volatility of the party system, as well as the transition from the single-member constituency electoral system – typical of socialistic states – to initially scarcely selective proportional representation systems.

From the constitutional point of view, the transition from the socialist to the liberal-democratic model occurred through the revision of the socialist constitutions (with limited exceptions), pending the approval of a completely new text, that was to be redacted by parliaments elected on the basis of the new pluralistic rules. In some cases, for example Albania or Poland, before the adoption of the new constitutions, temporary/interim constitutions were adopted. In some countries of the former Yugoslavia, the adoption of the new constitutions preceded the dissolution of the State (Serbia, Croatia, Macedonia). Only in one case the constitution of the interwar period was restored, and it was Latvia, with the 1922 Constitution. In Lithuania the pre-war constitution was symbolically restored for just one hour. The political debate on the reintroduction of pre-war constitutions as a symbol of continuity with that period and denial of socialist regime was very heated in the Baltic states and in Czechoslovakia. Only in Hungary the old 1949 constitution has been continuously amended, originating in 2011 a completely new text, that substituted the previous one, mainly for political reasons and that received many contestations.

By the end of this period, the democratic structuring of society and political system took over the disintegration of the old system, with the emergence of a new pluralistic political culture. The most advanced countries were admitted into the Council of Europe and the path to EU membership began. Transitional justice measures (especially lustration)[9] are also to be included in the long 'deconstruction' phase of the previous system.

Between 1999 and 2000 a turning point towards a truly pluralistic and pro-European path occurred also in Croatia and in the Yugoslav Federation (which united only Serbia and Montenegro), as a result respectively of Tuđman's death and of the electoral defeat of Milosević.

For what concerns the constitutional courts, they have been very active from the beginning of the transition to democracy, also because they were given large competences. They substituted the legislator, especially in the initial phase after the transition. While waiting to make a decision on the limits of the penetration of European law into domestic

9 A. Di Gregorio, *Epurazioni e protezione della democrazia. Esperienze e modelli di "giustizia post-autoritaria"*, cit.

legal order and on the boundaries of national sovereignty, they focused on the interactions between state powers, which is particularly delicate issue in countries where both the constitution and the political practice lead sometimes to a hybrid semi-presidentialism.

2.2.2 1999-2004

The second phase is characterized by the preparations to join the European Union, that also included a series of constitutional amendments. As we are going to see, these modifications were not only made to introduce the so-called 'European clauses' in the constitutions and to restructure the system of sources of law in order to facilitate the harmonization with European law. In facts, at the same time, they went to modify the government's frame by reducing the influence of the head of State and strengthening that of the prime minister and the government.[10]

As for the EU membership, it should be remembered that the 'democratic conditionality' process has been developed precisely in the perspective of the great enlargement to Central and Eastern European countries, putting in place mechanisms which have been later applied in the context of European Neighborhood Policy. The application process was much more complex than the previous ones and raised specific problems of 'democratic' consistency. Apart from the necessity to be compliant to the aforementioned Copenhagen requirements – set by the European Council in 1993 – there was the issue of national sovereignty, a principle that was very emphasized in the constitutions, as an obvious reaction to the previous limitation of sovereignty.

Although European institutions were concerned about a possible 'protective' or 'defensive' attitude towards the newly acquired sovereignty, new constitutions were equipped from the outset, or through later constitutional amendments, to address the impact of the external sources of law by providing appropriate delegation clauses of sovereign powers combined with safeguard clauses. The contribution of constitutional courts in the debate on national sovereignty and on limitations to the penetration of European law prompted interesting insights, although a kind of paradox can be found in the desire to defend their fundamental constitutional values, when EU membership was at beginning seen just as a guarantee of the continuation of the democratic transformation.[11]

10 Please refer to A. Di Gregorio, 'Riforme costituzionali ed integrazione europea: il caso dei nuovi membri dell'Est', *Diritto pubblico comparato ed europeo*, No. IV, 2004; A. Di Gregorio, 'Forme di governo e transizione democratica nell'Europa post-socialista', *in* L. Montanari, R. Toniatti & J. Woelk (Eds.), *Il pluralismo nella transizione costituzionale dei Balcani: diritti e garanzie*, cit.

11 This is the opinion of W. Sadurski, *Constitutionalism and the Enlargement of Europe*, Oxford, Oxford University Press, 2012, pp. 208-209.

2.2.3 2004-2018

While the process of harmonization with the requirements of European conditionality continues for the Western Balkan countries,[12] the period following the admission into the European Union for the first nine former communist countries (entered in 2004, 2007 and 2013) was marked by the strong impact of economic and migratory crisis, which produced Euroscepticism and the rise of populism. This had consequences on the political institutions (governmental crisis and early elections sometimes caused by street protests).[13]

From the constitutional point of view, some real crisis occurred that affected the balance of powers (a very wide project of constitutional amendment in Romania), the writing of new constitutions (Hungary) or indirect modifications of the constitution through ordinary legislation in particularly sensitive matters such as constitutional justice, judiciary, the power of attorney, the restriction of fundamental rights (meeting, association, freedom of the media, personal freedom, etc.), as happened in Poland as of November 2015, or further constitutional changes in order to refine the autonomy of the judiciary, also on the recommendation of the Council of Europe and the European Union (Bulgaria, Albania). A certain adjustment of the constitutional law of the new members states has been also required by budgetary rules (fiscal compact, budget balance),[14] by the ratification of the Lisbon Treaty, by a series of judgments of constitutional courts confronting the Court of Justice of the EU on the defence of sovereignty (Holubec case of the Czech Constitutional Court of 31 January 2012, the migrant quota case of the Hungarian Constitutional Court of 30 November 2016, etc.).

As for the countries of former Yugoslavia, some of them adapted their constitutions to obtain the EU integration (Croatia 2010), others completely renewed theirs (for example – as a result of the dissolution of the Union of Serbia and Montenegro – a new Constitution of Serbia originated in 2006 and of Montenegro in 2007 – while in Kosovo a proclamation of independence was made and, in 2008, a Constitution was redacted.).

12 Albania, Serbia, Montenegro, Macedonia, Kosovo, Bosnia-Erzegovina. However, the prospects of entrance into the EU have been delayed and the conditionality requirements have become harder.

13 *See* A. Di Gregorio, 'I processi di trasformazione politico-costituzionale ai confini dell'Unione europea: riflessioni sull'espansione del modello democratico e sui suoi limiti', *Diritto pubblico comparato ed europeo*, No. III, 2014, pp. 1041-1070.

14 *Cf.* M.A. Orlandi, 'Vincoli di bilancio europei e ordinamenti dei Paesi dell'Europa centro orientale', *Forum costituzionale*, 15 November 2013, www.forumcostituzionale.it/wordpress/images/stories/pdf/documenti_forum/paper/0441_orlandi.pdf (last accessed September 2018).

2.3 Framing the New Constitutions

2.3.1 The Interim Period

The first constitutional amendments were the consequence of the political change that took place with the dynamics described in the first chapter of this volume. In several countries, they followed round table negotiations (which occurred in Poland, Hungary, Czechoslovakia, Bulgaria and GDR) and were introduced as amendments of the old socialist constitutions, being adopted by parliaments elected by non-pluralist rules.[15] Although chronologically this phase occurred during the last period of the socialist state, it marked as well the end of the old system – as principles inconsistent with that form of state and typical of liberal-democratic constitutionalism were introduced. Many of the novelties originated during this interim period were then transposed into the new constitutions, which were drafted with or without the technical assistance of the Venice Commission of the Council of Europe, an institution especially set up, in May 1990, to help the democratization process of these countries,[16] which subsequently played an important role in their constitutional developments. In this regard, it must be remembered that if the constitutions were not adopted on European pressure, still the access conditionality coincided with their implementation and consolidation.[17]

In the interim period, pending the adoption of a new constitution, each country had a different constitutional framework. Let us go through the different cases, reminding also the socialist constitutions.

Cases per Country

GDR *- Constitution of the German Democratic Republic of 7 October 1949.*

On December 1989, the Parliament (*Volkskammer*) of the GDR amended Article 1 of the 1949 Constitution to remove the leading role of the working class and of its Marxist-Leninist party. The new *Volkskammer* elected through competitive elections on 18 March 1990 further amended Article 1 by deleting the definition of the GDR as a "socialist state of

15 Although in Czechoslovakia through a process of resignation and subsequent cooptation of democratic personalities, the parliament, even in the absence of competitive elections, was composed of opposition figures.

16 *See* S. Bartole, 'International Constitutionalism and Conditionality. The Experience of the Venice Commission', *Rivista AIC*, No. 4, 2014.

17 *See* T. Cerruti, *L'Unione europea alla ricerca dei propri confini. I criteri politici di adesione e il ruolo dei nuovi Stati membri*, Torino, Giappichelli, 2010.

workers and peasants". With the constitutional amendment of 17 June 1990 the GDR was called a "liberal, democratic, federal and social state". The new government expressed the desire of accelerating the process of reunification with the German Federal Republic. With a constitutional law of 22 July 1990 the five Länder abolished in July 1952 were restored (Meklemburg, Brandenburg, Saxony-Anhalt, Thuringia and Saxony), whose representative assemblies were elected on 14 October 1990. On 31 August 1990 the Unification Treaty between the two Germanies was signed in Berlin, entering into force on 3 October 1990, after the ratification by the two parliaments with a two-thirds majority. With this Treaty (*Einigungsvertrag*) it was achieved "the entry of the GDR within the validity of the Basic Law": this choice of words, that avoided the term *Bundesrepublik,* was expressly made by the GDR parliament not to say that East Germany had been annexed to federal Germany, even if as a matter of fact that was what actually happened. On 3 October 1990 the GDR ceased to exist, becoming part of the Federal Republic of Germany under Article 23 GG with a treaty of 'membership' (*Beitritt*).[18]

Czechoslovakia - *Constitution of the Czechoslovak Republic of 9 May 1948 and Constitution of the Czechoslovak Socialist Republic of 11 July 1960 (the latter was profoundly amended by constitutional Act of 27 October 1968 to introduce a federal structure).*

The interim period concerns only the federal Constitution since the two Republics never adopted their own constitutions after the transformation of the state into a federation in 1968. The Constitution of 1960-1968 was amended or supplemented several times in the period 1989-1992, through fifty-one constitutional laws among which the most important were the following: no. 183/1989 of 29 November 1989 (on the cooptation of new MPs to replace communist MPs); no. 46/1990 of 27 February 1990 (prohibition of imperative mandate); no. 295/1990 of 19 July 1990 (more competences to the Republics); no. 556/1990 of 27 December 1990 (the so-called 'great competence law'); no. 23/1991 of 9 January 1991 (introducing the Charter of Fundamental Rights and Freedoms); no. 91/1991 of 1 April 1991 (on the Constitutional Court); no. 327/1991 of 18 July 1991 (on the referendum); no. 542/1992 of 25 November 1992 (on the 'termination' of the Czech and Slovak Federal Republic).[19]

It should be remembered that the federal parliament elected in June 1990 had a constituent purpose, even if the drafting of the new constitution failed because of the political impasse concerning the fate of the common state.[20]

18 P. Biscaretti di Ruffia, *1988-1990. Un triennio di profonde trasformazioni costituzionali*, cit., pp. 109 *et seq.*

19 Please refer to A. Di Gregorio, *Repubblica ceca*, Bologna, il Mulino, 2008. On the procedure for the adoption of the new federal constitution, which was never adopted *see* A. Di Gregorio & A. Vitale (Eds.), *Il ventennale dello scioglimento pacifico della Federazione cecoslovacca*, cit., pp. 109-144.

20 A special parliamentary committee and a committee of experts worked on the project for about two years. Please refer to A. Di Gregorio, *Lo scioglimento della Cecoslovacchia: aspetti politico-costituzionali*, cit.

Hungary - *Act XX of 20 August 1949 or Constitution of the Hungarian People's Republic.*

At the time of transition, after the negotiations of the round table, there have been several substantial changes. The main ones were the Act XXXI of 23 October 1989 and the Act XL of 1990.[21] Regarding the first Act, between 18 and 23 October 1989 the National Assembly introduced ninety-four amendments to sixty-one of the seventy-eight articles of the Constitution. The changes were ground-breaking, concerning both institutional architecture (parliament almost always in session, monocratic head of state, government responsible before the parliament, independent judiciary, constitutional court and court of auditors) and fundamental principles (in Art. 2 Hungary was defined as an "independent, democratic, rule of law based state in which the values of bourgeois democracy and democratic socialism are asserted in equal measure"; subsequent articles introduced the multi-party system – thus the leading role of the Marxist-Leninist party disappeared – and fundamental rights were defined as inviolable). After the first free elections of March 1990, the new National Assembly, between May and August 1990, managed to further amend most of the constitutional provisions, eliminating some ambiguous or compromise assertions, such as those related to democratic socialism and to the benefits of a planned economy, that were initially added to the principles on the market economy (Act XL/1990).[22]

Poland - *'Small constitution' or constitutional Act of 19 February 1947 on the system and sphere of activity of the main institutions of the Republic of Poland and Constitution of the Polish People's Republic of 22 July 1952.*

After the negotiations of the round table, a broad constitutional revision was adopted on 7 April 1989, but only the one of 23 December 1989 replaced the principles of a pluralist democracy to the socialist ones. Before the adoption of the 'small constitution' of 17 October 1992, four further amendments acts were adopted between March 1990 and the end of 1991 (greater autonomy to the local government, direct election of the President, removal of many socialist residues in the catalogue of rights, right to asylum). During the transitional period were therefore in force: a part of the 1952 Constitution (as expressly provided by constitutional Act of 23 April 1992 which generally repealed that Constitution),[23] the constitutional Act of

21 Before the broad constitutional amendment occurred through the Act XXXI/1989, the Constitution was amended by Act I/1989, which added to the text, among others, provisions for the protection of freedom of association and assembly. Then followed: Act II /1989 on the right of association, Act III/1989 on the organization and operation of political parties, Act III /1989 on the right of assembly. The protection of the freedom of association was constitutionalized with the constitutional amendment Act XXXI / 1989.

22 M. Ganino, 'Introduction Ungheria', *in* P. Biscaretti di Ruffia & M. Ganino, *Costituzioni straniere contemporanee* cit., pp. 391 *et seq.*

23 It was mainly the bill of rights, even if on 12 November 1992 President Wałęsa submitted to parliament a draft constitutional law that would have to supplement the 'small constitution' as a bill of rights, but was never approved until the adoption of the 1997 Constitution. Provisions regarding the courts and the attorney also remained in force from the old text.

17 October 1992 (promulgated on November 19) on mutual relations between the legislative and executive power and local communities or 'small constitution'[24] and, for the procedure of framing and adopting the new Constitution, constitutional Act of 23 April 1992 as amended by constitutional Act of 22 April 1994.[25]

Bulgaria - *Constitutions of the People's Republic of Bulgaria of 4 December 1947 and 18 May 1971.*

At the end of 1989, a still communist-led parliament changed some significant parts of the 1971 Constitution (eliminating the adjective 'socialist', allowing the formation of opposition parties, introducing national minorities' rights). Following the roundtable talks between the Union of Democratic Forces (which included several opposition forces) and the Bulgarian Communist Party (later renamed Bulgarian Socialist Party), on 19 January 1990 the People's Assembly approved a constitutional amendment which abolished the leadership role of the Communist Party. The amendment act of 3 April 1990 introduced into the Constitution the agreement reached at the roundtable on 30 March 1990 ("On Fundamental Ideas and Principles of the Draft Amendment to the Constitution of the PRB"), abolished other socialist principles and introduced democratic principles (democracy, political pluralism, division of powers). This Act also established the convening of the Grand National Assembly with the task of adopting a new constitution.[26]

24 This constitutional Act was approved against the opposition of the Centre Alliance and the Movement for the Republic (whose leader was the former prime minister Olszewski). According to these political forces, the text assigned the President 'quasi-dictatorial' competences (on the contrary, it significantly reduced the President's competences). There were also conflicts between the two houses on the adoption of the final text. Moreover, the text did not meet the favour of the then President Wałesa, to the point it was thought he would have exercised his power of veto. In the period between the adoption and the promulgation of the Act some centre-right deputies challenged the procedure for adopting it before the Constitutional Tribunal. On 17 November 1992, only two days before the expiry of the period for exercising the presidential veto, the TC, in a highly controversial decision, established that the Act was consistent with the Constitution. *See* 'Constitution Watch', *EECR*, Vol. 1, No. 2, Summer 1992, p. 13 and Vol. 1, No. 3, Fall 1992, pp. 12-14.

25 M. Ganino, 'Introduction to Polonia', *in* P. Biscaretti di Ruffia & M. Ganino, *Costituzioni straniere contemporanee*, cit., p. 289. According to this constitutional Act, the new Constitution would be drawn up by a constitutional commission made up of forty-six deputies of the *Sejm* and ten members of the Senate. The President, the Government and the Constitutional Tribunal would have a representative in the commission without voting rights. The constitutional initiative belonged to the same constitutional commission, to a group of at least forty-six deputies and to the President. The Constitution had to be approved by a two-thirds majority of the National Assembly (the meeting of the two houses). The President would have a right of veto on some provisions. In this case, in a third session of the Assembly the objections of the President would be rejected by the same two-thirds majority required for the adoption of the text. After the approval, the Constitution would be submitted to a popular referendum.

26 C. Filippini, 'Introduction to Bulgaria (1991)', *in* M. Ganino (Ed.), *Codice delle Costituzioni*, cit. *See* also 'Constitution Watch (Bulgaria)', *EECR*, Vol. 1, No. 1, Spring 1992, pp. 3-4.

Romania - *Constitutions of the People's Republic of Romania of 13 April 1948 and 24 September 1952; Constitution of the Socialist Republic of Romania of 21 August 1965.*[27]

There were no amendments to the socialist Constitution to mark the transition to the new form of state but a clear break, with the 'non-application' of the 1965 Constitution (although the latter was formally repealed only by the 1991 Constitution). In the interim period, the decree-laws of the Council of the National Salvation Front no. 2 of 27 December 1989 and no. 92 of 14 March 1990 acted as interim constitutional documents. The latter also established the procedure for the approval of the new Constitution by the parliament elected in May 1990 as a constituent assembly and called to resign one year after the adoption of the Constitution.

Lithuania - *Constitutions of the Lithuanian Soviet Socialist Republic of 25 August 1940 and 18 April 1978.*

Following the election of the Supreme Soviets of the Republics of the USSR held with more competitive rules in March 1990, a pre-constituent period characterized by a break with the soviet time began in the three Baltic countries, also on a constitutional point of view. The Lithuanian Act of 11 March 1990 proclaimed the restoration of the national independence (opposed by Moscow in a much harder way than in the other two Republics, with military intervention). A new declaration of independence was adopted in August 1991 after the failed coup d'état organized by conservative communists. The Declaration of Independence of 11 March 1990 established the revival of the 1938 Constitution. This fact, of highly symbolic though formal value, made the restored Constitution last only one hour, after which it was immediately replaced by a provisional basic law (that also established rules for the approval of the new constitution), amended several times.[28]

Estonia - *Constitutions of the Estonian Soviet Socialist Republic of 25 August 1940 and 18 April 1978.*

A first 'provisional' declaration of independence from the USSR was proclaimed in March 1990, while the break occurred through the Declaration of Independence of 20 August 1991, which dictated the interim rules establishing the convening of a constituent assembly for the approval of the new constitution that would subsequently be subjected to a referendum. During the transitional period, the last soviet Constitution was applied when non-contrasting with the principles of the Declaration of Independence.

27 A 1974 amendment introduced the office of the President of Republic.

28 'Constitution Watch (Bulgaria)', cit., p. 5.

Latvia *- Constitutions of the Latvian Soviet Socialist Republic of 25 August 1940 and 18 April 1978.*

Latvia opted for a neat break with the previous constitutional order and restored the 1922 Constitution. However, this happened through a series of steps with the temporary and partial reintroduction of the soviet constitution. In the first declaration of independence of 4 May 1990 ("On the renewal of the independence of the Republic of Latvia"), the Supreme Soviet of Latvia reintroduced Articles 1, 2, 3, 6 of the Constitution of 15 February 1922, in order to ensure continuity with it, on the assumption that in 1940 the Constitution was not repealed but only suspended. The Supreme Soviet then declared the full restoration of national independence on 21 August 1991, with a specific constitutional Act confirming the restoration of some articles of the 1922 Constitution and adopting a 9-point transitional Declaration. Nevertheless, the Constitution of the soviet Latvia remained in force, with the exception of provisions conflicting with the fundamental principles of the 1922 Constitution. Consequently, for a long time, Latvia continued to have in force two obsolete constitutions awaiting a more complete constitutional framework.[29]

Albania *- Constitution of the People's Republic of Albania of 14 March 1946 and Constitution of the People's Socialist Republic of Albania of 28 December 1976.*

In the parliament elected with the first free elections of 31 March 1991, former communists conquered the majority of mandates, as the opposition was still weak. In such a situation, a narrow draft amendment of the 1976 socialist Constitution drawn up by the Labor Party was abandoned, and the parliament decided instead to adopt a so-called 'small constitution' with provisional value, waiting to adopt a new constitution with a broad consensus. On 29 April 1991 the Constitutional Act No. 7491 'On the main constitutional provisions' was thus adopted. According to its final provisions, this Act would have been in force until the approval of the new constitution, the draft of which would be redacted by a special committee of the People's Assembly. The composition of the committee and the redaction and approval of the draft would have been decided by the Assembly itself. In any case, it was immediately decided to repeal the 1976 Constitution (Art. 45). This small constitution in its initial version was rather short but it was supplemented by subsequent amendments (especially after the electoral success of the opposition forces, i.e. the new Democratic Party, in the early elections of March 1992) to the point of becoming a nearly complete text, even if with some internal inconsistencies (a powerful role of the Assembly coming from the socialist system of government combined with politically active powers of the head of state).[30]

29 *Ibidem*, p. 4.

30 M. Ganino, 'La Costituzione albanese del 1998: alla ricerca dell'Europa', *Diritto pubblico comparato ed europeo*, No. I, 1999, pp. 25 *et seq*. Nine constitutional amendment Acts were adopted from February 1992 to November 1997. The VII Amendment (March 1993) included a bill of rights. In this, it can be observed

Yugoslavia and Its Former Republics - *Constitution of the Federal People's Republic of Yugoslavia of 31 January 1946 and Constitutions of the Socialist Federal Republic of Yugoslavia of 7 April 1963 and 21 February 1974 (the Constitutions of the components Republics were adopted in the same years).*

The constitutional revision of 25 November 1988 introduced some relevant innovations especially in the economic sector: the right of private ownership; the right to strike. The constitutional revision of 9 August 1990 enhanced citizens' rights, recognized the autonomy of the judiciary, political pluralism and also guaranteed an equal recognition of all types of ownership. Between 1990 and 1991 several constitutional amendments drafts were redacted – although they were never officially discussed – concerning in particular the reform of the federal structure (there were three main hypotheses: federal, confederative and cantonal). In January 1990 the XV congress of the League of Communists, after the interruption caused by the Slovenian delegation leaving the meeting, formalized a multi-party system: it was the beginning of the end of socialist Yugoslavia. During the process of framing the new constitution in Croatia, in October 1990, a draft confederal treaty was prepared and jointly sent by the Croatian and Slovenian governments to other Republics to be taken into consideration.[31] The project was inspired by the institutions of the European Community and proposed a monetary and customs union, a joint protection of civil rights, a common market with free movement of labour, capital and goods, and a common defence. The confederal organs would consist in a parliament with advisory functions, a council of ministers, an executive committee and a confederal court.

As in other former communist countries, the new constitutions were preceded by a series of amendments of the previous socialist constitutions which had been covering the role of interim constitutions.

In Slovenia, after the free elections of 15 April 1990, the 1974 Constitution was amended to abolish the adjective 'socialist' in the name of state. The Slovenian parliament passed a 'Declaration', on 2 July 1990, which established the sovereignty of the Republic of Slovenia and the primacy of the Constitution and legislation of Slovenia over those of the Yugoslav Federation. In September 1990, these innovations were introduced in the Constitution. The referendum held on 23 December 1990 (declared illegitimate by the Federal Constitutional Court in January 1991) responded positively to the idea of a sovereign and independent Slovenia, providing a waiting period of six months.

a big difference between the Albanian interim constitution and the 'small' Polish constitution of 1992, which on the verge appeared rather flimsy still relying on the relevant part of the 1952 socialist Constitution.

31 In *Vjesnik*, 12 October 1990. Please refer to B. Smerdel, 'On the Draft of an Agreement on Confederation of the Yugoslav Republics', *Informator*, Vol. 38, No. 3823, 1990, pp. 1-2.

In Croatia two major amendments to the 1974 socialist Constitution were adopted. The first, in January 1990, authorized multi-party elections. The second one, adopted after the elections of 10 May 1990 and entered into force in July 1990, repealed the symbols of Yugoslavia and of communism (including the adjective 'socialist') and the Cyrillic alphabet.

For what concerns Macedonia, the amendment of the 1974 socialist Constitution, approved on 6 September 1990, was particularly relevant: it introduced monocratic presidency and a parliament of 120 seats, thus favouring the calling of the first multi-party elections, held in November 1990. Although Macedonia proclaimed its independence in 1991, due to the political confrontation with Greece regarding the name of the country, the European Community and the UN did not formally recognize it until 1993.

In Bosnia-Herzegovina, with the LIX-LXXX amendments to the socialist Constitution in July 1990, the principles of multi-party system, the freedom of political organizations and the prohibition of violent overthrow of the constitutional order were introduced, opening the path to the first free elections. On the basis of these amendments the representative assembly was divided into two councils, the Citizens' Council – composed of 130 directly elected members – and the Council of Municipalities – composed of representatives elected by each municipality and urban community. With the constitutional Act implementing the amendments, it was established that several of them would be promulgated by 15 September 1990 (especially those related to different levels' elections). All the constitutional innovations introduced, and the implementing rules, favoured the ethnic element as a basis of political legitimacy.[32] The independence referendum was held between 29 February and 1 March 1992. The 99.44 percent of the 64.31 percent of eligible voters who went to the polls responded affirmatively. On 6 April 1992 the member countries of the European Communities recognized Bosnia-Herzegovina's independence, and so did the USA on the next day. On 22 May 1992 the country was admitted to the UN.

Serbia and Montenegro, the two remaining Republics of the former Yugoslavian federation, adopted a new federal Constitution in 1992 to manage the new common state of Yugoslavia. The drafting and adoption of the constitution took place during the civil war. The negotiations began in March 1992, when the leaders of the federal government and of the governments of the two Republics met to discuss the future of the Yugoslav state. The federal parliament, along with the Serbian and Montenegrin parliaments, set up a commission of experts to elaborate the draft, which was ready in just fifteen days. The text was to be approved by the parliaments of the two Republics before being submitted to the vote of the federal parliament. Both voted in favour of the text on 23 April 1992. Specifically, in the

32 V. Katz, 'Parliamentarism in Bosnia and Herzegovina in Conditions of Political Pluralism (1990-1995)', www.parlament.ba/Content/Read/183?title=Parlamentarizamubosni&lang=en (last accessed September 2018).

Serbian parliament, 153 votes were cast in favour, 29 against and there were three abstentions. The Serbian opposition parties criticized the lack of public discussion of the text. In the Montenegrin parliament, eighty-seven votes were cast in favour, one against and there were two abstentions. Thirty opposition MPs boycotted the final vote to show their protest on the close ties with Serbia. On 27 April 1992, the federal parliament approved the text with seventy-three votes in favour, one against and three abstentions. The thirteen deputies of Albanian origins of the Serbian Province of Kosovo boycotted the parliamentary session considering the procedure illegitimate and gravely manipulative.

In the 1992 Constitution of the 'Third' Yugoslavia, Serbia and Montenegro proclaimed themselves direct successors of the SFRY. The 1992 Constitution was amended in July 2000 (introducing direct election of the President and the strengthening of its powers) and then replaced by the Charter of Serbia&Montenegro (the links between the two Republics were already quasi-confederal).[33] The Yugoslavian Constitution of 1992 did not provide for the possibility of secession of the Republics.

Finally, it must be remembered that, even before the dissolution of socialist Yugoslavia, the Republics and the autonomous Provinces adopted their own constitutions. These were clearly inconsistent with the 1974 federal Constitution, even if the latter did not provide precise legal sanctions in the event of such conflicts.[34]

2.3.2 *The Adoption of the New Constitutions*

From a symbolic point of view, the adoption of new constitutions played a double function: firstly, they were called to introduce new democratic rules to replace the previous rules and practices in order to avoid the comeback of the past.[35] At the same time, the new constitutions had an 'internal' value (to legitimate the new form of state) and an 'external' relevance (to get democratic legitimacy from the international community, the so-called

33 For further information, P. Nikolic, *I sistemi costituzionali dei nuovi Stati dell'ex Jugoslavia*, Torino, Giappichelli, 2002.

34 The opinions expressed by the Constitutional Court to the federal parliament (which established that the 1974 Constitution could not be violated) were not legally binding given the limited nature of the constitutionality control in the socialist system: the Constitutional Court could only report to the assembly the existence of acts of the Republics inconsistent with the federal Constitution; Conversely, the Republics were not obliged to respect the opinions of the federal Constitutional Court. In short, the only arbiter of the conflicts remained the federal parliament. M. Rinaldi, 'Profili storici e giuridici della forma di Stato della Repubblica federale di Jugoslavia', *in* M. Cermel (Ed.), *La transizione alla democrazia di Serbia e Montenegro*, Venezia, Marsilio, 2002, p. 82.

35 M. Lesage, 'Introduction', *Constitution d'Europe centrale et oriéntale*, Paris, La Documentation française, 1995.

'certification of democracy'). Their nature has changed dramatically, if compared to the ideological manifestos of the past.

The new constitutions have been drafted in compliance with European and international standards, although, at the time of the adoption of the first ones, these parameters had not yet been formalized. There were only soft references to democracy in the documents concerning the recognition of new states.[36] Nevertheless, the new constitutions reflect their post-communist origin through 'remnants' and 'distancings': both aspects are in fact a legacy of the past. This can be deduced from the emphasis accorded to certain principles and rights: *e.g.* the prohibition of state ideologies, the strong role of assemblies (which is a socialist heritage), the introduction of instruments for the protection of democracy, etc.

From the point of view of the evolution over time, we can distinguish different stages of post-communist constitutionalism, not overlapping for all the countries:

1. Substantial revisions of the socialist constitutions in the sections concerning the basic principles (to introduce democratic principles) following procedures laid down by socialist constitutions (everywhere but Romania).
2. Adoption of interim constitutions, in some cases keeping partially in force the old socialist ones (Poland, Albania).
3. Restoring the constitution in force before the communist period (Latvia).
4. Immediate adoption of new constitutions after a longer or shorter period of application of the amended socialist ones (Bulgaria, Romania, former Yugoslav Republics).

In the countries of the former Yugoslavia a first generation of constitutions was followed by new or amended ones as a consequence of the political and state restructuring.[37]

The fast adoption of new constitutions (especially in Serbia, Bulgaria and Romania), considering the specific characteristics of the transition of these countries, meant that the framing process had been dominated by former communists. Although this seems paradoxical, these constitutions are nevertheless in line with the requirements of liberal-democratic constitutionalism (although, in some cases, there is a greater mixture of old and new aspects, especially regarding the right of private ownership, the state role, social

36 *Déclaration des pays de la CEE sur les lignes directrices sur la reconnaissance de nouveaux Etats en Europe centrale et en Union soviétique*, cit.

37 L. Montanari, 'Il principio di rule of law e la tutela dei diritti nei Balcani occidentali', *in* L. Montanari, R. Toniatti & J. Woelk (Eds.), *Il pluralismo nella transizione costituzionale dei Balcani: diritti e garanzie*, Trento, Università degli studi di Trento, 2010, pp. 206 *et seq.*, identifies three constitutional cycles: that of the 1990s (adoption of new constitutions in all the Republics of the former Yugoslavia), that of the early 2000s (constitutional amendments in Slovenia, Croatia, Macedonia, the constitutional Charter of Serbia and Montenegro), the last cycle (new constitutions of Serbia and Montenegro, Kosovo, the failed attempt to adopt a new constitution in Bosnia-Herzegovina). The third cycle, according to the author, is marked by a return to the national sovereignty with a smaller opening to external conditionality, also considering that the prospect of joining EU became less imminent. Please, *see also* M. Calamo Specchia *et al.* (Eds.), *I Balcani occidentali. Le Costituzioni della transizione*, cit.

rights, the participation of employees to the factory management). According to J. Elster and S. Holmes, this can be explained by the fact that the previous regime elites were much more interested in adopting new constitutions than the new leaders. Indeed, the first free elected parliaments in which former communists had the majority were much easier to control than the ones elected in countries such as Hungary, Poland and Czechoslovakia, where from the beginning of the transition the political landscape was plural and fragmented and the political forces of the past were soon marginalized.[38] One relevant incentive of the former communists was the desire to acquire legitimacy both internally and internationally, and to be recognized as democratic forces and as promoters of the new constitutional order. Both the Romanian and the Bulgarian constitutions, however, while providing a long bill of rights, had some important gaps that were subsequently filled under the impulse of the Council of Europe, with a series of constitutional amendments.[39]

Other constitutions, as well, that were adopted quickly specifically for state-building reasons (to mark a factual or legal secession, or the independence from a previous federation) later revealed inconsistencies and implementation problems and needed an even deeper revision. A clear case is that of Slovakia. The Constitution adopted in 1992, following the draft prepared by the Movement for a Democratic Slovakia of Vladímir Mečiar, included an unusual model of powers' division: theoretically it was a parliamentary system of government but the head of state, not directly elected, had a series of relatively important competences (the power to dissolve the parliament in certain circumstances, to adopt acts without countersignature, etc.), which according to some comments represented a remnant of the socialist constitutionalism.[40] Other inconsistencies were a certain paternalism in dealing with social rights; the inadequate protection of ethnic minorities' rights; the lack of autonomy of the central bank and some details about financial and tax legislation, etc.[41] Moreover, Articles 4 and 20 described the right of public ownership widely enough to cause concerns about the repealing of the privatization process.

It should also be remembered that in several countries (Romania, Albania, Slovakia) the constitution was submitted to a (popular) public discussion, as was the norm in the socialist period. This procedure, which usually preceded a confirmatory referendum, led

38 J. Elster & S. Holmes, 'New Constitutions Adopted in Bulgaria and Romania', *EECR*, Vol. 1, No.1, Spring 1992, pp. 11-12.

39 We refer in particular to the Romanian constitutional revision of 2003 (the guarantees of due process have been reinforced, the right of private property become stronger, other social rights have been introduced, the rights of minorities and the role of ombudsman have been strengthened, *etc.*: for an analysis *see* A. Di Gregorio, 'Romania. Le elezioni presidenziali e parlamentari del 2004: le prospettive della forma di governo alla luce della revisione costituzionale del 2003', *Diritto pubblico comparato ed europeo*, No. I, 2005, pp. 336-344).

40 P. Höllander, 'The New Slovak Constitution: A Critique', *EECR*, Vol. 1, No. 3, Fall 1992, pp. 16-17.

41 *Ibidem* «The étatist and paternalist ambitions, the authoritarian tendencies, the non functional ties among state organs, and the general obsolescence of the approved concept arouse in me doubts and fears about the framework this kind of constitution will create for the political and economic stabilization of Slovakia».

in some cases to take into account the observations / complaints of citizens or experts (*e.g.* Albania).

2.3.3 *The Procedures for the Approval of the New Constitutions and the Political Characteristics of the Constituent Processes*

Constituent Processes per Country

Serbia *(6 July 1990)*

The Constitution of Serbia approved by popular referendum on 6 July 1990, and entered into force in September of the same year, was adopted by the parliament elected in 1989 which initially included only delegates of the Communist League, then transformed into the Socialist Party (leader Slobodan Milosević) after merging with the Socialist Alliance (the first fully multi-party elections were held only in December 1990). This constitution certified the transition to the liberal-democratic form of state but also abolished the autonomy of the Provinces of Vojvodina and Kosovo.[42] The constitution also strengthened the position of the President. Considering that the federation still existed, there was no provision for the binding of international treaties on human rights. Such provision can be found, though, in the Constitution of 2006.

Being the first constitution adopted in the post-socialist region, it had some ambiguous characteristics and contained many legacies of the past – duties alongside rights, many social rights, death penalty, etc. – but at the same time it incorporated the main elements of Western constitutionalism, including a broad catalogue of freedoms, rights and duties of man and citizen. Like other constitutions adopted immediately after the transition to democracy, by political forces derived from the past regime,[43] it is the expression of the desire on the one hand to control the transition (for example by avoiding punishment of the old ruling class) and by another to obtain an international recognition (pluralism and protection of rights seemed inevitable even to former communists).

42 The Kosovo Albanians declared their independence on the 2nd of July 1990 and adopted their own constitution the following September. The Serbian government did not recognize these developments and therefore the exclusion of Kosovo Albanians from the constituent process worsened the conflict situation in the Province.

43 *See* the cases of Bulgaria and Romania, even if their parliaments had already been renewed through pluralist electoral procedures and therefore opposition forces were represented.

***Croatia** (22 December 1990)*

Croatia held the first free multi-party elections in April-May 1990, and witnessed the success of the Croatian Democratic Union or HDZ (thanks to a nationalistic platform and the appeal to restore an independent Croatia). The new constitution was elaborated immediately after, and adopted by the *Sabor* (parliament of Croatia) within a period of five months, on 22 December 1990 (hence its denomination the 'Christmas Constitution').[44] The 16 MPs representing the Serbian minority walked out before the final vote as a form of protest, as their objections were not being included in the revised draft. The Constitution, in fact, included an article that allowed Croatia to secede from the Yugoslav federation with a two-thirds majority vote from the legislature.[45] As a reaction, the regions of Croatia inhabited by Serbs proclaimed their independence after a referendum that took place in August 1990 and expressed the intention not to follow Croatia in case of secession from Yugoslavia. In May 1991 the President of Croatia submitted the question of independence to a referendum.[46] The positive outcome was accepted by parliament on 25 June 1991 with the Declaration "On the establishment of a sovereign and independent Republic of Croatia". This decision included an invitation to the other Republics of Yugoslavia to begin the process of "dissociation from the Yugoslavian Federation" and the one for the formation of "an alliance of sovereign states". A constitutional law was added in 1991 to settle the minority rights dispute.

The drafting of the new constitution began in July 1990 during the first meeting of the parliamentary committee for constitutional questions. On 12 August the President decided to set up another commission, composed of 229 members of different parties and professions to ensure the widest popular participation. This commission made public its project in mid-September. The debates continued until the last day before the decisive meeting of the Sabor, and 5-5 different projects were made public in the meantime. The most important compromises were reached in the last two weeks under the influence of President Tuđman, who accepted several proposals from the opposition parties against the most radical nationalist

44 P. Nikolić, 'I nuovi Stati della ex Jugoslavia (aspetti costituzionali)', *Diritto pubblico comparato ed europeo*, No. III, 1999; P. Nikolić, 'La disgregazione della Jugoslavia socialista. Formazione e sviluppo della nuova Jugoslavia e dei membri costitutivi della Federazione. Aspetti costituzionali', *in* S. Gambino (Ed.), *Europa e Balcani: Stati, Culture, Nazioni*, Padova, Cedam, 2001.

45 Art. 140: "The Republic of Croatia will remain part of the SFRY until a new agreement is reached by the Yugoslav Republics or until Sabor decides otherwise". Moreover, the second paragraph of this article authorized the "organs of the Republic" to take the necessary measures to protect the sovereignty, territorial integrity and interests of the Republic in all cases where these interests were endangered by actions of the federal institutions or of institutions of the other Republics or Provinces.

46 The 84.94 percent of voters participated in the vote and a majority of 93.24 percent answered yes to the question "Do you agree that the Republic of Croatia as a sovereign and independent State, that guarantees cultural autonomy and all civil rights to Serbs and other nationalities in Croatia can become part of an alliance with the other Republics?"

exponents of his party.[47] Because of this climate some crucial issues, such as bicameralism, were not resolved at that time and the discussions on the matter continued after the adoption of the constitution.[48]

With the constitutional amendment Act of 21 February 1991, the invalidity of all federal legislation inconsistent with the new Constitution was established on the Croatian territory. Soon after that, the government of the self-proclaimed Serbian province of Krajina in Croatia declared the invalidity of Croatian laws on its territory, unless they were in conformity with the federal Constitution and with its own regulations.[49]

Bulgaria *(12 July 1991)*

The Grand National Assembly – an *ad hoc* body already established for the adoption of the 1879 Constitution of Tărnovo – was elected in June 1990. Although all the parties in parliament had presented their own constitutional project, the constitutional process was dominated by the socialist party (formerly communist) together with the social-democratic party. These political forces slowed down the activity of the constitutional commission in an attempt to postpone the elections from the set date in May to October 1991. Protesting against this behaviour and against the constitutional project of the socialist forces, thirty-nine representatives of the Union of Democratic Forces left the Assembly on 14 May 1991. The Constitution was adopted on 12 July 1991, with 309 votes out of 400 and is considered the first democratic constitution of a sovereign country of post-socialist Europe. The Constitution was not submitted to a referendum (the socialists feared that the 'Group of 39' could mobilize the electorate against its approval), it was challenged by some ministers in office and also by President Želev who symbolically refused to sign it.[50]

47 For further information, *see* B. Smerdel, 'Republic of Croatia: Three Fundamental Constitutional Choices', *Croatian Political Science Review*, Vol. 1, No.1, 1992, pp. 60-78. Following A. Lijphart, 'Constitutional Choices for New Democracies', *Journal of Democracy*, Vol. 2, No. 1, Winter 1991, p. 72, "In this process several hard decisions were faced by 'the constitution-makers'. Two of them – a choice between majority elections and proportional representation, and between the parliamentary or presidential form of government, are common to architects of new democratic constitutions in all countries of the post-communist era in Eastern Europe."

48 G. Casper, 'European Convergence', *The University of Chicago Law Review*, Vol. 58, No. 2, 1991, pp. 441-446.

49 The Croatian Constitutional Court declared this decision unconstitutional while the federal Constitutional Court declared the unconstitutionality of the amendment of the Croatian Constitution of the February 1991.

50 'Constitution Watch (Bulgaria)', cit., pp. 3-4.

***Macedonia** (17 November 1991)*

Following the first multi-party elections of November 1990 and his consequent election as the first President of the Republic (January 1991) Kiro Gligorov, in May 1991, promoted the adoption of a new constitution and the request for independence. A special parliamentary constitutional commission redacted a constitutional draft in four months.

In this country, the most heated debates concerned the relationship with the Albanian minority, which contested their lack of recognition as 'constitutive people' in the draft constitution approved in the first reading on 23 August 1991. For this reason, the Albanian minority did not participate in the referendum of 8 September 1991, in which 95 percent of voters expressed their support for independence. The confrontation continued in October and November (the Albanian deputies left the house in sign of protest on 10 November, the date scheduled for the final approval of the Constitution). On 17 November 1991, however, the parliament approved the text without the amendments requested by the Albanians, with ninety-six votes in favour over 120 (all deputies of the Albanian parties and three deputies from other parties voted against). The Constitution came into force on 21 November 1991, the same date of the proclamation of independence.[51]

***Romania** (8 December 1991)*

The Constitution was adopted by the parliament in a constituent session[52] on 21 November 1991 and submitted on 8 December to a confirmatory referendum. The procedure included two phases: the elaboration of 'Theses' regarding the main political choices and the drafting of a detailed text. A constitutional commission of the parliament was established in June 1990, composed mainly of members of the National Salvation Front (they were twenty-six, including some external experts) – a political force that held over 70 percent of the seats in the two houses. The 'Theses' were subjected to a preventive public debate inside and outside the country (several foreign experts were consulted).[53] The debate lasted from February to June 1991. From 10 September 1991, the text was discussed in parliament, article by article, and over 1000 amendments were presented. About 145 were accepted, including some proposed by the opposition and by the Hungarian minority. The final text was adopted on 21 November, with 414 votes in favour, which was more than the two-thirds majority required.

51 On 6 January 1992 the Constitution was amended to specify that Macedonia did not intend to create a 'Greater Macedonia' with the provinces of Greece and Bulgaria.

52 The first free elections were held in May 1990 on the basis of a governmental decree which provided for the election of a parliament with a constituent mandate. The two houses of parliament should have been dissolved in case they did not adopt the constitution within 18 months after their election.

53 For further details please refer to M. Ganino, 'Premessa a Romania', *in* P. Biscaretti di Ruffia & M. Ganino, *Costituzioni straniere contemporanee*, cit., pp. 344-345.

According to a decree of December 1989, a constitutional referendum had to take place within thirty days after the parliamentary approval: the limited time available made it impossible to carry out an extensive information campaign, however about two-thirds of voters participated and 77.3 percent voted yes. The voters of Transylvania - where the Hungarian minority predominantly lived and lives- were mainly against the new Constitution, which entered into force immediately after the referendum approval.

***Slovenia** (23 December 1991)*

The Constitution was approved by the Assembly of the Republic on 23 December 1991. The declaration of independence of 25 June 1991 – "Fundamental Constitutional Act on the independence and sovereignty of the Republic of Slovenia" – expressly recalled in the Constitution's preamble, had a pre-constituent value. The procedure for the approval of the Constitution was the one provided for by the old socialist Constitution, although a public consultation was avoided. The government appointed a commission of constitutional experts headed by Miro Cerar, a professor of law at the University of Ljubljana. During the drafting of the Constitution, different foreign constitutions were taken into consideration, such as German, Austrian, Italian, along with the previous socialist constitutions.[54]

***Estonia** (28 June 1992)*

A 'Constituent Assembly' was established in September 1991, not through direct elections (the USSR still existed) but by selecting its members within some existing institutions elected in 1990 (thirty members of the Supreme Soviet and thirty members of the 'Estonian Congress', a parallel parliamentary body composed of citizens of Estonian nationality).

Four constitutional projects were submitted to the Constituent Assembly, as well as the 1938 Constitution. Only three of these projects were seriously considered (the one set aside reinforced presidential powers). Ultimately, the debate both in the Assembly and in the public opinion focused mainly on the returning in force of the 1938 Constitution and on the project presented by the Estonian National Independence Party (ENIP), the main party of that period. The idea of bringing into force the 1938 Constitution was rejected for several reasons: 45 years had passed; the text strengthened the President's powers in a dictatorial manner and was connected with a period of authoritarian degeneration. The Assembly therefore decided to work on the ENIP project, against which no real opposition had been advanced, at least until a month before the referendum, when a movement called 'Restitution' proposed again to reintroduce the 1938 constitutional text, on the basis of the principle of legal continuity, a principle that was considered essential in order to compel Russia to fully

54 A. Perenić, 'La nuova Costituzione slovena', *Quaderni costituzionali*, 1994, pp. 307 *et seq.*

recognize the independence of Estonia and withdraw troops from its territory. In the end, the proposal to adopt a new constitution on the basis of the project supported by the National Independence Party prevailed. The Constitution was confirmed in the referendum of 28 June 1992, by about 90 percent of those entitled to vote. The right to vote, however, was granted only to those who had Estonian citizenship from before 1940, and to their descendants, thus excluding the Russian-speaking population (about a third of the residents). Along with the Constitution, a specific act was passed to implement it.[55] The Estonian Constitution, in force since 4 July 1992, is the first constitution adopted by a Republic of the former USSR.

***Slovakia** (1 September 1992)*

The elaboration of the constitutional draft began in February 1990. According to the proposals presented by the government, a unicameral parliament should have been established, and important powers should have been given to the government and the head of state. No provision was made for a separation from the federal state. In June 1991, the parliament created a commission composed of representatives of different parties. The draft was made public in December 1991 and submitted to popular debate. The process underwent significant changes following the June 1992 elections, in which the National Democratic Movement for a Democratic Slovakia obtained the majority of mandates. On 17 July 1992, the parliament adopted the Declaration of sovereignty and on 28 July 1992 the final version of the government draft was presented to the parliament. The debate was rather heated because the opposition parties, especially the Christian-democratic party and the Hungarian minority parties, challenged different aspects of the draft (which was also formally inconsistent with the federal constitution still in force). The Constitution was approved on 1 September 1992, and entered into force on 1 October, with the exception of some articles, whose entry into force was suspended until 1 January 1993.[56] The draft was redacted hastily, and for this reason it was soon necessary to introduce amendments, both concerning the system of guarantees and the form of government. According to some authors, since this Constitution is the basis of an independent state, the dissolution of the federal state would have occurred since 1 October 1992.[57]

55 M. Mazza, 'La Costituzione dell'Estonia (1992)', *in* M. Ganino (Ed.), *Codice delle Costituzioni*, Vol. III, cit., pp. 47-49.

56 For further details please refer to A. Di Gregorio, 'La Costituzione della Slovacchia (1992)', *in* M. Ganino (Ed.), *Codice delle Costituzioni*, Vol. III, cit., pp. 299 *et seq.*

57 'Constitution Watch', *EECR*, Vol. 1, No. 3, Fall 1992, p. 10.

***Montenegro** (12 October 1992)*

The Constitution of Montenegro of 12 October 1992 was adopted following the procedure set out in Amendment LXXXII, item 1, para. 7 of the 1974 Constitution. The same considerations that were made about the 1990 Constitution of Serbia, regarding the mixture of old and new aspects and the lack of a strong role for international law, can also apply to this Constitution.

***Lithuania** (25 October 1992)*

In the summer 1990, a constitutional commission composed of legal experts was established to draft the new constitution. A new commission, including also MPs, was constituted on 10 December 1991. At the end of April 1992, two constitutional drafts were presented: one was the expression of the majority of the commission, which proposed the parliamentary system of government. The other, preferred by the minority – but supported by the movement *Sajudis*, which had the majority in parliament and composed the executive – favourable to a presidential form of government.[58] In the end, a compromise was found between the two positions and the final draft, approved on 13 October 1992, was submitted to a referendum on 25 October 1992, the same date of general elections, together with the constitutional Act "On the procedure for entry into force of the Constitution". The Constitution was approved by the 56.7 percent of the voters. On 6 November 1992, an Act on the procedure for implementing the Constitution was also adopted. In its Final Provisions (Art. 150), the Constitution establishes that a series of constitutional Acts are part of the Constitution: "On the State of Lithuania" of 11 February 1991, "On the non-alignment of the Republic of Lithuania to Post-Soviet Eastern unions" of 8 June 1992, "On the procedure for entry into force of the Constitution" of 25 October 1992 and "On membership of the Republic of Lithuania in the European Union" of 13 July 2004.

***Czech Republic** (16 December 1992)*

The drafting of the Czech Constitution started after the June 1992 elections, which foreshadowed an imminent separation of the two Republics. In the summer of 1992, two commissions were formed, one by the government and one by the parliament, composed by representatives of all parties. The two projects merged into one text, presented to the parliament in early November. Nevertheless, the influence of the government draft was

58 M. Mazza, 'La Costituzione della Lituania (1992)', *in* M. Ganino (Ed.), *Codice delle Costituzioni*, Vol. III, cit., pp. 111-112. The confrontation between the two positions was harsh. The supporters of a strong presidency (who accused the parliamentary draft of anarchy) organized a referendum on 23 May 1992 to introduce an amendment to the provisional fundamental law of 11 March 1990 in order to bind the final constitutional draft. The referendum did not reach the expected high quorum (50 percent of those entitled), even though 69.5 percent of the voters voted in favour of the question.

prevalent, and this caused harsh criticism from the opposition. Among the most debated issues were the formation and role of the upper house[59] and the competences and methods of election of the President (the then head of state Havel pressed for a President elected directly by citizens and with more competences, while the premier Klaus did not agree). The territorial question has also been source of heated discussions: since the collapse of the communist regime, the political forces of Moravia insisted to obtain greater autonomy. The Constitution was adopted on 16 December 1992 and entered into force on the 1st of January 1993. The Charter of Fundamental Rights and Freedoms, derived from the federal constitutional law adopted in 1991, was added as a fundamental component of the constitutional order. During the parliamentary debate, the rank to be given to the Czechoslovakian Charter of Rights between the sources of law, as well as its content, was a subject of great debate.[60] In addition, at an early stage, it was proposed to restore the 1920 Czechoslovakian Constitution (whose content was resumed in several sections of the current constitution) or to rielaborate the previous federal Constitution as amended since 1989. However, a desire for innovation prevailed, though with the preservation of the 1991 catalogue of rights, which was already in line with the Council of Europe standards.

***Latvia** (15 February 1922)*

The first parliament (*Saeima*) democratically elected on 5 June 1993 confirmed on 6 July 1993 the decision to restore the Constitution of 15 February 1922. However, this Constitution did not have a catalogue of fundamental rights – prepared at that time but never approved by parliament – which was introduced with a constitutional amendment in 1998 – the new chapter VIII. In the transitional period, the Act No. 380 of 1991 "On the rights and obligations of the citizen and the person" (repealed with the 1998 constitutional revision) had been applied as a provisional bill of rights. The constitutional framework has been perfected with constitutional amendments in 1996 – introducing the constitutional court – and in 1997 – extending the mandate of the parliament and the head of state from three to four years.

With the 1998 constitutional amendments – which came into force on 6 November – it was also established that Latvian is the official state language. Considering that around 30 percent of the Latvian population is Russian-speaking, this provision has been very contro-

59 The members of the Christian-democratic movement threatened to leave the coalition government if the upper chamber had not been included in the constitutional draft; those who opposed regarded this as an attempt by the members of the Federal Assembly to maintain their seat following the dissolution of the Federation.

60 The ODS considered it contained too many social rights: while allowing the opposition not to amend it, the liberals of Klaus insisted to keep the text separate from the Constitution itself. In their opinion, this would facilitate its later amendment. *See* 'Constitution Watch', cit., p. 4 and A. Di Gregorio, *Repubblica ceca*, cit.

versial, especially in view of the application process to entry into the EU. It is very likely that the introduction of this provision was the quid pro quo offered to the nationalist party 'Fatherland and Freedom' (LNNK) in order to obtain their vote on the bill of rights. In fact, the *Saeima* had failed on several occasions to reach the two-thirds majority required for the approval of the constitutional amendments.

Bosnia and Herzegovina *(14 December 1995)*

The constitution is the Annex No. 4 of the General Framework Agreement for Peace in Bosnia and Herzegovina, known as the Dayton Treaty, signed on 14 December 1995.

In the last phase of the Dayton negotiations, the parties of the conflict (Bosnian Muslims or Bosnia, Serbs of Bosnia,[61] Croats of Bosnia, Serbs of Yugoslavia and Croats of Croatia) were kept in isolation until they reached an agreement. The draft was 'checked' by the International Contact Group and therefore cannot be considered democratic nor representative. In fact, the initial draft was written by a committee composed of diplomats and experts from the Contact Group and then presented separately to the parties to receive comments and proposals. The representatives of the Contact Group then decided which of these comments and proposals would be communicated to other parties. The procedure continued until an agreement was reached. The constitution was considered ratified by the signing of the peace agreement in Paris on 21 November 1995. An important part of the agreement consisted in accepting the presence of NATO peacekeeping forces to ensure the respect of the agreement itself.

The constitution adopted in Dayton proved to be inappropriate in the long term for the country, both for what concerns its legitimacy (there was no 'patriation' of the constitution), and for what regards the form of government and international influence in the sources of law and in the administration of the country. The Venice Commission itself, in its March 2005 opinion,[62] criticized the 'Dayton system'. Last but not least, there is the problem of making the constitutions of the two entities consistent with the federal one.[63]

61 In the final stage of negotiations, the Serbs of Bosnia were represented by the Serbs of Yugoslavia, as the leader of the Bosnian Serbs had been indicted as a war criminal and was not allowed to participate.

62 CDL-AD (2005) 004 *Opinion on the Constitutional Situation in Bosnia and Herzegovina and the Powers of the High Representative adopted by the Venice Commission at its 62nd plenary session* (Venice, 11-12 March 2005), www.venice.coe.int/webforms/documents/?pdf=CDL-AD(2005)004-e (last accessed September 2018).

63 For a reference to the constitutional amendment bill prepared and not approved for few votes in 2006, please refer to L. Montanari, 'La tutela dei diritti nelle nuove Costituzioni dei Balcani occidentali', *in* M. Calamo Specchia, M. Carli, G. Di Plinio & R. Toniatti (Eds.), *I Balcani occidentali. Le Costituzioni della transizione*, Torino, Giappichelli, 2008, p. 178, and to the opinion of the Venice Commission of 7 April 2006.

***Poland** (25 May 1997)*

A new constitution could not be adopted in the first two post-communist legislatures because of the fragmented nature of the parliaments elected respectively in 1989 and 1991.[64] However, thanks to the existence of an interim constitution, the adoption of a new text was not imperative. In any case, since December 1989 two different constitutional committees were established within the *Sejm* and the Senate. In April 1991, the Senate made public its first draft, which included a long bill of rights and a presidential form of government. The *Sejm* draft, presented in September of the same year, contained a broad list of economic and social rights and outlined a parliamentary form of government.

The Constitution was adopted at the end of the legislature that followed the elections of 1993, when there was a wider political majority. The constitutional committee set up in 1993 examined eight different drafts (some presented by the committee itself, others by political parties,[65] by the citizens, the head of state and the Senate).[66] The most relevant differences among them concerned the strengthening respectively of the President or of the government/prime minister, in order to be able to avoid the institutional conflict which characterized the first years after the transition. In the end, an intermediate solution was adopted. As required by the constitutional Act of 23 April 1992, the new constitution was approved, after long debates, on 2 April 1997 by the two houses meeting as National Assembly (451 votes in favour, forty against and six abstentions), and then ratified via referendum on 25 May – the votes in favour being only 53 percent. The Constitution entered into force on 17 October 1997 and expressly repealed the provisions still in force provided by the Constitution of 22 July 1952, by the 'small constitution' of 17 October 1992 and by the Act of 23 April 1992 on the procedure for elaborating and adopting the constitution of the Republic of Poland.

64 The parliament elected in 1991, where more than twenty parties were represented, was dissolved early, in 1993. Following J.P. Massias, *Droit constitutionnel des Etats d'Europe de l'Est*, cit., p. 145, several parties believed that the *Sejm* elected in 1991 did not have the right to adopt the new constitution because the electoral system had applied a 5 percent threshold that had prevented most of the right-wing parties from being represented. For this reason, the Act on the procedure for drafting and adopting the new constitution was amended in 1994 to enable also a group of 500,000 citizens to present a draft constitution. In the original version, the subjects allowed to propose a draft were the constitutional commission itself, the President and a group of fifty-six members of the National Assembly.

65 Democratic Union, Alliance of Democratic Right, Confederation of Independent Poland, Center Agreement, (a joint project of) Polish Farmer Party and Union of Labor. For more information, J.P. Massias, *Droit constitutionnel des Etats d'Europe de l'Est*, cit., p. 147.

66 M.Ganino, 'Premessa a Polonia', cit., pp. 309-312.

***Albania** (22 November 1998)*

Since the end of 1990, several constitutional projects were introduced to the parliament, on the initiative of both the government and the opposition parties.[67] Following the elections of July 1997, where the socialist party and its allies obtained the majority of mandates, the parliament (Assembly of the Republic), with its decision no. 339 of 3 September 1997, set up a constitutional committee with the aim of redacting a constitution draft, that – once approved – would have been submitted to a confirmatory referendum. The committee was composed of twenty-one members, twelve of which belonged to the government coalition. The opposition led by Berisha (leader of the centre-right Democratic Party) boycotted the process demanding the call of a constituent assembly. As in other former socialist countries, and following a practice in vogue in the previous form of state, the project was submitted to public discussion in different forums, with the participation of foreign experts.[68] The public debate was taken into account in the final wording of the text, that was finally approved on 21 October 1998. The referendum was called by the President of the Republic, in accordance with the decision of the Assembly no. 393 of 21 October. Fearing not to reach enough votes, the Assembly introduced an amendment into the referendum act to change the quorum's criteria from the majority of those entitled to the majority of voters. The referendum took place on 22 November 1998.

The assistance of the Council of Europe, through the Venice Commission, had been constant and its suggestions were generically approved. Besides, Albania's admission to the Council of Europe in November 1995 was consented on the condition that, within three years, a new constitution was to be adopted to eliminate all references to death penalty and to ensure the independence of the judiciary. The 1997 Polish Constitution was also taken into consideration, especially the chapter regarding sources of law. Despite the length of the constituent period and the external assistance, the new Constitution – once promulgated – still needed further amendments especially in relation to the autonomy of the judiciary.

67 The first project was finalized in December 1990. The second was drawn up as the March 1991 elections approached. A new committee – composed of exponents of the five parties represented in parliament and of judges and other experts – was appointed to develop a third project. Among the most debated issues were: the form of government (the desire to limit the President's role prevailed), the bill of rights (if it should be more or less detailed and if social and economic rights should or not be included), the structure of the judicial power and local self-government, the powers of the constitutional tribunal, the proclamation of an 'ideological' inspiration of the Republic (market economy or social democracy). For these details *see* 'Constitution Watch', *EECR*, Vol. 1, No. 2, Summer 1992, p. 2. A new constitutional draft promoted by President Sali Berisha, which significantly strengthened the President's powers, was rejected with a popular referendum on 9 November 1994. The procedure followed on that occasion was of dubious constitutionality, since the project was not initially approved by the parliamentary majority as the interim constitution required. Later, Berisha expressed its opposition to the strengthening of presidential powers, favouring the parliamentary model.

68 M. Ganino, *La Costituzione albanese del 1998*, cit., pp. 29-30.

***State Union of Serbia and Montenegro** (4 February 2003)*

The "Proceeding Points for the Restructuring of Relations between Serbia and Montenegro" of 14 March 2002 were processed with the intermediation of European Union. They were approved by the federal authorities and by the individual Republics and became the new constitution on 4 February 2003 (Constitutional Charter of the State Union of Serbia and Montenegro). The bill of rights was adopted separately ("Charter of Human and Minorities Rights and Civil Liberties") following the same procedure used to adopt the constitution, of which the Charter was an integral part, as required by Article 8.[69]

The 2003 constitution originated a new form of state, that replaced the 1992 Federation and established an 'expiring' system (Art. 60). The Charter, with Article 65, provided for the amendment – or the replacement with new texts – of the two existing constitutions of the constituent Republics, within six months since its adoption, in order to guarantee their compliance with itself and with the Charter of Rights, but this has not been done.

***Serbia** (29 October 2006)*

The new Constitution was approved by the National Assembly on 30 September 2006 and submitted to a popular referendum on 28-29 October. The opinion of the Venice Commission was adopted later (19 March 2007). The constitution-making process took place mainly internally and rather hastily. The lack of international influence is highlighted by the several assertions of Kosovo belonging to Serbia,[70] that can be justified by the fact that Serbia has not yet officially recognized the independence of its former autonomous Province. For what concerns the catalogue of rights, international influence is indirect, it can be perceived through some contents taken from the Charter of Rights of the Union of Serbia and Montenegro.[71] There are fewer social rights and guarantees, while property rights are made

69 On the complex events that led, with the assistance of the European Union and the Council of Europe, to the transformation of the 1992 federal Yugoslavia (the so-called 'third' Yugoslavia) into a confederation, ie Union of Serbia and Montenegro in 2003 (waiting for the secession of Montenegro which took place in a disciplined and constitutional manner in 2006), please refer to T. Cerruti, 'Recenti vicissitudini di uno Stato balcanico: il caso jugoslavo. Da un federalismo dubbio ad una confederazione a termine?', *Diritto pubblico comparato ed europeo*, No. I, 2003, pp. 3 *et seq.* and J.O. Frosini & F. Rinaldi, 'L'avverarsi della "condizione sospensiva" costituzionale per l'esercizio dello ius secessionis in Serbia-Montenegro', *Diritto pubblico comparato ed europeo*, No. IV, 2006, pp. 1495 *et seq.*

70 L. Montanari, *Il principio di Rule of Law*, cit., pp. 224-225. The Author considers the definition of the status of Kosovo in the new Serbian Constitution, which does not take into account the situation existing since 1999 and the indications of the Venice Commission, as a demonstration of its focusing on national issues and contesting the international interference. But there are reasons for this attitude: the Constitution was drafted and approved very quickly and through a referendum to anticipate the ruling of the International Court of Justice on Kosovo's declaration of independence. Serbs wanted to reiterate that the autonomous provinces belonged to Serbia and demonstrate the broad popular support for this new constitutional disposition.

71 Following L. Montanari, *La tutela diritti nelle nuove Costituzioni dei Balcani occidentali*, cit., p. 170.

safer. On the subject of minority rights, the 1990 text seemed more advanced, though less detailed.

Montenegro *(22 October 2007)*

With the referendum of 21 May 2006, Montenegro decided to secede from the Union of Serbia and Montenegro and formally announced its independence on 3 June. Then, on 22 October 2007, on the basis of the Act on the adoption and promulgation of the new Constitution of Montenegro (Act 66/06), the parliament adopted the Constitution. The process of drafting the new constitution lasted from June 2006 to October 2007. The international influence was more significant than in Serbia,[72] also because, after the secession, Montenegro had to submit a new application for admission to the Council of Europe. On 13 July 2013, the parliament approved sixteen amendments to the Constitution that were added at the end of the text and declared to be integral part of the same.[73]

Kosovo *(9 April 2008)*

The 2008 Constitution was preceded by an interim constitution redacted by the international community (*Constitutional Framework for Provisional Self-Government in Kosovo*), adopted by the Special Representative of the UN Secretary on 15 May 2001, on the basis of the powers conferred by Resolution 1244 (1999) of the Security Council. The Declaration of Independence by the Assembly is dated 17 February 2008.[74] During the elaboration of the Constitution there has been a phase were foreign experiences[75] were studied, and close

72 Unlike the opinion issued for the Serbian Constitution of 2006, in the case of Montenegro the opinion of the Venice Commission was adopted before the adoption of the Constitution (the main stages of the constitution-making process are recalled), on 5 June 2007.

73 As for differences compared to the 1992 Constitution: some socialist remnants are eliminated, such as death penalty (expressly forbidden); the international law is included as a source of binding law; the self-dissolution of parliament disappears; the provisions concerning the formation and dismissal of government are clearer (there are also checks instruments such as interpellations and parliamentary inquiries), as well as those for the management of the emergency states and for the President's elections; the discipline of local self-government is longer; an organ of self-government of the judiciary has been introduced; there is a special section on the economic system (which also speaks of the central bank, the court of accounts, *etc.*).

74 Serbia has requested an opinion from the International Court of Justice, which was rather ambiguous, albeit substantially in favour of Kosovo's independence, thus encouraging a series of further unilateral declarations of secession with questionable motivations (Abchazia, Ossetia, Crimea, *etc.*). On the subject, *see* E. Milano, 'Il parere consultivo della Corte internazionale di giustizia sulla dichiarazione di indipendenza del Kosovo: qualche istruzione per l'uso', www.sidi-isil.org/wp-content/uploads/2010/02/Milano-su-Kosovo.pdf (last accessed September 2018) and especially L. Gradoni & E. Milano (Eds.), *Il parere della Corte internazionale di giustizia sulla dichiarazione di indipendenza del Kosovo. Un'analisi critica*, Padova, Cedam, 2011; P. Hilpold, 'The International Court of Justice's Advisory Opinion on Kosovo: Perspectives of a Delicate Question', *Austrian Review of International and European Law*, Vol. 14, No. 1, 2013, pp. 259 *et seq.*

75 M. Mazza, *L'ordinamento costituzionale del Kosovo*, Napoli, Jovene, 2008.

attention was given also at the influences of the previous experience of the interim UN Administration. The Constitution was approved on 9 April and entered into force on 15 June 2008.

***Hungary** (18 April 2011)*

A political climate favourable to the adoption of a completely new constitution, after several unsuccessful attempts – of which, the closest to a final adoption occurred during the 1994-1998 legislature, when the socialist party had the majority of seats – arose after the spring elections of 2010, where the centre-right coalition led by the Fidesz movement obtained over two-thirds of the seats. Thanks to this high majority, to the relatively easy procedure for constitutional amendments – that required only a two-thirds majority of the MPs – and to the absence of an explicit procedure disciplining a total revision or the adoption of a new constitution; the approval of the constitution could happen on 18 April 2011, despite the strong opposition made not only by other parties, but also by civil society and European institutions. The new Hungarian Fundamental Law entered into force on 1 January 2012 and underwent six major revisions in the two following years – a seventh amendment, after a failed attempt in 2016, has been approved on June 2018 – on questions of principle, demonstrating how its adoption represented an event of strong ethical and political division within the country and abroad.

2.4 Fundamental Principles and Bill of Rights

2.4.1 *Main Features, Preambles and Principles*

In the socialist understanding of law, the constitution was not only the basis of the State but also of society. Accordingly, the section on the principles characterizing the form of State was full bodied and enjoyed a super-constitutional status. These principles were mostly included in the preamble, a real manifesto of the Marxist-Leninist ideology, but there was also a special section on the economic system (public ownership of the 'means of production', limitation of private activities, planned economy, etc.).

On the other hand, post-socialist constitutions have a completely different nature, as well as a different structure and effectiveness. They are meant to repudiate the socialist model and therefore they contain an explicit rejection of the leading role of a single party and emphasize the importance of political and party pluralism and free elections.[76]

Bills of rights are usually placed at the beginning of the constitutions, after preamble and principles, with some significant exceptions: Hungary until 2011 (the text followed the framework of the 1949 Constitution, where rights were listed after the organizational part) and Latvia, where the 1998 constitutional amendment added the bill of rights to the text of 1922, placing it after the section on the constitutional institutions. Not all bills of rights are included in the same text of the constitution. This is the case, for example, of the Czech Republic, whose Charter of Rights and Freedoms, adopted in 1991 at a federal level, remains as a separate document with the same rank as the constitution. Similarly, for the Union of Serbia and Montenegro, the Charter of Human Rights and Minorities and Fundamental Freedoms was adopted after the adoption of the 2003 Constitution.[77] The Croatian constitutional law on the rights of minorities also stands outside the constitutional text.

Preambles, where they exist,[78] are not formally binding, except the case of Fundamental Law of Hungary (please refer to Art. R, para. 3). In countries characterized by the presence of substantial ethnic minorities, the contents of preambles have been object of heated discussions, because of the accentuation of the national character of the state (the focus on the dominant nation). Such are the cases of Slovakia, Croatia, Macedonia, Latvia. Even after the Ohrid agreements that ended the Macedonian civil war in 2001, constitutional and legislative reforms aimed at improving the integration of the Albanian 'minority' have not succeeded in amending the preamble in the way Albanians asked for – that is to say, to be regarded as a constituent people of the land, like the Macedonians – even though the constitutional amendments adopted after the agreement gave a wide space to the protection of minorities, inter-ethnic and inter-religious dialogue.[79] Equally particular is the history

76 According to the socialist constitutions, the power was formally unique and derived from the people, who expressed it through directly elected assemblies. Because of the leading role of the communist-inspired party (single or hegemonic) and the lack of pluralism, the assemblies resulted in a homogeneous expression of this party (not having the other parties gathered in the 'national fronts' any bargaining or ideological power). Furthermore, the rule of imperative mandate was applied. The elections were fictitious, but they were the expression of massive support to the regime. Despite the formally prevalent role of representative bodies, the executives in fact prevailed. For bibliography on the socialist state, please refer to Chapter 1.

77 In this Charter, as pointed out by L. Montanari, *Il principio di rule of law*, cit., p. 220, in addition to the reference to ECHR dispositions, the case law of the European Court of Justice (*see* Art. 13 on the principle of equality) and the Charter of Nice (*e.g.* Art. 11 on the prohibition of cloning) are also evoked.

78 Bulgaria, Estonia, Lithuania, Poland (long preamble), Czech Republic (both the Constitution and the Charter of Rights), Slovakia, Slovenia, Hungary (very long), Croatia (very long, with strong emphasis on identity and sovereignty), Albania, Macedonia, Montenegro 1992 and 2007, Kosovo, Bosnia and Herzegovina. In some cases, the faith in God is invoked (Poland; Albania, with reference to religious coexistence).

79 The Albanian minority always contested the wording of the preamble, which it believed would confer a preferential position on the Macedonian people. The Ohrid agreement, which ended with the international mediation the civil war of 2001, had urged the elimination of any reference to ethnic groups from the

of the long preamble of the Latvian Constitution introduced in June 2014.[80] For what concerns the preamble of the new Hungarian Fundamental Law, it is a text characterized by a strong identity, reflecting the new Christian-conservative ideology of the ruling party.[81]

As for fundamental principles, the ones that define the new form of state (separation of powers, rule of law, democracy) are clearly set out and emphasized. However, self-promotion is not enough "to ensure the effective existence of the vaunted characteristic while representing the solemn announcement of the change".[82] This declaratory approach resulted in the incorporation into a single 'block' of a set of principles that in old democracies have been introduced and applied during a secular constitutional evolution, commonly making unnecessary to expressly state the same principles in the constitutional text. Division of powers and democracy, where not expressly declared, can be deduced from the provisions concerning state structure, political and party pluralism and free elections. As we shall see, the fundamental characteristics of the new form of state are expressly withdrawn from constitutional revision (*e.g.* Romania, Czech Republic, etc.). Alternatively, the amendment of the relevant provisions is extremely complicated (*e.g.* Lithuania, Latvia, Estonia, Poland, etc.). Among the fundamental principles we also find sovereignty, which usually defines and qualifies a state. Sovereignty is not a feature to be considered in an abstract way, it must be evaluated keeping into account also the participation in supranational organizations

preamble. However, the Macedonian nationalists opposed to a similar transformation, and eventually a compromise was reached on the following wording "citizens of the Republic of Macedonia, the Macedonian people, as well as citizens living within its borders who are part of the Albanian, Turkish, Wallach, Serbian, Rom, Bosnian and others populations'". The original version stated as follows: "Proceeding from the historical, cultural, spiritual and statehood heritage of the Macedonian people and their centuries-long struggle for national and social liberty and the creation of their own state.... Macedonia is established as a national state of the Macedonian people, in which full equality as citizens and permanent coexistence with the Macedonian people is provided for Albanians, Turks, Vlachs, Roma and other nationalities living in the Republic of Macedonia...."

80 Adopted after more than a year of public debate, the preamble emphasizes the fundamental principles on which the state is based, according particular importance to the concepts of 'Latvian nation' and 'Latvian language'. Two years after the failed constitutional referendum on the recognition of the Russian language as the second official language, the preamble reaffirmes the uniqueness of the Latvian language as state language (as already provided for in Art. 4 of the Constitution and now also in para. 5 of the preamble), while ensuring respect for national minorities. A. Angeli, 'Latvia. A New Preamble to the Constitution Adopted', 23 July 2014, http://nad.unimi.it/latvia-a-new-preamble-to-the-constitution-adopted/ (last accessed September 2018).

81 G.F. Ferrari, 'Premessa a Ungheria (2011)', *in* M. Ganino (Ed.), *Codice delle Costituzioni*, cit.; B. Fekete, 'The National Avowal of the Fundamental Law: An Unorthodox Deconstruction', *in* Z. Szente, F. Mandák & Z. Fejes (Eds.), *Challenges and Pitfalls in the Recent Hungarian Constitutional Development. Discussing the New Fundamental Law of Hungary*, Paris, L'Harmattan, 2015.

82 M. Ganino, 'Democrazia e diritti umani nelle Costituzioni dei Paesi dell'Europa orientale', *in* M. Ganino & G. Venturini (Eds.), *L'Europa di domani: verso l'allargamento dell'Unione*, cit., p. 130. On the 'self-qualifications' *see* L. Pegoraro & S. Baldin, 'Costituzioni e qualificazioni degli ordinamenti. Profili comparatistici', *in* L. Mezzetti & V. Piergigli (Ed.), *Presidenzialismi, semipresidenzialismi: modelli comparati e riforme costituzionali in Italia*, Torino, Giappichelli, 1997.

and the interpretation of constitutional jurisprudence. Other particularly relevant principles, given the socialist past of these countries, are those of legality and constitutionality (with the supervision of the constitutional courts). Sometimes a call for a social version of democracy can be found, with reference also to 'social justice'.

The rule of law principle is included in every constitution, in preambles, fundamental principles sections and in asserting the supremacy of law and constitution. The rule of law can be interpreted strictly, as a principle of legality and constitutionality, to which is given an effective content after the rhetoric of socialist legality, or as a summary of the characteristics of the liberal-democratic constitutionalism. The Serbian Constitution of 2006 includes a detailed description of the rule of law principle in Article 3.[83]

Fundamental principles outlining the new form of state and included in preambles or in specific sections on fundamental principles are therefore the following: democracy, rule of law, pluripartidism, separation of powers (with the specification of balance and mutual control in the most recent Constitutions of Serbia and Montenegro), social state (in Serbia both the old and the new Constitution speak of "social justice", the same do Constitutions of Montenegro 2007 and Kosovo 2008), market economy. Further characteristics of post-socialist constitutions are the emphasis put on sovereignty and identity and the nationalistic tone: despite the presence of specific clauses limiting sovereignty, there are references to self-determination, to the 'nation',[84] to the protection of compatriots abroad. Another typical feature of these constitutions is that they provide a broad list of rights for ethnic minorities (with positive discrimination and emphatic arrangements on languages and alphabets, especially in the countries of the former Yugoslavia). Moreover, they tend show a peculiar relationship between state and religion (a rather negative attitude towards the churches is noted in the Serbian Constitution of 2006, because of the vagueness of certain formulations)[85]; they include the right of 'resistance' (it can be found in constitutions of Estonia, Lithuania, Czech Republic, Slovakia and Hungary).

83 This article details the components of the rule of law: free and direct elections, constitutional guarantees of human and minority rights, division of powers, independent judiciary, respect for the constitution and the law by the authorities; moreover, it is said that "the rule of law is a fundamental prerequisite for the Constitution which is based on inalienable human rights".

84 The nationalistic tendency in Art. 51 of the Serbian Constitution of 1990 was very strong: in introducing the duty of defense of the Republic, this article specified that no one would have the right to recognize or sign an act of capitulation, or accept or recognize the occupation of the Republic of Serbia or a part of it. The betrayal was considered a crime against the nation and punished as a serious criminal offense. All this is an expression of the period in which the Constitution was adopted.

85 Pursuant to Art. 44, para. 3 Constitutional Court can ban a religious community if its activities violate the right to life, to physical and mental health, personal and family integrity, children's rights, public order and if they incite to religious, national or racial intolerance.

2.4.2 Fundamental Rights

The socialist constitutions, generically speaking, featured wide and detailed bills of rights' sections. However, the fruition of said rights suffered different types of limitations: they were aimed to the building of a communist society; civic liberties were subordinated to social rights, the state had to provide the means for the exercise of rights, etc. Moreover, the absence of an effective system of enforcement and monitoring – as well as the lack of an independent judiciary – made those rights ineffective.

As a general rule, in defining the bill of rights, constitutional framers were inspired by international documents adopted within UN, OSCE and Council of Europe. Many rights are described with the same wording as in the ECHR. However, a distinction should be made between the different generations of post-communist constitutions. Only in a second phase the framers received the assistance of the Venice Commission, while in the beginning the transposition of European and international standards has been indirect, culturally mediated, or facilitated by the signing and ratification of the main international treaties.

The reference to international covenants on human rights is particularly emphasized in the most recent constitutions, and particularly in those of the countries of the former Yugoslavia, who were subjected to a strong international conditioning during and after the civil wars that bloodied the region. The closest connection with the international treaties on human rights is expressed in the Constitution of Bosnia and Herzegovina. The Dayton Constitution, in fact, does not include a proper bill of rights, but one built through a series of references to several different international treaties, which are considered directly applicable, regardless of their ratification. The same applies to guarantees, which are largely 'internationalized' (*see* for instance the Human Rights Chamber, then replaced by a Constitutional Court: both institutions are partly composed of international members).[86] It should be remembered that beside the Constitution, which is included in Annex no. 4 of the Dayton Treaty, the Annex no. 6 of the same Treaty is specifically dedicated to the protection of human rights.[87]

Apart from post-conflict situations settled with the international intervention or mediation (Bosnia-Herzegovina, Union of Serbia and Montenegro, Kosovo, constitutional amendments in Macedonia after 2001), the international conditioning on constitutional texts – in particular on the bills of rights and guarantees system – is obviously more intense

86 Some details regarding the complex composition of these institutions can be found in L. Montanari, 'La tutela dei diritti in Bosnia ed Erzegovina: il complesso rapporto tra Camera dei diritti umani, Corte costituzionale e Corte di Strasburgo', *in* G.F. Ferrari (Ed.), *Corti nazionali e Corti europee*, Napoli, ESI, 2006.

87 Therefore, as L. Montanari, *La tutela dei diritti nelle nuove Costituzioni dei Balcani occidentali*, cit., p. 176, points out, there are three categories of rights provided by the Constitution in Art. II ("Human rights and fundamental freedoms"): those included in the ECHR, which is directly applicable and prevails over conflicting laws; the rights expressly listed; the rights recognized in international treaties indicated in Ann. I of the Constitution (and related to Ann. 6).

for the EU candidate countries. In fact, if we consider, for example, the Western Balkans, it has been stronger in the second constitutional cycle.[88] The reference to ECHR is also present in the Albanian Constitution, where Article 17, para. 2 states that limitations of constitutional rights and freedoms through legislation "may not infringe the essence of the rights and freedoms and in no case may exceed the limitations provided for in the European Convention on Human Rights". This is a clear example of the Venice Commission assistance in the drafting the 1998 Constitution (Art. 17 as a matter of facts 'constitutionalizes' ECHR for what concerns rights restrictions. This also implies a reference to the case law of the Strasbourg Court). Article 53 of the 2008 Kosovo Constitution provides that

> Human rights and fundamental freedoms guaranteed by this Constitution shall be interpreted in a manner consistent with the decisions of the European Court for Human Rights.[89]

Article 20, para. 1 of the Romanian Constitution states that

> constitutional provisions concerning the citizens' rights and freedoms shall be interpreted and enforced in conformity with the Universal Declaration of Human Rights, with the covenants and other treaties Romania is a party to.

In case of inconsistency between those international sources and domestic laws, the firsts prevail, unless there are more favourable provisions of the Constitution or the laws. Article 89 of the Latvian Constitution provides that the state recognizes and protects the fundamental human rights not only in accordance with the Constitution and laws but also with international treaties that are binding on Latvia. In the new Serbian Constitution, a significant emphasis is put on international rights protection, including the protection of minorities, with a reference not only to international standards on human rights and minorities but also to the "practice of international institutions which supervise their implementation" (Art. 18).

As for Montenegro, the 1992 Constitution, although it did not include an explicit reference to international law and international organizations, provided that "citizens have the right to address international institutions to protect their rights and freedoms guaran-

88 Different things are the so-called 'European clauses', introduced almost everywhere after the adoption of the constitutions through specific constitutional amendments.

89 On the other hand, the provisional constitution of 15 May 2001 did not contain a real bill of rights, referring to a series of international conventions (*see* the preamble and Chapter 3, which listed a series of international treaties). Instead, the rules relating to the rights of ethnic, religious and linguistic communities and their members were established directly (Chapter 4), and the membership of Kosovo to the Yugoslavian Federation was also affirmed.

teed by the Constitution" (Art. 44, para 2). We have to consider that – having been expected that it was Serbia that would have succeed in the international commitments of the country – when Montenegro requested the separation, it had to apply for admission to the Council of Europe. The new born country, therefore, committed to introduce in its Constitution the same fundamental principles along with a protection of rights equivalent to that provided for by the Charter of the Union of Serbia and Montenegro, which was written under international influence[90] (even though the 1992 Constitution was far more advanced in the rights protection than the 1990 Serbian Constitution). Here, too, the constitution-making process was subjected to the constant advice of the Venice Commission.[91] The Constitution of 2007 is even clearer. In fact, Article 24 ("Limitations of human rights and liberties") uses the same wording of the ECHR as for the limitation of rights. Also, Article 17 specifies that rights and freedoms must be exercised not only on the basis of the Constitution, but also "of confirmed international treaties".

For what concerns the bills of rights' content, in addition to traditional freedom and political rights they also include social rights albeit with significant differences, according to the different characteristics and speed with which the transition to democracy occurred. While civic and political rights are considered directly applicable, social rights' enforcement generically require the implementation through legislation. As for new generation rights, that is to say the ones related to environment, privacy, cloning, biotechnology, data and consumer protection, etc., the more recent the constitutions are, the more these rights are foreseen. The Croatian Constitution of 1990 (Art. 37: protection of personal data, Art. 58: protection of veterans) and the Serbian Constitution of 1990 (rights of the disabled, Art. 38, c. 3; Art. 39, para. 1) were rather precocious in this respect. Equally precocious was Montenegro in matters of environmental protection, having adopted the Declaration on the Ecological State of Montenegro on 20 September 1991. The interest to this aspect was confirmed by the Montenegrin Constitution of 1992, which conferred to the state the protection of the sanctity and purity of nature (preamble) and defined Montenegro as an ecological state (Art. 1). It also specifically provided for the protection the environment at Article 65. The 2007 Constitution, too, emphasizes the ecological quality of the state: in addition to the preamble ("the state is responsible for the preservation of nature, sound environment, sustainable development") *see* Articles 1 (Montenegro is again defined an "ecological state"), 23, 78. The protection of the environment is an express limitation to the freedom of enterprise guaranteed by Article 59. In general, the 2007 Constitution of Montenegro, being one of the last adopted in Europe, contains several references to new generation rights: Articles 27 (biomedicine: cloning ban, etc.), 43 (protection of personal

90 L. Montanari, *La tutela dei diritti nelle nuove Costituzioni dei Balcani occidentali*, cit., pp. 172-173.

91 Commission's preliminary opinion of 5 June 2007.

data), 48 (conscience objection), 68 (protection of persons with disability), 70 (consumer protection).

Many new generation rights are also included in the 2006 Serbian Constitution,[92] as they already were in the Croatian Constitution of 1990 (Art. 37: protection of personal data; Art. 58: protection of war veterans). The rights of disabled people were already provided for in the 1990 Serbian Constitution (Art. 38, para. 3, Art. 39, para. 1). In the new Hungarian Fundamental Law too, there are new generation rights (or prohibitions) such as the denial of eugenic practices (Art. III, para. 3: "Practices aimed at eugenics, the use of the human body or its parts for financial gain, as well as human cloning shall be prohibited"), the protection of personal data and access to data of public interest – which also represents a distance from the past – (Art. VI, para. 2). Furthermore, Article X, para. 2 states that "the state shall have no right to decide on questions of scientific truth; only scientists shall have the right to evaluate scientific research" and Article XX, para. 2 prohibits genetically modified agriculture in order to protect human health and promote access to healthy food and beverages. Among the elements indicating the Hungarian authoritarian degeneration, which occurred also through continuous changes in the constitutional text, it is to be taken into account the restriction suffered by certain fundamental freedoms, with the VII constitutional amendment act entered into force on 29 June 2018. Specifically, the right of expression and meeting (new version of Art. VI, which formally concerns the rights of privacy), of circulation (Art. XXII), as well as the right to asylum (new version of Art. XIV).

As mentioned, the reference to the welfare state is present almost everywhere, as well as a long list of social rights, especially in constitutions adopted immediately after the transition from the communist rule. However, the implementation of these rights can be problematic if confronted with the level of protection and guarantee existing in socialist constitutions. With the transition to market economy, it was necessary to preserve only those rights that could be secured within a reasonable period of time or alternatively proclaim them all but with fewer guarantees. Undoubtedly, this last approach has been seen as a regression into the social policy of the state and has favoured the temporary return to government of the former communists. Different choices in this respect were made by the divergent political majorities elected for the constituent assemblies. It can be noticed, for example, the discrepancy between the Czech and the Slovak Constitutions with specific reference to social rights – which are more relevant in Slovakia, because of a different

92 Art. 6: prohibition of conflict of interests; Art. 15: gender equality; Art. 24, para. 3: prohibition of cloning; Art. 42: protection of personal data; Art. 63: freedom to procreate or to not procreate (para.1; but the State encourages parents who decide to have children and supports them, para. 2); Art. 66, para. 3: rights of children with disabilities; Art. 69, para. 4: social assistance for disabled, war veterans and war victims (this protection exists in several Republics of the former Yugoslavia); Art. 74: right to the environment; Art. 90: consumer protection; Art. 100, para 2: protection of gender representation also in parliament.

context and transition path, although both lists of rights derive from the common Czechoslovakian bill of rights adopted in 1991.[93] In the Constitution of the Czech Republic it is expressly stated that a series of social rights may be claimed only within the confines of the laws implementing the relative provisions (Art. 41 of the Charter). Similar provisions are included in the Constitutions of Albania (Art. 59, para. 2) and Poland (Art. 81). Among the social objectives of the state, the Albanian Constitution also includes "the protection of national cultural heritage and particular care for the Albanian language" (Art. 59).

For what concerns the links with the past, both socialist residues (stronger in the countries of the former Yugoslavia) and distancing provisions can be found. For what concerns these last ones, let us mention the following: prohibition of usurpation of power, prohibition of unconstitutional parties or associations (very detailed is the Serbian Constitution of 2006),[94] prohibition of torture, forced labour, forced medical experiments, censorship. Other distances are subtler, for example in the 1992 Constitution of Montenegro, Article 20 ("Personal inviolability") protects the physical and psychological integrity of persons; Article 24, para. 2 prohibits the use of force against a detained suspect and any forcible extraction of a confession or statement; in Article 77, para. 2 (independence of deputies) it is specified that deputies decide and vote according to their convictions and cannot be recalled. In the Serbian Constitution of 1990, within the right of petition provided by Article 48, it is also included the right to "publicly criticize the work of state and other organs and organizations", as well as "high-ranking officials". The Serbian Constitution of 2006 in Article 51 ("Right to information") specifies that

> Everyone shall have the right to be informed accurately, fully and timely about issues of public importance. The media shall have the obligation to respect this right. Everyone shall have the right to access information kept by state bodies and organizations with delegated public powers, in accordance with the law.

The new Hungarian Fundamental Law, too, protects the right to access data of public interest (Art. VI, para. 3).

Even in terms of economic rights, the distance from the past is evident: the pillars of market economy – that is to say the freedom of enterprise and ownership – are provided, and the possibility to expropriate ownership is limited to cases of public utility and behind adequate compensation. Some constitutions define the nature of the economic system:

93 *See* the introductions to the two constitutions of A. Di Gregorio, *in* M. Ganino (Ed.), *Codice delle Costituzioni*, cit.

94 Art. 5, paras. 3 and 55, para. 4: the Constitutional Court can dissolve these associations, among other reasons, if they incite racial, national or religious hatred or violate guaranteed human or minority rights; *see also* Art. 2, para. 2: "no state body, political organization, group or individual may usurp the sovereignty from the citizens, nor establish government against freely expressed will of the citizens."

market economy (Romania), social market economy (at the beginning, in Hungary) or socially and ecologically oriented market economy (Slovakia, Art. 55). In the constitutions of the countries of former Yugoslavia there is a special section on the economic system (Montenegro 1992 and 2007, Serbia 1990 and 2006, Macedonia, Slovenia). In general, ownership rights and economic initiative are included among the fundamental freedoms to mark the break with the past.

2.4.3 *Regulation, Limits and Protection of Rights*

For what concerns the regulation of rights and their possible limitations, constitutions refer to the adoption of specific legislations. This 'reserve of law' often implies the adoption of laws by absolute or qualified majority – the so-called organic or cardinal laws, that are usually reserved for the regulation of rights and of the main constitutional bodies. For example, in the 2011 Hungarian Fundamental Law, specific 'cardinal laws' – adopted by a majority of two-thirds of the deputies present – regulate rights of citizenship (Art. G), protection of family (Art. L), protection of personal data and access to data of public interest (Art. VI), freedom of the press (Art. IX), voting rights (Art. XXIII), rights of national minorities (Art. XXIX). Article 83 of the Constitution of Montenegro of 1992 listed a series of subjects regulated by laws passed by a majority of votes of the total number of deputies, including legislation regulating the manner in which the freedoms and rights are exercised. In the Croatian Constitution, Article 17 provides for the possibility of curtailing fundamental constitutional rights (with the exception of certain ones, such as right to life, prohibition of torture, freedom of thought and religion) in the event of war or other states of emergency, by a two-thirds majority of all representatives or, if the parliament is unable to convene, by an act of the President. Article 83 of the same Constitution states that, by a two-thirds majority vote of all deputies, the parliament shall adopt (organic) laws in order to regulate the rights of national minorities while, by a majority vote of all deputies, it shall adopt organic laws elaborating, among other matters, constitutionally established human rights and fundamental freedoms. In Romania, organic laws passed with an absolute majority of members of parliament shall be adopted to regulate, among other things, the protection of rights and legitimate interests violated by public authorities (Art. 52), the rights of social protection and labour (Art. 73), the status and the use of language of national minorities (Art. 73), the general statutory rules of religious cults (Art. 73), citizenship (Art. 5), the right of private property (Art. 136). Article 18 of the 2006 Serbian Constitution require that human and minority rights guaranteed by the Constitution shall be implemented directly and that "the law may prescribe the manner of exercising these rights only if explicitly stipulated in the Constitution or necessary to exercise a specific right owing to its nature" (but no reference is made to laws adopted with a special majority).[95]

Even where they are not explicitly made exempt from constitutional amendments, fundamental rights are defined inalienable and imprescriptible. A law is provided for their regulation, often protecting the essential content at constitutional level.[96] Rather ambiguous references to 'morality', as a limit to the exercise of a series of fundamental rights, can be found in the constitutions of Romania, Serbia 2006, Montenegro 2007. Similarly, an ambiguous limitation on the freedom of speech is provided by Article IX, para. 5 of the Hungarian Fundamental Law, which states that

> The right to freedom of speech may not be exercised with the aim of violating the dignity of the Hungarian nation or of any national, ethnic, racial or religious community. Persons belonging to such communities shall be entitled to enforce their claims in court against the expression of an opinion which violates the community, invoking the violation of their human dignity, as provided for by an Act.

Equally restrictive is the provision of Article XXII, para. 3 introduced with the 4th constitutional revision of 25 March 2013, according to which

> In order to protect public order, public security, public health and cultural values, an act or a local government decree may, with respect to a specific part of public space, provide that staying in public space as a habitual dwelling shall be illegal.

As for the protection of rights, in addition to the introduction of constitutional courts (please, refer to the specific chapter of this volume), states of emergency are also regulated in detail, in order to avoid authoritarian backslidings (especially in the Balkan constitutions: *see* Art. 17 of the Constitution of Croatia, Art. 25 of the 2007 Constitution of Montenegro,

95 "The law may prescribe manner of exercising these rights only if explicitly stipulated in the Constitution or necessary to exercise a specific right owing to its nature, whereby the law may not under any circumstances influence the substance of the relevant guaranteed right." Art. 20, para. 1 provides for the limitation of human and minority rights with the same wording as the ECHR: "Human and minority rights guaranteed by the Constitution may be restricted by the law if the Constitution permits such restriction and for the purpose allowed by the Constitution, to the extent necessary to meet the constitutional purpose of restriction in a democratic society and without encroaching upon the substance of the relevant guaranteed right."

96 *See, e.g.* Art. 17, para. 2 of the Constitution of Albania; Art. 49, para. 2 of the Constitution of Romania; Art. 13, para. 4 of the Constitution of Slovakia; Art. 4, para. 4 of the Charter of Rights of the Czech Republic; Art. 31, para. 3 of the Constitution of Poland; Art. 11 of the Constitution of Estonia; Art. 18 and especially Art. 20 of the Constitution of Serbia of 2006; Art. I, para. 3 of the Hungarian Fundamental Law; Art. 55, para. 4 of the Constitution of Kosovo.

Art. 170 of the Constitution of Albania). The admissible restrictions of fundamental rights during the emergency situations are generally defined directly by the constitutions (sometimes in a very general manner, as happens in the Macedonian Constitution), that also specify the ones that absolutely cannot be limited.

The institution of 'ombudsman' or parliamentary commissioners (they are named differently in every country),[97] in their most recent evolution – they have been transformed from administrative control bodies into instruments of protection of rights – is widespread. These bodies can appeal to the constitutional courts as collectors of citizens' requests: this is a particularly important function in countries where there is no possibility for individuals to appeal directly to the constitutional courts. The public prosecutor figure that can be found in the 1990 Constitution of Serbia (Art. 103) and in the 1992 Constitution of Montenegro (Art. 105) is comparable to an ombudsman, as its role is to defend constitutionality and legality. It is an evident socialist heritage. In some countries, the ombudsman is provided for only at legislative level: Latvia (National Human Rights Office, Act No. 392 of 1996), Czech Republic (Public Defender of Rights, Law of 8 December 1999).

According to the Norwegian-born sociologist Jon Elster, who analysed the contents of new constitutions – in some cases only of constitutional drafts – in 1991, many provisions on fundamental rights had two main shortcomings, the first being the rule of law for their implementation (not contemplated in USA's legal order, Elster's homeland of adoption), and the second that freedom of speech, assembly and religion were limited by the reference to public morality or security.[98] However, many of the detected flows were eliminated from the final text of the constitutions, or were removed by subsequent constitutional amendments (*e.g.* limitations on the right of private property). This does not apply to the 2006 Serbian Constitution which provides in Article 46 (freedom of thought and speech) the possibility of restricting by an act this freedom, among other reasons, in order to protect the morality of a democratic society, as well as national security. The same limitation is provided for in the regulation of freedom of assembly (Art. 54). As mentioned above, some references to 'morality' as a limitation to the exercise of rights is also contained in the

97 Albania (People's Advocate, Arts. 60-63), Montenegro 2007 (Protector of human rights and liberties, Art. 81), Slovenia (Ombudsman for Human Rights and Fundamental Freedoms, Art. 159), Slovakia (Public Protector of Rights, Art. 151a), Romania (Advocate of the People, Arts. 58-60), Bulgaria (Ombudsman, 2006 constitutional amendment, Art. 91.a), Croatia (Ombudsperson, Art. 93), Hungary (Commissioner for Fundamental Rights, Art. 30), Poland (Commissioner for Citizens' Rights, Arts. 208-212; Commissioner for Children's Rights, Art. 72), Lituania (Seimas ombudsmen, Art. 73), Estonia (Chancellor of Justice, which has also other competencies, Arts. 139-145), Kosovo (Ombudsperson, Arts. 132-135), Serbia 2006 (Civic Defender, Art. 138).

98 J. Elster, 'Constitutionalism in Eastern Europe: An Introduction', *University of Chicago Law Review*, Vol. 58, No. 2, 1991, pp. 465-466. The Author believes that the rights regulated by the constitutions in a more controversial manner were those of minorities (especially in Romania and Bulgaria), of free disposal of property, the right to decent living conditions and the limitations mentioned above to freedom of expression, assembly and religion.

Montenegrin Constitution of 2007 (*see* Art. 47 on freedom of expression, fifty-one on the right to obtain information and fifty-two on freedom of assembly).

Lastly, for what concerns the protection of rights, we find a peculiar situation in Bosnia-Herzegovina: Annex 6 establishes the Commission on human rights. This originally included the office of the Ombudsman, which is still provided, and the Human Rights Chamber, which ceased its activities on 31 December 2003, on the basis of an agreement that transferred its competences to the Constitutional Court.[99]

2.4.4 *The Rights of Ethnic-National Minorities*

Special attention is paid by the constitutional texts to the protection of ethnic-national minorities, due to the great complexity of these countries. This heterogeneity, which is partially given also by religious complexity, is the result of events dating back in some cases to the end of the First World War and in others to the disintegration of the socialist federations, and it originates different phenomena, which should be so differentiated:

- 'quasi-constitutive' peoples[100];
- Russian-speaking minorities,[101] which amount to significant proportions of the population in Estonia and Latvia[102];
- large but territorially concentrated minorities with a strong kin-state reference (Hungarians in Slovakia, Romania and Vojvodina, Turks in Bulgaria);
- minorities belonging to the people of former rulers[103];
- minorities without specific protection (Roma).

Provisions on the protection of ethnic and national minorities were already present in the constitutions of the 1920s; however, they did not go beyond purely formal proclamations. Currently the issue of a strong protection, starting from the constitutional level, is a particularly sensitive one especially in the Republics of the former Yugoslavia, where the protec-

99 Please refer to L. Montanari, *La tutela dei diritti nelle Costituzioni dei Balcani occidentali*, cit., p. 196, and to the opinion of the Venice Commission of 13 December 1999.

100 The Albanians in Macedonia, for example, which amount to over 40 percent and are territorially concentrated in the north-western region, on the border with Albania.

101 Moved after 1940.

102 They were over 28 percent in Estonia, over 32 percent in Latvia and about 8 percent in Lithuania immediately after the collapse of the USSR. Today the percentages are lower. Please refer to A. Di Gregorio, *Democratic transition and linguistic minorities in Estonia and Latvia*, Briefing requested by the PETI committee, European Parliament, edited by Policy Department for Citizens' Rights and Constitutional Affairs, Directorate-General for Internal Policies, April 2018.

103 Russian-speaking population in the Baltic countries, Serbs in the Republics of the former Yugoslavia, Hungarians in Romania, Slovakia and Vojvodina, Turks in Bulgaria.

tion of minorities becomes a 'litmus test' for the protection of human rights.[104] A typical form of protection of democracy in these countries consists in the prohibition of incitement to racial or religious hatred, to war, to the violent overthrow of the constitutional order or to the violent attack on territorial integrity, even if this prohibition can be seen as a general limitation to the freedom of expression of thought and association, as well as of religion and press.[105] On the other hand, the right not to declare or express thoughts, religion or nationality seems to be a distancing from the past.[106] Another form of protection of the recently conquered democracy, taken in order to protect peaceful coexistence and national independence, consist in the prohibition to form parties on a national or religious basis. Are also to be taken into account the dispositions, that can be found in all the constitutions, on the prohibition to discriminate on the basis of several reasons, among which the national origins.

The legislative implementation of minority rights has taken place, however, after the adoption of the constitutions, thanks to the encouragement of the Council of Europe and the European Union (it is one of the Copenhagen criteria). The most important document, at European level, is the Council of Europe Framework Convention on the Protection of National Minorities, approved on 10 November 1994 and entered into force on 1 February 1998, after reaching the required number of ratifications. Under the influence of this document, the former communist countries have adopted a series of regulations for the protection of minorities, even if, taking advantage of the programmatic nature of the Convention, many have tried to 'nationalize' it, limiting its application to the minorities already recognized in the national constitutions (Slovenia, Macedonia, Poland).[107] This has frustrated the initial ambition of the Council of Europe, who wanted to make the

---

104 *See* F. Palermo & J. Woelk, *Diritto costituzionale comparato dei gruppi e delle minoranze*, Padova, Cedam, 2011. On the former Yugoslavia Republics *see* M. Dicosola, *Stati, nazioni e minoranze. La ex Jugoslavia tra revival etnico e condizionalità europea*, Milano, Giuffré, 2010; Id., 'Strumenti di tutela giuridica della comunità Rom negli Stati dell'ex Jugoslavia', *in* P. Bonetti, A. Simoni & T. Vitale (Eds.), *La condizione giuridica di Rom e Sinti in Italia*, Milano, Giuffrè, 2011, pp. 527-552.

105 Please refer to: Art. 9, para 2 cost. Albania; Art. 20, para. 3 cost. Macedonia; Art. 50, paras. 2 and 55, para. 1 cost. Montenegro 2007; Art. 37, paras. 2, 42, and 43 cost. Montenegro 1992; Art. 63, para. 1 cost. Slovenia; Art. 44, para. 3 cost. Kosovo; Art. 5, paras. 3 and 43, para. 4 cost., 44, paras. 3, 49, and 50, paras. 3 and 55, para. 4 cost. Serbia 2006; Art. 44, paras. 2 and 46, para. 6 cost. Serbia 1990; Art. 39 cost. Croatia.

106 For the national affiliation *see* Art. 34, para. 3 cost. Montenegro 1992, Art. 3, para. 2 Czech Charter of rights, Art. 12, para. 3 cost. Slovakia, Art. 47, para. 2 cost. Serbia 2006, Art. 49, para. 2 cost. Serbia 1990.

107 *Cf.* K. Gál, 'The Council of Europe Framework Convention for the Protection of National Minorities and its Impact on Central and Eastern Europe', *Journal on Ethnopolitics and Minority Issues in Europe*, Winter 2000, www.ecmi.de/fileadmin/downloads/publications/JEMIE/JEMIE05Gal30-07-01.pdf (last accessed September 2018). As the author points out, the Convention contains many programmatic provisions that leave wide discretionary implementation to the states. It also does not contain a definition of minority and therefore several states (Bulgaria, Denmark, Estonia, Germany, Switzerland, Macedonia) have ratified it with a declaration introducing a restrictive interpretation of the term 'national minority'. *See also* C. Filippini, 'La disciplina costituzionale sulle minoranze nei paesi dell'Europa orientale e l'adesione all'Unione europea', *in* M. Ganino & G. Venturini (Eds.), *L'Europa di domani verso l'allargamento dell'Unione*, cit., pp. 333-361.

Convention the European reference document on the protection of minorities, as – unlike the OSCE Copenhagen Document of 1990, which set up minority rights as a political declaration of intent – it had formulated these rights in a purely legal form.

Between the two different possible approaches to the question, the 'general' and potentially anti-minority one – based on the principle of equality and non-discrimination, and the 'inclusive' and plurinational one – based on affirmative actions that however could appear as 'discriminations', it is the first one that prevailed, with some exceptions, in the countries. It grants individual rights to minority members as individuals (with collective rights existing only in Hungary, Slovenia, Croatia, Estonia, Montenegro, Serbia).[108] At the same time, there are some 'reverse discriminations' in favour of the majority nation.[109]

Among the rights granted to minorities, those related to the protection of language and culture prevail (but the protection of the language of the dominant nation is also emphasized, *see* Albania, Serbia, Latvia). In some cases, specific political rights are also granted, such as the right to a guaranteed parliamentary representation: in the constitution in Romania, Article 62, para. 2; Slovenia, Article 80, para. 3 and Article 64, para. 6 (in the latter case with a right of veto of the Italian and Hungarian minorities, similar to the Belgian 'sonnette d'alarme'); Montenegro 2007, Article 79 point 9; Kosovo, Article 64[110]; Serbia 2006, Article 100, para. 2; in the legislation in Poland, Croatia, Montenegro. In rare cases, special institutions for the protection of minorities are built up.[111] In other cases, in municipalities where a certain percentage of the population belongs to a specific minority, it enjoys greater rights.[112]

An important aspect, especially in the countries of the former Yugoslavia, is that of the alphabet, as this is also a national symbol. In the 1992 Constitution of Montenegro, the para. 3 of Article 9 ("Language and Alphabet") provided that

> In the municipalities in which the majority or a substantial number of the population consists of national minorities and ethnic groups, their respective languages and alphabets shall be in official use.

108 Already in the Estonian Constitution of 1920.

109 Romania, Art. 6, para. 2 cost., Slovakia, Art. 34, para. 3, Macedonia until the 2001 constitutional amendment, Bulgaria Art. 11, para. 4.

110 *See also* the mandatory approval of constitutional amendments by the two-thirds of minority representatives: Art. 144, para. 2.

111 There was a specific parliamentary commissioner in Hungary until 2011. Instead, according to the new Fundamental Law, now one of the deputies of the Commissioner for fundamental rights has this function. In Kosovo it is the Consultative Council for Communities under the authority of the President of the Republic; in the 1992 Constitution of Montenegro the Republican Council for the Protection of Rights of National and Ethnic Groups; in Croatia the Council for National Minorities foreseen by the constitutional Act on minorities in 2002.

112 *See, e.g.*, in Macedonia, V amendment to the Costitution, Kosovo Art. 59, para. 6, Serbia 2006; Art. 79, Montenegro 2007; Art. 79, para. 3, Estonia; Art. 52, para. 2, *etc.*

Articles 67 to 76 were explicitly devoted to the rights of national and ethnic groups. However, the exercise of these rights should not conflict with the Constitution, the principles of international law and the principle of territorial integrity of the country (Art. 75). The 2007 Constitution strengthens the protection of minorities (as mentioned in the preamble: Serbs, Bosnians, Albanians, Muslims, Croats and others), also in the light of international law, and it reinforces the prohibition of discrimination and intolerance in general (Arts. 7 and 8). With regard to language, in addition to the Montenegrin, among the official languages are mentioned Serbian, Bosnian, Croatian and Albanian (Art. 13: apart from the last one, the others consist in different versions of the same language). There is a special section in the catalogue of rights dedicated to minority rights (Arts. 79-80), which is, however, shorter than the homologous section of the 1992 Constitution and no longer provides for the Council for the protection of minorities. The new "Protector of rights" is introduced, though, along with a prohibition of forced assimilation. The clause that conditioned the exercise of minority rights to the respect of territorial integrity of the country, as well as of the constitution and international treaties, has been deleted. There is no explicit reference to the rights of local self-government of minorities, as it was before. The right of persons belonging to minority nations and other minority national communities to be represented in the national or local bodies (where they constitute a substantial share) is confirmed and defined as "positive action" (Art. 79).

In the Serbian Constitution of 2006 Article 1 defines the Serbian Republic "a State of Serbian people" and of all citizens who live in it, not explicitly mentioning minorities. The provisions on the use of language and alphabet (Art. 10) are more restrictive than in the Constitution of 1990 (Art. 8),[113] when Serbia was still part of Yugoslavia, since they directly proclaim Serbian language and the Cyrillic alphabet[114] as official, while the rules on the use of other languages and alphabets are left to the law. For the protection of minorities, we must refer to Article 14 ("Protection of national minorities"), to the general prohibitions contained in Article 21 ("Prohibition of discrimination"), to the auspices of Articles 48 ("Promotion of respect for diversity") and 49 ("Prohibition of inciting racial, ethnic and religious hatred": this being an evident post-war disposition). A specific section of the chapter on human rights, freedoms and rights of minorities (Chapter 3) is dedicated precisely to the rights of "persons belonging to national minorities" (Arts. 75-81) which ends with an incitement to the spirit of tolerance (Art. 81).

113 Which stated as follows: "In the Republic of Serbia, the Serbo-Croatian language and the Cyrillic alphabet are officially used, and the Latinic alphabet is officially used in the manner established by law. In the regions of the Republic of Serbia inhabited by national minorities, their languages and alphabets are also officially used, in the manner established by law."

114 Art. 10 ("Language and Script"): "Serbian language and Cyrillic script shall be in official use in the Republic of Serbia. Official use of other languages and scripts shall be regulated by the law based on the Constitution" (in 1990 the other alphabets and languages were directly mentioned in the constitution).

In Croatia, the 2002 constitutional Act on the protection of minorities sought to remedy the lack of implementation the homologous act of 1991. In Macedonia, the necessity to prevent other ethnic conflicts led to the Ohrid agreements and to a series of constitutional amendments in November 2001.[115] These amendments were aimed to increase the protection of the Albanian minority (even if, as mentioned above, the concept of 'minority' is hardly applicable in presence of percentages of this magnitude), through greater cultural and linguistic rights but also through a greater political participation at national and local level.

As aforementioned, in several countries there are cases of reverse discrimination, or of protection of the main nation (the nation which gives the name to the state), that cause ambiguity. Moreover, particularly sensitive is the relationship between minority rights and freedom of expression, including the freedom to form political parties. In fact, there are a number of restrictions precisely linked to the ethnic-national identity, regionalism, separatism (in Albania, Romania, etc.). Both in Romania and in Bulgaria minorities' rights are treated in contradictory terms: on one hand they are broadly envisaged, but on the other political parties that have an ethnic basis or who undermine territorial integrity of the country are banned (Art. 11, para. 4 cost. of Bulgaria; Art. 8, para. 2, const. of Romania). Moreover, the territorial integrity and unity of the state are underlined in both cases. For example, Article 30, para. 7 of the Romanian Constitution, limits the freedom of expression by prohibiting the incitement to territorial separatism. Likewise, Article 40, para. 2 considers political parties that militate against the integrity of Romania to be unconstitutional.

The presence of Russian-speaking minorities in Estonia and Latvia has been problematic especially at the beginning of the post-independence period because of the numerical relationship between this minority and the titular nation: at the time of independence just over 50 percent of the population was ethnically Latvian in Latvia. There are no specific sections on the protection of minorities in the constitutions of the Baltic countries,[116] but only general non-discrimination provisions based on a number of requirements, including ethnic ones. Only the Constitution of Estonia pays a greater attention to the rights of

115 Please refer to E. Ferioli, 'La sovranità "condivisa" della Repubblica di Macedonia (FYRoM): un recente caso di procedimento di revisione costituzionale etero diretto', *Telescopio, Quaderni costituzionali*, 2001, www.forumcostituzionale.it/wordpress/wp-content/uploads/pre_2006/171.pdf (last accessed September 2018). *See also Journal of Ethnopolitics and Minority Issues in Europe*, No. 1, 2002, www.ecmi.de/publications/detail/issue-12002-65 (last accessed September 2018).

116 Art. 114 of the Constitution of Latvia states that persons belonging to ethnic minorities have the right to preserve and develop their language and their ethnic and cultural identity. Art. 37 of the Constitution of Lithuania provides that citizens belonging to ethnic communities have the right to foster their language, culture, customs. Art. 45 states that ethnic communities of citizens shall autonomously manage the affairs of their ethnic culture, education, charity and mutual assistance. Ethnic communities have the support of the State.

minorities.[117] In all three cases, the possession of citizenship is assumed, although discriminations took place in Estonia and Latvia precisely through a particularly severe legislation on citizenship.

2.5 The Sources of Law

A clear hierarchy of the sources of law is a requirement closely linked to the principles of a democratic state, since in the socialist system – notwithstanding the introduction of the principle of socialist legality – political directives prevailed over legal sources.

The regulation of the sources of law in a democratic state concerns the form of state, the frame of government and also territorial organization.[118] However, only in a few cases (Poland, Albania, some countries of the former Yugoslavia)[119] the hierarchy of sources is expressly provided for by the constitution; in the other cases it can be deduced from certain provisions, for example those concerning the resort to the court against administrative acts or the competences of constitutional courts.

With regard to Poland, Title III of the Constitution (Arts. 87-94) is entitled "The sources of law". Article 87, para. 1 lists these sources distinguishing them in "Constitution, statutes,

117 Art. 37, para. 5 states that the language of teaching in national minority educational institutions is chosen by the educational institution; following Art. 49 everyone has the right to preserve their ethnic identity; Art. 50 gives minorities the right, in the interests of their culture, to establish self-governing agencies under the conditions and pursuant to the procedure provided in the National Minorities Cultural Autonomy Act. Following Art. 51, para. 2 in localities where at least one half of the permanent residents belong to a national minority, everyone has the right to receive responses from government agencies, local authorities and their officials also in the language of the national minority (this percentage is considered too high by the Council of Europe's body monitoring the implementation of the Framework Convention). This provision is reinforced by Art. 52, para. 2 according to which, in localities where the language of the majority of the residents is not Estonian, local authorities may, to the extent and pursuant to a procedure provided by law, use the language of the majority of the permanent residents of the locality as their internal working language. Finally, Art. 104 provides that among the acts that may only be passed and amended by a majority of the members of the *Riigikogu* there is also the National Minorities Cultural Autonomy Act.

118 L. Pegoraro, 'Il sistema delle fonti giuridiche nelle Costituzioni dell'Est europeo', *Quaderni costituzionali*, No. 1, 1995, pp. 111-127. Following Pegoraro, p. 112, "The constitutional discipline of the sources of law not only testifies the nature of transpositions and influences of the models, at the same time revealing the degree of resistance of the previous experiences and the revival of more remote ones, but also allows to perceive the way in which the constituent power intended the transition to a new form of state and new forms of government." According to Pegoraro, the discipline of the system of sources of law affects both the relations between the people and the government (laws on fundamental freedoms adopted by qualified majority, limitations on urgency decrees, *etc.*) and relations between the supreme state organs (role of the head of state in the legislative procedure, reserves of law, *etc.*).

119 There is a chapter on "Constitutionality and legality" in the constitutions of Slovenia, Yugoslavia 1992, Montenegro 1992 and 2007, Serbia 1990 and 2006, Macedonia (although here the title is different: "Guarantees of fundamental rights and freedoms"). A special chapter on constitutionality and legality was included in the constitutions of the socialist Yugoslavia.

ratified international agreements, and regulations".[120] Article 94 adds to these sources also local legal enactments, issued by organs of local government and by territorial organs of government administration, on the basis of the law and within the limits specified by the statute.

For Albania, one shall refer to Article 4 (supremacy of the Constitution and its direct applicability) and especially to Chapter 1 ("Normative acts") of the seventh part of the Constitution (Arts. 116-120). Pursuant to Article 116, normative acts that have force on the entire territory of the Republic are: The Constitution, ratified international agreements, statutes, normative acts of the Council of Ministers. Acts issued by the organs of local government have a limited territorial effectiveness. Normative acts of ministers and other central institutions are effective on the entire territory within their jurisdiction. Unspecified "sub-legal acts issued on the basis of and for the implementation of the laws" are regulated by Article 118, and they include the regulations of the Council of Ministers and of each single minister (Art. 119).

In the new Hungarian Fundamental Law, Article T, para. 2 lists the sources of law which are below the constitution and "cardinal" laws, even if the hierarchy between them is not completely clear.[121] In other constitutions, the hierarchy of sources of law can be deduced from the sections related to the competences of different constitutional bodies. Sometimes the hierarchy is not clear. This is the case, for example, of the different kinds of international treaties, laws and sublegislative acts.[122] In some constitutions specific sections on the law (statute), or legislation, regulate in detail how to adopt and publish laws (Estonia, Latvia, Romania).

At the top of the sources of law there is the constitution, whose rigidity may have different levels. This means that there is a sort of internal hierarchy of the same constitutional provisions, more evident where explicit limits to constitutional amendments are provided. In many cases the provisions of the constitution are declared directly applicable (Bulgaria, Lithuania, Poland, the provisions on human rights and minorities of the 2006 Serbian Constitution). The second level in the hierarchy, after the constitution, are the sources of international law (on which *see* below).

For what concerns primary sources, some countries are provided with a special category of laws, comparable to the organic ones. These include, for example, acts that the Hungarian

120 However, not all types of treaties are above the law. In order to clarify their position among the sources of law, a systematic reading of different constitutional provisions is required.

121 "Legal regulations shall be the acts, the government decrees, the prime ministerial decrees, the ministerial decrees, the decrees of the Governor of the National Bank of Hungary, the decrees of the heads of autonomous regulatory organs and local government decrees. In addition, decrees of the National Defence Council adopted during a state of national crisis and decrees of the President of the Republic adopted during a state of emergency shall also be legal regulations."

122 Already noted by L. Pegoraro, 'Il sistema delle fonti giuridiche nelle Costituzioni dell'Est europeo', cit.

constitution uses for the regulation of many important issues which are adopted by a two-thirds majority of the present deputies (constitutional amendments or a new constitution are adopted by the two-thirds majority of the members of the National Assembly). While the old constitution (1989-2011) referred to them simply as "acts", the 2011 Fundamental Law calls them "cardinal" acts. We may find 'organic' laws in Romania – a long list, though not exhaustive, is included in Article 73 of the Constitution – that are approved by the majority of the members of the two chambers. In other constitutions, laws approved with special majorities do not have a specific name. For example, in Montenegro, Article 83 of the 1992 Constitution provided for laws approved by an absolute majority of votes to regulate matters of constitutional relevance (rights and liberties, constitutional bodies, referendums, etc.). The same happens in the 2007 Constitution (the list is longer: *see* Art. 91). There is also another category of laws approved by a majority of two-thirds of the MPs, concerning the electoral system and foreigners' property rights. Finally, Article 91 provides that the parliament can adopt – via a special procedure – laws regulating minority rights and the use of Army units in international forces (in the first round with two-thirds majority and in the second round, which can take place no earlier than three months later, with the majority of all MPs). In the Albanian Constitution, Article 81 provides for laws – that do not have a specific name – approved by three-fifths of all members of the Assembly, on subjects such as: elections, citizenship, referendum, codes, constitutional bodies, state of emergency, amnesty, status of public officials, administrative division. Then there are laws passed by a majority of all MPs (Art. 2, para. 3), necessary to take part in a system of collective security. In Estonia, Article 104, para. 2 of the Constitution includes a list of laws that can be adopted only by absolute majority of the members of the *Riigikogu* (on elections, citizenship, constitutional bodies, etc.). Generically, the relationships between these 'reinforced' or 'atypical' sources and the 'ordinary' laws is not clear, the distinction seems to be only that of competence *ratione materiae*. In Kosovo, Article 81 of the Constitution provides a list of laws of "vital interest", adopted by a qualified majority and with the participation of minority representatives, for issues that mainly concern rights of the latter. These laws require "for their adoption, amendment or repeal" both the majority of the Assembly deputies present and voting and the majority of the "Assembly deputies present and voting that are holding seats reserved or guaranteed to representatives of Communities that are not in the majority". In the Czech Republic, only certain laws must be approved by both chambers (Art. 40: the electoral law, laws regarding relations between the two chambers, laws enacting the standing orders of the Senate). Furthermore, if the Chamber of Deputies is dissolved, the Senate may adopt legislative measures, though with a series of limitations, which must then be ratified by the Chamber of Deputies at its first meeting (Art. 33). Lastly, the category of constitutional laws in Lithuania is rather peculiar: pursuant to Article 69, para. 3, constitutional laws are adopted by more than a half of all the members of the *Seimas* and can be altered by not less than a three-fifths majority vote of all the members of the *Seimas*. It is the same *Seimas*, and not directly the constitution, to establish the list of constitutional laws by a majority of three-fifths of its members.

In a very few cases the executive power is empowered to adopt delegated legislation or other primary sources: Albania (Art. 101: normative acts having the force of law in cases of necessity and emergency, similar to the Italian model)[123]; Romania (governmental ordinances on the basis of an enabling law, Article 108; ordinances in fields outside the scope of organic laws in case of necessity, which are subject to parliamentary approval, and urgency ordinances in exceptional motivated cases even in fields of competence of organic laws, Art. 115[124]); Latvia in special cases (Art. 81: when the parliament is not in session, the government can adopt regulations with the force of law in case of urgency and with a series of limitations).[125] In Hungary the government can adopt acts that derogate from laws in cases of preventive state of defence, unexpected attacks and extreme danger (Arts. 51, 52 and 53); in Macedonia the government adopts decrees having the force of law during the state of war or emergency (Art. 126, para. 1), the same happens in Montenegro.[126]

Decrees with the force of law of the head of state in the event of emergency or war are provided for by the constitutions of Slovenia (Art. 108, they have to be presented on the proposal of government, and they have to be submitted to the National Assembly immediately upon its next convening. Such decrees may restrict rights and freedoms), Kosovo (Art. 131, paras. 3 and 4: rights may be suspended, but within forty-eight hours the parliament have to provide its consent by two-thirds vote of the deputies present and voting), Hungary (Art. 50, para. 3) and Croatia (Art. 101, with various conditions including the approval of the Assembly). In Serbia, the significant role of the President in cases of emergency, foreseen by the Constitution of 1990 (Art. 83) has been reduced in favour of the Assembly with the Constitution of 2006. Only when the Assembly cannot meet, the emergency measures – which can suspend rights – are enacted by the government and co-

123 "The Council of Ministers, in cases of necessity and emergency, may issue, under its responsibility, normative acts having the force of law for taking temporary measures. These normative acts are immediately submitted to the Assembly, which is convened within 5 days if it is not in session. These acts lose force retroactively if they are not approved by the Assembly within 45 days."

124 *See* M. Ganino, 'Romania', *in* M. Ganino (Ed.), *Codice delle Costituzioni*, Vol. III, cit., p. 260.

125 "During the period between the sessions of the Saiema, the Government has the right, if there is an urgent need, to enact regulations that have the force of law. These regulations cannot amend the law concerning the Saiema elections, the laws governing the judicial system and court proceedings, budget and budget-related rights, as well as the laws adopted during the mandate of the current Saiema, and they cannot affect amnesty, state taxes, customs duties and loans and cease to be in force if they are not submitted to the Saiema not later than three days after the subsequent session of the Saiema has been convened." That article, however, was repealed by the constitutional amendment of 3 May 2007.

126 Art. 101; the wording of Art. 94 of the 1992 Constitution was similar, referring to decrees with the force of law adopted during the state of emergency, imminent danger of war or state of war, to be approved by the Assembly as soon as it was able to convene.

signed by the President (Art. 200, paras. 6 and 9). In Estonia, according to Article 109 const., if the *Riigikogu* is unable to convene, the President may, "in matters of national urgency", issue decrees with the force of the law, countersigned by the speaker of the *Riigikogu* and by the prime minister. When the *Riigikogu* convenes, the President presents the decrees and the parliament passes a law regarding their confirmation or repeal.

Below the laws, there are sublegislative acts, adopted by the government or, in some cases, by the head of state. Generally, sublegislative sources, including those of local authorities, are regulated in broad terms in the constitutions: their normative nature is rarely mentioned, sometimes their existence is only implied. For what concerns Albania, the executive decrees and orders are provided for by Article 100, para. 5.[127] As for limitations on the sphere of action of sublegislative acts, *see* the provisions of the Constitution of Estonia (Art. 110).[128] In Poland, regulations adopted by the bodies indicated in the Constitution "shall be issued on the basis of specific authorization contained in, and for the purpose of implementation of, statutes" (Art. 92), while resolutions of the Council of Ministers and orders of the prime minister and ministers are not considered to be normative (Art. 93).

Referendum can be considered as a source of law only where it proposes the adoption or the abrogation of a normative act. In Albania, according to Article 150 const., at the request of at least 50,000 voters, a referendum for the abrogation of a law or an advisory referendum (about issues of special importance) may be held; the Assembly also may decide to submit to referendum an issue or a draft law of a special relevance,[129] with the limits established by Article 151[130] and with a prior admissibility scrutiny by the Constitutional Court (Art. 152). In this case, as well, the Italian model was (partially) followed. In Lithuania, Article 69, para. 5 of the Constitution states that provisions of law can also be adopted by referendum (the procedure for calling and holding referendums shall be established by law: Art. 9, para. 4). Legislative referendums are also provided by the constitutions of Slovenia (Art. 90), Estonia (Art. 105), Hungary (Art. 8), Kosovo (Art. 81 only

127 "The Council of Ministers issues decisions and instructions."

128 The Constitution, the Acts listed in Art. 104 of the Constitution, laws which establish national taxes, and the national budget may not be enacted, amended or repealed by a decree of the President.

129 "The people, through 50 thousand citizens, who enjoy the right to vote, have the right to a referendum for the abrogation of a law, as well as to request the President of the Republic to hold a referendum about issues of special importance. The Assembly, upon the proposal of not less than one-fifth of the deputies or the Council of Ministers, can decide that an issue or a draft law of special importance be presented for referendum. Principles and procedures for holding a referendum, as well as its validity, are provided by law."

130 "A law approved by referendum is promulgated by the President of the Republic. Issues related to the territorial integrity of the Republic of Albania, limitations of fundamental human rights and freedoms, budget, taxes, financial obligations of the state, declaration and abrogation of the state of emergency, declaration of war and peace, as well as amnesty, cannot be voted upon in a referendum. A referendum upon the same issue cannot be repeated before 3 years have passed since it was held."

provides that "none of the laws of vital interest" listed in this Article may be submitted to a referendum), Latvia (Art. 72), Serbia 2006 (Art. 108), Croatia (Art. 87).[131]

2.5.1 *The Relations Between National and European/International Law*

Among the sources of law, those adopted at extrastatual level play an important role in the countries concerned, both for the strengthening of the catalogue of rights and for facilitating international and European integration. The international treaties, including those ratified by the parliament, are placed below the constitution, since a preventive control of their constitutionality is provided. The positioning of all 'external' sources in the hierarchy of sources of law is not an easy task, because not all international sources have the same rank. There are, for example, treaties ratified through qualified majorities, such as those to enter supranational organizations. The different ways in which treaties are ratified affect their hierarchical position.[132] Moreover, the characteristics of relations between internal and international/European sources of law evolved after the entry into force of constitutions, thanks to specific constitutional amendments and to the interpretation of constitutional courts. In some cases, there are special sections of the constitution devoted to Euro-Atlantic relations, introduced after the adoption of the constitutions (*see, e.g.*, constitutional revisions of Romania in 2003 and Croatia in 2010).

For what concerns the member countries of the European Union (entered in 2004, 2007 and 2013), they (almost) all have decided to adopt specific constitutional amendments to adapt their legal system.[133] Indeed, only the Polish Constitution included clauses for membership of supranational organizations, having been adopted in 1997, when the negotiations to enter in the EU had already begun. The 'European' constitutional revisions were almost all introduced close to the entrance, presenting a wider opening in Czech Republic, Slovakia, Hungary, Romania and Croatia, and a more cautious approach in the Baltic countries, Bulgaria and Slovenia, whose constitutions firmly underline national sovereignty.

131 On referendums in Central and Eastern Europe *see* S. Bagni, *Il popolo legislatore*, Bologna, Bononia University Press, 2017, pp. 98 *et seq.*

132 *See, e.g.*, differences between international customary and treaty law, international and EU law, 'special' international treaties (regarding fundamental rights, the membership in international organizations) and others, *etc.*

133 On this subject please refer to A. Di Gregorio, 'Riforme costituzionali ed integrazione europea: il caso dei nuovi membri dell'Est', *Diritto pubblico comparato ed europeo*, No. IV, 2004, pp. 2067-2093; A. Di Gregorio, 'La ratifica della Costituzione europea tra "vecchia" e "nuova" Europa', *Diritto pubblico comparato ed europeo*, No. IV, 2005, pp. 1598-1623; A. Albi, *EU Enlargement and the Constitutions of Central and Eastern Europe* Cambridge, Cambridge University Press, 2005; A. Albi, '"Europe" Articles in the Constitutions of the Central and Eastern European Countries', *Common Market Law Review*, Vol. 42, No. 2, 2005, pp. 399-423; T. Cerruti, 'L'adesione della Croazia all'Unione europea e i criteri politici', *federalismi.it*, No. 13, 2013.

As regards the content of the amendments, they range from the more pro-European approach of Slovakia to the more restrictive one of Estonia. The explicit mention of the European Union – whose peculiarity is therefore recognized by the presence of *ad hoc* accession clauses and procedures – is foreseen in the constitutions of Slovakia (which speaks of "European Communities" and "European Union"), Hungary (the new 2011 Fundamental Law mentions only the "European Union"), Latvia (it contains references to the access to "international organizations"), mentioning the EU only in regards to the accession referendum, hence considered an *ad hoc* type of referendum), Estonia, Bulgaria, Romania, Croatia. In other cases, revisions generally mention joining international organizations, while providing for a particular, and more complex, procedure to ratify the related treaties. For what concerns the reserves or limitations to the transfer of sovereign powers, the constitutions of the Czech Republic, Slovakia, Poland, Bulgaria, Romania and the 2011 Fundamental Law of Hungary do not specify anything, while in other cases rather general provisions may be found, or ones related to the protection of rights or sovereignty / independence of the country.

The Constitution of Bulgaria provides, in Article 5, para. 4, that every international treaty which has been ratified according to the procedure established by the Constitution and has entered into force is part of domestic law and prevails over domestic legislation in case of conflict, while Article 149, para. 1 introduces the primacy of general international law ("universally recognized standards of international law"). In Slovenia, Article 160, para. 1 of the Constitution states that the Constitutional Court decides on the conformity of laws and other regulations with the ratified treaties and with the general principles of international law. Moreover, as part of the process of ratifying an international treaty, the Court, on the proposal of the President, or of the government, or of a third of the deputies of the National Assembly, issues an opinion on the conformity of a treaty to the Constitution, and the National Assembly is bound by that opinion. Article 8 of the Constitution states the obligation of conformity of domestic law with general international law and international treaties, but only the latter are directly applicable. For Romania, *see* Article 11 const. (automatic entry into domestic legal order of international treaties ratified by parliament: it is not clear, however, whether all the ratified treaties are above the law or only those on human rights explicitly mentioned in Article 20). The constitutions of Poland (Art. 91) and Albania (Art. 122) refer only to treaties and not to general (customary) rules of international law, even if, respectively, Articles 9 (Poland) and 5 (Albania) refer to the respect of international law which binds the country. In the Hungarian Constitution – both in the old amended and in the new Fundamental Law (Art. Q, para. 3) – there is a greater openness to "generally recognized rules of international law". Beside Romania, also in Czech Republic (until the revision of 2001) and Slovakia, the constitution foresees the prevalence of the international treaties on human rights on domestic legislation (in

Slovakia, before the 2001 amendment, at the condition to guarantee a greater extension of the rights and fundamental freedoms).

The current or future candidate countries, thanks to the fact that their constitutions are relatively new, have already taken steps to adapt their legal system to the reception of European law. The 2006 Serbian Constitution has a special provision (Art. 16) on international relations which, while recognizing the direct applicability and superiority of international law over ordinary legislation, places the former below the Constitution.[134] Article 16, para. 1 recognizes the obligation to respect also customary international law. The Venice Commission has expressed criticism regarding the position of the ECHR among the sources of law in its opinion of 12 July 2007, but this is a situation common to almost all Member States of the Council of Europe.[135] Article 18 of the same Constitution establishes that the Constitution must ensure and implement human and minority rights guaranteed by the generally accepted rules of international law and ratified international treaties.

See hereunder a country-by-country overview of the different characteristics highlighted.

Poland

Poland applied for EU membership in 1994. In drafting the new constitution, therefore, a constitutional basis for the accession had to be constructed. However, the inserted provisions are not that broad, and they refer to generic international organizations, unlike some of the proposals that were discussed during the framing process, which were more pro-European.[136] The most important articles on the subject are those going from 87 to 91, included in the section on sources of law.

Pursuant to Article 87, para. 1, international treaties ratified are included among the sources of law. Article 90 authorizes the delegation of powers to international organizations

134 "The foreign policy of the Republic of Serbia shall be based on generally accepted principles and rules of international law. Generally accepted rules of international law and ratified international treaties shall be an integral part of the legal system in the Republic of Serbia and applied directly. Ratified international treaties must be in accordance with the Constitution."

135 According to L. Montanari, *Il principio di Rule of Law e la tutela dei diritti*, cit., p. 228, in the last constitutions or constitutional amendments in the Western Balkans, since the prospect of European accession became more distant, it is possible to observe a come back to the national interests. This means that, while in the complex phase of transition to democracy, international instruments have been considered to be indispensable, in a second moment these countries have returned to an ordinary model "characterized by subsidiarity and dialogue between the courts as instruments to ensure the effective implementation of European guarantee standards".

136 *See* M. Granat, 'La constitution de la République de Pologne face à son adhésion à l'Union européenne', *in* M. Ganino, G. Venturini (Eds.), *L'Europa di domani*, cit., p. 173; J. Sawicki, 'Più Europa nella Costituzione polacca?', *Nomos*, No. 1, 2002, pp. 139-144. The Constitutional Tribunal has clarified the most uncertain issues on several occasions.

by establishing the characteristics of the related treaties and their ratification procedures.[137] The Accession Treaty is therefore a special treaty, subject to a different process of ratification, that require majorities greater than those needed for constitutional amendments, whose adoption also involves the parliamentary opposition and potentially to call for a referendum. Furthermore, the procedure can be checked by Constitutional Tribunal (which can verify the ratification Act both *a priori* and *a posteriori*).[138] For the ratification of the Treaty of Accession to the European Union in 2003, the *Sejm* decided for parliamentary ratification.

For what concerns the relations between the sources of law, according to Article 91, para. 2 an international treaty ratified with the prior consent of a law prevails over the law if the latter is inconsistent with it. According to Article 91, para. 3 when it comes to a treaty ratified by the Republic of Poland which creates an international organization, the acts adopted by it are applied directly, prevailing in the event of conflict over national laws. The conflicts between internal and international sources of law can be detected and resolved both by the Constitutional Tribunal and by ordinary judges. Only the latter, though, have the task of guaranteeing the superiority of secondary law of the EU over laws and other internal acts. The jurisprudence on the conditions and limits of the penetration of European law into the internal legal system is now very rich.[139]

Polish Constitution makes a clear difference between the collocation of international treaty law and primary and secondary Community law (without specifically naming it). In a general manner, Article 9 prescribes that "The Republic of Poland shall respect international law binding upon it". There are references to international law in special cases, for example the ones concerning the relations between the state and the catholic church (fixed in a treaty concluded with the Holy See and in a specific act: Art. 25, para. 4), or those with reference

137 "The Republic of Poland may, by virtue of international agreements, delegate to an international organization or international institution the competence of organs of state authority in relation to certain matters. A statute, granting consent for ratification of an international agreement referred to in para. 1, shall be passed by the Sejm by a two-thirds majority vote in the presence of at least half of the statutory number of Deputies, and by the Senate by a two-thirds majority vote in the presence of at least half of the statutory number of Senators. Granting of consent for ratification of such agreement may also be passed by a nationwide referendum in accordance with the provisions of Article 125. Any resolution in respect of the choice of procedure for granting consent to ratification shall be taken by the Sejm by an absolute majority vote taken in the presence of at least half of the statutory number of Deputies."

138 Pursuant to Art. 133, para. 2 the President of the Republic before ratifying an international treaty may refer it to the Constitutional Tribunal with a request to adjudicate upon its conformity to the Constitution. Pursuant to Art. 188 the Constitutional Tribunal decides, among other things, on the conformity to the Constitution of statutes and international treaties, on the conformity of a statute to ratified international agreements whose ratification required prior consent granted by statute, on the conformity of legal provisions issued by central state organs to the Constitution, ratified international agreements and statutes.

139 *See, among others*, B. Banaszak, 'Limitation of Sovereignty by the European Integration – The Polish Approach', *in* R. Arnold (Ed.), *Limitation of National Sovereignty through European Integration*, Dordrecht, Springer Verlag, 2016, pp. 99-108.

to the protection of minorities' language (Art. 27: "Polish shall be the official language in the Republic of Poland. This provision shall not infringe upon national minority rights resulting from ratified international agreements"). Other references to international law concern the extradition of Polish citizens[140] (which is prohibited by Art. 55, with the exception of the obligations deriving from ratified international treaties or from laws implementing a legal instrument adopted by an international organization of which Poland is a member, even if there are further conditions; the latter are not required if the extradition concerns genocide crimes, crimes against humanity, war or aggression) and asylum (Art. 56, para. 2: refugee status is granted in accordance with the international treaties of which Poland is a part). Freedom of association in trade unions and employers' organizations may be limited by law, as far as allowed by international treaties to which Poland adheres (Art. 59, para. 4).

Lastly, with reference to defence, on the basis of Article 116, para. 2 the *Sejm* may adopt a resolution on a state of war not only in the event of armed aggression against the territory of the Republic of Poland, but also when an obligation of common defence against aggression arises by virtue of international agreements. The principles for deployment of the Armed Forces beyond the borders of the Republic of Poland shall be specified by a ratified international agreement or by statute; the same applies to the presence of foreign troops on Polish territory, and their movements across the territory (Art. 117).

Czech Republic

The 1993 Constitution did not include a general provision for the transposition of international law, nor provisions on integration into international organizations. It adopted a classic dualistic approach, with the exception of human rights treaties, which were considered to be above the law.[141] The special status of these treaties was underlined by the fact that no prior constitutional review was foreseen, while the Constitutional Court could repeal laws or sublegislative acts if they were inconsistent with such treaties.[142]

140 Which is prohibited under Art. 55, with the exception of obligations stemming from an international treaty ratified by Poland or from a statute implementing a legal instrument enacted by an international organization of which the Republic of Poland is a member, under certain conditions; the same conditions are not required if an extradition request is made by an international judicial body established under an international treaty ratified by Poland, in connection with a crime of genocide, crime against humanity, war crime or a crime of aggression, covered by the jurisdiction of that body..

141 As established by Constitutional Court, references were mainly to the ECHR and its additional protocols, but also to the UN Pacts of 1966.

142 These treaties, unlike the others, pursuant to Art. 39, para. 4 cost. were ratified by a majority of three-fifths of all the deputies and three-fifths of the senators present (the same majority required for the approval of constitutional laws). Because of the ambiguity of the constitution, which did not clarify the relationship between constitutional laws (including the Constitution) and human rights treaties (that is, whether they were equiordinated sources of law or not), interpretative differences arose. On this subject, please refer to A. Di Gregorio, 'Giustizia costituzionale e diritto internazionale nei paesi dell'Europa centro-orientale e balcanica', *in* M. Ganino & G. Venturini (Eds.), *L'Europa di domani*, cit., pp. 285-332 and M. Ganino *et al.*,

The relationship between international/European and national law has changed with the constitutional amendment Act of 18 October 2001 (the so-called *euronovela*), which introduced a special clause for the integration into supranational organizations and strengthened the role of international law. In fact, a general provision is added to Article 1 of the Constitution, which describes national sovereignty ("The Czech Republic is a sovereign, unitary, and democratic state governed by the rule of law, founded on respect for the rights and freedoms of man and of citizens"), on the necessity to comply to the obligations deriving from international law ("The Czech Republic shall observe its obligations resulting from international law"). The preferential position previously granted only to human rights treaties is extended to all international treaties – that is to say: superiority on national laws in case of conflict, a more complex ratification procedure which includes the same majority required for constitutional amendments. The key provision of the constitutional amendment Act is the new Article 10, which changes the very conception of the relationship between domestic and international law, establishing that "Promulgated treaties, to the ratification of which Parliament has given its consent and by which the Czech Republic is bound, form a part of the legal order; if a treaty provides something other than that which a statute provides, the treaty shall apply". This is a general incorporation rule that applies not only to treaties ratified after the 2001 constitutional amendment Act but also to the previous ones, provided that they meet the requirements of Article 10. The constitutional amendment Act added to the Constitution the new Articles 10a and 10b concerning the accession to international organizations and the relations between legislative and executive branches in this respect.[143]

Article 143 of the Constitution refers to the membership of international organizations dealing with collective defence.[144]

'Corti costituzionali e Corti europee: i casi di Federazione di Russia, Polonia, Repubblica ceca, Ungheria', *in* G. F. Ferrari (Ed.), *Corti nazionali e Corti europee*, Napoli, ESI, 2006, pp. 123-139.

143 Art. 10a: "Certain powers of Czech Republic authorities may be transferred by treaty to an international organization or institution. The ratification of a treaty under paragraph 1 requires the consent of parliament, unless a constitutional act provides that such ratification requires the approval obtained in a referendum." Art. 10b: "The government shall inform the parliament, regularly and in advance, on issues connected to obligations resulting from the Czech Republic's membership in an international organization or institution referred to in Article 10a para. 1. The chambers of parliament shall give their views on prepared decisions of such international organization or institution in the manner laid down in their standing orders. A statute governing the principles of dealings and relations between both chambers, as well as externally, may entrust the exercise of the chambers' competence pursuant to paragraph 2 to a body common to both chambers."

144 Pursuant to Art. 43, para. 1 "Parliament decides on the declaration of a state of war, if the Czech Republic is attacked, or if such is necessary for the fulfilment of its international treaty obligations on collective self-defense against aggression." Para. 2 establishes that "The parliament decides on the Czech Republic's participation in defensive systems of an international organization of which the Czech Republic is a member." Following para. 4 of the same Art., the government may decide to send Armed Forces outside the national territory, with some time limitations, in order to participate "in peace-keeping operations pursuant to the decision of an international organization of which the Czech Republic is a member, if the receiving state consents".

Article 87 (jurisdiction of the Constitutional Court) gives the Court the power to decide on the measures necessary to implement a decision of an international tribunal which is binding on the Czech Republic, in the event that it cannot be otherwise implemented. On the other hand, Article 95, para. 1, in the wording following the 2001 constitutional amendment, assigns to ordinary judges, and no longer to the Constitutional Court, the power to "judge whether enactments other than statutes are in conformity with statutes or with international treaties" since "in making their decisions, judges are bound by statutes and international treaties which form a part of the legal order". A large part of legal scholars did not agree with the abolition of the competence of the Constitutional Court to check the compatibility between laws or sublegislative acts and human rights treaties.[145] The Court itself claimed that such control could still be carried out (in the *obiter dicta* of a judgment of 25 June 2002). The pretext to continue the practice of referring to the ECHR (and to other human rights treaties) lies in the general rule of Article 1, para. 2 const. on the observance of international law, which is addressed to all the state organs.[146]

Slovakia

While in the original version of the Constitution only a "state union" with other countries was envisaged (thinking of a possible rapprochement with the Czech Republic), the constitutional amendment Act of 23 February 2001 (constitutional law n. 90/2001) provides, among other things, the adjustment of constitutional legal order to European and Euro-Atlantic integration. Indeed, with this amendment, the accession of Slovakia to European Communities and European Union, as well as to collective mutual security organizations is explicitly envisaged. The superiority over internal laws of some types of international treaties, ratified by a qualified majority – the same required for constitutional amendments – is recognized.[147]

The new para. 2 of Article 1 of the Constitution states that "The Slovak Republic recognizes and honours general rules of international law, international treaties by which it is bound and its other international obligations". The most important innovations are included in the new drafting of Article 7, which absorbs and integrates the previous provisions of Article 11. Article 7 now provides for the participation of Slovakia in different supranational institutions, including those of collective mutual security. However, no mention is made to

145 For the different positions of the legal scholars concerning the interpretation of the new Art. 95, *see* J. Stulakova, 'Repubblica ceca. Prime applicazioni del diritto internazionale tra giudice ordinario e Tribunale costituzionale dopo la riforma del 2001', *Diritto pubblico comparato ed europeo*, No. II, 2004, pp. 1049-1051.

146 Many legal scholars criticized this approach of the Court. *See* I. Šlosarčík, 'Constitutional Changes in the Czech Republic and Case-Law of the Constitutional Court in 2000-2002', *European Public Law*, Vol. 10, No. 1, 2004, pp. 3-18.

147 For a comment on this constitutional amendment, please refer to A. Di Gregorio, 'Riforme istituzionali ed avvicinamento all'Europa dei paesi dell'Est: il caso della Slovacchia', *Nomos*, No. 3, 2001, pp. 109-131.

sovereign limitations, that are hence only implicitly deductible.[148] It is also explicitly stated that "Legally binding acts of the European Communities and European Union shall have primacy over the laws of the Slovak Republic. Undertaking of legally binding acts that require implementation shall be executed by law or a government ordinance pursuant to Article 120, paragraph 2".[149] Paragraph 5 of Article 7 reports the contents of the previous Article 11 by providing that "International treaties on human rights and fundamental freedoms, international treaties whose execution does not require a law and international treaties which directly establish rights or obligations of natural persons or legal persons and which were ratified and promulgated in a manner laid down by law shall have primacy over the laws". The previous limitation, that conditioned this supremacy to the guarantee of a greater amplitude of fundamental rights and freedoms, is repealed.

The constitutional amendment Act specifies in which cases the parliament must express its consent to the ratification of international treaties, and with what majorities (Art. 86). For the ratification of an international treaty, as per Article 7, paras. 3 and 4, the consent of the absolute majority of all the deputies is required (Art. 84, para. 3), while for the ratification of an international treaty as per in Article 7, para. 2 (*i.e.* EU membership) the consent of at least three-fifths of all deputies is needed (Art. 84, para. 4), that is to say the same majority requested for the adoption of the constitution, the constitutional amendments laws, constitutional laws and to declare war. As a result, the type of international treaties that Slovakia can subscribe to is greatly expanded, and the list of treaties that are considered to be above the laws, or as a direct source of rights and obligations, is extended.[150] The consequence of

148 Firstly, para. 1, as the previous single paragraph of Art. 7, provides that "The Slovak Republic may enter into a state union with other states upon its free decision". The decision to join the aforementioned union or to withdraw from it is adopted through a constitutional law, which is confirmed by referendum. The second paragraph directly mentions the phenomenon of European integration, establishing that "The Slovak Republic may, by an international treaty ratified and promulgated in a manner laid down by law, or on the basis of such treaty, transfer the exercise of a part of its rights to the European Communities and European Union". Art. 7, para. 3 states that "The Slovak Republic may, with the aim of maintaining peace, security and democratic order, under the terms laid down by an international treaty, join an organization of mutual collective security".

149 To Art. 120 a new para. 2 is added, which authorizes the government "to issue ordinances in order to execute the European Agreement establishing an association between the European Communities and their Member States, of the one part, and the Slovak Republic, of the other part, and to execute international treaties stipulated in Article 7, paragraph 2".

150 In the original text of the Constitution, treaties concerning fundamental rights were placed above the laws, while other treaties ratified by parliament were considered to be on the same level as ordinary laws (with the exception of those approved by constitutional law). In this way, as it is written in the explanatory note attached to the amendment Act, it was recognized the inadequacy of "the previous type of relationship between international and domestic law, the collocation of dispositions and rules of international law in the state legal system and in the hierarchy of the sources of law, the conditions for the application of the norms of international law in the internal legal system as well as the resolution of possible legal conflicts between international law and the Constitution of the Slovak Republic".

this approach is the new provision of Article 144, para. 1, according to which "Judges are independent in execution of their function and bound solely by the Constitution, constitutional laws, international treaties stipulated in Article 7, paragraphs 2 and 5 and laws". It follows that, in the event of conflict between an internal law and an international treaty provided for in Article 7, para. 5, judges will have to give preference to the latter.

The reference to international treaties is expressly included in the parameter of constitutionality in all cases of normative control (previously this reference was limited to the verification of sublegislative acts) and also in the examination of individual applications (Art. 125). The Constitutional Court has been given new powers, among them the right to rule on the conformity to the Constitution, or to the constitutional law, of the concluded international treaties that require the consent of the National Council of the Slovak Republic (Art. 125 a).[151] The procedure for individual applications is also partially amended. Article 127 adds to the violation of constitutional rights and freedoms also that of human rights and fundamental freedoms that derive from an international treaty that the Slovak Republic has ratified, and that has been promulgated in the ways foreseen by the law.

Estonia

The commission of constitutional law experts appointed on 14 May 1996 by the government in order to ascertain the necessity of constitutional amendments came to the conclusion that the entry in the EU would not directly compromise the national independence, as the EU was seen more as a confederation than a federation.[152] However, constitutional amendments were suggested to prepare the text for European integration. As stated in the opinion of the Venice Commission in 1998 on the constitutional amendment draft presented by the Estonian government,[153] it was necessary to introduce a general provision on the delegation of competences to the European Union, since Article 1 of the Constitution emphasized national sovereignty. Furthermore, considering the diffuse control of constitutionality of laws, an enabling clause that explicitly stated the constitutionality of the transfer of a series of competences would have confirmed the direct binding efficacy and prevalence of European law, avoiding the possibility that the Estonian courts, in compliance to Article 152 const. ("When

151 Such action may be brought by the President of the Republic or the government before submitting the treaty for ratification to the National Council of the Slovak Republic. If the Court establishes that it is not in conformity with the Constitution or the constitutional law, the treaty cannot be ratified.

152 T. Kerikmäe, 'Estonian Constitutional Problems in Accession to the EU', *in* A.E. Kellermann, J.W. De Zwaan & J. Czuczai (Eds.), *EU Enlargement. The Constitutional Impact at EU and National Level*, cit., pp. 291-300.

153 *Avis sur les problèmes constitutionnels soulevés par l'adhésion de l'Estonie à l'Union européenne*, adopté par la Commission lors de sa 35e session plénière (Venise, 12-13 juin 1998), www.venice.coe.int/webforms/documents/default.aspx?pdffile=CDL-INF(1998)010-f (last accessed September 2018).

determining a case, the courts refuse to give effect to a law or other legislation or administrative decision that is in conflict with the Constitution"), did not apply primary and secondary European law.[154]

In spite of the government's intention to propose a broad constitutional amendment act, concerns about the high degree of Euroscepticism in the country convinced the parliament to simply integrate the Constitution with the so-called 'third constitutional Act'. This Act, approved in 2002, confirmed by referendum[155] and then entered into force on the 14 December 2003, provided for a general interpretative clause stating that in case of entrance into the Union, the Constitution must be applied in the light of the Accession Treaty. According to most Estonian constitutionalists, this 'third constitutional Act', both from a substantial and a procedural point of view, was not consistent with the Constitution, as it circumvented the three severe amendment procedures – which do not provide for the possibility of adopting an independent constitutional law beside the Constitution – and did not remove the conflict between Community law and the Constitution.[156]

As for the rank of international law in the Estonian legal order, according to Article 3, para. 2 "Generally recognized principles and rules of international law are an inseparable part of the Estonian legal system". According to Article 120[157] "The procedure for the conduct of relations between the Republic of Estonia and other states and between the Republic of Estonia and international organizations is provided by law". Article 121 const. includes among the treaties that should be ratified and denounced by the parliament those thanks to which the Republic of Estonia becomes a member of international organizations or unions.[158] However, as provided for by Article 123 "The Republic of Estonia may not enter into international treaties which are in conflict with the Constitution. When laws or other legislation

154 The opinion also noted that both the Constitution and the draft of the constitutional amendment Act did not grant European citizens the right to stand for election in local elections and the right to vote and stand for the elections of the European Parliament. The Commission suggested to change the provision on the competence in issuing the currency (reserved by Art. 111 of the Constitution to the Bank of Estonia) and to add a provision on the right of EU citizens to be members of political parties. It also suggested to provide for a clearer division of competences in Community matters between the President and the government.

155 The referendum in question was not the one that according to Art. 162 const. is necessary to amend the fundamental provisions of the Constitution (although the heading of the constitutional law referred to this article), since none of these provisions have been formally amended. Under this constitutional law, "Estonia may belong to the European Union, provided the fundamental principles of the Constitution of the Republic of Estonia are respected" (Art. 1). "When Estonia has acceded to the European Union, the Constitution of the Republic of Estonia is applied without prejudice to the rights and obligations arising from the Accession Treaty" (Art. 2).

156 The criticisms of legal scholars not only concerned the form of the third constitutional Act but also the fact that the 'constitutional amendment Act' was much more limited than the draft prepared by the commission of experts and evaluated by the Venice Commission.

157 Arts. 120-123 are included in the Chapter IX "Foreign Relations and International Treaties".

158 No special majority is required for the ratification of these treaties.

of Estonia are in conflict with an international treaty ratified by the *Riigikogu*, provisions of the international treaty apply". According to Article 122, para. 3 the ratification of international treaties which modify the borders of Estonia requires a two-thirds majority of the members of the *Riigikogu*.

Regarding the right to vote, as per Article 156, para. 2, people permanently residing on the territory of the local government and which have the age of 18 have the right to vote in local council's elections, as provided by law. Regarding the extradition, Article 36, para. 2 provides that "No citizen of Estonia may be extradited to a foreign state, except under conditions prescribed by an international treaty and pursuant to a procedure provided by such treaty and by law". Article 106 establishes that the ratification and denunciation of international treaties cannot be submitted to referendum. Finally, according to Article 128, para. 1, on the proposal of the President, the *Riigikogu* declares a state of war, orders mobilization and demobilization, and decides on the use of the Defence Forces to fulfil international obligations of the Estonian government.

Latvia

Although the European Association Agreement had already been signed in 1995, the debate on the amendment of the constitution began in Latvia only in August 2000, when a special working group was set up by a prime minister's decree to draw up proposals on the matter. According to the report presented by the group, there were several constitutional obstacles to the entrance into the European Union. In the first place, Article 1 of the Constitution proclaims independence. For what concerns the sovereignty, which is conferred to the people by Article 2, it was not considered to be an obstacle to the integration. In fact, Latvia could always secede from the Union, after having joined it, and therefore the last word on this matter remains with the sovereign people.

Several proposals were made during the parliamentary debate on constitutional amendments. The more 'limited' version (which was eventually chosen) proposed to add to the Constitution a special European integration clause. Other proposals suggested to amend several articles of the Constitution, to introduce a new chapter on EU membership or even replace the old 1922 text with a completely new Constitution.

The constitutional amendment Act of 8 May 2003 changed only Articles 68 and 79. The first one now authorizes the delegation of sovereignty to international organizations and provides for the related procedures and conditions ("for the purpose of strengthening democracy"),[159] while the new version of Article 79 concerns the regulation of referendums on European issues.[160]

Latvia, therefore, limited its sovereignty only through a parliamentary procedure, derogating from the constitutional provisions on revision and introducing a new type of referendum which, although binding, does not replace the ratification of the Accession Treaty.[161]

Other references to international law are provided for in Article 89 ("The state shall recognise and protect fundamental human rights in accordance with this Constitution, laws and international agreements binding upon Latvia") and Article 98, para. 2 ("A citizen of Latvia may not be extradited to a foreign country, except in the cases provided for in international agreements ratified by the *Saeima* if by the extradition the basic human rights specified in the Constitution are not violated").

Lithuania

The Constitution of Lithuania emphasizes the principles of independence and sovereignty but follows a monistic approach and incorporates international treaties ratified in the domestic legal system (Art. 138, para. 3).[162] These treaties are therefore directly applicable, unless they require implementing provisions. On 22 June 1999, the *Seimas* approved a new

159 Following the new version of Art. 68, "All international agreements, which settle matters that may be decided by the legislative process, shall require ratification by the *Saeima*. Upon entering into international agreements, Latvia, with the purpose of strengthening democracy, may delegate a part of its state institution competencies to international institutions. The *Saeima* may ratify international agreements in which a part of state institution competencies are delegated to international institutions in sittings in which at least two-thirds of the members of the *Saeima* participate, and a two-thirds majority vote of the members present is necessary for ratification. Membership of Latvia in the European Union shall be decided by a national referendum, which is proposed by the *Saeima*. Substantial changes in the terms regarding the membership of Latvia in the European Union shall be decided by a national referendum if such referendum is requested by at least one-half of the members of the *Saeima*."

160 "An amendment to the Constitution submitted for national referendum shall be deemed adopted if at least half of the electorate has voted in favour. A draft law, decision regarding membership of Latvia in the European Union or substantial changes in the terms regarding such membership submitted for national referendum shall be deemed adopted if the number of voters is at least half of the number of electors as participated in the previous *Saeima* election and if the majority has voted in favour of the draft law, membership of Latvia in the European Union or substantial changes in the terms regarding such membership."

161 According to the working group, the 'European' amendments would not have required a specific constitutional referendum because EU membership would not have touched the principles of sovereignty, independence and democracy included in Arts. 1 and 2 of the Constitution (for the amendment of which, in accordance with Art. 79 const., it is necessary a specific referendum with a minimum participation quorum of 50 percent of those eligible).

162 "International treaties ratified by the Seimas of the Republic of Lithuania shall be a constituent part of the legal system of the Republic of Lithuania."

law on international treaties that establishes the supremacy of the treaties ratified on the domestic legislation.[163]

As for the membership of international organizations, the 1992 Constitution already included a specific provision (Art. 136: "The Republic of Lithuania shall participate in international organisations provided that this is not in conflict with the interests and independence of the state"). Nevertheless, a special working group built up in 1998 proposed to introduce in the Constitution a provision on the delegation of sovereign powers to the European Union and on direct applicability and superiority of Community law. However, no agreement was reached on these changes and in the end the parliament approved only two amendments of 'technical' nature. In June 2002, Article 119 was amended to give all permanent residents, including non-citizens, the right of active and passive vote in local elections (with effect from 2006) and in January 2003 Article 47 was amended to allow foreign natural and legal persons to purchase agricultural land (provision with effect from 2011).[164] The working group considered unnecessary a constitutional referendum, as EU membership would not concern sovereignty. Nevertheless, a referendum regarding the entrance was called in application of Article 9, para. 1 const., according to which "The most significant issues concerning the life of the state and the nation shall be decided by referendum".

With regard to extradition, Article 13, para. 2 prohibits the extradition of a Lithuanian citizen to another state unless an international treaty ratified by the Republic of Lithuania establishes otherwise. Article 105 confers to the Constitutional Court the power to give opinions on the constitutionality of international treaties. Article 135, para. 1, states that in implementing its foreign policy, Lithuania must follow the universally recognized principles and norms of international law and contribute to the creation of an international legal system based on law and justice.

The *Seimas* shall impose martial law, announce mobilization or demobilization, adopt a decision on use of the armed forces when a need arises to defend the Homeland or to fulfil the international obligations of the state of Lithuania (Art. 142, para. 1).

Finally, Article 150 declares that the constitutional Act "On membership of the Republic of Lithuania in the European Union" of the 13th of July 2004 – establishing the modalities

163 V. Vadapals, 'Lithuania: The Constitutional Impact of the Enlargement at National Level', *in* A.E. Kellermann, J.W. De Zwaan & J. Czuczai (Eds.), *EU Enlargement. The Constitutional Impact at EU and National Level*, cit., pp 347-368.

164 The previous version of the same article, according to the constitutional amendment of 20 June 1996, provided that such subjects could acquire, under certain conditions, only non-agricultural lands and only for certain purposes.

of such membership,[165] the relations between sources of law[166] and between government and parliament in matters falling within the competence of the EU – is a constituent part of the Constitution.[167]

Slovenia

Article 8 of the 1991 Constitution, introducing the monistic principle, is an opening to the international law.[168] However, it was considered insufficient to allow the entrance into the EU and to ensure the direct application of secondary Community law – as it refers only to ratified and published treaties.[169] Accordingly, a constitutional amendment Act was approved on 27 February 2003 – adding a new article (Art. 3a), to the Constitution, and amending Articles 47 and 68 – whose provisions apply to both the EU and NATO.

The new Article 3a regulates the transfer of the "exercise" of sovereign powers (a wording that seems to have less impact on national sovereignty) and also conditions the EU's accession to the compliance with certain condition.[170] As for the government-parliament relations

165 "The Republic of Lithuania as a Member State of the European Union shall share with or confer on the European Union the competences of its State institutions in the areas provided for in the founding Treaties of the European Union and to the extent it would, together with the other Member States of the European Union, jointly meet its membership commitments in those areas as well as enjoy the membership rights" (point 1).

166 "The norms of European Union law shall be a constituent part of the legal system of the Republic of Lithuania. Where it concerns the founding Treaties of the European Union, the norms of European Union law shall be applied directly, while in the event of collision of legal norms, they shall have supremacy over the laws and other legal acts of the Republic of Lithuania" (point 2).

167 "The Government shall inform the Seimas about the proposals to adopt acts of European Union law. As regards the proposals to adopt the acts of European Union law regulating the areas which, under the Constitution of the Republic of Lithuania, are related to the competences of the Seimas, the Government shall consult the Seimas. The Seimas may recommend to the Government a position of the Republic of Lithuania in respect of these proposals. The Seimas Committee on European Affairs and the Seimas Committee on Foreign Affairs may, according to the procedure established by the Statute of the Seimas, submit to the Government the opinion of the Seimas concerning the proposals to adopt the acts of European Union law. The Government shall assess the recommendations or opinions submitted by the Seimas or its Committees and shall inform the Seimas about their execution following the procedure established by legal acts" (point 3).

168 *See* F. Grad, 'Constitutional Principles and Accession to the European Union: Case of Slovenia', *in* M. Ganino & G. Venturini (Eds.), *L'Europa di domani. Verso l'allargamento dell'Unione*, cit., p. 269.

169 According to Art. 8, "Laws and other regulations must comply with generally accepted principles of international law and with treaties that are binding on Slovenia. Ratified and published treaties shall be applied directly."

170 "Pursuant to a treaty ratified by the National Assembly by a two-thirds majority vote of all deputies, Slovenia may transfer the exercise of part of its sovereign rights to international organisations which are based on respect for human rights and fundamental freedoms, democracy, and the principles of the rule of law and may enter into a defensive alliance with states which are based on respect for these values. Before ratifying a treaty referred to in the preceding paragraph, the National Assembly may call a referendum. A proposal is passed in the referendum if a majority of voters who have cast valid votes vote in favour of the same. The National Assembly is bound by the result of such referendum. If such referendum has been held,

regarding European issues, the National Assembly's position towards the government is stronger in Slovenia than in other former communist countries, although formally the Constitution expresses a semi-presidential form of government. The 2003 amendment took this into account.[171]

Article 47 of the Constitution has been modified for what concerns the extradition, taking into consideration the membership of supranational organizations.[172] Article 68, concerning the right to private property, has been amended in order to provide the possibility for foreigners to acquire property rights on real estate, under the conditions provided by law or by a treaty ratified by the National Assembly.[173]

Article 153, para. 2 regulates the relations between domestic and international sources of law.[174] Among the powers of the Constitutional Court, Article 160 includes the one to verify "the conformity of laws and other regulations with ratified treaties and with the general principles of international law". In the process of ratifying a treaty, the Constitutional Court "on the proposal of the President of the Republic, the Government, or a third of the deputies of the National Assembly, issues an opinion on the conformity of such treaty with the Constitution. The National Assembly is bound by the opinion of the Constitutional Court".

a referendum regarding the law on the ratification of the treaty concerned may not be called. Legal acts and decisions adopted within international organisations to which Slovenia has transferred the exercise of part of its sovereign rights shall be applied in Slovenia in accordance with the legal regulation of these organisations."

171 According to Art. 3a, para. 4, "In procedures for the adoption of legal acts and decisions in international organisations to which Slovenia has transferred the exercise of part of its sovereign rights, the Government shall promptly inform the National Assembly of proposals for such acts and decisions as well as of its own activities. The National Assembly may adopt positions thereon, which the Government shall take into consideration in its activities. The relationship between the National Assembly and the Government arising from this paragraph shall be regulated in detail by a law adopted by a two-thirds majority vote of deputies present."

172 "No citizen of Slovenia may be extradited or surrendered unless such obligation to extradite or surrender arises from a treaty by which, in accordance with the provisions of the first paragraph of Article 3a, Slovenia has transferred the exercise of part of its sovereign rights to an international organization." This article seems to refer to the International Criminal Court.

173 This article had already been amended in 1997 to allow foreigners to purchase the land with a clause of reciprocity, which was repealed in 2003. The 1997 amendment was adopted to respect the opinion of the Constitutional Court according to which the European association agreement was in conflict with the Constitution. *See* P. Vehar, 'Constitutional Problems in the Period of Pre-accession in the Republic of Slovenia', *in* A.E.Kellermann, J.W. De Zwaan & J. Czuczai (Eds.), *EU Enlargement. The Constitutional Impact at EU and National Level*, cit., pp. 369-374.

174 "Laws must be in conformity with generally accepted principles of international law and with valid treaties ratified by the National Assembly, whereas regulations and other general acts must also be in conformity with other ratified treaties."

Hungary

To get a complete picture of the adaptation of the Hungarian constitutional order to the European integration, it is worth considering what was done before the adoption of the 2011 Fundamental Law and therefore the 'European' amendment Act of the old Constitution. The reference is to the constitutional amendment Act of 17 December 2002, which had opted for the minimum adjustments necessary to join the EU, deliberately leaving the solution of future and potential conflicts to the Constitutional Court. This applies especially to the supremacy of Community law, given the clearly dualistic nature of the Hungarian legal order.[175] The theory of the 'common exercise' of state sovereignty was also adopted.

The rather long amendment Act consisted of eleven Articles. The Constitution was integrated with an Article 2/A to authorize the entrance into the European Union[176]; a fourth subparagraph was added to Article 6 pursuant to which: "The Republic of Hungary shall contribute to the construction of European unity in order to achieve freedom, well-being and security for the peoples of Europe". Other provisions introduced by the constitutional amendment Act concerned the 'special' reserve of law (*i.e.* approved by a two-thirds majority of the deputies present) for the regulation of the elections of members of the European Parliament (Art. 71, para. 3); the election of members of the European Parliament on the basis of direct, secret, universal and equal scrutiny (Art. 71, para. 1); the competence of the President of the Republic to call elections for the European Parliament (Art. 30/A, para. 1, letter d); the assignment to the government of the task of representing Hungary in the institutions of the European Union featuring the participation of governments (Art. 35, para. 1 letter k); the granting to the citizens of other EU Member States of the active and passive voting rights in local elections (with some limitations) and in elections to the European Parliament. Finally, Article 35/A on the responsibility of the government towards the parliament in European matters was included, which required the approval by a two-thirds majority for laws concerning parliament's control, as well as the obligation of the government to submit information

175 Art. 7 of the old amended Constitution provided that "The legal system of the Republic of Hungary accepts the generally recognized principles of international law and must harmonize domestic law with obligations assumed under international law". Three categories of international treaties were identified: those concluded by the parliament with an ordinary majority, the EU Treaty (ratified by the parliament with a two-thirds majority, the same as constitutional revision and special laws), treaties concluded by the executive (President and government).

176 "On the basis of a treaty, the Republic of Hungary, in the interest of its participation as a Member State of the European Union, may exercise certain constitutional powers jointly with the other Member States to the extent necessary for the exercise of rights and the fulfillment of obligations conferred by the Treaties on the foundation of the European Union and the European Communities; the exercise of these powers can take place independently as well as through the institutions of the European Union. For the ratification and for the promulgation of the treaty indicated in the first paragraph it is necessary the vote of two thirds of the deputies."

on issues related to European integration. The same constitutional amendment Act called a referendum for the entrance into the European Union on 12 April 2003.

As for the 2011 Fundamental Law, the wording of Article E is not very different from that of the old Article 2/A: "In order to enhance the liberty, well-being and security of the people of Europe, Hungary shall contribute to the creation of European unity". In its role as a Member State of the European Union and by virtue of an international treaty "Hungary may – to the extent necessary for exercising its rights and fulfilling its obligations stemming from the Founding Treaties – exercise certain competences deriving from the Fundamental Law, together with the other Member States, through the institutions of the European Union".

With the VII constitutional amendment, which came into force on 29 June 2018 as part of a package of measures directed to a further protection of national and cultural identity, a paragraph is added to the preamble of the constitution which states that "We proclaim that protecting our identity, as it is rooted in our historical Constitution, is a fundamental duty of the State". Furthermore, in para. 2 of Article E a clarification is added according to which "The exercise of powers under this Paragraph must be consistent with the fundamental rights and freedoms set out in the Fundamental Law, and it must not be allowed to restrict Hungary's inalienable right of disposition relating to its territorial integrity, population, political system and form of governance".[177] General binding rules of conduct may be laid down in European Union legislation within the framework set out in the para. 2 of Article E. The authorization to recognize the binding nature of the international treaties referred to in para. 2 is conferred to the parliament with the favourable vote of two-thirds of its members. Article 19 regulates government-parliament relations in European affairs.[178] Article XXIII lays down conditions for the exercise of voting rights for European citizens.[179]

For what concerns the relations between domestic and international law, pursuant to Article Q, paras. 2 and 3 "In order to comply with its obligations under international law, Hungary shall ensure that Hungarian law be in conformity with international law. Hungary shall accept the generally recognized rules of international law. Other sources of international

177 This provision is strengthened by the new para. 4 of Art. R pursuant to which "Each and every body of the State shall be obliged to protect the constitutional identity and the Christian culture of Hungary".

178 "The National Assembly may request information from the Government on the Government position to be represented in the decision-making procedures of the intergovernmental institutions of the European Union, and may take a position on the draft placed on the agenda in the procedure. In the course of the decision-making of the European Union, the Government shall act on the basis of the position taken by the National Assembly."

179 In particular, para. 2 states that "Every adult person recognised as a refugee, immigrant or resident in Hungary shall have the right to vote in elections of local government representatives and mayors". However, para. 6 specifies that "Everyone having the right to vote in elections of Members of the National Assembly shall have the right to participate in national referendums. Everyone having the right to vote in elections of local government representatives and mayors shall have the right to participate in local referendums".

law shall become part of the Hungarian legal system by promulgation in legal regulations". Pursuant to Article 1 para. 2 d) the National Assembly "shall authorize the expression of consent to be bound by international treaties falling within its functions and powers". Article 8, para. 3 forbids the holding of national referendums on any obligation arising from international treaties. Following Article 9, para. 4 a) the President of the Republic "shall, on the basis of authorization by the National Assembly, express consent to be bound by international treaties". Article 22, para. 1 establishes that a resigning government "may not express consent to be bound by international treaties".

Some provisions on criminal matters ensue.[180]

With regard to the competences of the Constitutional Court, Article 24, as amended after the IV and V amendments to the Fundamental Law, gives to the Court the power to check the conformity of any legal instrument with any international treaty, being able to establish the annulment in case of conflict. Finally, Article 45 assigns to the Hungarian Defence Forces the task of collective defence and peacekeeping duties deriving from international treaties as well as humanitarian activities in accordance with the rules of international law. Article 47 regulates the powers of the parliament and the government respectively to authorize both the use abroad of the Hungarian armed forces and the dislocation of foreign ones on the national territory, always in order to fulfil the country's international obligations.

Romania

In its initial version of 1991, the Constitution of Romania already had a number of provisions suitable to promote the relations between domestic and international law. This refers in particular to Articles 10 and 11.[181] Furthermore, the aforementioned Article 20 provides for the precedence, in case of inconsistencies, of the covenants and treaties on fundamental

180 Following Art. XXVIII, paras. 4, 5 e 6: "No one shall be held guilty of or be punished for an act which at the time when it was committed did not constitute a criminal offence under Hungarian law or, within the scope specified in an international treaty or a legal act of the European Union, under the law of another State. Paragraph 4 shall not prejudice the prosecution or conviction of any person for any act which, at the time when it was committed, was a criminal offence according to the generally recognised rules of international law. With the exception of extraordinary cases of legal remedy laid down in an Act, no one shall be prosecuted or convicted for a criminal offence for which he or she has already been finally acquitted or convicted in Hungary or, within the scope specified in an international treaty or a legal act of the European Union, in another State, as provided for by an Act."

181 Art. 10 ("International Relations"): "Romania fosters and develops peaceful relations with all the states, and in this context, good neighbourly relations, based on the principles and other generally recognized provisions of international law." Art. 11 ("International and National law"): "The Romanian State pledges to fulfil as such and in good faith its obligations as deriving from the treaties it is a party to. Treaties ratified by Parliament, according to the law, are part of national law." If such treaties are inconsistent with the Constitution, their ratification shall only take place after the revision of the Constitution (Art. 10, para. 3).

human rights ratified by Romania over domestic statutes, except when the Constitution or national laws foster more favourable provisions.

Notwithstanding the foregoing, in 2003 the Romanian parliament considered it necessary to adopt a broad constitutional amendment Act aimed, among the rest, to adapt the Constitution to Euro-Atlantic integration. In addition to the membership clauses and procedures (included in the new Title VI, entitled "Euro-Atlantic integration"), the right of Romanian citizens to elect and be elected for the European Parliament is introduced (Art. 38) together with the right for EU citizens to elect and be elected in the local public administration bodies (Art. 16, para. 4). The European Union is expressly mentioned in Articles 148, 44, para. 2 (on land ownership),[182] 135 g (the state must secure "the implementation of regional development policies in compliance with the objectives of the European Union"), 137, para. 2 (once Romania has acceded to the EU, the circulation and replacement of the national currency by that of the EU may be acknowledged through an organic law).

For what concerns the two articles of Title VI, Article 148 ("Integration in the European Union") establishes the procedure for joining the EU and the relations between the sources of law,[183] while Article 149 ("Accession to the North Atlantic Treaty") sets the ones for joining NATO.[184]

Article 75, para. 1, states that the Chamber of Deputies "shall debate and adopt the bills and legislative proposals for the ratification of treaties or other international agreements and the legislative measures deriving from the implementation of such treaties and agreements". Pursuant to Article 91, para. 1, the President of the Republic, in the name of Romania, concludes the international treaties negotiated by the Government and submits

182 "Foreign and stateless persons shall only acquire the right to private property of land under the terms resulting from Romania's accession to the European Union and other international treaties Romania is a party to, on a mutual basis, under the terms stipulated by an organic law, as well as a result of lawful inheritance."

183 "Romania's accession to the constituent treaties of the European Union, with a view to transferring certain powers to community institutions, as well as to exercising in common with the other Member States the competencies stipulated in such treaties, shall be carried out by means of a law adopted in the joint session of the Chamber of Deputies and the Senate, with a majority of two thirds of the number of Deputies and Senators. As a result of the accession, the provisions of the constituent treaties of the European Union, as well as the other binding community regulations shall take precedence over the opposite provisions of the national laws, in compliance with the provisions of the accession act. The provisions of paragraphs 1 and 2 shall also apply accordingly for the accession to the acts revising the constituent treaties of the European Union. The Parliament, the President of Romania, the Government, and the judicial authority shall guarantee that the obligations resulting from the accession act and the provisions of paragraph 2 are implemented. The Government shall send to the two Chambers of the Parliament the draft mandatory acts before they are submitted to the European Union institutions for approval."

184 "Romania's accession to the North Atlantic Treaty shall take place by means of a law adopted in the joint session of the Chamber of Deputies and the Senate, with a majority of two thirds of the number of Deputies and Senators."

them to the parliament for ratification. Other treaties are concluded, approved or ratified according to the procedures set by law.

Following Article 118, para. 1, the Romanian Army, on the basis of the international treaties of which the country is a part, shall contribute to collective defence in military alliance systems, and participate in peace keeping or peace restoring missions. Para. 5 of the same article states that foreign troops may enter, station, carry out operations, or pass through the Romanian territory only under the terms of the law or the international treaties Romania is a party to. Article 119 confers to Supreme National Defence Council the task of organizing and coordinating the activities concerning Romania's participation in international security keeping and in collective defence in military alliance systems, as well as in peace keeping or restoring missions. Pursuant to Article 18, para. 2 "The right of asylum shall be granted or withdrawn under the provisions of the law, in compliance with the international treaties and covenants Romania is a party to". Pursuant to Article 19, para. 2 it is possible to waive the prohibition of extradition of Romanian citizens, in compliance with the international agreements Romania is a party to, according to the law and on a reciprocity basis. Para. 3 specifies that foreign citizens and stateless persons may be extradited only in compliance with an international covenant or in terms of reciprocity.

Finally, Article 146 (competences of the Constitutional Court) let. b) gives the Court the power to rule on the constitutionality of treaties or other international agreements, upon request of the presidents, of the two chambers, or at least of fifty deputies or twenty-five senators. Article 147, para. 3 regulates the consequences of the unconstitutionality of treaties by establishing that they cannot be ratified.

Bulgaria

To understand the characteristics of the relations between domestic and international legal order in Bulgaria, it is necessary to refer to both the original version of the Constitution and the amendments introduced in 2005 (constitutional Act 18/2005).

Article 5, para. 4 const. provides that "Any international treaty, which has been ratified according to a procedure established by the Constitution, which has been promulgated, and which has entered into force for the Republic of Bulgaria, shall be part of the domestic law of the land. Any such treaty shall take priority over any conflicting standards of domestic legislation". Pursuant to Article 85, the National Assembly shall ratify or denounce by statute the international treaties which are of a political or military nature, the ones concerning the participation of the Republic of Bulgaria in international organizations, those that provide for a modification of the state borders, impose financial obligations on the state, provide for the participation of the state in arbitral or court settlement of international disputes, affect fundamental human rights, or simply require an express ratification. The 2005 constitutional amendment Act added to this list treaties which grant the European Union powers arising from the Constitution. The adoption of an act to ratify such international treaties shall require a majority of two-thirds of all national representatives. Finally, Article 85 establishes that the conclusion of international treaties, which require amendments to the Constitution, shall be preceded by the passage of the said amendments. Among the powers of the Constitutional Court, Article 149, para. 4, includes the possibility to rule on the consistency of any international treaty concluded by the Republic of Bulgaria with the Constitution, prior to the ratification of such treaties, as well as on the consistency of any domestic laws with universally recognized standards of international law and with the international treaties whereto Bulgaria is a party.

Among the powers of the Grand National Assembly, Article 158, para. 2, includes the possibility to change the territory of the Republic of Bulgaria, and the ratification of any international treaty providing for such changes. Following Article 24, para. 1 the foreign policy of the Republic of Bulgaria shall be implemented in accordance with the principles and standards of international law. Article 25, para. 4, as rephrased by the 2005 amendment Act, states that no citizen of the Republic of Bulgaria may be surrendered to another state or to an international court for the purposes of criminal prosecution except where this is provided for in an international treaty which has been ratified, and that has been promulgated and entered into force. Similarly, pursuant to Article 27, para. 2 Bulgaria grants asylum to foreigners persecuted for their convictions or actions in defence of internationally recognized rights and freedoms. Article 100, para. 5 confers to the President the possibility to declare the state of war, also in response to the urgent need to honour international commitments.

As for the European Union, the reference to this organization was explicitly introduced with the 2005 constitutional amendment: pursuant to Article 4, para. 3, "The Republic of Bulgaria shall participate in the building and development of the European Union".[185]

Croatia

A specific debate on the constitutional revision has been launched in Croatia since the country's entrance into the EU pre-accession programs.[186] In particular, the debate was about the possibility of amending the procedures for joining supranational organizations, the

185 Other changes related to participation in the EU introduced with the same constitutional amendment Act are as follows: Art. 22, para. 1 (land ownership for foreigners); Art. 42, para. 3 (elections of members of the European Parliament and the participation of citizens of the European Union in elections of local authorities); Art. 105, paras. 3 and 4: "The Council of Ministers shall inform the National Assembly on matters concerning the obligations arising for the Republic of Bulgaria from its membership of the European Union. Where participating in the drafting and adoption of acts of the European Union, the Council of Ministers shall inform in advance the National Assembly and shall render account for the actions thereof."

186 *See* T. Cerruti, 'L'adesione della Croazia all'Unione europea e i criteri politici', cit., p. 15.

relationship between national and international sources of law, the relations between constitutional bodies and the same concept of national sovereignty.[187]

The 2010 constitutional amendment Act introduced a specific chapter regarding the membership of the Union (Arts. 143-146) and amended other provisions. Article 2, para. 4, of the Constitution establishes that the Croatian parliament and people shall directly, independently, and in compliance with the Constitution and law, decide upon association in alliances with other states. Para. 5 of the same Article states that the Republic of Croatia may conclude alliances with other states, retaining its sovereign right to decide upon the powers to be so delegated and the right to freely withdraw therefrom.

Section VII of the Constitution is devoted to the "International Relations", and is divided into two sub-sections: "International treaties" (Art. 139-141) and "Association and dissociation" (Art. 142). Pursuant to Article 139, international treaties may be concluded, depending on their nature and content, by the parliament, the President of the Republic or the government.[188] Article 141 states that international treaties which have been concluded and ratified in accordance with the Constitution, that have been published and which have entered into force shall be a component of the domestic legal order and shall have primacy over domestic law. Article 142 states that a procedure entailing the association of the Republic of Croatia into alliances with other states may be initiated by at least one-third of the deputies of the parliament, the President of the Republic or the government. However, any procedure for the association of Croatia into alliances with other states, if such association leads, or may lead, to a renewal of a "South Slavic state union" or to any form of "consolidated Balkan state" is prohibited. This association shall be first decided by Parliament, with a two-thirds majority of all members, and then submitted to a referendum, to be approved by the majority vote of all voters. Such a referendum shall be held within thirty days from the date on which the decision has been passed by the parliament. The same procedure is applied to conditions and procedures for the dissociation of the Republic of Croatia.

Section VIII is expressly devoted to the European Union and is divided into four sub-sections: "Legal grounds for membership and transfer of constitutional powers" (Art. 143); "Participation in European Union institutions" (Art. 144); "European Union Law" (Art. 145); "Rights of European Union citizens" (Art. 146).[189]

187 Art. 2, para.1, states that "The sovereignty of the Republic of Croatia is inalienable, indivisible and non-transferable", but it has not been amended.

188 Pursuant to Art. 140, the parliament ratifies "international treaties which require the adoption of amendment to laws, international treaties of military and political nature, and international treaties which give rise to financial commitments for the Republic of Croatia. International treaties which grant an international organization or alliance powers derived from the Constitution of the Republic of Croatia shall be ratified by the Croatian Parliament by a two-thirds majority of all deputies".

189 Following T. Cerruti, *L'adesione della Croazia all'Unione europea e i criteri politici*, cit., p. 16, the amended provisions can be divided into three groups: those requested during the accession negotiations (amendments

Following Article 143, Croatia, as a Member State of the European Union, "participate in the creation of European unity in order to ensure, together with other European states, lasting peace, liberty, security and prosperity, and to attain other common objectives in keeping with the founding principles and values of the European Union. Pursuant to Articles 140 and 141 of the Constitution, the Republic of Croatia shall confer upon the institutions of the European Union the powers necessary for the enjoyment of rights and fulfilment of obligations ensuing from membership". Article 144 establishes that citizens of the Republic of Croatia shall be directly represented in the European Parliament where they shall, through their elected representatives, decide upon matters falling within their purview. The government shall report to the parliament on the draft regulations and decisions in the adoption of which it participates in the institutions of the European Union. In respect of such drafts, regulations and decisions, the Croatian parliament may adopt conclusions which shall provide the basis for the government's actions in the European Union's institutions. Parliamentary oversight by the Croatian parliament of the actions of the government in European Union institutions shall be regulated by law. The Republic of Croatia shall be represented in the Council and the European Council by the government and the President of the Republic in accordance with their respective constitutional powers. Article 145 regulates the relations between domestic and European sources of law.[190] Article 146 lists the rights deriving from the European Union citizenship to Croatian citizens.[191] All rights shall be exercised in compliance with the conditions and limitations laid down in the founding treaties of the European Union and the measures undertaken pursuant to such treaties. All rights guaranteed by the European Union *acquis communautaire* shall be enjoyed by all citizens of the European Union.

Article 7 regulates the use of Croatian armed forces, or of foreign forces on the Croatian territory, in relation to the international commitments assumed on the basis of ratified

to the provisions on extradition, on the central bank, the introduction of an audit body, the electoral rights for European citizens, the reform of the judiciary, *etc.*), those deemed 'appropriate' and others apparently not related to the accession (on constitutional judges, armed forces, ombudsman, etc.).

190 "The exercise of the rights ensuing from the European Union acquis communautaire shall be made equal to the exercise of rights under Croatian law. All the legal acts and decisions accepted by the Republic of Croatia in European Union institutions shall be applied in the Republic of Croatia in accordance with the European Union acquis communautaire. Croatian courts shall protect subjective rights based on the European Union acquis communautaire. Governmental agencies, bodies of local and regional self-government and legal persons vested with public authority shall apply European Union law directly."

191 Freedom of movement and residence in the territory of all Member States, active and passive voting rights in European parliamentary elections and in local elections in another Member State in accordance with that Member State's law, the right to diplomatic and consular protection of any Member State, the right to submit petitions to the European parliament, complaints to the European ombudsman, to apply to European Union institutions and advisory bodies in the Croatian language as well as in other official languages of the EU and to receive a reply in the same language.

treaties.[192] According to paras. 8 and 9, the armed forces of Croatia or of allied states may cross the national border for the purpose of military exercises and training, within the framework of international organizations to which the Republic of Croatia has acceded, or is in the process of acceding, and for the purpose of rendering humanitarian assistance, pursuant to a decision by the government, with the prior consent of the President of the Republic.

Article 9 considers as an exception to the denial of extradition of a Croatian citizen the execution of an extradition or surrender decision made in compliance with an international treaty or the *acquis communautaire* of the European Union. Article 33 forbids granting asylum to foreigners and stateless persons if they are accused of non-political crimes contrary to the fundamental principles of international law, but prohibits the extradition of foreigners who are legally in Croatia except for the cases of enforcement of decisions based on an international treaty or law. According to Article 31, no one may be punished for an act that, before being done, was not defined as a punishable offence by domestic or international law. It also excludes the statute of limitations for offences that are not subject to statute of limitations under international law.

Pursuant to Article 93, para. 1, the Ombudsperson is a commissioner of the Croatian parliament responsible for the promotion and protection of human rights and freedoms enshrined not only in the Constitution and the laws but also in the international legal instruments ratified by Croatia. Courts shall administer justice according to the Constitution, law, international treaties and other valid sources of law (Art. 118, para. 3). Following Article 133, para. 4 (rights of local self-government), the rights specified in this Article shall be exercised by European Union citizens in compliance with law and EU *acquis communautaire.*

Albania

Article 5 of the Albanian Constitution provides for a generic obligation to respect international law ("The Republic of Albania applies international law that is binding upon it") and Article 17 refers to the requirements set by the ECHR to justify the limitations on the rights and

192 In particular, para. 4 states that "The Republic of Croatia may render assistance to allied states in case of armed aggression on one or more thereof as stipulated under ratified international treaties, pursuant to a decision of the Croatian Parliament proposed by the Government of the Republic of Croatia with the prior consent of the President of the Republic of Croatia". These are decisions adopted by a majority vote of all of parliament's members. If the President of the Republic denies his/her consent, the parliament shall make the decision by a two-thirds majority of votes of all of its members.

freedoms provided for in the Constitution.[193] For what concerns criminal cases and international law, *see* Articles 29 and 39.[194]

Section VII of the Constitution is dedicated to the sources of law. Articles 121-123 refer to international treaties, providing that certain types of treaties must be ratified by law (Art. 121), including those of accession to international organizations (Art. 123).[195]

The majorities required for the ratification are not specified, referring to the law for details. In any case, it is clearly provided that the ratification of treaties implying for Albania to transfer state prerogatives to international organizations require the total majority of the votes, though the Assembly may decide to proceed with the ratification via referendum (Art. 123). An international agreement that has been ratified by law prevails over domestic laws that are not compatible with it (Art. 122, para. 2). The acts issued by an international organization prevail, in case of conflict, on the laws of the country, when the agreement ratified by the Republic of Albania for its participation in said organization expressly provide for the direct applicability of the norms issued by the organization itself (Art. 122, para. 3).

The Constitutional Court decides on the compatibility of the law with the Constitution or with international agreements as provided for in Article 122; on the compatibility of international agreements with the Constitution, prior to their ratification; on the compatibility of normative acts of the central and local bodies with the Constitution and international agreements (Art. 131).

Finally, Article 171, para. 2 establishes that "(...) when a common defence obligation derives from an international agreement, the Assembly, upon proposal of the President of the Republic, declares the state of war and decides on the state of general or partial mobilization or demobilization".

193 As para. 2 of this Art. states, "These limitations may not infringe the essence of the rights and freedoms and in no case may exceed the limitations provided for in the European Convention on Human Rights."

194 Art. 29, para. 1, states that "No one may be charged or declared guilty of a criminal offence that was not considered as such by law at the time of its commission, with the exception of cases, that at the time of their commission, according to international law, constitute war crimes or crimes against humanity". Following Art. 39, para. 2 "Extradition may be permitted only when it is expressly provided in international agreements, to which the Republic of Albania is a party, and only by judicial decision".

195 "The Republic of Albania, on the basis of international agreements, delegates to international organizations state powers for specific issues. The law that ratifies an international agreement as provided for in paragraph 1 of this article is approved by a majority of all members of the Assembly. The Assembly may decide that the ratification of such an agreement be done through a referendum."

Bosnia-Herzegovina

Since the Dayton Constitution is an annex to an international treaty, international law and institutions played a particularly relevant role in its redaction, so it is possible to define it a true 'international' constitution.[196]

According to point 1 ("Human Rights") of Article II ("Human rights and fundamental freedoms") of the Constitution, "Bosnia and Herzegovina and both Entities shall ensure the highest level of internationally recognized human rights and fundamental freedoms. To that end, there shall be a Human Rights Commission for Bosnia and Herzegovina as provided for in Annex 6 to the General Framework Agreement". Point 2 of the same Article ("International Standards") states that the rights and freedoms set forth in the European Convention for the Protection of Human Rights and Fundamental Freedoms and its Protocols shall apply directly in Bosnia and Herzegovina and shall have priority over all other law. Point 8 ("Cooperation") establishes that all competent authorities in Bosnia and Herzegovina shall cooperate with and provide unrestricted access to: any international human rights monitoring mechanisms established for Bosnia and Herzegovina; the supervisory bodies established by any of the international agreements listed in Annex I to the Constitution; the International Tribunal for the Former Yugoslavia[197]; and any other organization authorized by the United Nations Security Council with a mandate concerning human rights or humanitarian law.

According to Article III, point 2, of the Constitution, the constitutive Entities of Bosnia-Herzegovina shall provide all necessary assistance to the government of Bosnia and Herzegovina in order to enable it to honour its international obligations. Each Entity may enter into agreements with states and international organizations, with the consent of the Parliamentary Assembly, which may provide by law that certain types of agreements do not require such consent. Point 3 of the same Article provides that "the general principles of international law shall be an integral part of the law of Bosnia and Herzegovina and the Entities".

Among the powers of the collegial presidency (Art. V, point 3) there are the representation of Bosnia and Herzegovina in international and European organizations and institutions; the application for membership in such organizations and institutions of which Bosnia and Herzegovina is not a member (lett. c); the negotiation, denunciation, and, with the consent of the Parliamentary Assembly, ratification of the treaties of Bosnia and Herzegovina (lett. d).

196 However, the Preamble speaks in the name of the constituent peoples: "Bosniacs, Croats, and Serbs, as constituent peoples (along with Others), and citizens of Bosnia and Herzegovina hereby determine that the Constitution of Bosnia and Herzegovina is as follows (...)" and subsequently recalls a series of international treaties. Ann. I to the Constitution lists additional fifteen human rights treaties to be applied in Bosnia and Herzegovina.

197 And in particular shall comply with orders issued pursuant to Art. 29 of the statute of the tribunal.

The composition of the Constitutional Court (Art. VI, point 1) is peculiar, showing a strong international influence. It consists of nine members, three of whom – who must not be citizens of Bosnia and Herzegovina or of neighbouring countries – are selected by the President of the European Court of Human Rights after consultation with the collegial presidency. The Court decides, among other things (Art. VI, para. 3), on the issues referred to it by any court in Bosnia-Herzegovina concerning the conformity of a law – from whose validity the court's decision depends – not only to the Constitution but also to the ECHR and its protocols. It also decides on the existence / scope of application of a general rule of international public law, relevant to the decision of the court *a quo* (letter c).

For what concerns the composition of the Central Bank (Art. VII), an international influence can be found only in the first term of the board of directors (the governor was appointed by the International Monetary Fund, after consulting the collegial presidency and could not be a citizen of Bosnia-Herzegovina or of a neighbouring state).

Macedonia

The 1991 Constitution of Macedonia contains some general references to international law even in the section on fundamental principles. There is also a special section (VI), devoted to "International Relations" (Arts. 118-121).

Article 8 includes among the fundamental values of the constitutional order of the Republic of Macedonia "the basic freedoms and rights of the individual and citizen, recognized in international law and set down in the Constitution" and also the "respect for the generally accepted norms of international law".

Article 29, para. 1, states that foreigners in the Republic of Macedonia enjoy freedoms and rights guaranteed by the Constitution, under conditions regulated by law and international agreements. Para. 3 specify that extradition of a foreigner can be carried out only on the basis of a ratified international agreement and on the principle of reciprocity.

According to Article 98, para. 3, the courts judge not only on the basis of the Constitution and laws but also on that of international agreements ratified in accordance with the Constitution.

As regards the section devoted to international law and supranational integration, Article 118 considers the international agreements ratified in accordance with the Constitution as part of the internal legal order, and states that they cannot be changed by law. In that way, it recognizes their supremacy over the national legislation. International agreements are concluded in the name of the Republic of Macedonia by the President of the Republic of Macedonia, but they may also be concluded by the government, when it is provided by law (Art. 119).

The procedures for joining a union or association with other states, or an international organization, are more complex, and demand the involvement of the parliament. The Constitution distinguishes the two cases, and it seems to consider the first one as a sort of confederation, as super-qualified majorities are required for the approval of accession.[198]

Constitutional amendments adopted in 2011, following the Ohrid agreements, involve an even stronger role of international law. While Amendment XXV only reiterates that the courts judge on the basis of ratified international treaties, Amendment XXX provides that the Office of the Public Prosecutor performs its duties on the basis not only of the Constitution and the laws, but also of international treaties ratified in accordance with the Constitution. Amendment XXXII echoes that citizens of Macedonia cannot be extradited to another country, except on the basis of a ratified international treaty and of the decision of a court.

Serbia

While the 1990 Constitution, having been adopted by a republic part of a federation, did not contain, as aforementioned, references to international law, the 2006 Constitution has several ones, starting from the commitment to the "European principles and values" provided for in Article 1. Article 16 ("International Relations") para. 2, states that "Generally accepted rules of international law and ratified international treaties shall be an integral part of the legal system in the Republic of Serbia and applied directly". However, "ratified international treaties must be in accordance with the Constitution" (para. 3). According to Article 99, the National Assembly ratifies international treaties when the obligation of their ratification is stipulated by the law. Pursuant to Article 105, the National Assembly shall adopt, by means of majority vote of all deputies, laws on the conclusion and ratification of international treaties. Article 108, para. 2, forbids to hold a referendum on duties deriving from international treaties. In the part devoted to the hierarchy of the sources of law ("Constitutionality and legality", Arts. 194-195), and in particular in Article 194, para. 4, it is stated that "Ratified international treaties and generally accepted rules of international law shall be part of the legal system of the Republic of Serbia. Ratified international treaties may not be in noncompliance with the Constitution". According to para. 5, "Laws and other general acts enacted

198 Art. 120 states that "A proposal for association in a union or community with other states or for dissociation from a union or community with other states may be submitted by the President of the Republic, the Government or by at least 40 Representatives. The proposal for association in or dissociation from a union or community with other states is accepted by the Assembly by a two-thirds majority vote of the total number of Representatives. The decision of association in or dissociation from a union or community is adopted if it is upheld in a referendum by the majority of the total number of voters in the Republic". As regards the membership in an international organization, Art. 121 establishes that "A decision of association or dissociation concerning membership in international organizations is adopted by the Assembly by a majority vote of the total number of Representatives of the Assembly and proposed by the President of the Republic, the Government or at least 40 Representatives of the Assembly".

in the Republic of Serbia may not be in noncompliance with the ratified international treaties and generally accepted rules of the international law".

Article 17, in accordance with the international treaties, grants foreigners in the Republic of Serbia all rights guaranteed by the Constitution and law, with the exception of rights to which only the citizens of the Republic of Serbia are entitled. Article 85, para. 1, gives foreign – both natural and legal entities – the right to obtain real estate property, in accordance with the law or international treaties.

According to Article 18, para. 2, the Constitution should guarantee and directly implement human and minority rights provided by the generally accepted rules of international law and by ratified international treaties. Para. 4 of the same article establishes that provisions on human and minority rights shall be interpreted to the benefit of promoting values of a democratic society, pursuant to valid international standards in human and minority rights, as well as the practice of international institutions which supervise their implementation. According to Article 22, para. 2, citizens shall have the right to address international institutions in order to protect their freedoms and rights guaranteed by the Constitution. As noted above, the reference to the Constitution rather than to the international documents that these institutions are called to protect is rather anomalous. The mention of international law is included also in Article 75, para. 2, regarding the protection of minorities.

The Serbian Army can perform missions based on the principles of international law which regulate the use of force (Art. 139).

Courts are bounded by international law, both treaties and customary, as established by Article 142, para. 2.[199] As specified in Article 145, para. 2: "Court decisions are based on the Constitution and law, the ratified international treaty and regulation passed on the grounds of the law". Public Prosecutor's Office shall perform its function on the grounds not only of the Constitution, the law and the regulations made under the law but also of ratified international treaties (Art. 156, para. 2). The Constitutional Court (Art. 167) decides on the compliance of the laws and other general acts with the Constitution, the generally accepted norms of international law and ratified international treaties, and on the conformity with the Constitution of ratified international treaties.

Montenegro

While the 1992 Constitution included limited references to international law,[200] it has an important place in the new Constitution of 2007, starting from the preamble (which refers

199 "Courts shall be separated and independent in their work and they shall perform their duties in accordance with the Constitution, Law and other general acts, when stipulated by the Law, generally accepted rules of international law and ratified international contracts."

200 Para. 2 of Art. 44 ("Citizens and international organizations") provided for the citizens' right to address international institutions to protect their freedoms and rights guaranteed by the Constitution; para. 2 of

to the cooperation on equal basis with other nations and states, and to the European and Euro-Atlantic integration).

Concerning the exercise of rights Article 17, para. 1, states that "rights and liberties shall be exercised on the basis of the Constitution and the confirmed international agreements". Article 56 provides that everyone shall have the right of recourse to international organizations for the protection of their own rights and freedoms guaranteed "by the Constitution" (this is the same anomaly noted in the 2006 Serbian Constitution and the 1992 Montenegrin Constitution). The protector of human rights and liberties shall exercise duties on the basis of the Constitution, the law and "confirmed international agreements", observing also the principles of justice and fairness (Art. 81, para. 2). According to Article 12, para. 3, citizens of Montenegro shall not be expelled or extradited to other states, "except in accordance with the international obligations of Montenegro".

Article 15 deals specifically with relations with other states and international organizations. In particular, paras. 2 and 3 provide that "Montenegro may accede to international organizations. The Parliament shall decide on the manner of accession to the European Union". Nevertheless, considering what had happened in the past, para. 4 specifies that Montenegro "shall not enter into a union with another state by which it loses its independence and full international personality".

Concerning the status of international treaties among the sources of law, Article 9 states that "the ratified and published international agreements and generally accepted rules of international law shall make an integral part of the internal legal order, shall have the supremacy over the national legislation and shall apply directly when they regulate relations differently than the national legislation". The parliament shall "confirm international agreements" (Art. 82). Furthermore, as required by Article 91, para. 4, by a two-thirds majority of the total members, the parliament approves at second reading the laws regulating, among other things, the use of Army units in international forces. This is linked to the provisions of Article 129, para. 1, according to which the Army defends the independence, sovereignty and territory of Montenegro in accordance with the principles of international law governing the use of force; and para. 3, according to which members of the Army may be part of international forces.

Art. 67 ("Protection of identity") established that the protection of rights of members of national and ethnic groups was exercised in accordance with the international protection of human and civic rights; Art. 74, para. 2 granted to members of national and ethnic groups the right to participate in the regional and international non-governmental organizations, and the right to address international institutions for the purpose of the protection of their freedoms and rights, guaranteed by the Constitution. With reference to the special rights guaranteed to ethnic and national groups, Art. 75 provided that these could not be exercised if in conflict with the Constitution, the principles of international law and the principle of territorial integrity of Montenegro (*reverse discrimination*).

Courts shall rule not only on the basis of the Constitution and laws but also of confirmed and published international agreements (Art. 118, para. 2). As in other constitutions of the former Yugoslavia, there are rules on the relations between sources of law. Article 145 provides that "The law shall be in conformity with the Constitution and confirmed international agreements" while other regulations shall be in conformity with the Constitution and the law. As a consequence, the Constitutional Court shall decide on the conformity of laws with the Constitution and confirmed and published international agreements (Art. 149). According to Article 152, para. 1, "when the Constitutional Court establishes that a law is not in conformity with the Constitution and confirmed and published international agreements" such a law shall cease to be valid on the date of publication of the decision of the Constitutional Court.

Kosovo

In the Constitution of Kosovo there are many openings to international law, especially because of the origins of the independence of the country and of the Constitution itself, which is in part deriving to the previous temporary instrument adopted at a UN level. The numerous references to international law, and the general international influence on the legal system, have been kept until the adoption of the 2012 constitutional amendments, to allow a soft succession of constitutional systems.

The preamble of the Constitution already expresses the Kosovo's vocation for Euro-Atlantic integration ("With the intention of having the state of Kosovo fully participating in the processes of Euro-Atlantic integration"). Article 2, para. 3, states that: "The Republic of Kosovo, in order to maintain peace and to protect national interests, may participate in systems of international security". Article 16, para. 3, provides respect of the international law, while Articles 17-19 and 22 deal with the relations between internal and external sources of law. While Article 17 is rather general, authorizing the country to conclude international treaties and to participate in international cooperation "for the promotion and protection of peace, security and human rights", Article 18, para. 1, defines the ratification procedure (the treaties concerning the membership of the Republic of Kosovo to international organizations are ratified by two-thirds vote of all deputies of the Assembly). The details of the ratification procedure are established by law. Pursuant to Article 19, para. 2, ratified international agreements and legally binding norms of international law have superiority over the laws.

Article 20 is dedicated to the "delegation of sovereignty" and establishes that "the Republic of Kosovo may on the basis of ratified international agreements delegate state powers for specific matters to international organizations. If a membership agreement ratified by the Republic of Kosovo for its participation in an international organization explicitly contemplates the direct applicability of the norms of that organization, then the law ratifying the international agreement must be adopted by two thirds (2/3) vote of all deputies of the Assembly, and those norms have superiority over the laws of the Republic of Kosovo". As for regulation of rights, Article 3, para. 2 states that "The exercise of public authority in the Republic of Kosovo shall be based upon the principles of equality of all individuals before the law and with full respect for internationally recognized fundamental human rights and freedoms, as well as protection of the rights of and participation by all Communities and their members". Article 22 states that human rights and fundamental freedoms guaranteed by a series of international agreements and instruments are directly applicable and, in case of conflict, they prevail over provisions of laws and other acts of public institutions.[201] Pursuant to Article 53, human rights and fundamental freedoms guaranteed by the Constitution shall be interpreted consistently with the decisions of the European Court of Human Rights. Article 121, para. 2, gives foreign natural persons and foreign organizations the possibility to acquire ownership rights over real estates in accordance with the law or international agreements. Article 122, para. 1, confers to the people of Kosovo the enjoyment of the natural resources of the Republic, provided that they do not infringe on the obligations stemming from international agreements on economic cooperation. Article 123, para. 3, links the activity of local self-government bodies to the respect not only of the Constitution and the internal laws, but also of the European Charter on Local Self-Government.

For what concerns criminal matters, according to Article 33, para. 1, no one shall be charged or punished for any act which did not constitute a criminal offence under the law in force at the time it was committed, except for acts considered genocide, war crimes or crimes against humanity in the international law. The citizens of Kosovo shall not be extradited from Kosovo against their will except for cases when otherwise required by international law and agreements (Art. 35, para. 4).

As for ethnic minorities, Article 58, para. 2, states that "the Republic of Kosovo shall promote a spirit of tolerance, dialogue and support reconciliation among communities and respect the standards set forth in the Council of Europe Framework Convention for the Protection of National Minorities and the European Charter for Regional or Minority Lan-

201 Universal Declaration of Human Rights, European Convention for the Protection of Human Rights and Fundamental Freedoms and its Protocols, International Covenant on Civil and Political Rights and its Protocols, Council of Europe Framework Convention for the Protection of National Minorities, Convention on the Elimination of All Forms of Racial Discrimination, Convention on the Elimination of All Forms of Discrimination Against Women, Convention on the Rights of the Child, Convention against Torture and Other Cruel, Inhumane or Degrading Treatment or Punishment.

guages". Article 59 confers to the members of the communities a series of rights, to be used individually or collectively, and in conformity to the law and international standards.[202]

The composition of the Assembly of Kosovo shall respect the internationally recognized principles of gender equality (Art. 71, para. 2). Similarly, the principles of gender equality recognized at international level shall be respected in the composition of the civil service (Art. 101, para. 1) and of the judiciary (Art. 104, para. 2).

Security institutions shall act in accordance with internationally recognized democratic standards and human rights (Art. 125, para. 2). Para. 3 of Article 125 provides that Kosovo fully respects all applicable international treaties as well as the relevant international law, and cooperates with international security organs and regional counterparts. International cooperation is required for Security Forces (Art. 126, para. 1), the Security Council of the Republic (Art. 127, para. 3: on the basis of Art. 131, para. 8, during the state of emergency the Security Council shall cooperate with the international authorities), the Police (Art. 128, para. 5), the Civil Aviation Authority (Art. 130, para. 2).

It is within the jurisdiction of the Constitutional Court (Art. 113) to examine the compatibility of a proposed constitutional amendment with binding international treaties ratified under the Constitution.

International agreements and other acts relating to international cooperation that are in effect on the day the Constitution enters into force continue to be respected until such agreements or acts are renegotiated / withdrawn, in accordance with their terms, or until they are superseded by new international agreements or acts covering the same subject areas and adopted pursuant to the new Constitution (Art. 145 "Continuity of International Agreements and Applicable Legislation"). Articles 146-162 ("Transitional Provisions") establish for the transitional period – which lasted four years and ended with the adoption of a special constitutional amendment on 7 September 2012 – provisional bodies with a strong international footprint and a general international supervision, including the presence of international armed forces.

2.6 Constitutional Amendments and Revisions

Particularly relevant are the provisions regarding constitutional amending, since procedural complication and limitations to the amending power are among the fundamental features

202 These are rights connected to the education, use of community symbols, establishing of media in the language of community, contacting people of the same community, language or religion in other countries, *etc.* Special provisions are dictated for the Serbian minority.

of a democratic, rule of law state.[203] A special section on the amending of the constitution is not necessarily included in every text, sometimes the relevant clauses can be found in the general list of parliamentary competences. This is the case when the procedure is rather simple and it is carried out in the parliamentary arena (Hungary, Czech Republic, Slovakia, Croatia). In other countries, procedures are much more complex. There are different methods depending on the articles or sections to be amended, thereby confirming the internal differentiation or hierarchy of constitutional provisions that we have already mentioned above.

For what concerns who is entitled to propose a constitutional amendment, bill or a new constitution, they are generally institutional subjects, even if in some cases specific percentages of voters enjoys the right of initiative. This is foreseen in Latvia (Art. 78: not less than one-tenth of the electorate), Lithuania (Art. 147: not less than 300,000 voters), Romania (Art. 150: at least 500,000 citizens with the right to vote), Slovenia (Art. 168: at least 30,000 voters), Macedonia (Art. 130: 150,000 citizens), Serbia 1990 (Art. 132: at least 100,000 voters) and 2006 (Art. 203: at least 150,000 voters), Montenegro 1992 (Art. 117: at least 10,000 voters). The Hungarian Fundamental Law allows even a single member of the parliament to present a draft amendment of the constitution or a draft of a new Fundamental Law.[204]

As for procedures, there are different kinds which are sometimes alternative[205]: 'total' revision procedure with the convening of a special constituent assembly (Bulgaria)[206]; parliamentary procedure (Czech Republic, Slovakia, Hungary, Kosovo, Croatia, Bulgaria, Bosnia-Herzegovina, Macedonia); optional referendum (Slovenia, Poland for the amendment of chapters I, II and XII, Albania and Serbia in some cases); mandatory referendum.[207]

203 Socialist constitutions did not provide for explicit limitations to constitutional amendments and the procedure was not particularly complex. However, thanks to political homogeneity and a strong party discipline even ordinary legislation was approved unanimously. Public consultation preceding the adoption of laws, constitutional amendments and new constitutions, conferred legitimacy to the system. This consultation has been used also for the adoption of some new democratic constitutions (Croatia, Albania, Romania, Slovakia). *See* M. Ganino, *La revisione costituzionale in Europa orientale*, in S. Gambino & G. D'Ignazio (Ed.), *La revisione costituzionale e i suoi limiti: tra teoria costituzionale, diritto interno, esperienze straniere*, Milano, Giuffrè, 2007.

204 The draft of the Fundamental Law of 2011 was officially submitted to the parliament by a single member of the Fidesz.

205 M. Ganino, *La revisione costituzionale in Europa orientale*, cit., pp. 454-484.

206 This is a historical heritage (it derives from the Constitution of Tărnovo) already followed for the adoption of the current Constitution of 1991. The total revision procedure is applied for the adoption of a new constitution or for the amendment of some specific provisions.

207 In Lithuania a special referendum is called for the amendment of Art. 1. In this case the three-fourths of citizens entitled to vote must answer yes. To amend Chapters I and XIV of the constitution a 'simple' referendum is required. In Latvia a referendum is required to amend Arts. 1, 2, 3, 4, 6, 77; in Estonia to amend Chapters I e XV; in Romania in every case; in Serbia and Montenegro the referendum is mandatory to amend certain parts of the constitution. *See* further for more details.

The most complex revision procedure is that envisaged by the Constitution of Estonia, which provides for three different procedures with different 'strictness' in Arts. 163-168. The simplest ones are those of Czech Republic, Slovakia and Hungary, as they are entirely carried out in parliament.

As for the expressly provided limitations to constitutional changes, there are three main different kinds: those referred to time, those to circumstances and those to content. These last ones, which we may call 'substantive', are explicitly foreseen in very few cases and generally include the democratic character of the state, as well as fundamental rights or characteristics of the national state (Czech Republic, Art. 9, para. 2, cost: "essential requirements for a democratic state governed by the rule of law"; Romania, Art. 152, paras. 1 and 2: national, independent, unitary and indivisible character of the state, the Republican form of government,[208] territorial integrity, independence of the judiciary, political pluralism, official language, suppression of fundamental rights and freedoms or of their safeguards; Bosnia and Herzegovina, Art. X, para. 2: no amendment may eliminate or diminish any of the rights and freedoms referred to in Art. II or alter the same Art. X).

The 'circumstantial' limitations, generally related to the prohibition to amend the constitution during the state of war or emergency, are provided for in the constitutions of Estonia (Art. 61), Lithuania (Art. 147), Romania (Art. 152; *see also* Art. 63, para. 4: the amendment of the Constitution is forbidden during the period of prorogation of the houses of parliament), Albania (Art. 177), Serbia 2006 (Art. 204), Montenegro 2007 (Art. 156). Lastly, 'time' limitations are related to the prohibition of re-examination of a draft amendment rejected by parliament or via referendum before the lapse of a certain amount of time, usually one year (Estonia one year, Art. 168; Lithuania one year, Art. 148; Albania a year from the rejection by the parliament and three from the referendum, Art. 177; Serbia 2006 one year, Art. 203; Montenegro 1992 one year, Art. 117; Montenegro 2007 one year, Art. 155).

There are also implicit or 'implied' limitations, that are usually detected by constitutional law scholars or jurisprudence, and mainly derive from the principles that describe the state as democratic or from the use of adjectives such as 'irrevocable', 'unchangeable', 'immutable' or 'fundamental' to characterize fundamental rights.

For what concerns the procedures to adopt constitutional amendments, there are different possible burdens, that include both qualified majorities for the final approval of the draft and different readings, as well as the possibility or the obligation to call a referendum.

As regards the parliamentary procedure, the number of votes required for the parliamentary approval of acts amending the constitution in some cases coincide with the majorities required for the ratification of international treaties limiting sovereignty (Czech

208 At the time of the adoption of the Constitution the introduction of this limit was somewhat controversial considering the warm reception given to former King Michael I during his visit to Bucharest in April 1992.

Republic, Slovakia, Slovenia, Latvia, Hungary, Croatia). For bicameral procedures, like those in Poland, Romania and Czech Republic, the participation of the upper house is always mandatory, with the exception of Slovenia, where the upper house is an institution representing economic, social, professional and local interests.

In Bulgaria, for the approval of a 'simple' constitutional amendment draft, a majority of three-fourths of all national representatives, taking three votes on three different days, is required; if the motion received less than three-fourths but more than two-thirds of the votes of all national representatives, the said motion shall be eligible for a new consideration not earlier than two months and not later than five months thereafter (Art. 155). In Estonia, where there are three different procedures, the majorities of votes required vary from the absolute to the four-fifths; the same parliament decides in the third reading of the project what procedure and majority it will use (Arts. 163-166). In Latvia, amendments are approved in three readings by a majority of not less than two-thirds of the members present in sittings, when there are at least two-thirds of the members of the *Saeima* participating (Art. 76). In Lithuania, the amendments are adopted by not less than two-thirds of all the members of the *Seimas* in two readings (Art. 148). In Poland, a bill to amend the Constitution is approved by the *Sejm* by a majority of at least two-thirds of votes in presence of at least half of the statutory number of deputies, and by the Senate by an absolute majority of votes in presence of at least half of the statutory number of senators (Art. 235). In Czech Republic, a majority of three-fifths of all deputies and three-fifths of present senators is required for the adoption of a constitutional amendment act or other constitutional acts (Art. 39). In Slovakia, the agreement of at least a three-fifths majority of all members of parliament is required to pass and amend the Constitution and constitutional laws (Art. 84). In Romania, at least two-thirds of the members of each chamber – and in case of disagreement between the chambers at least three-quarters of the number of deputies and senators in joint session – are needed to adopt the draft or proposal of revision (Art. 151). In Hungary, the votes of two-thirds of the members of the National Assembly are required in order to adopt a new Fundamental Law or the amendment of the Fundamental Law (Art. S). In Slovenia, the National Assembly adopts acts amending the Constitution by a two-thirds majority vote of all deputies (Art. 169). In Croatia, the decision to amend the Constitution shall be made by a two-thirds majority of all deputies (Art. 149). In Albania, a proposed amendment is approved by not less than two-thirds of all members of the Assembly (Art. 177). In Serbia, both in the 1990 Constitution (Art. 132) and in the 2006 Constitution (Art. 203) it is a two-third majority of the total number of deputies (in 1990 there was also a referendum). The same majority is required by the two constitutions of Montenegro (1992: Art. 117 and 2007: Art. 156). In Kosovo, any amendment shall require for its adoption

> the approval of two thirds (2/3) of all deputies of the Assembly including two thirds (2/3) of all deputies of the Assembly holding reserved or guaranteed seats for representatives of communities that are not in the majority in the Republic of Kosovo (Art. 144).

In Bosnia-Herzegovina, the Constitution may be amended by the Parliamentary Assembly, which consists the session of the two houses, with a two-thirds majority of those present and voting in the House of Representatives (Art. X). In Macedonia, the decision to amend the Constitution is eventually approved by the Assembly by a two-third majority vote of the total number of deputies, after the same majority decided to proceed with the amendment and the absolute majority confirmed the project, then submitted to public debate (Art. 131).

As for constitutional referendums, it is mandatory in Romania for any change to the Constitution (Art. 151). In Estonia, a referendum is mandatory to modify the General Provisions (Chapter I); those on the Amendment of the Constitution (Chapter XV); and if the *Riigikogu* requires it during the third reading of the draft amendment, by the majority of three-fifths of its members (Arts. 162-164). In Latvia, a referendum is mandatory for the modification of Articles 1-4, 6 and 77 (Art. 77) and also for the constitutional amendment Acts of popular initiative, if the *Saeima* does not approve them (Art. 78). At least a half of the electorate shall vote in favour (Art. 79). In Lithuania, the referendum is mandatory to change Article 1 and Chapters I and XIV (Art. 148). In the case of Article 1 the amendment shall be approved by a majority of not less than three-fourths of the citizens of Lithuania with right to vote. The referendum was mandatory for any amendment of the Constitution according to the Serbian Constitution of 1990, and should have been approved by more than one-half of the total number of voters (Art. 133), while in the Serbian Constitution of 2006 the constitutional referendum is in general optional, it has to be requested by the Assembly, but it became mandatory for the modification of some parts of the Constitution (the preamble, the principles, human and minority rights and freedoms, the system of authority, proclamation the state of war and emergency, derogation from human and minority rights in the state of emergency or war or the proceedings of amending the Constitution, Art. 203), and it is adopted by the majority of voters who participate in the referendum. In the 1992 Constitution of Montenegro, the referendum was mandatory to change the status of the Republic, the form of government and the frontiers[209] (Art. 2) while according to the 2007 Constitution it is mandatory to amend

209 Moreover, if the proposal to amend the Constitution concerned fundamental parts of the same (status of the country, form of government, restriction of rights) or the adoption of a new Constitution, after the approval of the text, the Assembly should have been dissolved and a new Assembly would have been convened within ninety days from the day the amendment was adopted deciding by a majority of two-thirds of all members on the approved amendments or on the text of the new Constitution (Art. 119).

Articles 1-4, 12-15, 45, 157[210] and a majority of minimum three-fifth of the total number of voters is required (Art. 157). In Poland, the referendum is optional, at the request of the same subjects who have the right to propose constitutional amendments (at least one-fifth of the statutory number of deputies; the Senate; or the President of the Republic), for the amendment of chapters I, II and XII, the majority of voters are required (Art. 235). In Slovenia, the referendum is optional for any constitutional amendment law, at the request of at least thirty deputies (Art. 170) and a double quorum is required for the approval (if a majority of those voting voted in favour of the amendment, provided that a majority of all voters participated in the referendum). The referendum is optional also in Albania, where the Assembly decides, with the majority of two-thirds of its members, which amendments are to be approved with it. In any case, the constitutional amendment is submitted to a referendum, after its parliamentary approval, when this is required by one-fifth of the members of the Assembly (Art. 177). It should also be noted that the Hungarian Fundamental Law explicitly excludes a referendum on "any matter aimed at the amendment of the Fundamental Law" (Art. 8).

As aforementioned, Bulgaria provides for the possibility of a so-called 'total revision' of the constitution. This total revision, as in other countries where it is foreseen, concerns not only the adoption of a totally new constitution, but also the modification of the fundamental features of the state.[211] This means that, although with further procedural burdens, these features can actually be modified. In these and other cases the reference to constitutional jurisprudence is essential.[212]

Among the countries examined, only in Romania and Kosovo the constitutional court has the obligation to comment on any constitutional amendment bill (respectively Art. 146, a) and Arts. 113 and 144, para. 3 const.). In the new Hungarian Fundamental Law, if the President of the Republic finds that any procedural requirement laid down in the Fundamental Law with respect to the adoption of the Fundamental Law or the amendment of the Fundamental Law itself has not been met, he or she shall request the Constitutional

210 Concerning the main characteristics of the state (sovereignty, territory, symbols), citizenship, language and alphabets, religion, relationship with international organizations, right to vote and constitutional amendment referendum.

211 Following Art. 158 const. it is up to the Grand National Assembly to adopt a new Constitution, resolve on the matter concerning a change of the territory of the Republic of Bulgaria, and ratify any international treaties providing for such changes. It also makes decisions on matters concerning changes in the form of state organization and of the form of government, on the matters concerning amendment of Art. 5, paras. 2 and 4 (on the direct applicability of the Constitution and on the superiority of international treaties ratified on internal laws) and of Art. 57, paras. 1 and 3 (on the inalienability of the fundamental rights and on the restriction of rights in case of war and emergency). Lastly, it rules on the matters of amending and supplementing chapter nine of the Constitution ("How the Constitution is amended and supplemented. Adoption of a new Constitution").

212 *See* in particular Decs. 3/2003 and 9/2016 of the Bulgarian Constitutional Court concerning the form of government, which is interpreted in a very broad sense.

Court to examine the issue. The latter may review the amendment of the Fundamental Law only in the light of to the procedural requirements laid down in the Fundamental Law for its making and promulgation (Arts. S and 24).

The public debate on the draft amendment to the constitution, which is a socialist legacy, remains only in the constitutions of Macedonia (Art. 131, para. 2) and Montenegro (2007, Art. 156, para. 4).

Different procedures for the modification of different parts of the constitution, as seen, are provided for by the constitutions of Bulgaria,[213] Estonia,[214] Latvia (Arts. 1, 2, 3, 4, 6, and 77 are amended through a referendum), Lithuania (referendum with a simple majority, a high majority or no referendum at all, depending on articles to be amended), Poland (a more complex procedure with an optional referendum is provided for the modification of chapters I, II and XII), Montenegro 1992 (the same procedure is provided for the revision of fundamental principles and for the adoption of a new constitution). Different procedures are also foreseen in the Constitution of Serbia of 2006 (mandatory referendum for the modification of some parts) and in the 1992 Constitution of Montenegro.[215]

The procedure for amending the constitution and for the adoption of a new constitution coincides in Hungary, Slovakia, and Montenegro 2007. In Slovakia and Czech Republic, constitutional acts are approved with the same procedure as the constitutional amendment acts.

In some Republics of the former Yugoslavia (Serbia, Montenegro, Macedonia) together with the constitutional amendment act, an act implementing the amendments is adopted; moreover, there are various parliamentary resolutions, always adopted with qualified majorities (approval of the proposal, adoption of the constitutional amendment act, adoption of the act of implementation), which probably replace the different readings.

---

213 'Ordinary' revision and revision by the Grand National Assembly for the modification of some sensitive parts or for the adoption of a new Constitution: it is the National Assembly that decides by a two-thirds majority to hold elections for the GAN, which approves the modifications or the new Constitution with the majority of the two-thirds of the members, that is to say a majority lower than the one of three quarters required for the approval of 'ordinary' revisions.

214 Art. 163 distinguishes three variants, the choice is up to the same parliament (except for the modification of the chaps. I and XV), on the occasion of the third reading of the project. These are the following three procedures: approval with referendum, decided with the majority of three-fifths of deputies; in two different legislatures, procedure decided by absolute majority; in urgent procedure, if four-fifths of the deputies so decide.

215 If the revision concerned some fundamental parts or the adoption of a new constitution, the Assembly had to be dissolved and the new Assembly would have to decide on the revision with a two-thirds majority (Art. 119). In the cases provided for by Art. 2, para. 4 a mandatory referendum was foreseen.

2.7 Final Remarks

2.7.1 *Some Remarks on Constitutional Peculiarities of the Countries of Former Yugoslavia*

A general feature of the 'first cycle' constitutions of the Republics of former Yugoslavia is that they were adopted on the basis of principles contrasting with those of the socialist federal Constitution, which was still in force. The procedures followed to adopt the new constitutions were also in contrast with those provided for in the 1974 Constitution, and the same can be said for the declarations of sovereignty and independence of the Republics. However, the 1974 Constitution did not contain provisions allowing the constitutional crisis under way to be resolved. Even the Federal Constitutional Court, that was asked by the federal parliament to give opinions on the legitimacy of some republican constitutional acts, could not provide final solutions, due to the limitation of its role in the socialist system. The break-up of the federation took place precisely following the continued adoption by the Republics of acts inconsistent with the federal Constitution, even though in all the three Yugoslav socialist constitutions the right of self-determination of the peoples was theoretically foreseen.[216] The obstructionist activities of the Republics (with the exception of Serbia and Montenegro) were added to these measures. They withdrew their representatives from the federal institutions, thus preventing any agreed solution of the crisis.[217] For these reasons, Nikolic speaks of "constitutional deficit", and therefore of a lack of democratic legitimacy, of the new constitutions of the states of the former Yugoslavia.[218] According to Gambino, due to the constituent and/or constitutional amendment procedures used, we can speak of "an uncertain legal basis for the formation of the new States and a largely formal constitutionalism, except for Slovenia".[219]

---

216 Art. 1 of the fundamental principles of the 1974 Constitution established that "The nations of Yugoslavia, proceedings from the right of every nation to self-determination, including the right to secession ...". In a similar manner were drafted Art. 1 of the 1946 and of the 1963 Constitutions. On secessions in general please refer to R. Scarciglia, *Profili costituzionali della secessione: dall'esperienza canadese all'indipendenza del Kosovo, Il diritto della Regione*, No. 5-6, 2009, pp. 163-177.

217 *See* S. Gambino, *Potere costituente e transizioni democratiche nell'area balcano-occidentale*, in M. Calamo Specchia et al. (Eds.), *I Balcani occidentali. Le Costituzioni della transizione*, cit., pp. 33-34.

218 P. Nikolic, *I sistemi costituzionali dei nuovi Stati dell'ex Jugoslavia*, cit. However, the same author, in *La disgregazione della Jugoslavia socialista. Formazione e sviluppo della nuova Jugoslavia e dei membri costitutivi della federazione. Aspetti costituzionali*, in S. Gambino (Ed.), *Europa e Balcani. Stati, culture, nazioni*, Padova, Cedam, 2001, p. 198, states that "the legal foundation of the formation of the new states was the adoption of new Constitutions".

219 S. Gambino, *Introduzione*, in P. Nikolic, *I sistemi costituzionali dei nuovi Stati dell'ex Jugoslavia*, cit., p. 14.

For what concerns the contents of these constitutions, while scholars emphasize the international conditioning,[220] especially in those of the second cycle, the imprinting of socialist constitutionalism is underestimated. As a matter of facts, the continuity, at least formal, with socialist constitutionalism appears to be significant. The following socialists residues can be detected: the role of the prosecutor in the protection of constitutionality and legality, a special constitutional section on constitutionality and legality, the competences of constitutional courts, which are drown quite literally from those provided in the socialist constitutions (*self-saisine, actio popularis*, suspensive powers, control of legality, etc.), the participation of workers in the companies' management,[221] the emphasis on social rights (Montenegro 1992) and on workers' rights, the introduction of duties as well as rights,[222] a certain mixture of old and new in the section on economic system,[223] the upper house in Slovenia as a chamber representing economic, social and professional interests, the initial appointment of judges for a limited period of time followed by a subsequent confirmation,[224] the public discussion of draft laws and constitutions or of constitutional amendments, a special constitutional section on the economic system, the adoption of special constitutional acts to implement constitutional amendments, the strong role of the parliaments (in some cases, they can self-dissolve), the lack of the countersignature for the acts of the President of the Republic, who is not called head of state,[225] the attribution to the President of a sort of emergency legislative function,[226] etc.

---

220 L. Montanari distinguishes between 'conditioned' drafting of the bill of rights (in general, all the constitutions of the Western Balkans), 'guided' drafting (Albania, Montenegro, Macedonia, Serbia & Montenegro), 'internationalization' of the constitutions and bill of rights (Bosnia and the interim Kosovo Constitution). L. Montanari, *La tutela dei diritti nelle nuove Costituzioni dei Balcani occidentali*, cit., p. 165.

221 Serbia 1990: Art. 58, para. 2 ("The employed persons manage a socially-owned enterprise and participate in management in other kinds of enterprises and other organizations where they work, or where they invest their resources, in accord with the law and the collective agreement"); Croatia: Art. 56, para. 4 ("Employees may, in conformity with law, participate in decision-making process in their places of employment"); Slovenia: Art. 75 ("Employees shall participate in the management of commercial organisations and institutes in a manner and under conditions provided by law"). Art. 65 of the Constitution of Montenegro creates the "Social Council" to resolve conflicts between workers and employers, consisting of representatives of trade unions, employers and the government.

222 Montenegro 1992: pay taxes, participate in the prevention or elimination of the state of emergency. Serbia 1990: duties include the obligation to help people in need and to participate in the elimination of general dangers (Art. 54).

223 Serbia 1990: state, social and cooperative ownership (Arts. 55 and 59). Serbia 2006: Art. 82, para. 3 "The impact of the market economy on social and economic status of the employed shall be adjusted through social dialogue between trade unions and employers".

224 Serbia 2006: Art. 146, para. 2 "Exceptionally, a person who is elected a judge for the first time shall be elected for the period of three years". Similarly, Art. 147.

225 In the Republics of the former socialist Yugoslavia the collegial presidency was not considered a head of state.

226 In the socialist Yugoslavia the power to issue decrees with the force of law was the exclusive prerogative of the collegial presidency or of its president.

The recurrence of these aspects can be found not only in the first post-socialist constitutions but also in the following ones. After all, in the socialist period, Yugoslavia represented a peculiar, different and absolutely *sui generis* system of which positive aspects must be remembered. Precisely the loss of such a cohesive and participated social system could have led to some subsequent political setbacks, as the model offered by European Union does not provide answers from this point of view. In addition, some of the characteristics in the bills of rights that seem derived from the European Conventions on Human Rights, represent the wish to take distance from the socialist system, as we already noticed (prohibition of torture, of compulsory medical treatments, of censorship, of forced labour, etc.).

Bills of rights of these constitutions are long and detailed, however such abundance may seem to indicate a certain insecurity.[227] There is a lack of a rational construction, with cases of duplication and lack of a logical order. One of the best structured constitutions is that of Albania, thanks also to the assistance of the Venice Commission. As for the new generation rights, they are mainly environmental rights (as already highlighted, in the 1992 Constitution of Montenegro), privacy, personal data protection, conscience objection, prohibition of cloning, freedom of procreation, consumers protection, sport's rights, prohibition of a cruel treatment of animals. Another common feature of these constitutions is the reference, among the social rights, to the assistance of war veterans and victims of war, a clear consequence of the painful genesis of the new statehood.

The influence of international rights charters, including the EU Charter of Fundamental Rights (Nice Charter), is evident, both for what regards the new rights and for the provisions dedicated to specific categories of persons (children, women, the elderly, the disabled).[228] As in almost all the other former socialist countries, we find here the duty to respect international treaties which, once ratified, prevail over conflicting domestic laws. However, the principle of the highest level of protection applies in general.[229]

As for the international influence, it does not seem different here from what other former socialist countries have experienced, apart from a few specific cases (Bosnia-Herzegovina, Serbia & Montenegro, the 2001 revision of the Macedonian Constitution, the 2001 provisional constitution of Kosovo). The admission into the Council of Europe, and the application process for the entrance into the European Union are common features for the whole area and there are no significant differences from the other former socialist

227 L. Montanari, *La tutela dei diritti nelle nuove Costituzioni dei Balcani occidentali*, cit., p. 180.

228 A broad reference in the bill of rights to the fundamental rights of liberal constitutionalism and to the human rights of international conventions was necessary because these countries, unlike other Central-Eastern Europe, could not refer to the traditions of the first post-war period, when national identities had been compressed in the state of Serbs, Croats and Slovenes, especially after the transformation into the Kingdom of Yugoslavia with the 1931 Constitution which also marked a restriction of rights with respect to the 1921 Constitution. L. Montanari, *La tutela dei diritti nelle nuove Costituzioni dei Balcani occidentali*, cit., p. 166.

229 *See* for instance Art. 15, para. 5 of the Constitution of Slovenia.

countries. With specific reference to the advices of the Venice Commission, these have been more or less relevant, depending on the period of adoption and / or amendment of the constitutions.

2.7.2 *The Evolution of Constitutionalism in CEBBE Countries Between Progress and Degeneration*

Thirty years after the end of the communist system, the analysis of constitutional development of the countries emerging from that political regime, which were initially considered to be a constitutional laboratory, may become more accurate by trying to underline previous cultural traditions[230] and highlighting the paradigmatic value of this kind of constitutional transition.

We can make different kinds of considerations. Firstly, the heterogeneity of these countries is wide, despite the unifying effect of the pan-European constitutionalism represented by the Council of Europe and the European Union. This leads us to approach with caution the debates on the degeneration of the rule of law and, more broadly, of the liberal-democratic constitutionalism in these countries. The belief that a global degeneration is taking place comes from the observation of what happened in recent years in two countries that had been at the forefront of political-constitutional transformations, namely Poland and Hungary.

Another peculiar feature of the transition to democracy in this part of Europe has been the length of the transformation process, which gave origins to a proper 'constitutional law of transition', as well as to the questioning of the transition outcomes many years later. Indeed, what happened in 1989 left an indelible aftermath in some political forces, both in terms of dealing with the communist past and as a challenge to the path chosen to overcome the socialist form of state. This happened especially in Poland and Hungary, the countries that have in fact experienced the most negotiated transition of the area.

Another important aspect to be considered is the existence of constitutional traditions, and their continuing influence on the new constitutional law. These are complex traditions since – as we have seen – we can refer both to those deriving from the constitutions of the interwar period and to the socialist residues, although the latter are more hidden or can be confused with general or even innovative aspects of the contemporary democratic constitutionalism. To give examples, in addition to the aspects we have highlighted in the countries of the former Yugoslavia, we can find, in other countries, a specific role of the prosecution organs in the protection of legality, the public discussion of draft laws and constitutions, a peculiar system of appeal in court proceedings, the quasi-normative role

230 References to the previous constitutional experiences are included in most of the new constitutions.

of the directives of the supreme courts, the 'formalist' approach of legal scholarship (though in process of evolving), the popular recall of the elected representatives. Some remnants of the past were present at an early stage, for example the limitations of the effectiveness of the constitutional case law (until 1999 in Poland and until 2003 in Romania the parliament could overcome the unconstitutionality of a law voting with a qualified majority), a certain 'positivism' in the reasoning of the courts, not only the constitutional ones, a greater role of social rights, the limitation of property rights, the existence of duties as well as rights, the lack of distinction between public and private sphere.[231]

Ultimately, in the constitutions of the countries examined we may find three main influences: pre-socialist traditions (above all in the forms of government or in institutions of direct democracy), socialist remnants (especially in the countries of the former Yugoslavia), Western models (above all in the bills of rights). Additionally, explicit 'distances' from the socialist model can be found, which are at the same time a symptom of the 'stickiness' of the past. Finally, in the first years after the transition constitutional courts (in some cases existing since the socialist period) have played an active role, which over time has caused problems in the relationship with the executive power – it is one of the reasons that can explain the 'idiosyncrasy' towards these courts of the right-wing governments in Hungary and Poland. Equally original is the fact of providing in the constitutions not only for the binding nature of international treaties, in particular of those concerning fundamental rights, but also, thanks mainly to later constitutional amendments, for the special role played by the European Union law. However, as the analysis of constitutional case law will show, this privileged role, clashing with the 'sovereign' resistance of these countries, will lead over time to the adoption of relevant decisions in terms of 'counter-limits' or constitutional identity.

We can, thus, list the constitutional innovations of these countries: new generation rights (bioethics, environment, privacy, etc.), peculiar forms of government (different variants of semi-presidentialism), particular approaches to Europe (special provisions for the limitation of sovereignty, referendums for entry into the EU, emphasis on constitutional identity), the leading role of constitutional courts (especially in the initial moment in order to clarify the principle of separation of powers), sovereignty and the national principle.

From the combination of European and local constitutional models, original solutions arose, although they are still object of ongoing adjustments. We should continuously monitor the institutional practice of these countries because their instability could have repercussions on European stability.

231 This is the summary of the characteristics of the post-socialist constitutionalism made by C.R. Sunstein, 'Something Old, Something New', *EECR*, Vol. 1, No. 1, 1992, pp. 18-21. For a critique of Sunstein's position *see* H. Schwartz, 'In Defense of Aiming High', *EECR*, Vol. 1, No. 3, 1992, 25-28, reminding that social and economic rights are not a socialist residue but a feature of post-war European constitutionalism.

As for the external influences, as noted by J. Elster, some countries may have been tempted to adopt constitutions *à la carte*, taking cues from here and there without worrying about them actually being effective. In any case, the challenge faced by these countries was really huge: to create a new civil society, replace communist rules and build new rules where there were missing, give birth to a new political system, a new economic system, address old and new problems of ethnic and national homogeneity. In short, "democracy to be stable, needs a constitutional framework; constitutionalism, to be legitimate, needs a democratic pedigree".[232]

232 J. Elster 'Making Sense of Constitution-Making', *EECR*, Vol. 1, No. 1, 1992, pp. 15-17.

3 The Systems of Government

Jan Sawicki

3.1 The Position of Parliament

The comparative analysis of systems of government in this large area starts from a focus on the role played by the parliamentary institutions. Such an approach may seem to be provocative, since the democratization which coincided with the constituent processes in the area put an end to the predominance – much more declaimed than it was effective – of the legislative assemblies in the socialist systems, the main fruit of the asserted unity-unitariness of state power.[1] Indeed, contrary to appearances, the introduction of the separation of powers, at times even too emphasized, allowed parliaments in these countries to exploit some potentialities which in the past had been frustrated by the real fact that the ruling party was permanently in office.[2] Such potentialities have been expressed in a con-

1 Paradoxical as it may seem, it is the Hungarian Fundamental Law of 2011, which by ideological option of its drafters should represent the most evident departure from socialism, the one which calls to life an essential feature of that system, by prescribing (Art. 1, para. 2, lett. g) that Parliament shall dissolve "representative bodies whose operation is in conflict with the Fundamental Law". It is the claim to take upon the political assembly an oversight power, not only on acceptance of a particular political direction, but even on compliance with the Constitution from other bodies, which reveals marks of the assembly-centred conceptual idea that was predominant, at least rhetorically, under the previous system. This is all the more evident since the organs, whose task is normally to guarantee compliance with the Constitution by the active political institutions, can usually adopt a variety of sanctions against those subjects, which, in turn, only in extreme cases can lead to their dissolution or resignation.

2 A significant peculiarity of the current Czech Constitution (Art. 6) lies in the provision according to which political decisions emerging from the will of the majority manifested in free elections "shall take into consideration the interests of the minorities". It is a form of limitation of power *tout court*, which does not pass through the channels of the traditional separation of powers, and it is qualified by V. Kutlešić, *Les Constitutions postcommunistes européennes. Étude de droit comparé de neuf États*, Bruxelles, Bruylant, 2009, p. 39, as an option for a pattern of 'consensus democracy'. It was not to be taken for granted, as it is now quite common in this area to interpret the lawful conquest of an electoral majority as a mandate to decide in an unlimited way, as legitimized by the 'sovereign' (people), with risks of prevarication. According to J. Filip, P. Molek & L. Vyhnárek, 'Governance in the Czech Republic', *in* N. Chronowski, T. Drinóczi & T. Takács (Eds.), *Governmental Systems of Central and Eastern European States*, Warsaw, Oficyna Wolters Kluwer Polska, 2011, p. 177, the Czech constitutional order include among minorities only the ethnic and national ones, but according to the International Covenant on Civil and Political Rights, from which the Czech Republic is bound, even linguistic and religious minorities must be protected. Although Art. 6 of the Czech Constitution does not refer explicitly to any minority, it is to be considered, according to the authors mentioned above, that the protection of minorities referred to here should be interpreted extensively, until finding corollary and implementation in additional provisions such as qualified majorities to amend the Constitution, qualified minorities who can start a session of the Chamber of Deputies, the right of a

tradictory way, even not always in a positive one,[3] but as a matter of fact, for instance, the ordinary parliamentary assemblies, in one way or another, have everywhere played an essential role, not only formally but also in fact, in the development of the constituent processes.[4] That has proven true by noting that not only, as obvious, were the new constitutions submitted to the adoption by the various assemblies, but also that they happened most of the times to be the outcome of compromises reached within the assemblies themselves, and only rarely they were the fruit of an imposition by charismatic personalities or anyway by the executives.[5] The importance of parliaments is also to be found in the fact that virtually everywhere the existence of the government is bound to the confidence which it enjoys by an elective assembly.[6] It should also be noted that parliaments are the political arena on which the new actors of pluralism, political parties, measured their strengths. Another support to this assertion can be found in the generalized lack of confidence these young or renewed democracies showed towards the idea of conferring primary legislative powers to the executives (with a few exceptions, Romania for instance). To sum up, for various reasons it is cautious to not underestimate the centrality of the representative organ, even despite the fact that in several cases, and for different reasons, a factor of national unification and unity of political direction has been pursued elsewhere, for example in the office of President of the Republic.

It is not by chance that the accentuation of 'presidential' appearances in the system of government, even though modulated in a different manner, has extinguished, after an

---

minority group of deputies or senators to initiate proceedings before the Constitutional Court or even the proportional mechanism of transformation of votes into seats within the Chamber of Deputies, in addition to guaranteeing the protection of human rights and fundamental freedoms, of which every type of minority has the greatest need.

3 In the case of Slovakia, for example, the strict and detailed enumeration of powers of the Slovak National Council (Art. 86 of the Constitution) was criticized by part of the doctrine (C. Cibulka & L. Mokrá, 'The Slovak Republic', *in* N. Chronowski, T. Drinóczi & T. Takács (Eds.), *Governmental Systems of Central and Eastern European States*, cit., p. 683), since it seems to have an ambiguous harmony relation with the principles of constitutionalism. Above all, an extremely detailed list could be reductive of the overall position of parliament, as if it should be adopted in order to prevent trespassing.

4 A good example here is the case of Hungary, as evidenced by A. Arato & Z. Miklósi, 'Constitution Making and Transitional Politics in Hungary', *in* L.E. Miller (Ed.) with L. Aucoin, *Framing the State in Times of Transition*, Washington, USIP, 2010, p. 350.

5 The significant exceptions of Serbia and Croatia – at least at an early stage – should be mentioned in this respect (*see* P. Nikolic, 'La transizione costituzionale nell'ex-Jugoslavia', *in* S. Gambino (Ed.), *Costituzionalismo europeo e transizioni democratiche*, cit., p. 162), which not by chance were related to nationalism factors. The role of the Klaus government in the Czech constituent process should also be taken into account (*see* A. Di Gregorio, *La Costituzione della Repubblica ceca*, cit., p. 212).

6 Despite the effective effort at rationalizing the parliamentary system, along with the strengthening of the executives, by way of 'constructive no confidence' votes and by protecting them from assaults coming from non-cohesive majorities, it should be noticed that there are still occasionally traces of an assembly-centred vision, as evidenced by some aspects of Art. 65 of the Estonian Constitution (Parliament, or the *Riigikogu*, has a set of appointment powers for state positions; it 'authorizes' the prime ministerial candidate to form his/her cabinet).

initial blaze,[7] wherever it had appeared, sooner or later followed by shifting towards power relations in which the binomial government-parliamentary majority plays a crucial role, whereas the head of state has shown protagonism only very occasionally. This has been a very uniform trend.

3.1.1 *The Structure of Parliaments*

As far as the structure of parliaments is concerned, the great majority of states of the recently democratized former socialist area – the countries which once belonged to the Warsaw Pact and the states of former Yugoslavia – chose unicameralism (Bulgaria, Estonia, Latvia, Lithuania, Slovakia, Hungary, Albania, Kosovo, Macedonia, Montenegro and Serbia). Only Poland, Czech Republic, Romania, Slovenia and Bosnia-Herzegovina opted in favour of a bicameral structure.[8] Of course, even the unicameral option, and not only the opposite one, deserves an explanation. In general, the only acceptable justification for the existence of two chambers, in the socialist countries, was the one based on the federal structure of the state.[9] Wherever the state structure was not multiethnic, with ethnic groups largely prevailing within specific portions of the national territory, a single Parliamentary Assembly became the obvious choice, as a symbol of the state unitary power. Therefore in this area the parliament or Yugoslavia was bicameral whereas Czechoslovakia (from 1968 to 1969) was represented by a Federal Assembly (which in turn was bicameral) and by two parliaments for each of the Czech and Slovak components; still different looked the situation of those countries which regained a state sovereignty as a consequence of the collapse of the USSR. In the peculiar turnover of organs and functions which led to the current bicameralism of the Czech Republic, the Senate replaced the old Federal Assembly (constitutional law no. 1/1993) following the 'velvet divorce' from Slovakia, even though it had been established at a later stage,[10] whereas the Chamber of Deputies expresses continuity with the Czech National Council within the socialist Czechoslovak federation. Only in Poland, Romania, Czech Republic are the 'second' chambers elected by universal suffrage,

---

7 A. Di Gregorio, 'Forme di governo e transizione democratica nell'Europa post-socialista', *in* L. Montanari, R. Toniatti & J. Woelk (Eds.), *Il pluralismo nella transizione costituzionale dei Balcani*, cit., pp. 31 *et seq.*

8 In Croatia a House of autonomies existed until 2001.

9 *See* among many M. Volpi, 'L'organizzazione costituzionale', *in* G. Morbidelli, L. Pegoraro, A. Rinella & M. Volpi, *Diritto pubblico comparato* (5th ed.), Torino, Giappichelli, 2016, p. 490, according to whom "bicameralism is adopted by the non federal socialist states, which are inspired by an assembly based theoretical approach" (an approach which in turn reflects a radical vision of the principle of popular sovereignty, partly deriving from the French revolutionary constitutions).

10 In addition the Senate performed the task of 'recovering' a part of the Czech deputies of the Federal Assembly which was dissolved together with Czechoslovakia, beside a role of taking the place of the lower house on particular occasions.

in the latter case with a partial renewal every second year, whereas in the former two countries elections take place simultaneously.

After the regime change, instead, the bicameral option spread a bit more, yet, above all, where (re)adopted it started to be justified on different grounds. In general, it can be accepted that the reasons for choosing bicameralism, no longer based on the need to protect the territorial division of the state, lie in the necessity to 'share' public power as much as possible, in needs of "counterpower and guarantee".[11] Paradoxically, it is precisely the Czech Republic, which after the separation from Slovakia, at the time of the 'velvet divorce' of 1992, has been transformed into a unitary state, the country which preserved a form of bicameralism within it. The same thing occurred for the Republic of Bosnia-Herzegovina, although the peculiar institutional set-up of this state – on which a strong international influence has been exercised after tragic war events – is justified by the conditions of extreme multi-ethnicity with which it coexists.[12]

The cases of Poland and Romania differ. In the first country, the existence of two chambers is rooted back in the centuries, although it was otherwise justified in the twentieth century. The reform which was agreed upon at the round table negotiations, in the spring of 1989, took the opportunity of combining the re-establishment of the Senate, an institution from the past (which had been abolished when a soviet-style system was imposed), with the trick that was necessary at the moment to alter a balance of power which was far from satisfactory in the first chamber, the *Sejm* (after the 'semi-free' elections).[13] In Romania,

11 F. Lanchester, 'Forma di governo parlamentare nell'Europa centro-orientale', *in* S. Bartole & P. Grilli di Cortona (Eds.), *Transizione e consolidamento democratico*, cit., p. 79. Similarly F. Frison-Roche, *Le «modèle semi-présidentiel» comme instrument de la transition en Europe post-communiste. Bulgarie, Lituanie, Macédonie, Pologne, Roumanie et Slovénie*, Bruxelles, Bruylant, 2005, p. 223, according to whom "il ne fait aucun doute qu'en Pologne et en Roumanie, les constituants voulaient un instrument supplémentaire de contre-pouvoir et non pas adopter simplement une formule de seconde chambre, dite 'de réflexion'", adding the motto "diviser pour affaiblir", where weakening is referred to the executive.

12 Here the second chamber (House of Peoples) takes on the role of ethnic mediation assembly, with fifteen delegates elected with a second degree procedure among the Croatian, Bosnian and Serbian ethnic groups: M. Calamo Specchia, L. Fabiano, 'Istituzioni e tecniche dei processi di democratizzazione nell'area balcanica (sistemi elettorali, partiti politici e società civile)', *in* L. Montanari, R. Toniatti & J. Woelk (Eds.), *Il pluralismo nella transizione costituzionale dei Balcani*, cit., p. 177. The fact that the members of this chamber are defined as 'delegates' by the Constitution of Bosnia-Herzegovina testifies the binding mandate they have to act within by the ethnic-territorial assemblies that elect them (this is a clear institution of the socialist past). The compromise pattern between ethnic components, recurring throughout the Constitution, is confirmed by the fact that the decisions of the compound State, although governed by the classical majority principle typical of representative democracies, must preferably be taken (Art. IV, para. 3 of the Constitution) with the consent of at least one third of each component, in the absence of which conciliation procedures are required.

13 An accurate recognition of the circumstances under which the Senate was reestablished in Poland can be found in J. Ciemniewski, 'Bicameralism Under the Constitutional System of the Third Republic of Poland', *The Sejm Review (Przegląd Sejmowy. Fifth Special Edition)*, 2014, pp. 66 *et seq.* (also available at http://orka.sejm.gov.pl/przeglad.nsf/xWgRokuAng/2014/$File/ps5_2014_eng.pdf (last accessed September 2018).

under the 1991 Constitution, an almost equal bicameralism was provided for, until 2003, when it was weakened in the context of a wider amendment.[14] The current order provides for a peculiar 'division of labour' between the Chamber of Deputies and the Senate, in which each assembly has priority ("first invested Chamber"), but not exclusive power, over a specific category of legislative acts.[15] Unusual is the case of Slovenia, where the existence of a National Council as second chamber determines what is described in that country as an 'incomplete bicameralism', bearing in mind the extremely limited role that chamber performs in the legislative process, so that it qualifies halfway between a legislative and a consultative institution. This, combined with a composition which represents specifically social, economic and professional interests as such, reminds of a long gone period,[16] and makes it possible to compare the said institution, among the countries of Western Europe, only to the Irish Senate.

In general, even when a bicameral structure has been preferred, the belief in the principle of popular sovereignty made it necessary to choose universal suffrage for the election of the 'upper' chamber as well, as results from the cases of Poland, Romania, Czech Republic (in the latter case the emphasis put on the national character of each election to a legislative assembly, which elsewhere imposed a simultaneity of elections, gave way to the idea that of a partial renewal of a third of senators every second year).[17] Where it was not justified by specific peculiarities of the form of state, this remark is sufficient to show the limits of any structural differentiation between the two chambers, which in turn has possible repercussions on the reasonableness of a significant functional separation. In the case of Poland and Romania common sittings of the two parliamentary chambers, for specific purposes, are also provided for.[18]

14 Romania is currently the only EU state – apart from Italy – in which the government must enjoy the confidence of both chambers.

15 In a consultative referendum of December 2009 77.8 percent of voters chose the abolition altogether of the Senate, but that was never achieved due to a lack of agreement in Parliament on how to amend the Constitution accordingly.

16 Even if a part of the doctrine doubts of the parliamentary nature of this assembly, the National Council seems now to have become, in fact, the second Chamber of the country. A mixed composition organ of forty members, in which local communities, employers, employees, farmers, craftsmen, tradesmen and professionals are represented as such, is entitled with a veto power over the acts passed by the National Assembly, which can only be outvoted by the latter with an absolute majority. According to F. Frison-Roche, *Le «modèle semi-présidentiel»*, cit., p. 233, within a ten year period, the Council only used this power 55 times, and one in four times the veto was not overridden by the Assembly. In the view of the author, the role played by the National Council is more one of legal expertise than that of a political institution; hence the attention paid by the public to its opinions, which must be taken at least into account by the deputies.

17 It was a choice made by the Czech constitution-makers in full awareness; the aim was to design for the Senate a role of substitute, especially when the Chamber was dissolved, in order to adopt legislative measures which could not be delayed. *See* A. Di Gregorio, *Repubblica ceca*, cit., p. 81.

18 In the case of Poland it is about, above all, relationships with the head of state (oath, but also start of an impeachment procedure). In the case of Romania (Art. 65) the spectrum of the foreseen activities is much wider, including decisions on the status of members of parliament and the adoption of the state budget.

There is an additional reason of interest as a consequence of bicameralism, where this has been implemented. The existence of two chambers elected by universal suffrage encouraged a certain degree of differentiated experimentalism when it comes to electoral system, at times even based on constitutional provisions. So, whereas the Romanian Constitution is silent as to the election formulas to be adopted for the two chambers,[19] the Polish one (Art. 96) imposes the adoption of a proportional formula for the Chamber, or *Sejm* – by the way, enforced in a way which is not beyond any doubt – and is silent as for the Senate, which in fact is elected since 2011 under a British-style first-past-the-post system. The case of the Czech Republic differs, since the first two sections of Article 18 of this Constitution expressly foresee proportional representation for the Chamber of Deputies and a majority system for the Senate.[20] The distinction of functions, with an additional stress on the power of the 'lower' chambers, limits the reasons of interest for the possible differentiated functioning of the elected assemblies, but also circumscribes the risks of dysfunctionality of the system which could derive from the adoption of alternative electoral formulas.

Of course the impact of the election system, and of the possible constitutional preference for one of them, does not get exhausted to bicameral systems. Among the examined states even the House of State of Slovenia is subject to a proportional formula following an amendment passed in 2000 (Art. 80.4 of Slovenian Constitution),[21] which goes so far as fixing a national threshold of four percent of votes, as already provided for in Estonia and Latvia. It has been observed, though, that even when texts are silent, some preference for proportional representation indirectly appears.[22] It is not surprising that this – even where not imposed – is the dominating trend in young democracies, which followed a tough totalitarian past, whose legacy left difficult cleavages to cure, a lack of mutual recognition and fears of long lasting abuse of power by the victors of an individual election.

3.1.2 *The Status of Members of Parliament*

Nearly everywhere the status of members of parliament is subject to an accentuated protection. Verification of credentials is a subject where differentiated patterns have been

19 A system based on proportional representation was put in place until 2008, when it was replaced by a mixed system (E. Veress, 'The Governmental System of Romania', *in* N. Chronowski, T. Drinóczi & T. Takács (Eds.), *Governmental Systems*, cit., p. 558. For more details M. Ganino, 'La Costituzione della Romania', *in* Id. (Ed.), *Codice delle Costituzioni*, cit., p. 262.

20 But under the Czech system the Senate, unlike the Chamber, can never be dissolved, also because of the functions described above.

21 The provision enters upon the subject of legislation, prescribing that there should be "due consideration for the fact that voters have a decisive influence on allotment of seats to the candidates", which must be interpreted as a propensity for an open list system with preferential vote.

22 V. Kutlešič, *Les Constitutions postcommunistes*, cit., p. 75.

adopted, whereas other classic institutions of parliamentarism are arranged in a basically uniform manner. In several states a tendency may be observed in favour of attracting the verification of credentials still into the sphere of interior autonomy (as can be ascertained from Arts. 82, 76, 18 of, respectively, the Slovenian, the Slovak, the Latvian Constitutions); on the other hand some Constitutions are silent on the verification of parliament's members by the assemblies themselves, and mention instead the competence of judicial organs such as the Supreme Court to decide on the validity of elections (Poland, Art. 101), or the Constitutional Court to solve possible legal challenges (Bulgaria, Art. 66). With these options, which do not seem to be majoritarian, confidence is shown on the one hand towards the independence of such organs from political pressures, on the other towards their political neutrality (the case of the Polish Supreme Court deserves here much attention).

As mentioned, it is univocal – despite some slight drafting differences – the regulation of the parliamentary mandate, since everywhere principles of liberty and the absence of bonds and instructions on behalf of the voters (or parties) are proclaimed. As far as the immunities are concerned, a high standard of protection of parliaments, before still of individual members, can be observed in the field of inviolability, where in various states (Latvia, Lithuania, Poland, Czech Republic, Romania, Slovakia, where a deputy can even refuse to witness in a process), a parliamentary authorization is needed to indict a parliamentarian (in Latvia the authorization is extended even to the imposition of administrative sanctions). In Bulgaria a 2006 constitutional amendment states that with the consent of the investigated deputy no authorization is requested. Only in Hungary some important aspects of the parliamentarian's inviolability remain quite vague (Art. 4 of 2011 Fundamental Law) and reserved to a cardinal law. It is true that cardinal laws (provided for by Art. T, section 4 of the Fundamental Law) must be adopted with a two-thirds majority of those present – which poses other problems – but in this case what takes place is a de-constitutionalization of what should be directly regulated at the highest possible level. Moreover, in Hungary parliament may, by a two-thirds majority of those present, declare the forfeiture of office of one member due to loss of qualifications, to incompatibilities, or to an absence from parliamentary activities prolonged for more than a year. It is an unusual provision in comparative perspective. It is true that the reasons justifying such a possible decision are circumscribed – even though the wording "loss of qualifications" is vague and indefinite. But it is also a matter of fact that the forfeiture of the mandate does not occur in this case automatically, nor does it depend on a personal decision of the concerned deputy, or, in hypothesis, on a final judgment by a court of justice, yet it is referred to the assembly to which the member himself belongs; the text makes it possible to imagine potential situations, in which a majority – even if qualified –[23] could cleverly interpret an obscure provision and in this way deprive some minority of its rights.[24]

Everywhere parliamentary votes are strictly unobjectionable, but quite often opinions and views expressed by members of parliament when performing their functions are also protected, sometimes adding the specification that such opinions are immune from legal prosecution provided they are expressed inside the Parliament's buildings.

Many constitutional texts provide for a more or less extensive catalogue of incompatibilities, but only some (Bulgaria, Estonia) prescribe that a member of parliament forfeits its mandate or is suspended when he or she takes up a government post. The Constitution of Romania rejects such a choice as well, even though, among the constitutional legal orders of the whole area, it is the country which is more influenced by cultural echoes of France and by its current semi-presidential system of government.

3.1.3 *Parliaments in the Law-Making Process*

In the Constitutions of this area the role of parliaments is regulated in such a way as to make sure they can enjoy a high standard of autonomy from the standpoint of organization and in rules of procedure. Many provisions are aimed at granting legislative assemblies the highest possible functionality. The most extreme case here seems to be that of the Czech Republic, where (Art. 39.2 of the Constitution) the structural quorum to deliberate, apart from constitutional laws and other decisions to be taken by qualified majority, is lowered even to one-third of members of each chamber.

The positive attitude towards the institution is confirmed by the decisive role it plays in the law-making process, which in general does not privilege the executive power, neither at the initiative stage[25] nor, above all, in the decisive steps in which the final decision on an act are taken. Even in these countries, for the same reasons recurring in the most consolidated democracies, the rate of success of governmental initiatives is higher than that of other institutions entrusted with the power of legislative initiative, whereas as far as the adopted laws are concerned, the majority of them start their process from an initiative by the executive power. Nonetheless the phenomenon proves true only to a lesser extent than

23 The two-thirds majority seems apt to avoid the risk that representatives of the opposition could be dismissed from their functions, under legal pretences, but in fact for political reasons. It's proper to remark that, right in Hungary, the combination of the electorate's choices and the electoral system, which developed in recent years, made it possible for a party, *Fidesz*, to win more than two thirds of the seats both in the 'constituent' elections of 2010 and in the subsequent ones of 2014 and 2018.

24 The Bulgarian Constitution (Art. 72.1, No. 2) is even more peculiar, by entrusting to the National Assembly the power to declare forfeiture of office – or not – of a deputy for premeditated criminal offence.

25 In Bulgaria, for instance, no preferential treatment is accorded to the executive; moreover, the legislative initiative belongs to each deputy, without setting a minimum number of members in order to start procedures on a bill.

it is in some 'recognized' Western democracies. Some anomalous circumstances must in addition be noted, like the one that is currently taking place in Poland: namely the fact that a government, even if solid in the support it gets from its majority, to pursue its program may prefer to use the artifice of fictitious parliamentary initiatives since these make it possible, according to the rules of procedure of the *Sejm*, to bypass hearings and discussions with external subjects which could be cause for embarrassment and in any case slow down the procedure. Yet in the Czech Republic (Art. 44, para. 3 of the Constitution) the government enjoys the right to ask the Chamber of Deputies to "terminate its discussion" on a government project within these months from its submission, if it had linked to that the request of a vote of confidence.[26] Even in systems based on one chamber, as in Bulgaria, mechanisms are provided for two readings of a bill in two consecutive sessions. But sometimes, as it happens in the Czech Republic (Art. 39, para. 2 of the Constitution) or in Slovakia (Art. 87), the legislative procedure is designed in a very thin way, and the Constitution confines itself to indicate the requested deliberative majorities in the chambers, leaving to the rules of procedure the regulation of several matters, even of principle; at times the law-making process enjoys a more analytical discipline, as in Poland, Romania or Hungary (especially as for the intervention of other organs or powers in this activity, in particular by the head of state).

The legislative initiative is usually characterized by a high level of institutional pluralism. It is obvious that members of parliament are the first holders of this power, although they do not always enjoy it individually and in some cases (Art. 41 of the Czech Constitution, Art. 118, para. 1 of the Polish Constitution) it is only the Senate as such – therefore after a majority vote took place in it – which may submit bills that eventually start from the first chamber, whereas only seldom specific provisions confer the legislative initiative to a minimum number of deputies, which may or may not coincide with what is necessary to establish a parliamentary group.[27] The grant of this power to the governments is also traditional, and in this respect the current Constitutions chose to get rid of the old socialist vision which saw the executives as institutions strictly subordinated to the assemblies.

A peculiarity of these countries lies instead in the fact that occasionally even the heads of state are granted a power to formally initiate bills in parliaments, which apparently is not seen as a sign of partisanship on their behalf nor is it seen as something that lies in contrast with their duty to represent the national unity (this faculty belongs to the presidents

26 Moreover it is always the government who may have a say on all bills under parliamentary scrutiny; a project cannot be said to be approved by the government unless the latter has decided within thirty days after its submission.

27 It's the case of Poland, where, in the silence of the Constitution, the *Sejm* rules of procedure reserve the legislative initiative to a minimum of fifteen deputies, which coincide with the number needed to form a group. This norm, as evident, is a narrow interpretation of Art. 118 of the Constitution, which in turn is perhaps intentionally vague.

in Poland, Latvia, Lithuania, Hungary). Here again it is not very important the modality of election of the head of state, as shown by the fact that it is elected by parliament in Hungary and Latvia.[28] It is also true that presidents use rare if not sporadic of this faculty, even if sometimes it is about occasions either of prestige or linked to particular functions attributed to this office.[29] It is unusual the granting of the legislative initiative to the President of the Republic, under the Estonian Constitution, which is confined to the field of constitutional amendment (Art. 78, para. 1 no. 8 in connection with Art. 103, para. 1 no. 5), a faculty which remains shared with a fifth of parliamentary members (Art. 161). Indeed an initiative power in this field is also recognized to the President of Romania, but in this case it's not a strictly presidential competence as it depends on a proposal coming from the government.[30] Some systems made an effort at enlarging the number of subjects entitled to submit bills, with the evident aim of improving the democratic nature of the system. Among the Constitutions which made this faculty broader the Serb one can be found (Art. 107 with regard to the assemblies of the autonomous provinces, and – in matters related to their competences – to the Ombudsman or the Central Bank) as well as the Romanian one ("a superior unity of territorial self-government", Art. 41, para. 2).

As for the direct initiative by the people, or by significant fractions thereof, it is permitted in some countries, particularly in Latvia (in the high quota of at least a tenth of the electors). Lithuania, Poland, Romania (with the exception of the tax system, international questions, amnesty and pardoning power), Slovenia. Notwithstanding the democratic authenticity of the purpose, which is beyond any doubt, even in this area of Europe the political impact of this institutions remains quite reduced.

As for the procedure in strict terms, the Constitutions of the interested area regulate it with differentiated modalities and intensity, not without traces of originality. So, even in a unicameral system like that established by the Bulgarian Constitution, it is determined that the laws are usually adopted following two votes which take place in two different sittings (Art. 88; a similar provision may be found in Art. 89 of the Slovenian Constitution). So, the Latvian Constitution (Art. 74) envisages forms of possible involvement of the people through referendum which seem to be inspired by the experience of the Weimar

28 As for the second case, it's even more peculiar if one considers that the 1922 Latvian Constitution, re-entered into force in 1993, is inspired according to the prevailing doctrine to the "Westminster model" much more than any other country in this area (M. Mazza, 'La Costituzione della Lettonia (1922)', *in* M. Ganino (Ed.), *Codice delle Costituzioni*, cit., p. 94; D. Ilianova, 'The Governmental System of Latvia', *in* N. Chronowski, T. Drinoczi & T. Takacs (Eds.), *Governmental Systems*, cit., p. 400. In fact, some particular aspect of this form of government will be scrutinized afterwards.

29 It is also true that presidents use rare if not sporadic of this faculty, even if sometimes they are occasions of prestige or linked to particular functions attributed to this office.

30 E. Veress, 'The Governmental System of Romania', *in* N. Chronowski, T. Drinoczi & T. Takacs (Eds.), *Governmental Systems*, cit., p. 559.

Constitution.[31] In some cases a limited substitutive legislative power by the Senate is also arranged, on the government initiative, when the Chamber of Deputies is dissolved (Art. 33 of the Czech Constitution) as well as the power to issue decrees with the force of law by the government when parliament is in recess (Art. 81 of the Estonian Constitution). In cases such as this, however, precautionary limitations are established, both in terms of subject matter and as power of the chamber to re-examine legislative acts passed during its inactivity.

It appears natural that the framework concerning the legislative procedure is more detailed in bicameral systems. In the case of Romania, in particular, a vast constitutional revision of 2003 fixed a sort of "functional differentiation of the two chambers",[32] that is to say that each chamber has competence to discuss with priority some categories of laws. In particular, the Chamber of Deputies enjoys priority on acts to ratify international treaties and on a wide range of organic laws, and the Senate on the remaining laws. The distinctiveness of such a double 'privilege' lies in the fact that each chamber with priority competence has a deadline to decide on the relevant project – usually forty-five days, raised to sixty for codification acts – and after expiry thereof a particular act is deemed to have been implicitly adopted. In fact, therefore, the truly privileged house is the one which is called to examine a bill as the second one, since its decision is usually the final one; and it is the Chamber of Deputies which in conclusion prevails over the Senate, paradoxically just because the latter has wider competences in the first reading.[33]

The case of Poland differs significantly, as here, on the one hand there is no functional differentiation by subject-matter between the two assemblies, and on the other there is a strong privilege in favour of the lower chamber (*Sejm*) in the scrutiny of bills, as all legislative initiatives must start from there, whereas the Senate only enjoys the power to amend or fully reject a "law" (so, literally, Art. 121 of the Constitution) submitted to it by the *Sejm*,

31 M. Mazza, 'La Costituzione della Lettonia', cit., 92. The referendum is in fact seen as a faculty for the people to prevent the entry into force of a law recently adopted by the Parliament (*Saeima*), provided at least half the number of voters who took part at the last parliamentary election vote in it, and the majority of these persons voted against the entry into force. More information on the limited use of this instrument in the last decades can be found in D. Ilianova, 'The Republic of Latvia', *in* C. Kortmann & J. Fleuren & W. Voermans (Eds.), *Constitutional Law of 10 New Member States. The 2004 Enlargement*, Dordrecht, Wolters Kluwer, 2006, p. V-32.

32 M. Ganino, 'La Costituzione della Romania', cit., p. 262.

33 The 2003 amendment was favourably assessed (M.A. Apostolache, 'Considerations on the Bicameral System in Romania', *Tribuna Iuridica*, Vol. 4, No. 2, 2014, p. 64), for fixing a specialization of the functions by repealing a conciliation process and removing the confrontational nature of the legislative process by attracting the role of reflection assembly in the first competent chamber and speeding up the timing with deadlines on it. But there are dissenting opinions as well, as that by I. Deleanu, *Instituții și procedure constituționale. în dreptul Roman și în dreptul comparât*, Bucharest, 2006, p. 188, according to whom the moderation effect on bicameralism is almost inexistent in conditions of non-effective functional difference, and as a consequence of that one may say that "the Romanian Parliament is a unicameral system in a Bicameral coat".

amendment or rejection which in turn the *Sejm* itself may reject with an overall majority.[34] The Polish Constitution goes into further details of the legislative procedure, either by imposing a three reading for each bill in the lower house, or because of important features of participation by the President of the Republic at the end of the process, an aspect that will be discussed further on.

3.2 The Head of State

3.2.1 *The Modalities of Election as a Possible Key to Interpret the System of Government*

The legal doctrine has already noted how, regardless of problematic and controversial classifications of the system of government, in several countries of this area "a certain protagonist role of the President, an individual person raised on top of the state" had initially appeared.[35] Even though that protagonist role was weakened when the transition was accomplished, or in subsequent phases of consolidation of the young democratic institutions, nevertheless the role played by heads of state often remained incisive, in a way that deserves to be assessed.[36]

An empirical evidence to be taken in account, in order to estimate the position accorded to the head of state, in these young democracies, lies in the length of the respective mandates. The meaning of this detail, perhaps more important on a symbolic level than on a practical one, should not be overestimated. Anyway, in a majority of the surveyed cases, the length of presidential terms of office exceeds that of parliamentary assemblies, or of the most important chamber of parliament. Parliamentary terms of office nearly everywhere last four years, whereas the presidential mandate usually lasts a year longer. An exception is that of Latvia and another one used to be that of Romania, prior to the 2003 constitutional amendment, already mentioned, when it was decided to lengthen the presidential mandate from four to five years. This overwhelming trend can surely be explained with the will to pay homage to the dignity of an office, like that of President of the Republic, whose prestige must be emphasized even from this aspect. Except that, especially in the countries where

34 The nature of amendments which the Senate may pass was in turn interpreted in a restrictive way (J. Sawicki, 'Polonia', *in* R. Dickmann & A. Rinella (Eds.), *Il processo legislativo negli ordinamenti costituzionali contemporanei*, Roma, Carocci, 2011, pp. 300 *et seq*).

35 A. Di Gregorio, *Forme di governo e transizione democratica*, cit., p. 19.

36 An articulated enumeration of conjectures on the reasons for that, despite the prevailing option for direct election, is offered by M. Ganino, C. Filippini & A. Di Gregorio, 'Presidenti, Governi e Parlamenti nell'Europa orientale (Polonia, Lituania, Ungheria, Repubblica ceca): l'equilibrio innanzitutto', *in* A. Di Giovine & A. Mastromarino (Eds.), *La presidenzializzazione degli esecutivi nelle democrazie contemporanee*, Torino, Giappichelli, 2007, pp. 142 *et seq*.

the source of legitimacy is the same, that is to say the popular one, the timing difference of the two terms can be cause for some drawback, like that of making situations of *cohabitation* more likely to happen, conditions whose dysfunctionality are more or less acute based on the extension of the effective presidential powers but above all on the stability of party systems, which in turn is influenced by the self-discipline of political actors and their mutual recognition. From this standpoint, it is uncommon the option made in 2003 by Romania, the country that more than anyone else has looked at France as a source of institutional inspiration, and yet took a choice, in this respect, opposed to the change to the French Constitution which was introduced in 2000.[37]

A unit of value to judge the role that each Constitution assigned to the President is certainly to be found in the modalities for his-her election, even though one has to point out that it is an 'easy' key to interpretation, and it is useful only in a limited way.[38] Following this traditional scheme, out of the countries which are examined here, ten elect their head of state at universal suffrage, and the remaining five use an electoral college, in most of the cases composed on parliamentary basis. Because of difficult premises based on the multiethnic composition of the state, the system of election is somewhat mixed in Bosnia-Herzegovina, where there is a collective joint presidency formed by each of the three ethnic groups (Bosnian, Croat, Serb) – elected by the people within the respective community – for a term lasting four years within which each community holds the top office in rotation for a period of eight months.

In general, therefore, the direct election prevails, even though the predominance of the presidential role in the system of government proved recessive especially once democracies appeared to be consolidated. It is an apparent paradox that the control, if not the close interpretation of the presidential powers goes 'hand in hand' with a growing acceptance for his-her direct election,[39] as witnessed by the decision taken by the Czech Republic,

37 *See* M. Ganino, 'La Costituzione della Romania', *cit.*, p. 260, who observes what has been confirmed in practical experience, namely that in this way chances of *cohabitation* become more frequent, which is just what reformers of the French Constitution desired to prevent.

38 F. Frison-Roche, *Le «modèle semi-presidentiel» come instrument de la transition en Europe post-communiste. Bulgaria, Lituanie, Macedonie, Pologne, Roumanie et Slovenie*, Bruxelles, Bruylant, 2005, avoids the most widespread interpretation and offers an original gateway for the prevailing option in favour of the direct election. That choice could be due to demands of political balance with the aim to prevent a predominance of individual actors, and therefore interprets cases of *cohabitation* as desired and designed on purpose, rather than unintended consequences.

39 The Czech Republic is the most significant case in this respect. The presidential office, which from the beginning (in reality since the Czechoslovak Constitution of 1920) was assigned through a parliamentary vote – while Czechoslovakia was still existing, before the dissolution which occurred in 1992 – and granted to the historic leader of the democratic dissidence Vaclav Havel, immediately proved to be anything but a symbolic and ceremonial institution. According to M. Kindlová & V. Pavlíček, 'The Czech State', in C. Kortmann, J. Fleuren & W. Voermans (Eds.), *Constitutional*, cit., p. II-6, right from the beginning the President so elected "became a very strong political participant, initiating constitutional amendments, actively intervening in the preparation of the new Constitution and using his legislative initiative in various

which through a vast constitutional revision in 2012 made this choice after more than two decades of parliamentary election.[40] Still more significant the case of Slovakia, which adopted a vast constitutional reform in 1999, including the direct election of the head of state while, at the same time, reducing his active political powers.[41]

Estonia, Latvia, Hungary, Albania and Kosovo in particular opted for indirect election. An institutional architecture is not always the result of a choice made with full determination and awareness, as it may also be the outcome of unwanted or not fully wanted consequences with respect to some premises. The reasons for introducing or keeping indirect election may be opposed to those which suggested the opposite choice, as the advantages of a strong democratic legitimacy may have appeared less attractive than those offered by a not too exposed and more low profile position. In some cases (Hungary) the decision may have been imposed by mutual fear of the rival political factions at the beginning of the transition (Communist party in power versus the democratic 'proto-parties' in opposition) with respect to the possibility that the opponent could turn out to be the victor.[42] In the case of Kosovo, which confirms the peculiarity of constituent processes dominated by the influence of the international community, the latter is in fact the strength which was able to impose the indirect election, for fears of rebirths of nationalistic outbreaks had the opposite option prevailed.[43]

---

field". Even after the democratic transition was consolidated and proved successful, according to the same authors (p. II-35), "the constitutional poker of the President of the Republic in some areas means that his constitutional position in the Czech Republic is more powerful than is usually for a head of state in parliamentary Republic". Moreover, "the position of the President of the Republic therefore even exceeds the normal situation in presidential Republic". All this, it has to be repeated, in a context of parliamentary election, before the subsequent developments which will be described afterwards.

40 On this subject A. Di Gregorio, 'La Costituzione della Repubblica ceca', p. 217, where it is pointed out as the debate on direct election was dragged from the years of transition with projects presented in this regard to each parliamentary term. In any case, the reform – which appears rather alien to the national traditions of parliamentarianism – has not been accompanied by a formal modification of the presidential powers, and leaves room for practice on the will or capacity of the successive Presidents for the other to widen one's sphere of influence, so that it is premature to draw definitive conclusions.

41 A. Di Gregorio, 'La Costituzione della Slovacchia', *in* M. Ganino (Ed.), *Codice delle Costituzioni*, cit., p. 305. Remarks are also made by G. Mezeznikov, 'La Slovaquie', *in* J.M. De Waele & P. Magnette (Eds.), *Les democraties européennes. Approches comparées des systèmes politiques nationaux*, Paris, Armand Colin, 2010, p. 386, where it is precisely stressed how the introduction of direct election had been favoured by the *impasse* experienced during the election by parliament a year prior to the enactment of the reform.

42 It must be acknowledged, though, that the final decision in favour of a parliamentary election was taken in a long forgotten but hard fought referendum of November 1989, when the country was almost evenly split (50.1 against 49.9 percentage points, or roughly 6000 votes in difference). Actually the question put to the voters concerned the necessity to hold presidential ahead of parliamentary elections – with the Workers' Socialist Party confident of gaining victory for its candidate – but the opposite decision, emphasizing the election of parliament, let the presidential election overshadowed by the former, thus frustrating the very idea of direct election. *See* A. Arato & Z. Miklosi, *Constitution Making and Transitional Politics*, cit., p. 351.

43 F. Korenica & D. Doli, *Constitutional Law in Kosovo*, Alphen aan der Rijn, Wolters Kluwer, 2012, 78: "the international state-builders' desire to establish a constitutional system that functions on the basis of the consociational principles of governance made it a priority to 'impose' a president appointed by the Parlia-

With regard to the election by these criteria, a specific feature should be noted. Whereas Latvia, perhaps because it has called to life in 1993 its own 1922 Constitution[44] is very synthetic in this respect, it worth noting the extreme detail used by the other (and more recent) Constitutions in regulating the electoral procedure, showing unwillingness too much space to practice, conventions, parliamentary procedures or other sources of law of hybrid nature (even though these are known in the area). Hungary is an interesting case in this perspective, because of the detail used by the Basic Law (Art. 11) in regulating the procedure, for instance with regard to the submission of candidacies, subject to written support by at least a fifth of members of parliament,[45] and multiple subscriptions are null and void. Only in Estonia (Art. 79 of the Constitution), in case after three unsuccessful ballots the president is not elected, the task is transferred to a special college, of which a limited number of representatives of local councils is also part.[46]

With regard to the vast majority of countries where the election by universal suffrage has been chosen, almost everywhere the pattern of the two rounds election was adopted, with a possible runoff in the very frequent case no candidate wins a majority of votes at the first ballot.[47] The right to submit nominations is usually given to significant fractions of the national electorate, and sometimes a limited number of parliamentarians is added to that (Czech Republic, Slovakia). An explicit privilege for existing parties, and even not exclusive, can only be traced in this sporadic provision; otherwise, even when assuming

ment". Still: "In societies driven by social and/or ethnical cleavages, like that of Kosovo, the risks posed by rule-of-majority model of democracy always preoccupy international state-builders. [...] Furthermore, it would far easier for the international presence in Kosovo to impose political criteria for the office of president if he/she is appointed via the agreement of political parties in Parliament." Adhesion to the pattern of consensual democracy advocated by A. Lijphart's political science is here evident.

44 M. Mazza, 'La Costituzione della Lettonia', *cit.*, p. 98.

45 In Hungary as elsewhere, through qualified majorities to be reached in the first round, concern is shown in order to make sure the winner is as representative as possible; but subsequent electoral rounds are also provided for, in order to prevent stalls in the continuity of the highest state office. But what matters most is the high quorum, starting from one fifth (Hungary, Estonia) to one fourth (Kosovo) of the parliamentarians entitled to submit a nomination. If on the one hand this rationalizes the contest, by limiting it to those who take part in it standing some chance, on the other it prevents minority groups from submitting symbolic candidates, who could in fact be representative of wider sections of the public opinion, and could be able to prove it. In Albania, where high qualified majorities are provided for in the initial ballots, the Assembly must even be dissolved as a consequence of not being able to elect a president at the fifth ballot.

46 Deepenings on the election of the Estonian president according to this special procedure in K. Merusk, 'The Republic of Estonia', *in* C. Kortmann, J. Fleuren & W. Voermans (Eds.), *Constitutional Law*, cit., p. III-19, where it is stated that, apart from the first election after the regained independence, never again was a president elected at the first three ballots, and always it was necessary to resort to election by the enlarged college, in which local councils have an overwhelming weight, over two-thirds of votes.

47 More details are provided by F. Frison-Roche, *Le «modèle semi-présidentiel»*, cit., p. 66, where some peculiarity is observed, like that of the Lithuanian Constitution, where (Art. 81.1) a candidate is deemed to have been elected provided he/she won more than half of valid votes, but with the additional condition that at least half of the electorate took part in the election; but even a candidate who won the vote of at least one third of the eligible to vote is elected, when turnout was lower than the absolute majority of the latter.

that the higher capacity of mobilization in the collection of signatures is connected to the already established parties, one must recognize that the openness to the electorate may also turn out to be in favour of independent candidates, able to mobilize because of the attractiveness they exert on public opinion (thereby marking a departure from the traditional French method of *parrainages*), thus giving way to a higher potential participation.

3.2.2 *A Classification of Presidential Powers*

It is now worth giving an overview, though short, of the powers granted to presidents in the countries which make part of this geographic area. In order to understand what real strength has been given to the heads of state in each of them – based on the written texts – it is perhaps pointless to classify powers based on criterion of the subject-matters on which they are exercised, whereas it is more productive to assess which of them effectively belong to the holder, and which ones are shared or even only formally belonging to the president, as the actual decision as to their exercise – by way of the countersignature or other – is in practice put in the hands of other subjects or organs.

Before examining this, it's worth to make another preliminary remark. Nearly all the Constitutions in force in this area, together with those which opted forum the direct election of the head of state, do not confine themselves to portray his or her as the supreme representative of the Republic or guarantor of sovereignty, safety and territorial integrity of the state, but they also use more or less strict formulas to underline how much this office must represent the national unity (Art. 80 of the Romania Constitution, which then qualifies it as a "mediator between the state powers, as well as between state and society") or "embody" it (Art. 92 of the Bulgarian Constitution), guaranteeing the right functioning of the constitutional organs or of the public authorities (Art. 101 of the Slovak Constitution; Art. 80 of the Romanian Constitution; Art. 94 of the Croat Constitution), presiding over the respect of the Constitution (Art. 126 of the Polish Constitution)[48] and similar expressions. Such political definitions are beyond discussion, though they may remain indefinite or vague.[49] From a wording like this one can draw a hope, expressed by the constituents, that the

48 Right in this regard F. Frison-Roche, *Le modele semi-presidentiel*, cit., p. 98, finds out, especially in the case of Poland and Romania, the stronger similarities with the 1958 French Constitution.

49 The last cited author – *Ibidem* – observes that even in the case of Romania – to some extent one of the most similar to the true semi-presidential system of the fifth French Republic – the global position of the head of state is not so legally exposed, despite the formula of "guardian of the Constitution", identical to the expression adopted in the French Constitution, and that because of the competences, already mentioned, of "mediator between the powers of the state and between state and society", which make him more of a conciliator between conflicting interests than of someone who decides in first person. According to this analysis, the functions of mediator – designed in order to prevent abuses of power by the heads of state – are even not worth those of arbitrage, which would exclude a political protagonism put in place by the president.

presidency would not necessarily be weak, ceremonial, symbolic, but that it should be obliged to pay respect to a an interpretation of the high office as much *super partes* as possible.[50]

It is a commendable commitment, or at least understandable, both in general and in particular because of the starting conditions for this young democracies. However one of the most prominent Polish constitutional scholars, already several years ago, cast a doubt, although the doubt was worded in very cautious terms: if it could be realistic to expect that presidents who are so elected could *ever* deliver guarantees of neutrality or impartiality, when they had to use specific slogans during their electoral campaign, in which they submitted a political program for whom they also called for support in parliament, "with a dependency which becomes all the more explicit as greater are the ambitions of the president to actively influence state policies".[51] After so many years this doubt is only gaining in strength. It is not intended here to involve old concepts like that of the *pouvoir neutre* or *moderateur* which, according to Constant, could also be an elective head of state, nor is it intended to resort to the Schmittian image of the 'guardian of the constitution', a dangerous one as it was based on the dialectic expedient according to which the president could hold his office, and pretend in addition the office was arbitral, as, according to the Weimar Constitution he was elected "by the whole people",[52] when reality proves that the whole electorate, or all the people, may certainly enjoy political rights but every president is in fact elected only by a fraction of the electorate, the one which identifies more in his/her figure or political program (and, to remain within the Schmittian theme of criticism against parties, it is difficult even today to be competitive in running for public elective offices without the support of at least one among these subjects). To sum up, it remains a fact that, if someone is elected by universal suffrage, he will unavoidably be forced to act somehow as a political leader; and therefore it will be even more difficult for him to qualify as the constitutional guarantor, in a gasping squaring of the circle. This is precisely the situation many young democracies in this area had to face.

So, even if one would include many countries in this area within the category of semi-presidentialism, only because they adopted the direct election of the head of state, often

50 Paradoxically it is the Czech Constitution, originally providing for a parliamentary election of the president, the less persistent in this regard.

51 W. Sokolewicz, 'Tra sistema parlamentare e presidenziale: presidenza limitata ma attiva in Polonia e in Romania', *in* S. Bartole & P. Grilli di Cortona (Eds.), *Transizione e consolidamento democratico*, cit., p. 29.

52 C. Schmitt, *Il custode della Costituzione* (translation into Italian by A. Caracciolo), Milano, Giuffrè, 1981, p. 211. The author seems to argue that just because of this feature a "neutral, mediator, regulating and preserving" power could be formed, as opposed to chaotic party pluralism above all (about Ebert and Hindenburg: "It will have to be recognized that these two presidents, each in his own way, fulfilled his difficult task better than any head of state who could not understand what would remain of *régner* if *gouverner* disappeared completely").

adding to that his formal inclusion in the executive power,[53] what would result from that are only weak versions of that system, even with some case of apparent semi-presidentialism.[54]

This can be demonstrated by a brief legal-empirical analysis of the more considerable powers that are usually put into the hands of the heads of state, especially when it comes to forming the government, to the causes which determine the termination thereof, to the dissolution of parliamentary assemblies as a remedy to permanent crises of the political majority or even – possibly – as a consequence of a lack of satisfaction or approval on the part of the president towards the parliamentary majorities themselves. The presidential powers can also be assessed from the standpoint of their effective capacity to resort to forms of direct democracy through the referendum, possibly even at odds with the political direction pursued by other constitutional organs, to ascertain if the head of state can open channels of direct 'dialogue' with the people, bypassing the representative organs. Such powers can also be assessed from other points of view, for instance the possibility for presidents to influence or affect the legislative process, both at the initiative stage or at the moment of their enactment. The survey can also be extended to an assessment of presidential influence in the field of the federative power according to the old criterion introduced by John Locke, in foreign relations and defence. A key of interpretation of all these functions and the real balance of power in their exercise must of course take into account, albeit not exclusively, the countersignature, one of the most traditional institutions of the parliamentary system of government, or of the parliamentary component of semi-presidential systems.

53 As it is the case in Romania, where E. Veress, 'The Governmental System of Romania', *in* N. Chronowski, T. Drinóczi & T. Takács (Eds.), *Governmental Systems*, cit., p. 565, rejects any legal formalism by stating that "in Romania the President is also a member of the 'government' – as Romania's political system is a semi-presidential one. But this situation is true only for those cases where the president comes from the same party to the prime minister or the parliamentary majority. In other cases the President is not a member of the Government but the part of the authorities controlling the activity of the Government: from the view of political scientists the President in such cases belongs to political opposition. The President can act as a quasi member of the opposition when the prime minister and the President come from two different coalitional parties and the relation between the coalition members is tainted". *Cohabitation* is a political situation already familiar to the French fifth Republic, as it is known. But it's also known that in those situations the role of the president used to move towards that of a 'pure' parliamentary form, whereas very different is the situation which could occur in Romania, where his role could even turn into that of representative of the opposition (as in fact it happened for some time in Poland, as it will be shown below). Much depends, in situations like this, on the spirit of loyal cooperation between institutions and political actors.

54 For quite extensive discussions on the reception of this system of government in the considered area, *see* R. Elgie (Ed.), *Semipresidentialism in Europe*, Oxford, Oxford University Press, 1999, A. Rinella, *La forma di governo semi-presidenziale. Profili metodologici e "circolazione" del modello francese in Europa centro-orientale*, Torino, Giappichelli,1997, M. A. Orlandi, *Quando il semipresidenzialismo passa all'Est*, Torino, Giappichelli, 2002, or the several essays in A. Giovannelli (Ed.), *Il semipresidenzialismo: dall'arcipelago europeo al dibattito italiano*, Torino, Giappichelli, 1998.

3.2.3 *The Presidential Influence on the Formation and the Termination of Governments*

With regard to the modalities of formation and appointment of the governments, it is first of all worth to point out that everywhere, even where the president enjoys some significant influence, the government – or the prime minister – is anyway bound to a relation of confidence with at least a Parliamentary Assembly. This aspect will be deeper discussed hereinafter, but since now it can be stated that this circumstance limits the potential semi-presidential features of the surveyed systems and inhibits any possible development in a presidentially accentuated direction (apart from possible amendments oriented this way or, which is worse, tacit or factual changes, fruit of stretches or open violations of the constitutional texts). Several Constitutions, beyond the modalities of presidential election, provide for procedures as to forming of the government which are actually quite detailed and recall features of a rationalized parliamentarism.

Thus, by way of example, we can mention the case of Romania, where the presidential appointment to the office of prime minister (Art. 103 of the Constitution) takes place after consultation with "the party that obtained the absolute majority in the parliament", or, in the absence of this, with all the parties represented there.[55] Or that of Bulgaria, where there is a detailed procedure (inspired by the Greek model) according to which the President is even bound to confer the task to the candidate presented by the largest numerically parliamentary group (Art. 99 of the Constitution), followed, in case of unsuccessful attempt, from assignment to a candidate of the second group, then again from one entrusted to another parliamentary group.[56] Greater presidential discretion, inferred in the light of the

55 Similar is the regulation established by Art. 127 Serbian Constitution. As summarily says Pajvančić, 'The Governmental System of Serbia', *in* N. Chronowski, T. Drinóczi & T. Takács (Eds), *Governmental Systems*, cit., p. 623: "Participation of the President of the Republic in deciding on the most important issues in the constitutional system of Serbia is limited in its extent, quality and scope of competence." As for Romania, V. Perju, 'The Romanian Double Executive and the 2012 Constitutional Crisis', *International Journal of Constitutional Law*, Vol. 13, No. 1, p. 251, recalled how the first three Presidents of the country following the democratic transformation (Iliescu, Constantinescu, Băsescu), although at times claimed in the abstract the power to indicate the prime minister as their own autonomous choice, in practice, always referred to the candidates indicated by the majority forces in Parliament.

56 According to E. Tanchev & M. Belov, 'The Governmental System of the Republic of Bulgaria', *in* N. Chronowski, T. Drinóczi & T. Takács, *Governmental Systems of Central and Eastern European States, cit.*, p. 99, the Bulgarian President "performs integrative, representative, guaranty and arbitrage functions" and not much else, according to schemes that are then best exemplified, leaving no space for extensive interpretations. In a similar sense, C. Filippini, 'La Costituzione della Bulgaria', *in* M. Ganino (Ed.), *Codice delle Costituzioni*, cit., p. 5, which points out that the presidential powers of prerogative in the 1991 Constitution were even reduced if compared to those which had been introduced with the April 1990 revision to the old Socialist Constitution of 1971, due to the fact that the Bulgarian Socialist Party – former Communist – was losing hope of controlling this position, hence fearing to lose control of the transition process. *See also* J.-P. Massias, *Droit constitutionnel des États de l'Europe de l'Est*, cit., pp. 310 *et seq.*, who makes it clear that in this country, as elsewhere, the role of the President is that of a mediator, qualified as "pouvoir moral",

generality of the provisions in this regard, is found in the Slovak Constitution (Arts. 102 and 110). The case of the Polish Constitution of 1997 can be considered intermediate, which represents the formally conclusive phase of a process of incremental adaptations inaugurated in 1989, where the process of formation of the government is subjected to a series of steps[57] that seem to evoke those foreseen by the Article 63 of the German Fundamental Law of 1949, with the peculiarity that the vote of confidence is collegial and not focused on the dominant figure of a chancellor as in Germany. There is in Poland a possibility of giving rise to 'presidential' governments, on the condition that by this adjective it is understood that, as an extreme remedy, the candidacy to the office of premier is the result of a personal initiative of the President, and meets a smaller favour by of the Diet (*Sejm*) in the form of a relative majority rather than absolute vote, but certainly not in the sense that the head of state can impose a solution with the obvious hostility of the parliamentary institution.[58]

As for the presidential possibility of influencing the composition of the government in terms of the ministerial structure, the experience of Slovakia can be paradigmatic here.

---

being located outside of each of the three classic powers. The same author observes (*Ibidem*, p. 318) how any dualism in the forming of the government is excluded, and this to the full advantage of the Parliament, since the latter must cast a vote with all constitutive effects, electing the Prime Minister and following, on his proposal, each of the ministers (Art. 84, No. 6), and it also has to express an advice on any change to the structure, always on the proposal of the Prime Minister. One might ask, in light of this, if the Bulgarian parliamentary form of government does not reveal even a trace of assembly dominance (after all, the Bulgarian Constitution qualifies the form of government as a parliamentarian, despite the direct election of the head of state).

57 Analysed by R. Balicki, 'Head of State', *in* B. Banaszak *et al.*, *Constitutional Law in Poland*, Wrocław, Wolters Kluwer, 2012, p. 123, who also claims that "the President also plays an active role in the process of forming the government". C. Filippini, *La Polonia*, Bologna, Il Mulino, 2012, p. 84, notes the gradual reduction of presidential powers in the Polish legal system – from the first revision of 1989 to the Socialist Constitution of 1952, to the constitutional law of 1992, bearing the c.d. "Small Constitution", to the 1997 Constitution – just in this respect. It is no longer possible to form 'governments of the president', the obligation to consult for the appointment of ministers of the interior, foreign, defence is suppressed, residual accountability of the government is envisaged, which is responsible for decisions on all policy questions which are not reserved to other organs of the state and territorial self-government (with limits to possible extensive interpretations of presidential attributions). Moreover, B. Banaszak, *Outline of Polish Constitutional Law*, Wrocław, Wydawnictwo Uniwersytetu Wrocławskiego, 2005, points out (p.111) that, even in government reshuffles, the President may be obliged to carry out certain actions, having his activity "a purely formal character, as he has no legal competence to oppose or suspend the decisions concerning the changes in the government".

58 With regard to the situation in Bulgaria, the possibility exists (Art. 99.5 of the Constitution) to form an 'official' government that could also be qualified as presidential, if an agreement has not been reached in the National Assembly to elect one with substantial fiduciary procedure (similar provision in the Croatian Constitution, Art. 112). However, according to the jurisprudence of the Constitutional Court of this country, this government "can exercise extremely limited powers because of its temporary nature and because it does not originate from the Parliament" (Decision No. 20/1992, cited by C. Filippini, 'La Costituzione della Bulgaria', cit., p. 7). That such government has the nature of a caretaker administration is confirmed by the mandatory provision, in the same paragraph, of the contextual call of elections: the fact that a new Parliament will be elected, therefore, is the only circumstance capable of justifying, however for a very short time, the formation of a government that rests on the sole personal presidential confidence.

In this country the ministerial reshuffles have been the subject of discussion, since the original text of the Constitution, with the assertion that appointments and removal of ministers were carried out by the President on the proposal of the head of government, left room for interpretation. In particular, it was wondered whether this proposal required the head of state to comply with the Prime Minister's proposals, or whether the former, taking into account the proposal, could deliberate in a different way. After conflicts in this respect the Slovak Constitutional Court decided in the second sense. However, it is significant that a subsequent revision of the Constitution has clearly established that the President is always bound by the Prime Minister's proposal.[59]

The situation, in this matter, is not fundamentally different in the countries that have opted for the non-direct presidential election. Probably the smallest influence in the formation of the government is assigned to the President in Hungary, but this derives from a model of chancellorship, already present previously and further strengthened by the Basic Law of 2011, together with the combination of the party system and the electoral system, already mixed but with prevalence of majority mechanisms, and modified in 2011 accentuating the latter.[60] The case of Hungary is yet another confirmation of how much the political landscape, in turn influenced by the mechanism of transformation of votes in seats, also conditions the interpretation of the formal requirements relating to relations between the constitutional bodies, as it is a system that since the beginning of the democratic transition, in contrast with almost all neighbouring countries and with similar wealth of historical experience, has chosen mixed electoral formulas (as well as Lithuania or Albania) but with a clear majority and single-member prevalence.[61] This, unlike what normally happened elsewhere, has encouraged the formation of fairly compact one-party majorities at the end of the elections, corroborating the features of rationalization and chancellorship already present in the constitutional provisions.

Considerations similar to those outlined above can be made with reference to the presidential powers to obtain, on his-her own initiative and with political motivations, the resignation of a government, which for hypothesis continues to enjoy the parliamentary confidence or which in any case has not ascertained the interruption of that relationship. The space for interventions of this kind is reduced to the minimum that can be imagined. There are no formulas so short as that contained in Article 8 of the French Constitution,

59 L. Cibulka & M. Mokra, 'The Slovak Republic', cit., p. 698.

60 G.F. Ferrari, 'La Costituzione dell'Ungheria (2011)', *in* M. Ganino (Ed.), *Codice delle Costituzioni*, cit., p. 395.

61 For an analysis of the Hungarian 'combinatorial' system, adopted from 1990 until 2010, *see* F. Lanchester, *Gli strumenti della democrazia. Lezioni di diritto costituzionale comparato*, Milan, Giuffrè, 2004, p. 241. The new formula, used since 2014, is instead described by G.F. Ferrari, 'La Costituzione dell'Ungheria', cit., p. 395-396. The experience now achieved allows us to conclude that, despite the change in some technical aspects, we cannot appreciate a significant difference in terms of the disproportionality of the system. The OECD reports after the 2014 elections, however, highlighted even gerrymandering phenomena.

concerning the appointment[62] and acceptance of the resignation by the Prime Minister, the latter often interpreted as meaning that the President of the Republic can impose those resignations. Indeed, in the case of Romania, for some time and by some still considered as the one that comes closest to the French prototype, the provision according to which "The President of Romania cannot revoke the Prime Minister" results from an amendment adopted in 2003.[63] Identical evolution, through an explicit revision process, occurred in Croatia.[64] Therefore, even if one prefers to define semi-presidential some of these systems because of the mode of election of the head of state, and perhaps also for the fact that in part of them (as in Poland and Romania) he is formally included within the executive power, there is no reason to believe that, from the point of view of the mentioned powers, any system comes close to the French model of 1958 (whose text in these respects has remained unchanged).

3.2.4 *The Presidential Involvement in the Activation of Instruments of Direct Democracy*

Some additional place is left to contemplate an active presidential role, in some situations, in the activation of mechanisms of direct democracy, or popular participation in representative democracy. Here Article 48 of the Latvian Constitution is relevant, according to which the President of the Republic has the power to propose the dissolution of Parliament (*Saeima*), but this proposal is bound to a mandatory confirmatory referendum.[65] In the event that more than half of the votes are expressed against the dissolution, however, the President is considered as automatically removed from his office (Art. 50). The provision, which is part of a context in which the exposition of the head of state is otherwise politically very small, suggests a purely presidential power to dissolve; however, the possible sanction is so heavy that it induces any head of state to use much caution in this respect. In the years of the democratization, following the reconquest of independence (1991), the mentioned

62 As aptly recalls M. Lesage, 'Il modello francese nelle nuove Costituzioni dei Paesi dell'Europa dell'Est', *in* S. Gambino (Ed.), *Costituzionalismo europeo*, cit., p. 152, "the French Constitution allows the President to appoint the Prime Minister without prior investiture by the Assembly. The Constitutions of Eastern Europe have chosen, in most cases, the most classic model of the Prime Minister previously invested by the Assembly".

63 M. Ganino, 'La Costituzione della Romania', cit., p. 259, who points out how previously – in 1991 and in 1999 – such removals, or resignations-revocations, had taken place twice, in the silence of the text about their admissibility.

64 T. Cerruti, 'La forma di governo della Croazia: da "presidenzialismo" a regime parlamentare', *Diritto pubblico comparato ed europeo*, No. IV, 2001, pp. 1818 *et seq.*

65 Ultimately, therefore, it is uncertain whether the topic of the referendum or rather the issue of dissolution should be included in the focus of the political conflict. It is even debatable whether the activated instrument is a referendum or a plebiscite.

power was, however, only used once in Latvia, in 2011, with a popular response clearly favourable to the presidential dissolution proposal.[66] That appears typical of certain rationalistic technicalities of some Constitutions enacted after the first post-war European period, but to some extent it is the opposite of the German Weimar Constitution, which – as we know – enabled the *Reichstag* to suspend the head of state with a qualified majority, with the obligation to hold a referendum which, in the event of an adverse outcome to the deposition, would have led to the dissolution of the Reichstag itself.[67]

Even in Romania the power to hold referendum belongs to the head of state (Art. 90), to "ask the people to express their will on problems of national interest". The absence, in the textual formulation, of substantial limits regarding the initiative and the object, as explained, becomes relevant in the perspective of an active President.[68] However, the ambiguity of the premise "after consulting Parliament", which is insufficient in itself, to clarify whether such consultation is also binding, should be underlined. So far, the practice seems to negatively answer this question, even if experience in itself shows that the referendum institution in Romania knows a rather uncertain implementation, and respect for the will expressed by the electoral body is not as faithful as one would expect.[69]

The President of Bulgaria does not have the power of initiative in referendum matters, since Article 98 of the Constitution specifies in this regard that the presidential calling of the referendum takes place "in the presence of a corresponding decision of the National Assembly". For what concerns Poland the subject is somewhat different. In this country the Constitution admits the possibility of holding deliberative popular votes "on matters of particular importance" (Art. 125 of the Constitution). The subjects authorized to hold such consultations are the *Sejm*, by an absolute majority of votes in the presence of at least half of its members, or the President of the Republic on authorization of the Senate, expressed by the same prior majority (and in this case – Art. 144, para. 3, para. 5 of the Constitution –, the decree convening the referendum is expressly taken from countersignature by the government).

The case of Poland is useful because it allows for a brief additional reflection on the subject. An institution like that of the referendum, undoubtedly inspired by the most

66 On this case, and on aspects of general theory which are related to it, *see* A. Kārkliņa, 'Dissolution of Parliament in Latvia: Legal Regulation and Practice', www.mruni.eu/upload/iblock/4ad/JUR-13-20-3-18.pdf (last accessed September 2018).

67 A different, and even more singular, tool of the Estonian Constitution (Art. 105) according to which the parliament (*Riigikogu*) can submit a draft law or another document of national interest to a referendum, with a decision taken by majority vote. If the popular vote gives a negative result with respect to the project, the parliament must be automatically dissolved. The provision is criticized for its irrationality, since it is not clear why the parliament should hold a popular consultation that puts at risk its own permanence in office (S. Baldin, 'I referendum arbitrali tra teoria e prassi applicative', *Federalismi.it*, No. 19, 2012, p. 7).

68 M. Ganino, 'La Costituzione della Romania', cit., p. 261.

69 As confirmed by the 2009 referendum for the overall reduction in the number of parliamentarians and the suppression of the Senate, advocated by President Băsescu and never implemented.

genuine democratic ideals, cannot be exempted from controls in the sense of mutual limitation between powers and organs of the state, under penalty of abuse and manipulation that ultimately risk being on course of collision with that underlying inspiration. At this point it becomes crucial to understand not so much who has the final formal power to call the consultation, which in some cases can be considered as a power-duty, as, on the one hand, who has the power of initiative in this respect, and, on the other, if such an initiative is binding for those with the final power to convene voters.[70] According to the law on national referendums, which in Poland dates back to March 24, 2003, it appears that the calling of a referendum by the *Sejm* can take place on its own direct impulse, but also at the request of the Senate, of the Council of Ministers or of a group of at least 500,000 citizens (Art. 63 in combination with Art. 61 of the Act). On the other hand, the wording of the regulations concerning the President (Art. 64 of the said law) makes it clear that the adoption of these decrees is based on his own initiative.

From the foregoing it appears that in Poland – but the reflection can be extended to other systems –[71] there exists the faculty for a fraction of the electorate to demand that the people be called upon to make decisions on certain topics. But the faculty is not equivalent to a guaranteed right of participation, since the ultimate decision on the matter belongs to the discretion of a legislative assembly, in other words to the dominant political majority in it (in the Polish case of the *Sejm*).[72] It follows that, in certain circumstances, a situation can arise for which the referendum becomes an instrument of which a dominant political structure takes advantage to consolidate its power, being able to choose, to deny or dispense

70 The Croatian legal system appears to be among the most open from this point of view, since there is the optional power for the parliament to hold referendum on various topics, a power also granted to the President of the Republic, provided that the question concerns matters relevant to the independence, integrity and existence of the Republic (Art. 87), and on condition that the proposal comes from the government and the relevant decree is countersigned. The parliament, however, is obliged to hold a binding referendum, with a wide choice of subjects, even when one tenth of the Croatian voters request it (Art. 87, para. 3). However, the law implementing the referendum provides that Parliament can turn to the Constitutional Court for a judgment of admissibility of the question, a fact which meets the critical opinion of a part of the doctrine (Z. Lauc & S. Ivanda, 'The Croatian Governmental System', *in* N. Chronowski, T. Drinóczi & T. Takács (Eds.), *Governmental Systems of Central and Eastern European States*, cit., p. 120), due to the fact that – in addition to the extreme procedural difficulties faced by voters to present their request – the power in question is attributed solely by the ordinary law on the referendum, without mention of it either in Constitution or in the (constitutional) law on the Constitutional Court. Also neighbouring Slovenia was inspired by great democratic openness, having made compulsory (Art. 90 of the Constitution) the convening of a legislative referendum when requested – along with the Council of State and a third of the deputies – even by 40,000 voters.

71 Consider the case of Estonia, where the referendum can be held on the exclusive initiative of the parliament, or *Riikikogu* (Art. 105 of the Constitution).

72 The case of Lithuania is slightly different, where Art. 9 of the Constitution, after having affirmed that "the most important matters concerning the life of the State and of the Nation are decided by referendum", it expressly states that the *Seimas* (the single chamber Assembly) should call it in the cases established by the law, while it may also be called if not less than 300,000 voters request it (a rather large fraction of the electoral body).

it, using direct democracy as a mere pretext or propaganda weapon.[73] In short, it is easy to reject 'inconvenient' referendum questions, even if they were not aimed at destabilizing the established authorities but solely at carrying out that merely arbitral function between representation and people that many remote-era theoreticians had aspired to realize. The question is of considerable importance, considering that often the political 'response' that rises from the depths of a country, the political direction that this shows to want to pursue, depends in an impressive way from the question or the questions that are addressed to it (and by those who address them), to the point that diametrically opposed can also be interpretations that these events are given at the international level.

In the light of what has been observed, it can therefore be concluded that in this geographical area the reception of French semi-presidentialism may appear, at least in part, more authentic and consistent with the prototype and the intentions to which it was inspired (Art. 11 of the French Constitution 1958) in this respect, that is to say that of the direct involvement of the people, than for the remaining powers examined here. Although it would be inaccurate, and ultimately unjust, to attribute to the constituents of these

73 Think of the political situation in Poland at the time of writing. The Parliament is dominated by a single party, the PiS (*Prawo i Sprawiedliwość*, or Law and Justice) which also holds the office of President of the Republic, in a context of strong concerns, internal and by the European institutions, for the respect of the constitution along with the principles of the rule of law. It happens that a sufficient number of subscriptions is deposited to request an opposition consultation on the reform of the school system recently approved by the government, but the latter makes no secret of its hostility in this regard, suggesting that it will be very unlikely for Parliament to be willing to follow up on referendum initiative (and in fact Parliament did not allow this vote to be called). On the other hand, the President of the Republic Duda announced for a year the idea of holding a consultative referendum, consisting of ten questions related to the revision of the same number of qualifying provisions of the 1997 Constitution (a doubtful referendum on the constitutional plan, since – among other things – the use of this instrument for the purpose is, if anything, subsequent and confirmatory of an already adopted revision law, as foreseen by Art. 235 of the Constitution). But in July 2018 the Senate, dominated by the PiS, rejected Duda's proposal, in part – according to widespread interpretations – because the idea of extending presidential powers to the detriment of those of the government, as in the intentions of Duda himself, was not appreciated; in part – above all – because all the polls predicted a failure in terms of voter turnout, not only for the foreseeable boycott of the opposition, with the risk of repercussions on the following electoral chances of the party and the President himself. It could be added, by way of example, that in Poland the government has long evoked the idea of a referendum on the EU measures concerning the relocation and reception of refugees and immigrants, which should have coincided with the general elections scheduled for the end of 2019 (if that was the case, Poland would follow the footsteps of Hungary, with its government referendum of October 2016, whose significant text read: "Would you like to allow the European Union to impose the re-allocation in Hungary of non-Hungarian citizens without approval of the National Assembly?". For the record, the No vote amounted to 98.36 percent of valid votes, but the consultation was invalidated for failure to reach the quorum, since only 44 percent of those eligible turned out). It is not a matter of complaining that this may be the next political destiny, but rather that legally this possibility exists, that is to say that referendums welcome to those in power – because they count on the possibility of winning them easily, using them in a demagogic key also as an instrument to improve its own electoral chances – can be held, whereas other referendums that are not acceptable to power may be rejected, in disregard for the proclamations of popular sovereignty brought by the constitution, and the principles that inspired the legislation on the referendum itself.

countries the intention to build a referendum of a substantially plebiscitary character, it is nevertheless true that the establishment of direct democracy, or forms of popular participation in representative democracy, remains in the area typically that of a referendum 'top-down' and not 'bottom-up'.[74]

3.2.5 *The Dissolution of Parliamentary Assemblies as Evidence Against an Excess of Presidential Powers*

According to the scheme previously mentioned, it is now appropriate to consider the presidential power of dissolution of the elective assembly (or of the assemblies, as in Poland and Romania). Although almost everywhere attributed to the President of the Republic in a formal way, this power is subject to varying degrees of limitation. Once more it can be observed that the limitations to which the presidential power of dissolution is subjected are circumstantiated in a manner similar to one another, beyond the title of legitimacy which derives from the mode of election of the head of state. Consider Poland among the countries in which the election takes place by universal suffrage, and Hungary among those who have opted for an indirect election. In the first legal system there are two circumstances that according to the Constitution legitimize what goes under the heading of 'shortening of the term of office': firstly, when, once terminated the last stage of a long procedure for the formation of the government, provided for by Articles 154 and 155 of the Constitution, the latter fails to obtain the confidence of the *Sejm* even by a relative majority of the votes; secondly, the dissolution is provided for by Article 225 of the Constitution if, within four months after the submitting by the government of the draft budget law, Parliament has not yet approved it and this was not transmitted to the head of state for the promulgation. In the first case, the dissolution is even mandatory, while the President remains left with a margin of choice only in the second. As for Hungary, it is envisaged (Art. 3 of the Fundamental Law of 2011) that the President can dissolve Parliament in the hypothesis that it has not been able to elect the Prime Minister indicated by the President himself within forty days of his proposal, or if the state budget has not been adopted by 31 March of each year. From this brief example we can deduce how limited are the margins

74 For this distinction, and more in-depth considerations in this regard, M. Luciani, 'Articolo 75', *in Commentario della Costituzione* (fondato da Branca e continuato da Pizzorusso), Bologna, Zanichelli, 2005, pp. 223 *et seq*. Similarly, T.E. Frosini, *Forme di governo e partecipazione popolare*, Torino, Giappichelli, 2008, p. 57, whose remarks are referred in particular to France, where "the referendum ends up losing its characteristic of being an institution that is formed from the beginning as manifestation of the popular will: it is no longer a request that comes from below, but rather is imposed from above". Even in some of the countries considered here, as we have seen, there is a similar risk of exploiting popular participation for the benefit of a political elite.

of choice attributed to the heads of state in these systems, which may even be slightly wider when they are elected in an indirect way.

There are some modest variations, such as that of Romania, where (Art. 89 of the Constitution) the dissolution is allowed if the Parliament does not grant the government a confidence vote within sixty days of the first vote, but only after at least two votes of refusal to grant it.[75] Still remaining in Romania, an interesting peculiarity can be seen starting from a case of impossibility of dissolution as an instrument of rationalization when a serious conflict of powers occurs. This refers to the possibility for the Parliament in a joint session to suspend, by an absolute majority of its members, the President of the Republic for "serious crimes, which violate rules of the Constitution" (Art. 95), with the Constitutional Court that precisely in this situation, however, seems to be reduced to an advisory role.[76] It seems indeed to be an exception to the principle of political unaccountability of a head of state, not the – rather usual – provision, on the contrary, of his empowerment, when the basis for asserting it is not a discretionary assessment of the power of political direction, but, on the contrary, doubts followed by investigations regarding specific crimes of constitutional importance. And the doubt that the first circumstance prevails over the second is also reinforced, and perhaps above all, by the merely consultative role played by the Constitutional Court in this situation. This exception to the political unaccountability of a head of state appears somewhat eccentric with respect to the canons of contemporary European parliamentary regimes,[77] re-echoing the approach of the German Weimarian Constitution of 1919 or even more that of the Austrian Constitution as amended in 1929, and presents furthermore a contradiction in terms. As well as in other constitutional regimes, a fully political body, such as parliament, is given the power

---

75 In general, for a restrictive interpretation of the presidential powers in the Romanian Constitution, and for a weak reinterpretation of the relative semi-presidentialism, I. Stanomir, 'Some Remarks on Romanian Semi-Presidentialism', *Comparative and European Public Law*, No. I, 2011, pp. 261 *et seq.*

76 As confirmed by V. Perju, 'The Romanian Double Executive and the 2012 Constitutional Crisis', cit., p. 259, with reference to the first of two attempts – which took place in 2007 – to remove President Traian Băsescu, in which the Constitutional Court interpreted Art. 95 as a legal sanction rather than as an instrument of ordinary and electoral politics. The Court then expressed the view that the suspension proceedings should only have been initiated if the President had committed "serious acts" against the Constitution, rather than whenever a political party or coalition had had sufficient votes to pass such a measure in parliament. Serious acts should be understood inter alia to interfere with the activities of other public authorities or acts aimed at disturbing the constitutional order or causing constitutional subversion. In any case, concludes the article, "the opinion of the Court is advisory only", hence any appearance of a judicial or even arbitration is removed from a conflict that should still safeguard the political irresponsibility of the head of the state. According to the same author (*Ibidem*, p. 263), "the political interpretation of the document is to be welcomed as a tool for preventing the presidentialization of the semi-presidential regime and for reinforcing the premier's role within the executive".

77 S. Soare & C. Preda, 'La Roumanie', *in* J.-M. De Waele & P. Magnette (Eds.), *Les démocraties européennes*, cit., p. 347, speak of eclecticism of the Romanian system of government even in this regard, adding that the Presidency of the Republic was the only public institution at the basis of constitutional crises (although this last statement can be partially corrected in the light of experience of more recent years).

to determine the suspension of another political body on the basis of legal considerations (serious crimes, violation of the Constitution), at the same time putting in a secondary role the subject who would have greater credibility or competence to judge on the merits. But the contradiction lies in the fact that what should be the final judgment is carried out by the people through a questionable arbitration function, consisting of a mandatory popular referendum with the task of resolving definitively on the dismissal of the president. Therefore, it is up to the people to determine not whether a head of state is performing well or badly according to political evaluations (which is normally assessed by elections, held at fixed intervals), but if it has committed constitutional offences. Even the provision of the referendum seems to be taken from Weimar, but with the peculiarity that if it gives a favourable response to the President, there is no provision for the dissolution of the Parliament.[78]

The political nature, at least in a large part, of the reasons that may underlie the initiation of such a procedure is confirmed by another very singular fact. The subsequent Article 96 of the Constitution, in fact, gives the House and Senate, meeting in common session, the power to indict the President "for high treason", by a two-thirds majority of the votes. First, the hypothesis of crime contemplated here could in part be absorbed also by the formulation of the previous Article 95, since the high treason – moreover still to be defined – would also be a serious violation of the Constitution, but, secondly, in this case the competence to decide is not of the people, with a referendum – typical expression of political will – but it is up to the High Court of Cassation and Justice, with a ruling of a jurisdictional nature. In Romania, therefore, there is a kind of duplication on the level of responsibility of the President of the Republic, but even if the parliament wanted to depose him by appealing to the people, without success, this does not bear consequences in the form of the threat of dissolution.[79] Proof of this attachment for the stability of the parliamentary terms of office is the fact that since 1996 there have been no more early legislative elections in Romania. This also confirms the favour that the parliament enjoys in the Constitution.

78 M. Ganino, 'La Costituzione della Romania', cit., p. 259, recalls how such a case has already occurred twice in the recent constitutional history, in both cases involving – for various reasons but without success, and also in different ways – President Traian Băsescu.

79 On the other hand, the Slovak Constitution (Art. 106, para. 3) adheres more closely to the Weimarian scheme, with the automatic dissolution of the National Council if the latter, acting by a majority of three fifths of all its members, called a popular vote, in fact a plebiscite, for the removal of the President of the Republic, then losing this plebiscite. Another difference with the Romanian case is that for which there is not even a hypothesis of a presidential functional crime, with the consequence that the form of Slovak government could even more deviate from the traditional principle of unaccountability of the head of state. Considerations in this regard in A. Di Gregorio, 'The Constitution of Slovakia', cit., p. 307, where the revision brought under Constitutional Law No. 9/1999 is mentioned, which has circumscribed some areas of excessive parliamentary centrality introduced with the 1992 Constitution, that in the 1990s had permitted informal practices of which the nationalist government of Vladimir Mečiar abused.

In the range of reasons justifying the power of dissolution, there are small variations on the theme, such as those of the Czech Republic, where the interruption of the legislature can also take place if the Chamber of Deputies does not give a ruling within three months on which the government had raised the question of confidence,[80] or in the event of too long suspensions of its activities, or of a prolonged inability to decide (Art. 35 of the Constitution). However, even in such cases the President of the Republic may proceed with the dissolution on a proposal of the Chamber itself, adopted with the consent of three-fifths of its members.[81] One wonders which legislative assembly can consent, besides by a majority so high, to be dismissed with reasons so critical in their regards.[82]

The above findings are such as to lead to the conclusion that it is not the heads of state who hold the fate of the respective national legislatures in their hands, but that the latter enjoy wide autonomy in determining, for better or for worse, their destinies. The detail with which the circumstances are taken such as to allow – and limit – the dissolution is similar in the unquestionably parliamentary forms (Czech Republic, even before the introduction of the direct election of the head of state, or even Hungary) and in those in which the head of State is directly elected (Poland, Romania, Bulgaria, Slovakia, although there is another case of 'arbitration' dissolution if the President has been confirmed in a referendum aimed at his revocation). In Albania (Art. 104) there is a hypothesis of dissolution, albeit formally presidential, at the express request of the Prime Minister if the government does not obtain a sufficient number of votes in favour of a question of confidence. A similar government impulse in the presidential dissolution is laid out with detail in the Serbian Constitution of 2006 (Art. 109). The cases of Romania and Lithuania are similar (Art. 89, paras. 3 and 58, para. 2 of the Constitution respectively), where the dissolution is excluded when the President's mandate enters its final semester.

Ultimately, from an overview of the systems belonging to this composite area not only emerges the hostility for forms of discretionary presidential dissolution, motivated with a desire to affect the national political direction, but on the contrary it becomes a general concern the safeguard, even before the stability of the executives from frequent and specious parliamentary 'ambushes', of the stability of the same legislature and its term of office.

80 The Senate can never be dissolved precisely because of the substitute function it must perform in these situations. It is elected by universal suffrage and is renewed for one-third every two years (Art. 16 of the Czech Constitution).

81 Self-dissolution is an additional possibility introduced with constitutional revision in 2009 (A. Di Gregorio, 'La Costituzione della Repubblica ceca', cit., p. 216). Apart from some regulations of the former Yugoslav area, it is also present in Poland (Art. 98, para. 3 of the Constitution), Hungary (Art. 3, para. 2 Basic Law).

82 Yet it is what happened in 2013, when the insistence of President Zeman in forming a technocratic government, in the presence of a narrow center-right majority hostile to it, has failed in parliament. One hundred and forty deputies out of two hundred, in this case, have voted in favor of what in fact presents itself as a self-dissolution.

What the constituents have generally wanted to protect is precisely the regular duration of the legislatures, perhaps as a protection of parliamentarism itself.

These countries did not, in principle, adopt models such as the French one or the British one, still in force, despite adjustments. These models, as it is known, identify respectively in the head of state and in the prime minister the actual engines of the decision-making process that leads to dissolving the political chamber, and provoke elections, in advance of the constitutional deadline of the legislature. In both cases mentioned, these are organs that fall within the executive power. In both, it is considered acceptable, if not almost inherent to the system, that the objective impossibility of continuing it must not necessarily be contemplated among the only causes of the early termination of the legislature, linked to minimum conditions of functionality of the legislative assembly; but that the subjective convenience, for political-strategic reasons, of the same holder of the power of dissolution, belonging – it should be repeated – to the executive, can be a sufficient justification, even if carefully motivated, to obtain early elections.[83] Certainly the constitutional experiences show how some provisions can be reinterpreted, adapted and partly bent to the needs or circumstances of the moment (consider how the institution of the question of confidence, as per Art. 68 of the German Fundamental Law, was sporadically used to resort to elections), but at least from the choices made by the constituents in the countries of the considered area it is quite unambiguous that the anticipation of the elections should only be considered as the last remedy for stalemates which are objectively not resolvable in any other way.

3.2.6 *The Role of the Presidents in the Law-Making Procedure*

Some traces of a more active involvement of the heads of state are to be found in the matter of the formation of laws. In the countries of the area in question it is not considered eccentric the idea that this organ possesses the legislative initiative, as shown by the Constitutions of Estonia (Art. 103, limited to the modification of the Constitution, which is already significant in itself); of Latvia (Arts. 47 and 65); of Lithuania (Art. 68); of Poland (Art. 118); of Hungary (Art. 6). In Bulgaria, the fact that the President is devoid of such a faculty can be much more than offset by the fact that he or she – together with a quarter of the members, a very high share – can promote amendments and additions to the Con-

83 This remains true despite the French constitutional review of 2000, which leads the presidential mandate to coincide substantially with the parliamentary term, and despite the British *Fixed-Term Parliaments Act* of 2011, which would exclude the calling of early elections as an expression, albeit with the caution of the case, of a substantial governmental will. In reality, in the first case the formal regulation of the power of dissolution has not been modified, eventuality that for various reasons remains not to be ruled out, and in the second one the recent – 2017 – affair of the British elections confirms how the will of the law can be interpreted and folded up to conform to the most traditional needs.

stitution according to an 'aggravated' parliamentary procedure and a 'super aggravated' one, both regulated by Chapter 9 of the Constitution[84] (a similar provision in Art. 161 of the Estonian Constitution). It is true that a President can hardly succeed in doing something in the matter, if he does not enjoy a qualified majority of parliamentarians willing to support his initiatives; nevertheless, it is an accentuated recognition of his position in an area of particular prestige for the direction of the State. Something in the subject has already been mentioned previously, and it is worth recalling here that the rate of effectiveness of the presidential initiatives, where foreseen, is almost everywhere scarce.

Greater effective political influence can be traced in the final phase of the legislative process, the one concerning the power to enact laws. This refers in particular to the potential presidential power to send back a law to parliament, the effectiveness of which depends largely on the procedures and majorities required for its possible re-approval, and possibly on the reasons – whether its prediction is inserted in the texts or based on interpretations of legal scholarship and jurisprudence – included in the referral itself. Thus, even in Bulgaria, which is recognized as the most parliamentary among the forms of government where the head of state is directly elected, the latter has a power to postpone the laws that must be passed by the National Assembly by a majority of its members (Art. 101 of the Constitution).[85] In different cases, like that of Hungary, there are no special majorities necessary with which the parliament should re-adopt a law postponed by the President, although the Hungarian is a case that still deserves some clarification.

It is the Constitution of Poland that presents the greatest potential presidential interference in the formation of laws.[86] With a very analytical discipline, it is established (Art. 122, para. 5) that the President of the Republic, at the end of a complex legislative procedure, can, with a motivated message, refer the law to the (only) Sejm, or Diet, for a review. The overcoming of this postponement can only take place with a vote, by the Diet, by a majority of three-fifths of those present in the presence of at least half of its members. It is, in fact, a potentially quite incisive veto power over the overall functioning of the form of government. While not even expressing the prototypical version of French semi-presi-

84 C. Filippini, 'La Costituzione della Bulgaria', cit., p. 11.

85 A similar provision in Art. 72 of the Lithuanian Constitution, in Art. 50, para. 2, of the Czech Constitution, in Art. 113 of the Serbian one.

86 It can be discussed how such a power of interference can be reconciled with that "inactive political arbitrator" spoken of by M.A. Orlandi, *Quando il semipresidenzialismo passa all'Est*, cit., p. 186, who also discusses a design of the constituents aimed at making the President a "neutral arbitrator among the active powers and substantially stranger to the influence of the parties". This may apply to the power of appointment of a large number of officials, to which reference is made (*Ibidem*, p. 189). But when it comes to referring laws to parliament for reconsideration, the question becomes complicated. Given the importance of the power in question, it is necessary to examine the personality of the President in office as well as the conformation of the parliament. At the present time, doubts are expressed about the presidency of Andrzej Duda, considered by many to be too compliant towards Jarosław Kaczyński, leader of the "Law and Justice" (PiS) party and in fact the true informal leader of the nation.

dentialism, it only can be understood in the context of its genesis. This dates back to the early stages of the democratic transition of Poland, which was pioneering in Central and Eastern Europe in early 1989. At a time when the previous system was partially liberalized with 'semi-free' elections leaving a limited area of competitiveness for the union and opposition movement Solidarity (*Solidarność*), it was deemed appropriate to assign to the President of the Republic (which, for a short time at the start of the transition, would have been General Wojciech Jaruzelski, the main representative of the old regime)[87] a role of restraining against possible leaks forward operated by a parliamentary majority that could have proved unpredictable, up to questioning the socialist principles of the state or the strategic-military alliance – formally still alive – with the Soviet Union. One of the means used was the postponement of the laws, to be overruled by the *Sejm* by a two-thirds majority (as foreseen since the constitutional revision of April 1989). This majority was indeed lowered with the Constitution of 1997 to three-fifths (with the exclusion then of the budget law: Art. 224 of the Constitution).

It is a matter of fact, however, that a power of referral with features of an effective veto has remained. Since political majorities of more than three-fifths are unlikely to be reached, it is clear that the head of state has a powerful instrument in Poland, above all as an obstacle to the political direction of government. And this is what almost always occurs in cases of cohabitation, revealing at this point a possible dysfunctionality of the Polish situation, which makes the President a stronger figure as an obstacle than as an impulse, which transforms it into a possible – but perhaps improper, and in any case informal – leader of the opposition, more than an authentic representative of the nation. When the conditions are created, the potential for the vanishing of the majority political direction is considerable, and the system's stability is dependent almost exclusively on spontaneous adherence to the principle of loyal collaboration between powers, only stated in the constitutional preamble. On the other hand, that it is a largely discretionary power seems confirmed – as well as the absence of countersignature – by the fact that the President, if he does not exercise it, can alternatively apply to the Constitutional Tribunal for this to verify the compliance of the law with Constitution (Art. 122, para. 2), and is bound to promulgate it only if such conformity has been established (Art. 122, para. 3). The fact that this last possibility can be exploited when there are legal doubts about the constitutional legitimacy of the law confirms that the 'veto' can be exercised due to the mere opposition of the President – here as a political actor, legitimized in this by the direct election – to the fact that a law enters into force (even if nothing prevents that considerations of this type fall

87 S. Ceccanti, *La forma di governo parlamentare in transizione*, Bologna, Il Mulino, 1997, p. 202, defined the position of the head of state in Poland, at that stage, as that of the guarantor of a 'finlandization' imposed by the fact that the choices policies of the country were free internally, yet bound to the Soviet hegemony (although declining) at an external level.

during the exercise of the veto).[88] The combination of these faculties shows how the head of state in Poland can play on different keys, when he intends to prevent a law from entering into force (or a government from implementing its own program).[89] In any case, this analysis presents reasons of interest for how a legal institution can, by a kind of inertia, survive the reasons that caused its genesis, even when these reasons are completely extinct, and continue to operate completely changing its meaning.

3.2.7 *The Presidents and Foreign Policy*

The last aspect that we had set ourselves to examine is the one relating to foreign policy. Here all the constitutions refer to a fairly traditional view of the previous experiences of Western Europe (but also of the same area, before the socialist experience). If we refer to the texts, there is almost no case where reference is not made to the high functions of representation of the President in relations with foreign countries or as far as defence is concerned (*ex multis*, Art. 80 of the Romanian Constitution: "The President of Romania represents the Romanian State and is the guarantor of national independence, unity and territorial integrity of the country", Art. 63, para. 1 lett. a) of the Czech Constitution: [The President] "represents the State abroad"; Art. 41 of the Latvian Constitution: "The President represents the State in international relations"). However, if we look a little deeper at the actual dynamics of powers, even in practice, we find out that rarely behind these statements of principle is there a role so incisive as to significantly exceed a ceremonial one.[90] Consider the question of international treaties. Even where the presidents are assigned not only the classic prerogative of the ratification, but also that of the relative negotiation – Czech Republic, Article 63, para. 1 lett. b, Slovakia, Article 102, para. 1 lett. a – it is envisaged that this attribution may be transferred to the government or to individual ministers, which in fact normally takes place. For the countries of the European Union a significant indication of the effective foreign policy strength of the relevant presidents is the fact that they, in place of prime ministers, participate in the summits of the European Council (as is the

---

88 A similar interpretation of the presidential veto power is accepted in Bulgaria: E. Tanchev & M. Belov, 'The Governmental System of the Republic of Bulgaria', cit., p. 101.

89 Broader remarks on these two institutions, on their respective use in practice and on the evaluation that has been given in doctrine in J. Sawicki, 'Polonia', cit., pp. 305 *et seq*. Similarly, as regards the Czech Republic, M. Kindlová & V. Pavlíček, 'The Czech State', *in* C. Kortmann & J. Fleuren & W. Voermans (Eds.), *Constitutional Law*, cit., p. II-39.

90 An exception seems to be that of Lithuania where the President (Art. 84, para. 1, No. 1) "decides the fundamental questions of foreign policy and, together with the Government, conducts foreign policy". Symptomatic that the head of state traditionally represents Lithuania in the European Council. There is however an author, A. Krupavicius, 'La Lituanie', *in* J.M. De Waele & P. Magnette (Eds.), *Les démocraties européennes*, cit., p. 56, which tends to diminish the presidential role, both as a whole and in this respect, stating that even in foreign affairs he cannot take initiatives except with the support of 'his' government.

case in France). As for those in the geographical area united by the socialist past, only Lithuania and Romania[91] share this practice. Although the constitutions of these Member States devote significant space to their membership of the European Union (also through subsequent revisions, such as those in the Czech Republic, Slovakia, Romania,[92] Croatia),[93] in general, the division of roles between constitutional bodies in this area it is not sufficiently clarified by the Constitution or even by the important revision laws that have been dedicated to the event, remaining entrusted to the law or even to practice with marginal risks of conflict, where the spirits of loyal cooperation do not prevail. In contrary cases the conflict may take legal connotations and be devolved to the jurisdiction of a court, as was the case in Poland with the decision of the Constitutional Tribunal in Kpt 02/08, issued in May 2009.[94]

91 In the case of Romania, which joined the EU in 2007, the decision was a suffered 'delivery'. V. Perju, 'The Romanian Double Executive', *cit.*, pp. 255 *et seq.*, reports with detail, shedding light on the clash between Prime Minister Victor Ponta and President of the Republic Traian Băsescu in 2012, which turned into a formal conflict of powers between the parties before the Constitutional Court. The conflict was resolved with a ruling substantially favourable to the second, on the basis of a rather textual interpretation of the Constitution – in particular of Art. 91 – which did not take into account, *inter alia*, the fact that this document – drawn up in 1991, 16 years before joining the EU, and when this event was not even taken into account – refers in the quoted article to rather traditional aspects of foreign policy, such as the signing of international treaties, accreditation of diplomatic representatives, in which much of Europe's relations are largely not involved, relations which in turn are much more susceptible to cause significant internal consequences, with respect to which the role of the government, responsible in front of the assembled rooms, is paramount. Moreover, the cited essay also refers to the exacerbation of the conflict due to the objectionable legal remedies adopted by the Ponta government in order not to publish the Constitutional Court ruling.

92 Which in 2003 even introduced a title No. VI, "The Euro Atlantic integration", composed of two articles consecrated each to the EU and NATO.

93 For the latter country we refer to Cerruti, 'L'adesione della Croazia all'Unione europea e i criteri politici', cit., pp. 15 *et seq.*

94 The judgment put an end to a formal dispute of allocation between powers (or organs) of the state. In the conflict, the late President of the Republic, Lech Kaczyński (PiS), claimed to participate in at least some summits of the EU. The government, then presided over by Donald Tusk of the Civic Platform (PO), did not wish for presidential interference in the European policy pursued by it, in compliance with the constitutional provisions. The Constitutional Tribunal, after paying homage to the 'majesty' of the presidential office, underlined the government's competence to define the guidelines of domestic and foreign policy (and of course, as influential on both, of the same European policy). Having drawn a distinction between the definition of European policies (which is always the responsibility of the Council of Ministers) and its possible representation in appropriate forums (which may also be delegated to the Head of State), the Tribunal essentially stated that the participation of the President of the Republic may be appropriate where decisions – especially if in the form of treaties – entail directly involving aspects such as the continuity of state power, territorial integrity, defense and command of the armed forces, which the Constitution solemnly attributes to the President. V. Perju, 'The Romanian Double Executive', cit., p. 255, offers a comparison between the judgments of the Polish and the Romanian constitutional court in the same type of conflict, highlighting the different conclusions reached by the two bodies. The Polish decision, apparently considered more favourably, is called 'far more nuanced', but perhaps without taking sufficient account of the fact that there is a textual data of the two Constitutions, which appears overall more favourable to the President of the Republic precisely in the case of Romania.

3.2.8 The Accountability of the President of the Republic

In the countries of this geographical area, in general, the principle of a traditional parliamentary approach of irresponsibility, for purely political reasons, of the head of state has taken root peacefully enough. This is tantamount to asserting that such institutions can be called to answer only for unlawful acts of a constitutional nature or at most legislative, and according to constitutionally established procedures and schemes which normally see a prior activation of the parliamentary assemblies in view of a formal indictment and a subsequent judgment by judicial bodies that have been made independent of interference and neutral with respect to political inclinations of a partisan type. On the one hand, the presidential institution must be preserved from actions which could be destabilizing for the State and, on the other, the impunity of someone who for a predetermined period holds office must be prevented; in other words the person must be distinguished from the function which is carried out, in the difficult attempt to reconcile the equality between persons with the inviolability of the function.[95]

From this premise, it is necessary to make a minimum differentiation between the presidential crimes contemplated in the texts of these constitutions to make use of the relative responsibility. These, with the synthesis of the case, are essentially of two types. The first is that of high treason, which in this form is recalled only by the texts of Bulgaria (Art. 103) and Romania (Art. 95), to which is added Lithuania (Art. 86) with the reference to the betrayal of the taken oath.[96] For the rest, the qualification of high treason remained one of the vaguely defined or definable, hard to qualify concepts of constitutional law.[97] However, it does not seem at all obvious, at least in doctrine, that the agreement with the enemy, in a strategic-military sense, or espionage activity, is to be understood as a dominant behaviour for the purposes of the classification of such a crime.[98] If it is not so, the feeling is strengthened that the high betrayal is essentially a duplicate, or a largely interchangeable figure, with the second type crime of which we intend to talk about, that is the violation

95 F. Frison-Roche, *Le «modèle semi-présidentiel»*, cit., p. 109.

96 From a systematic reading of the latter Constitution it appears that this oath is little more than a tautology, since the oath provided for in Art. 82 obliges the President-elect to state that he will be loyal to the Republic, to the Constitution and he will perform the duties of his office and be equitable. This is so true that the Lithuanian Constitutional Court, in its ruling of 31 March 2004 concerning the guilt of President Rolandas Paksas, stated that "a breach of the oath of office is always a gross violation of the Constitution and vice versa" (so V. Vaičaitis, 'The Republic of Lithuania', in J. Fleuren & W. Voermans (Eds.), *Constitutional Law*, cit., p. VI-29, to which reference should be made for the reconstruction of the related events).

97 Frison-Roche, *Le «modèle semi-présidentiel»*, cit., p. 109, with references to critical opinions by French legal scholars such as Olivier Duhamel, Yves Mény e Maurice Duverger.

98 This is the case, however, in the Czech Republic, where the Art. 65, para. 2, of the Constitution specifies under the category of high treason a behaviour "directed against the sovereignty and integrity of the Republic", but also adding to it a behaviour "against its democratic order", leading to the resulting confusion with the hypothesis of "serious violation of the Constitution", of which the same provision speaks earlier.

or attack on the constitution (which in some cases – Poland, Lithuania, Macedonia, Slovenia, Hungary – is complemented by serious violations of the law).

It is interesting to note in this regard that the Bulgarian Constitution does not distinguish between the two types of offence in the process necessary to ascertain and sanction it, while the Romanian Constitution does, as already mentioned previously. If on the one hand it can widen the field at least potential for presidential responsibility, on the other hand it risks further polluting the political nature of a sector that should remain as far as possible immune, given its delicacy. It is in any case peculiar that precisely in the circumstance of the "serious crimes, which violate norms of the Constitution", the suspension of the head of State by the parliament, which should be followed by a judicial ruling, is instead submitted to the people's vote in a referendum, a decision with a very political content and implications (with a merely advisory opinion of the Constitutional Court). And it is perhaps no coincidence that this was the procedure chosen twice to activate the responsibility towards a President, Traian Băsescu.[99]

Conversely, in all other cases, the parliamentary decision to indict is followed by a judicial decision for either acquittal or conviction. With regard to prosecution proceedings, they are generally regulated in a concise manner, although some texts govern them with more detailed. This is especially the case with Poland, Romania and Bulgaria, which have been inspired by German legislation in this regard, providing in each case, generally, high qualified majorities as a requirement for the respective heads of state to conduct such delicate checks of their work (two-thirds of the deputies in Bulgaria, two-thirds of the National Assembly in Poland, which is the joint session of the *Sejm* and Senate).[100] Precisely with regard to constitutional violations in Romania, here is the further peculiarity concerning the imposition of presidential accountability, as when the hypothesis is that of violating the Constitution, the decision to suspend the President – awaiting referral to the people's judgment in the referendum – is adopted only by the majority of Chamber and Senate members who are sitting in a joint session (the requirements to move high betrayal allegations, in accordance with Art. 96 of the Constitution, are the most stringent, as the majority to refer the head of state to the Supreme Court of Cassation and Justice reaches

99 The events related to both these constitutional conflicts (2007 and 2012), in which Parliament disregarded the advisory opinions No. 1/2007 and No. 1/2012 made by the Constitutional Court, opposed to the suspension of the President, are precisely reconstructed by S. Gianello, 'Il Presidente della Repubblica in Romania tra semipresidenzialismo mite e parlamentarismo a forte impronta presidenziale nella dottrina costituzionale e nella giurisprudenza della Corte costituzionale', www.forumcostituzionale.it/wordpress/wp-content/uploads/2015/05/gianello.pdf (last accessed September 2018). As proof of the facts, the 2007 referendum resulted in a clear victory for President Băsescu, while the one in 2012 saved the same personality only for failure to reach the quorum (with about 90 percent of favourable votes, this time, to his dismissal).

100 In Poland it is the Tribunal of State to rule on guilt (Art. 198 of the Constitution). This is a body of justice reserved to high officials of the State, which must be composed of professional judges, elected however by the *Sejm* for a period corresponding to its term. It is presided over by the first president of the Supreme Court.

two-thirds). Similar, indeed, is the case of Lithuania[101] where a presidential removal procedure has even ended positively (unlike in Romania). Here, due to some obscurity on the point in the constitutional text, it was not idle to ask the question of who actually can decide on the impeachment of the President. The Lithuanian solution, although very close to the Romanian one, is distinguished by two aspects: first, and more subtly, the ruling of the Constitutional Court takes the form of a 'conclusion',[102] if not a judgment, however, something more a mere advisory opinion; and secondly – with some contradiction – it must be followed by a parliamentary vote by the *Seimas* with which it is established whether or not to follow up with a possible guilty verdict.[103] This can be fatally linked to mere considerations of political opportunity; however, it remains true that a decision of the Constitutional Court of possible non-culpability of the President does not allow any opposite order by the parliament, as happened in Romania through the convening of questionable arbitration referendums.

In any case, the underlying defect of this whole system of sanctions is quite another. It is in the fact that in these countries – as elsewhere – the mechanisms of activation of the criminal-constitutional responsibility of the head of state, which in principle obey the criterion of separation of powers, in turn propitiated by the mere finding of otherness between constitutional organs, in practice respond to an eminently political impulse. In more explicit terms, one can well imagine a situation in which a president becomes the protagonist of serious constitutional offences – especially against third parties, perhaps organs with tasks of vigilance and guarantee – without this implying any questioning of his accountability, by parliament, for the simple fact that the political majority present in the latter coincides with the political affiliation of the former or even just because the president, for other reasons, enjoys a high popularity, so that the remaining political organs feel intimidated in some way and do not have the 'courage' to start a procedure against him. On the other hand, even a slight deviation from one's own powers, or from the overall role designed by the constitution, without causing serious or permanent alterations

101 As well as that of Montenegro, Art. 98, last paragraph, of the Constitution.

102 M. Mazza, 'La Costituzione della Lituania', cit., p. 117.

103 V. Vaičaitis, 'The Republic of Lithuania', cit., p. 30, which identifies this sequence: "the *Seimas* has the competence to initiate impeachment proceedings and has the power to make the final decision on whether or not to remove the president from office. Only the *Seimas* is competent to formulate impeachment charges and to appoint the *Seimas'* prosecutors and only members of parliament may vote to remove the president from office. Accordingly, the institution with power to impeach the president in Lithuania is the *Seimas*". However, it should be added that the Constitutional Court is the only body "with jurisdiction to determine if there are constitutional and legal grounds for the impeachment. In other words, parliament may not remove the president from office if the Constitutional Court is of the opinion that the president acted within the boundaries of his discretion and did not violate the Constitution. In this case, the role of the Constitutional Court is similar to that of a grand jury". *See also* G.T. Palubinskas, 'Democratic State-Building in Post-Communist Lithuania', *Lituanus. Lithuanian Quarterly Journal of Arts and Sciences*, Vol. 51, No. 4, www.lituanus.org/2005/05_4_2Palubinskas.htm (last accessed September 2018).

to the form of government or even the form of state, could cause strong tensions, and possibly a sanction (but here the role of judicial courts takes over) on the sole condition that political majorities do not coincide, in other words that there is a cohabitation. It is no coincidence that both procedures of political accountability – with legal pretexts – have been initiated in Romania, in a situation of this kind.

3.3 The Constitutional Position of the Government

3.3.1 The Powers of the Government in Constitutional Texts

An interesting profile under which to assess the position of governments in the legal systems of this area lies in the enunciation of their competences in constitutional texts. In general there is a greater detail than that observed on average in Western Europe, and this may indicate a greater circumspection towards the executives, since the criterion of the enumeration of attributions seems to be intended to delimit them (what reproduces at least in part the position of governments in previous socialist systems). In short, the distinction here to be made is that between countries that recognize to governments a range of general or even residual competences (in the broad sense of the term, that is to give them all the competences not expressly conferred to other state bodies) and countries that instead define attributions with an exactitude that even claims to be exhaustive. From this point of view, the comparative grid does not fully coincide with that concerning to the collegial-individual dichotomy in the government formation procedure described above.

In this perspective, the Constitutions of Bulgaria, Latvia, the Czech Republic, Romania, Slovenia respond to the logic of general-indefinite competence (in the last case Art. 114, para. 2 of the Constitution broadly refers to the definition of government activities), and in Hungary the broadest extensive notion of residual competence is given.[104] On the other hand, the Constitutions of Estonia, Lithuania, Poland, Slovakia prefer the criterion of enumeration or list of competences, although the Polish Constitution (Art. 146) presents a certain internal contradiction, with the setting of a dozen specific attributions and at the same time introducing the presumption of general jurisdiction "on the political issues of the state not reserved to other state organs or territorial self-government". In the latter case, it is clear that the enumeration is only an example of a range of broad powers.

104 The Hungarian Fundamental Law of 2011 (Art. 15), in addition to defining the government as "the general organ of the executive power", gives it responsibilities and competences "in all matters not expressly delegated by the Basic Law or by other provisions of the law responsibilities and responsibilities of another body". This is the most radical departure, at least on the lexical level, of the ancient parliamentary pre-eminence in the socialist systems.

3.3.2 *Parliamentary Confidence (a Decisive Institution Common to All the Area's Systems, Whether Semi-Presidential or Not)*

As is the case with all parliamentary systems, even in this geographical area, the government normally exercises the powers of an authentically 'governing body', and it does so through the established institution of parliamentary confidence. First of all, some lexical clarification should be carried out. A large part of the analysed constitutions uses the term "Government", while some (Poland, Bulgaria) prefer to use the more cautious wording of "Council of Ministers". Organs with the same qualities and the same role are often referred to in a different manner from country to country, and this has some significance on the symbolic level.[105] In any case, the vision of the government is dominant as a collegial and complex body, as a 'body of organs' within which a constitutional dignity is usually recognized also to individual members.

A qualifying aspect of the physiognomy of the government as an institution naturally lies in its formation. The constitutions of this area pay an unusual attention to the genesis of the executives, offering a rationalization that presents itself as one of the most complete disregards from previous socialist experiences.[106] An important aspect, by contrast with some Western European systems, is within the temporal limits set by different maps for the formation of the respective governments.

Even in these countries, as anywhere else, a differentiated position is attributed to the central or apical organ of the college. Having said this, it is not possible to speak of political pre-eminence everywhere for the benefit of this subject. An assessment of the prevalence of monocratic or collegiate data when it comes to the direction of government activities can be accomplished by the combination of legal-formal analysis with that linked to political practice. Naturally, the fact that a prime minister is more or less able to determine autonomously the political direction of the cabinet he presides over and impose on him, or rather be called upon to coordinate it on the basis of resolutions that must be previously agreed upon in a collegial way at the same cabinet, is a matter which is partly linked to the practice and to the changing conformation of a political system that only partly can be

---

105 Observed by V. Kutlešič, *Les Constitutions postcommunistes européennes*, cit., p. 109, which points out that, in the history of parliamentarianism, the term "Council of Ministers" accurately translated the qualities of this organ and its relations with the monarch. On the other hand, it is with the development of parliamentarianism that the organ that today is most often called parliament has made its appearance. From a practical point of view, however, this nominalist distinction does not have much significance, since the monarchical traditions of Poland and Bulgaria – the countries where this denomination is officially used – are not stronger than others.

106 It should be recalled that the official position of the governing body, in the socialist states, was that of an institution formally subordinated to the unlimited will of the assembly, almost relegated to the status of an administrative body (which was in fact more adherent to reality, since in fact the real decision-maker, compared to the official institutions of the state, was the dominant party).

determined by abstract prescriptions formulated once and for all in constitution. It has been affirmed that a sure political pre-eminence is found in the 'majority parliamentarianism' systems, where the political leader who wins the elections does not generally encounter any conflict in being appointed head of government; and that whereas, instead, coalition governments prevail, not directly pre-constituted following electoral consultations but deriving from agreements entered into by parliamentary groups, relatively detached from the results of the elections, the top of the government tends to limit its functions to those of a coordinator-mediator between the different components of the majority.[107] However, there is a minimum of constitutional data capable of providing clues to preferences expressed in this regard by the forces prevailing at the moment of the formation; and it easily happens that the conformation of the party system, also because of the chosen electoral system, confirms the preferences expressed in the drafting of the constitution, so that the political data coincides with the legal-formal one.

Thus, it appears that, in partial contrast with some Western European trends, the great majority of countries in this area have preferred to entrust their executive to a strong collegiality, sometimes – as in the almost extreme case of Bulgaria – with a first minister relegated to a role of *primus inter pares*[108] (analogous to the case of Macedonia).[109] In some cases, however, the practice, influenced by a spontaneous evolution of the party system, has ended up transforming into the pre-eminence of the president of the college what ought not to be strictly due to the will of the constituent. As far as Poland is concerned, the formal juridical provision that provides for collegiality starting from the same procedure of formation of the government – procedure for other aspects resembling, as already mentioned earlier, to that foreseen in the German Fundamental Law – has had to be adapted to a growing adherence, in practice, to the German model of the chancellorship (corroborated by the decadence of the entire Council of Ministers on the occasion of the resignation, however motivated, by its president, also called premier). The evolution in this sense of the Polish form of government, which has weakened the elements of semi-presidentialism, subject to the exceptions highlighted above, began a few years after the entry into force of the 1997 Constitution and culminated with almost two full terms of the premiership of Donald Tusk.

107 G. de Vergottini, *Diritto costituzionale comparato*, V Ed., Padova, Cedam, 1999, p. 546.

108 C. Filippini, 'La Costituzione della Bulgaria', cit., p. 6. The observation seems to be confirmed by the fact that out of Art. 105-116, consecrated to the Council of Ministers, the first three refer only to the organ in its collegiality, and only by Art. 108 the prime minister begins to be mentioned. Moreover, it results from E. Tanchev & M. Belov, 'The Governmental System', cit., p. 105, that the process of formation of the government in the Bulgarian Constitution of 1991 was inspired by the 1975 Greek Constitution, a fact which influenced both the geographical proximity and the political fragmentation of young democracies emerging from a long authoritarian phase.

109 K. Schrameyer, 'The Republic of Macedonia', in N. Chronowski, T. Drinóczi & T. Takács (Eds.), *Governmental Systems*, cit., p. 491.

In the perspective of constitutional provisions, the rate of collegiality of governments can be assessed by focusing on the modalities of the fiduciary investiture, observing whether this is aimed at the top or at the complex organ. If we keep this in mind, we must conclude that confidence in the only president of the college – which brings the form of government to a sort of chancellorship – is, in this area, an exception that confirms the rule. An individual confidence is placed in particular in Albania, Hungary and with some peculiarities in Estonia.[110] Lithuania, which presents a mixed system from this point of view, escapes this classification, as both an initial individual confidence vote and a subsequent collegial one are mandatory.

It is especially in Hungary that the major similarities with the German model are registered (*mutatis mutandis*), through the strengthening, by the Fundamental Law of 2011, of the monocratic principle which places the primacy of a prime minister over ministers appointed and removed by him. Even in the case of Hungary, moreover, this reinforcement is also found in the absence of the formal granting of an initial confidence vote on the political programme,[111] replaced by the election of the supreme organ of the executive by the parliament on the proposal of the President of the Republic (Art. 16, para. 3 of the Constitution). If at first sight the elective procedure may resemble the proper fiduciary procedure, a closer look will depart from that because it does not underline the sharing of political-programmatic lines, which are not the object of discussion either before or after election, while it is above all the personal characteristics of the elected person to establish himself at the centre of parliamentary elective deliberation.[112] Parliament is required to express itself within a period of fifteen days on the candidate proposed by the head of state, by a majority vote of its members. If this deadline should expire in vain – it should be pointed out that this is a rather unlikely eventuality in the current configuration of the Hungarian political system – the initiative to propose a new candidate must always start from the head of the state. In case of failure to elect even after this second procedure, it is up to the President of the Republic to dissolve the single-chamber Parliament, after hearing the outgoing Prime Minister still in charge for current affairs, the president of the chamber and those of the parliamentary groups. Even the procedure for appointing ministers, which is carried out by the head of state on the proposal of the newly elected prime minister, suggests a prevalence of the latter in the effective formation of the government, as confirmed both by the individual confidence and by the fact that this takes place before the formation

110 K. Merusk, 'The Republic of Estonia', cit., pp. III-30 *et seq.*, where the prime minister is described a *primus inter pares* as far as the direction of government business is concerned, and even when it comes to the coordination of its meetings.

111 G.F. Ferrari, 'La Costituzione dell'Ungheria', cit., p. 396.

112 Thus G. Romeo & E. Mostacci, 'La forma di governo', cit., p. 73. This seems to be confirmed by the fact that parliament can perform a series of control functions vis-à-vis the executive branch but appears to be excluded from the exercise of a real power of political orientation.

of the entire college. The use of the criterion related to individual or collegial confidence, as an indication of a greater or lesser concentration of power within the executive body, seems to be supported by a textual data. Indeed, it is precisely in the Hungarian Fundamental Law that "the Prime Minister determines the general policy of the Government" (Art. 18, para. 1, the italics are those of the writer), rather than stating, as is done in most of the remaining constitutions, that he or she coordinates or directs it on the basis of resolutions adopted by the Council of Ministers.

The case of Estonia is also peculiar, because here the prime minister charged – by the President of the Republic – to form the government is obliged to present a programme to the parliament within two months from assuming office; the subsequent parliamentary vote, which actually counts as one of confidence, formally gives the authorization to form the government, whose structure must then be presented to the President of the Republic for the final appointment.[113] The Prime Minister's proposals concerning the formation of the government (and the removal of ministers) are to be considered binding on the head of state. In Lithuania there is a complex procedure that sees first the appointment by the President of the Republic to a prime minister, which must be confirmed by a vote of confidence by a simple majority by the parliament (*Seimas*); then the 'premier', corroborated by the vote, must present the list of ministers to the President of the Republic; finally, the government formed in this way must appear again before the *Seimas* for a new vote of confidence, this time collegial, always with a simple majority.[114]

In other systems, as we said, the confidence relationship is characterized by a more or less marked collegiality, as evidenced by the clue of confidence or investiture to the complex organ rather than to its single top post. This is the case, for example, of Poland – as mentioned above – of Croatia, the Czech Republic, Latvia, Macedonia (Art. 90), Romania (Art. 103, para. 3 of the Constitution, where – absolute peculiarity, together with Italy –, both chambers have to grant confidence, in the case of Romania "with the majority vote of the deputies and senators" meeting in joint session), of Serbia (Art. 127), of Slovakia,[115] while in Slovenia a hybrid procedure is envisaged – with partial curtailing of the head of state – which first sees the election of the President of the Government (on the proposal of the President of the Republic) by the National Council, and subsequently, again by the National

113 M. Mazza, 'La Costituzione dell'Estonia', cit., p. 54.

114 M. Mazza, 'La Costituzione della Lituania', cit., p. 119.

115 Where, as reported by D. Cibulka & M. Mokrá, 'The Slovak Republic', cit., p.698, the Constitution was amended in the sense of binding the President of the Republic to the will of the head of government in the appointment and dismissal of ministers. The revision dates back to 2001 and overrules a previous judgment by the Constitutional Court (ÚS 39/93) which recognized instead the head of state a wider margin of appreciation in the decision on the fate of ministers. Moreover, in Slovakia there is also the forecast, normal at constitutional level for parliamentary assemblies but unusual for a government, for which (Art. 118 of the Constitution) the absolute majority of its members is required not only for the validity of a session, but also for the adoption of its resolutions.

Council, the election of ministers proposed by the President of the Government.[116] The case of Albania is also atypical, where an individual investiture of the Prime Minister by the President of the Republic is foreseen (Art. 96 of the Constitution), and only after the approval of the Prime Minister designated by the Assembly, an exposé of the programme takes place, with a request of confidence for the entire ministerial structure (Art. 97).

Another qualifying aspect of the parliamentary system, or in any case of the parliamentary elements present in the form of government of these countries, lies in the parliamentary majority required to confer confidence or to 'elect' the government or the prime minister. If compared with the majorities and the remaining conditions to be met in order to overthrow the governments themselves, or force them to resign, it makes clear the level of rationalization of the form of government which was achieved here.

First of all it should be noted that the vote of confidence or investiture, where the parliament has a bicameral structure, is reserved to the so-called lower chamber, a place where the full expression of the political will of the country is usually given. The exception to this is Romania (Art. 103, para. 3 of the Constitution), where the Chamber of Deputies and the Senate grant confidence in a joint session.[117] In any case, the requirement of the favourable vote of the majority of the members of an assembly is clearly prevailing. An absolute majority of members for the expression of confidence is required in Bulgaria, in Romania – with the deliberative chambers in joint session under the aforementioned Article 103 Cost. – in Hungary for the aforementioned prime minister's election vote and in Slovenia. The simple majority of the votes, in the presence of the quorum of the majority of members of parliament, is instead requested in Estonia, Latvia, Poland, Slovakia and the Czech Republic (where the quorum for deliberation amounts to just one-third). In these last three countries, however, the majority of votes to express confidence is counterbalanced by the absolute majority of members to approve the withdrawal thereof. These are among the most basic elements of rationalization, in which the constituent will was to facilitate the formation of governments in the face of disincentives for their removal.

116 This multiple and individual vote of confidence, inspired by an assembly-oriented ideology, is confirmed by the fact (Art. 112 of the Constitution) that each minister, before the vote, must appear before the parliamentary committee responsible for the relevant subject-matter in order to submit to an appropriate hearing.

117 In accordance with the fully multinational nature of the state (and the international process that gave rise to it), in the case of Bosnia-Herzegovina the President of the Council of ministers is appointed by the collegiate presidency of the state (composed of a Bosnian and a Croat, elected from the territory of the Federation, as well as a Serb elected from the territory of the Republika Srpska) pursuant to Art. V para. 4 of the Constitution. He then proceeds to appoint ministers in accordance with ethnic criteria. Here, in short, the mechanism of parliamentary trust seems replaced by another logic, which responds to the need to weigh up the ethnic groups that make up the federation. But the parliamentary form reappears in lett. c) of the same paragraph, where it is expected that the Council of Ministers should resign as soon as it takes a vote of no confidence by the Parliamentary Assembly, a complex body, composed of the House of Peoples (formed by delegates appointed by each of the ethnic groups) and the House of Representatives (which is elected by universal suffrage).

A similar case is that of Slovenia, where (Art. 111 of the Constitution) an absolute majority of deputies is expected in the first vote, but with the possibility of a subsequent resolution by majority vote if the outcome of the first vote has not proven fruitful.

3.3.3 *The Political Accountability of Governments*

Several countries provide as a further rationalization tool the possibility for the governments themselves to put at stake the previously obtained parliamentary confidence. This refers in particular to the Polish (Art. 160), Czech (Art. 71), Romanian (Art. 114), Slovak (Art. 114, para. 3), Macedonian (Art. 93), Albanian (Art. 104), Serbian (Art. 131), Slovenian (Art. 117), and Hungarian (Art. 21, para. 4) Constitutions. Only Romania, however, brings such an approach to the extreme limit of what is admissible in a still parliamentary regime; only it goes as far as to the version of a true semi-presidential system, conforming to the model established by the French Fifth Republic, which it follows even at the lexical level ("The Government can engage responsibility" [...] "about a program, a general policy statement or a draft law"). The feature in common with France is proven by the fact that it is not limited to linking the question of confidence to the approval of a text of government bill, but that it goes as far as to establish that the latter is to be considered approved only on the condition that the legislative – in this case the Chamber of Deputies and the Senate in a joint session – does not assume the responsibility of expressing the lack of confidence in the government by a majority vote of its members.[118] Even in other cases, however, (Slovakia or Slovenia), we can discuss of a real question of confidence put by the government, to which it is expressly connected "the vote on the adoption of a law or the vote on another question" (according to the terms of the Slovak Constitution, Art. 114, para. 3). In the Slovak legal system, however, the tool does not seem to be used frequently neither does it play a significant role in the functioning of relations between powers.[119] In this system too, therefore, an instrument that elsewhere – as in Italy – is used incisively in practice or in accordance with parliamentary rules of procedure, even in the silence of the constitution, expresses almost nothing of its potential. As for Poland, it appears that in the debate that preceded the adoption of the 1997 Constitution the question was raised whether to link the governmental initiative for the request of a renewed vote of confidence to the parliamentary approval of a specific provision. The text, like others, is silent in this

---

118 If anything, the form of government designed by the Romanian Constitution differs from the French one in that, with this as well as with other instruments – such as the legislative delegation or the emergency ordinances pursuant to Art. 115 of the Constitution – it undoubtedly strengthens the government to the detriment of the parliament, but does not achieve instead the further strengthening of the President of the Republic at the expenses of the cabinet.

119 D. Cibulka & L. Mokrá, 'The Slovak Republic', cit., p. 701.

regard. There has been an initial doctrinal division in this regard, where some have interpreted the silence as an opening to potentially very substantial developments, similar to the Italian ones, of the system of government. But the prevailing opinions, in addition to a well-established experience, lead us to the clear conclusion – comforted by the fact that amendments were rejected to expressly link the issue to the approval of concrete government documents – that the renewed request for confidence does not express any other value that which is intrinsic to the institution, even if the question remains open about the practical usefulness of such an institution.[120] However, it is undisputed that the rejection of a government request of confidence amounts to the obligation for the cabinet to resign.[121] If in most of the cases mentioned, such a situation highlights an overall preference of these laws for the legislature to the detriment of the executive – if the government has solicited the assembly and received a negative response, in short, the assembly remains and the government must go –[122] Albania and Slovenia constitute, the first with the Article 104 and the second with the Article 117 of the respective Constitutions, a relevant exception to all this. In Albania it is expected that if the request for confidence is approved by less than half of all members of parliament, the Prime Minister asks the President of the Republic to dissolve the latter (an act that must be issued without a doubt). Only in this case, therefore, a negative parliamentary response to a government request for repeated legitimacy is sanctioned with a sort of *aut simul stabunt aut simul cadent*. Only in the Albanian case, in short, the model provided for by Article 68 of the German Fundamental Law was adopted, with the peculiarity that in Albania the request for early elections must be accepted, since the alternative possibilities opened up in Germany do not exist.[123]

3.3.3.1 The Constructive No Confidence as a Further Rationalization Tool (and Its Low Impact on the System)

A known element of rationalization consists in the 'constructive no confidence'. There are few systems in the area that have chosen to adopt this legal arrangement on the substantial lines of the German federal model. Poland, Hungary, Slovenia and Albania have resorted

120 R. Mojak, *Parlament a rząd w ustroju trzeciej Rzeczypospolitej Polskiej* [Parliament and government in the system of the third Polish Republic], Lublin, Wydawnictwo Uniwersytetu Marii Skłodowskiej-Curie, 2007, p. 575.

121 In Poland, furthermore, this is a situation that can create a revocation of the government with a purely 'negative' vote, contrary to the rationalizing inspiration of the form of government, inspired by the vote constructive non confidence (Art. 158).

122 This can be understood, better than any other, by the example of the Slovak Constitution, which – Art. 115, para. 3 – when limiting the powers of the governments which resigned following a vote of no confidence or a rejection of the question of confidence, indicates how the exercise of those limited powers applies "until the new government is appointed".

123 In the case of Slovenia, the State Chamber is entitled to elect a new "President of the government" within thirty days, or to confirm the one in office with a new vote. Only if this does not happen, new elections must be held.

to this (the latter with a 2008 revision).[124] The choice was less surprising in the case of Hungary, as it is the country that since the beginning of the transition has made no secret of wanting to incorporate with a certain precision the German model of the 'Chancellorship', which is inherent in that way of taking note that the relationship of parliamentary confidence is exhausted.[125] In the case of Poland, the option denotes a certain eclecticism of the chosen form of government, alongside the undisputed institutional prestige enjoyed by neighbouring Germany. But ultimately we must take note of the extremely recessive role that this arrangement plays in the systems considered here,[126] which at first were attracted by a certain intellectual fashion, strengthened by its high reputation, and by the positive performance – also deriving from other reasons – of the country that first introduced and enforced it.

An explanation for this phenomenon cannot come from an analysis inspired by rigorous legal formalism, since the requisites for resorting to the instrument are not so strict –[127] which should favour its use – nor, of course, can one expect the explanation of its sporadic and very limited use from the wording itself. It is therefore necessary to resort to canons of interpretation closer to political science, which in this case help to interpret the living functioning of the constitution, what in fact *it is* beyond, but not necessarily in contrast, with what *ought to be*. The recessive position of the instrument can be attributed to the fact that the remaining instruments for the stabilization of the executives, and the legislatures themselves, have appeared on the whole sufficient.[128] But even where this had not

124 The case of Serbia is slightly more nuanced, as the Constitution (Art. 130) does not formalize the imposition of the constructive non confidence, but requires the formation of a new government, and the vote of confidence in it – obliging the head of state to take action in that sense – within thirty days of the resignation imposed on the previous government by a vote of parliamentary no confidence, under penalty of the mandatory call for early elections. Ultimately, it seems that the only thing that has been renounced is the immediate the election of the successor government, leaving the National Assembly a minimum amount of time necessary to reformulate its own guidelines. Furthermore, it is envisaged – at the last paragraph of the same article – that the negative result of a vote of no confidence required involves the prohibition of proposing a similar motion for the next 180 days.

125 In the Hungarian case only once the constructive distrust was enforced with effective success: this happened in April 2009, when Gordon Bajnai took the place of Ferenc Gyurcsány, however within the same coalition government between socialists and liberal-democrats. Furthermore, it should be noted that the constructive no confidence was applied in this case in a consensual atmosphere, since Gyurcsány himself, far from opposing his own replacement, had offered his resignation the previous month.

126 It's reported by I. Brinar & M. Žagar, 'La Slovénie', *in* J.-M. De Waele & P. Magnette (Eds.), *Les démocraties européennes*, cit., p. 406, that only twice in Slovenia, since 1990, has a government been forced to resign because of a constructive vote of no confidence.

127 As for the request to put a vote for the constructive no confidence, the required number goes from one-tenth of the deputies in Poland (Art. 158 of the Constitution) to one-fifth in Hungary (Art. 21) and Albania, passing by ten deputies out of ninety in Slovenia. As a matter of course, the absolute majority of members is normally required to elect an alternative candidate or government.

128 V. Perju, 'The Romanian Double Executive and the 2012 Constitutional Crisis', cit., p. 251, notes that the absence of the institution in Romania has not prevented that countless motions of no confidence put to the vote in that country – which we could call 'destructive' – were rejected by the parliament. According to S.

been the case, due to excessive party pluralism, insufficient discipline of political forces or the relative unwillingness to recognize each other, the preferred solution to a crisis in these systems seems to be moving in another direction. When – as happens more frequently – the crisis is fully endogenous within the majority of government, and for some reason it is considered appropriate, keeping the majority unchanged, to proceed with the replacement of the highest position, then it is easier that the latter tenders his/her resignation 'spontaneously',[129] having acknowledged that there are no longer the conditions to continue in office (if the balances have been altered by the majority, proceeding to a constructive no confidence vote could unnecessarily highlight internal disagreements). On the other hand, when the crisis is a prelude to a collapse of the majority or even to a radical mutation of the same during the legislature, the preferred way seems to resort to an early election, which – even where not easy to obtain – seems to be more respectful of popular sovereignty. Even in democracies like these, which always seem to be based on a certain centrality of the parliament, the immediacy of the relationship between the political majority and the elective body prevails, preference is given to a model of democracy in which voters determine that majority as directly as possible, and are immediately called upon to resolve any tensions within the majority itself.

With all this, it is not meant to devalue the potential of the instrument, which could someday start to re-develop in an unexpected way. It could also be argued, on the contrary, that the proof of the effectiveness of the constructive non-confidence is found in the little use that has been made of it (as indeed in Germany),[130] since the difficulty of overthrowing

Soare & C. Preda, 'La Roumanie', cit., p. 354, there have been dozens of them, and even 32 between 2000 and 2004.

129 Think of recent – at the time of writing – developments in Poland. Here it happens that the motions of constructive no confidence are tabled with some frequency, but almost only for demonstrative purposes, by oppositions who know they have no chance to overthrow the majority. But a paradoxical situation was reached in December 2017, when a motion of no confidence was filed by the opposition led by the Civic Platform (PO), with a view to replacing the sitting premier Beata Szydło (PiS) with Grzegorz Schetyna, leader of the PO. After the motion was largely rejected on 7 December – 239 votes against, 168 in favor and 17 abstentions – Szydło tendered her government's resignation in the hands of the President of the Republic Andrzej Duda the next 8 December only to be replaced by her former minister of economy Mateusz Morawiecki (for completeness of information, before formalizing her resignation Mrs Szydło had gone to make available its mandate at the headquarters of the PiS party, "Law and Justice", and its leader, the simple deputy Jarosław Kaczyński). There is no doubt that the bizarre sequence of events above described reflects the qualitative mutation of Polish democracy in the last two years; however, it remains that, in the aforementioned facts, there is nothing formally unconstitutional. But the majority party, which for some time had deemed it opportune to replace her at the head of the government, first protected her from an obsession with the opposition; and then he accepted the "spontaneous" resignation, for reasons of internal balance, completely circumventing the modalities of substitution of a cabinet that the Constitution shows to consider the most appropriate, and in any case omitting a parliamentary passage of preliminary assessment of the crisis.

130 Very emphatically, A. Ágh, 'La Hongrie', *in* J.M. De Waele & P. Magnette (Eds.), *Les démocraties européennes*, cit., p. 190, considers the adoption of constructive no confidence in his country as the cause of the fact that it became the most stable in Central Europe and that from 1990 onwards *all* the parliaments and almost all

a government with this type of vote can conceal how much easier it would be to do it in the presence of a merely 'destructive' mechanism. However, some conclusions must be drawn from the fact that, firstly, few of these countries have decided to adopt the constructive non-confidence,[131] and, secondly, even when this has been done, its use has become an exception that confirms the rule, also not written, of a different way to solve the cabinet crises or changes of orientation inside the assemblies, whether these take place for spontaneous internal settlements or for external influence due to changes in public opinion. In other words, even in these systems the preservation of the stability of parliamentary terms is seen as a good to be protected; but not to the point of sacrificing to this, as an absolute good, the unfolding of political developments and changes. In short, the stability of the legislatures cannot impose an artificial stability of governments.

3.3.4 *The Position of Ministers*

The ministers are part of the collegiate body called the council of ministers or government, and are holders of the political top of one of the sectors of competence of the state administration. In terms of the formal constitution, the level of autonomy, the relative weight in the system of ministers, or members of the governing body, can be considered inversely proportional to the specific strength conferred by the constitutional documents to the monocratic head of government. From this point of view, it is understandable that the individual strength of ministers is minor especially where, as in Hungary, the fiduciary relationship with the assembly is established only towards the prime minister.[132] The assessments of the case can however differentiate according to the functioning of the party system, which in turn is influenced by the electoral system. Similar considerations can be made with regard to the possibility of removing and replacing individual ministers, in addition to identifying the bodies that may be competent, on a formal or substantive level, to perform such reshuffles or replacements. Occasionally differentiations or graduations are established within the college, in the sense of providing for the vice-presidents of the

the governments have completed their constitutional mandates. The influence of the electoral system, and of the party system favoured by the latter, is somewhat left in second place (and in recent years it should be considered the exceptional stability not so much of the party system as such, but the prevalence of a single party over everyone else, and of an individual leader over the ruling party).

131 Furthermore, it should be noted that, even where the constructive no confidence has not been adopted, there have been cases of substitution of governments due to changes in the balance of power within the parliament during a parliamentary term (G. Mesežnikov, 'La Slovaquie', cit., p. 388), thus preserving stability.

132 With the addition (Art. 18, para. 4 of the Constitution) of the explicit provision of a double accountability of each minister, to the parliament and to the prime minister. But even before the new Fundamental Law it was possible to write (A. Ágh, 'La Hongrie', cit., p. 189), that the constructive no confidence concentrated on the prime minister made the remaining members of the college accountable only to him, even cancelling their traditional responsibility before the parliamentary assembly.

collegiate body (envisaged in Poland as a possibility, Art. 147, paras. 2 and 3), or the ministers with the capacity to perform vicarious functions in case of impediment or absence of the Prime Minister (two, chosen by the Prime Minister as in Estonia: Art. 93, para. 2, similarly in Lithuania, Art. 97, para. 2). It is often pointed out that ministers are placed in charge of or direct top management structures of the state administration such as ministries (Bulgarian Constitution, Art. 108, para. 3, Estonian, Art. 94); sporadically (as in the case of Hungary: Art. 17, para. 1 of the Basic Law or of Slovenia: Art. 114, para. 2 of the Constitution) an act of Parliament is required for the establishment of ministries, while Poland has made the original choice of placing the members of the government at the head not of ministries but of "sectors of government administration" (Art. 149), in accordance with an ordinary law of 1997 which identifies a large number of such sectors, over thirty. In this way every single government can modulate the number of its members, based on political or programmatic considerations, having the power to create ministries for unification or division, without having to change the law every time but 'playing' by means of mere decrees of execution on those sectors, which alone are predefined by law.[133]

The cohesion of governments that is inherent in contemporary parliamentary systems generally requires coherence in the ways in which individual ministers are appointed, and the regulations in this area are no exception to the principle. However, there is some margin of uncertainty, or necessity of interpretation, in order to the question to who belongs in concrete the will to appoint them, and if necessary to revoke them. It is quite common in the textual statements that the ministers are appointed by the head of state on the proposal of the prime minister, or premier. This is the case where the structure of the government is more collegial, as is the case in most cases (*e.g.* Czech Republic, Art. 68, para. 2, Poland, Art. 154, para. 1, Romania, Art. 95, para. 2, Lithuania, Art. 92, para. 2, Slovakia, Art. 111, Albania, Art. 98 of the respective constitutions), as to where it is more centralized on the figure of its summit, as is the case in Hungary (Art. 16, para. 7 of the FL). There are exceptions such as the one already mentioned in Slovenia, in the assembly type, where ministers are even formally appointed (and dismissed) by the State Assembly, a dominant branch of parliament, although on the proposal of the premier (in that country called President of the Government). Beyond this, however, the constitutions do not make it clear to the end – nor should they do so – to what extent the two institutions actually contribute to the choice of the governing body, leaving much to the practice here. In some

133 J. Sawicki, 'Governo e amministrazione in Polonia. Trasformazione della forma di stato, mutamenti costituzionali e difficile attuazione legislativa', *in* F. Lanchester (Ed.), *La barra e il timone. Governo e apparati amministrativi in alcuni ordinamenti costituzionali*, Milano, Giuffrè, 2009, pp. 347 *et seq.* Normally the number of ministries amounts at about half of the administrative areas required by law, so that each ministry encompasses roughly a couple of sectors. The faculty granted to the "premier" to modulate the number of ministers with portfolio based on the sectors is to be considered in itself as an implicit strengthening of his position, provided that this is allowed by coalition balances, where these are necessary.

order more marked by authentic semi-presidentialism, there is a more marked role of the head of the state, if not in the selection of ministers in positive, at least in a possibility to condition the procedure 'in negative', through a possibility of veto however rather informal as it is not imposed by the literal text of the constitution.[134] But precisely in cases like this – Lithuania and Romania, above all – it should be noted that such a surplus of influence can be obtained only by virtue of strongly shared practices and conventions,[135] possibly supported by the interpretation of constitutional jurisprudence, since never as in this case, in almost all the legal systems, the use of subtle expressions is found out, in part undefined and above all, however, almost identical to each other.

The constitutional position of ministers can also be conditioned by the question whether or not it is possible to express an individual vote of no confidence towards one of them, without this implying formal consequences for the collegiate body. As is well known, this is a qualifying point also in democracies of Western Europe. The constitutions of this geographical area seem less oriented to favour the removal of a single minister by the parliamentary assemblies than the possibility of doing so by the will of the executives themselves. However, they expressly admit to the individual minister's lack of confidence in the Polish Constitution – Article 159 – the Latvian one – Article 59 at the end – the Estonian one – Article 97, para. 5, while other texts maintain a more ambivalent attitude on this aspect (Lithuanian Constitution Art. 96, para. 2, which talks about the specific

134 That's what happened in the Czech Republic, with the very active presidency of Václav Klaus and in part also with the current one of Miloš Zeman. But it is also the case of Lithuania, where V.A. Vaičatis, 'The Lithuanian Governmental System', *in* N. Chronowski, T. Drinóczi & T. Takács (Eds.), *Governmental Systems of Central and Eastern European States*, cit., p. 457, reports how the President of the Republic, who usually "enjoys popular support", has considerable powers in selecting a particular minister. "As a rule, in choosing the candidate, the President must naturally confine his or her selection to candidates that have been nominated by a majority in Parliament, but he or she has the discretion to reject a particular candidate for ethical reasons, on grounds of political transparency or because of a possible conflict between the candidate's public and private interests" (on the basis of this 'added value' in terms of popularity, it is even stated that "the President who enjoys wide popular support may even convince the prime minister to resign, although he or she does not have *de iure* legal instruments to do so"). Something similar was found in Romania, albeit in a contradictory manner and with an abrupt jurisprudential overruling, which led the Constitutional Court within a single year – between 2007 and 2008 – to finally express a much more pronounced interpretation to favour of the presidential power to impose a veto to appointments proposed by the prime minister for ministerial positions, compared to the previous decision, more inspired by a form of parliamentary government (S. Gianello, 'Il Presidente della Repubblica in Romania', cit., p. 35, where he refers judgments No. 356/2007 and No. 98/2008). In the first place, it should be noted that the two rulings, made at a very short distance, were adopted without any formal legislative change having intervened in the meantime to justify their divergence in the matter; secondly that the same normative basis – Art. 85, para. 2 – limits itself to establishing that reshuffles or ministerial holidays are resolved with presidential appointments on the proposal of the prime minister. In the second ruling cited, the Constitutional Court has even come to create a norm by analogy, to establish that the President of the Republic may refuse for a single time, motivating, the appointment of a minister proposed by the Prime Minister, similar to the faculty that the text accords him – Art. 77, para. 2 – to request the parliament to review a law before promulgating it.

135 The case of Slovakia is different, as mentioned earlier.

responsibility of ministers before the *Seimas* as well as the President of the Republic). The way in which the Constitutions of Romania (Art. 106) and the Czech Republic (Art. 74) deal with the matter, does not leave the impression that these systems are conducive to individual no confidence. The case of Slovenia, which leans towards an assembly-oriented system according to which every minister can be removed by Parliament on the proposal of the prime minister, but only after a specific parliamentary hearing has taken place, is very particular.[136]

3.4 Electoral Systems and Parties as a Completion of the Form of Government

3.4.1 *The Constitutional and Legislative Framework of Political Parties*

Although not formally listed in the list of constitutional bodies, it is obvious to anyone the factual role that parties play in contemporary forms of government. Since these are regimes based on the principle of political representation, the incidence of electoral systems, which inevitably presupposes a position of the party as a prime actor of the struggle in the arena of representation, is also of primary importance. It is true that such systems are not normally considered directly at constitutional level – except in very general principles in rare cases – but they find their discipline in primary legislative sources such as the legislative one, whose materially constitutional relevance is recognized as a fact. These are topics on which, in an incidental but inevitable way, something has already been anticipated in the previous paragraphs.

As far as the parties are concerned, it must be said that they know in most of the constitutions of liberal-democratic imprint a treatment that is at least bare and general. In the case of the countries of the area considered here, their possible discipline had to be measured with a theoretical and practical problem of great importance, namely the encumbrance of a very recent past of political regimes substantially based on a single party – with at most one pluralism of mere façade –, a reality which marked a difference with the liberal-democratic systems of qualitative, even before quantitative, relevance. It is evident that the status of a party, its position in the legal system, change radically due to the fact that

136 I. Brinar & M. Žagar, 'La Slovénie', cit., p. 406. After all, this is what happens even before their appointment. On closer inspection it is a singular and attenuated form of assembly-oriented model, since the top position of the government is the *spiritus movens* of the action aimed at removing one of its ministers, but it cannot act in the first person and must involve the assembly in this; the removal cannot therefore be perfected with the vote of membership of a parliamentary committee. A hybrid between individual a parliamentary no confidence vote and prime-ministerial power is thus realized to remove one's own minister, a combination of two similar institutions, albeit conceptually to be distinguished.

it is the only one allowed or one of the many freely created as a form of expression of society, if only for the fact that pluralism of parties should avoid, at least in part, the risk of identification between them and the state. Moreover, precisely because of the burning and very recent historical experience, the discipline of the parties has had to measure, on the part of the constituent and the ordinary law-maker of first implementation, with a massive diffidence of very wide popular strata towards the very idea of political party, a sense of extraneousness that is enormously higher than what was seen in the aftermath of democratization in Germany after World War II or in southern European countries. It must also be said, however, that the theoretical-doctrinal reflection on the constitutional status of the parties in these countries seems to have been weaker than that consecrated to other aspects of public law, as if the doctrine had remained – or was relegated – to a scarcely formalized willing to recognize legal significance to this phenomenon.[137]

This does not rule out that in many cases, without perhaps the aid of great intellectual elaborations, the constituent bodies of these countries, at least those more aware of its impact on the form of state and government, have come to give a meaningful or original discipline of this important social body.[138] Interesting is the differentiation between one system and another, which emphasizes different sensitivities of the various constituent forces. Few are the systems that have systematically ignored the problem (Kosovo, Montenegro, Bosnia-Herzegovina, where just a very generic right of association is mentioned). Some countries did not consider it appropriate for their respective constitutions to spend particular reflections on political parties, barely mentioning them as acknowledging their existence.[139] In some cases there are rather generic or neutral definitions of their function,

137 It is significant that even in the Western-language studies produced in this subject a clearly dominating political science approach is used, focused the proliferation of parties, their organization, purely factual relations of force, while there is a lack of reflections of legal theory on their constitutional status. Examples of such studies include the following: P. Grilli di Cortona, *Da uno a molti. Democratizzazione e rinascita dei partiti in Europa Orientale*, Bologna, Il Mulino, 2000; R. Bugajski, *Political Parties of Eastern Europe: A Guide to Politics in the Post-Communist Era*, New York, The Center for Strategic and International Studies, 2002 (an impressive work of over 1000 pages dedicated to all the regulations included in the present discussion, but nowadays a bit 'dated' compared to the state of the facts); I. van Biezen, *Political Parties in New Democracies. Party Organization in Southern and East-Central Europe*, New York, Palgrave Macmillan, 2003; P.G. Lewis, *Political Parties in Post-Communist Eastern Europe*, London, New York, Routledge, 2000.

138 According to B. Kosowska-Gąstoł, P. Borowiec & K. Sobolewska-Myślik, 'Comparing Organizational Structures of Political Parties in Central and Eastern European Countries', *in* B. Kosowska-Gąstoł, P. Borowiec & K. Sobolewska-Myślik (Eds.), *Organizational Structures of Political Parties in Central and Eastern European Countries*, Kraków, Jagellonian University Press, 2016, p. 467, a high legal recognition of political parties is a common feature of these constitutions. It is rather peculiar of the area that such a recognition, unlike what happened above all with the constitutions of once totalitarian countries such as Italy (1947) or Germany (1949), occurred along with the foundation of many parties or has even anticipated it, shaping the new formations.

139 Like Art. 102 of the Latvian Constitution of 1922 (re-entered into force in 1990), or Art. 35 of the Lithuanian Constitution, symptomatic of the deep-rooted memory of the recent past for the specification that the membership of parties – as well as other forms of association – cannot be mandatory; or Art. 48, para. 1,

as in Hungary (Art. VIII, para. 3 of the Fundamental Law, where it is specified that political parties "contribute to the formation and manifestation of popular will"), in the Czech Republic (Art. 5 of the Constitution, according to which "the political system is based on free and voluntary formation and on free competition between political parties", although the Charter of Fundamental Rrights and Freedoms, with full constitutional value, also bears a reference to freedom of association), in Bulgaria (where – Art. 11, para. 3 of the Constitution – "the parties contribute to the formation and manifestation of the political will of the citizens", an almost identical expression in Art. 8, para. 2 of the Romanian Constitution, with emphasis on pluralism, in the first paragraph, as a condition and guarantee of constitutional democracy). Elsewhere, with different emphases, some principles are enunciated. The separation between the State and the parties has been perceived as a necessity in Slovakia, where this principle has been translated in terms of positive law (Art. 29, para. 4), even in the absence of a general definition, and in even more explicit terms the Bulgarian Constitution itself – Article 11, para. 2 – excludes that any political party, or ideology, can be proclaimed as a party or state ideology. Alongside this there are also limits to the legitimate formation of parties, as Bulgaria does again in the fourth and last paragraph of Article 11, with the prohibition of parties formed on an ethnic, racial or religious basis and those which pursue the aim of taking power by violent means. This accentuation was even stronger in the former Yugoslavia.[140]

This objective is then remarked in full in the Polish Constitution of 1997, whose authors in Article 13 wanted to draw the lines of a "democracy that defends itself", with an evocation of the German Fundamental Law in some aspects even more explicit,[141] referring both to some ideologies and to modes of action by which no legally existing party could legitimately be inspired (a corollary of this, the Constitutional Tribunal was envisaged as competent to judge the conformity to the Constitution of the ends and activities of the parties under Art. 188, para. 1, para. 4 of the Constitution). More circumscribed limits in the Romanian

of the Estonian Constitution, where it is specified that only Estonian citizens can belong to parties. Even more significant is the case of Slovenia, where in a broad catalogue of "human rights and fundamental freedoms" the association in parties is mentioned – Art. 42, para. 4 – in order to prohibit it to professional members of the armed forces.

140 It is highly significant that precisely in this area an identification between political party and violent methods is feared, along with the use of the armed public force to conquer power, to destroy the constitutional order and to incite ethnic, racial or religious intolerance, and prohibitions resulting from this fear are established. *See* Arts. 20 of the Constitution of Macedonia, 55 of Montenegro, 5 of Serbia. The Constitution of Kosovo evokes a situation of this kind but merely states that such organizations "may be prohibited by a decision of a competent court" (Art. 44, para. 3).

141 Art. 13: "Political parties and other organizations whose programmes are based upon totalitarian methods and the modes of activity of nazism, fascism and communism, as well as those whose programmes or activities sanction racial or national hatred, the application of violence for the purpose of obtaining power or to influence the State policy, or provide for the secrecy of their own structure or membership, shall be prohibited." Moreover, neither in this nor in any other place is there a definition of the sociopolitical function of constitutionally legitimate parties, or of their limits.

Constitution of 1991, which places them 'in respect of national sovereignty, territorial integrity, the legal system and the principles of democracy'. Not much attention, in general, is dedicated to the issue of internal democracy within parties, which crosses with that of the general democratic order.

But apart from the expressed prohibition of being inspired by totalitarian ideologies, a peculiar feature of the constitutional systems of this area – albeit sporadically translated into positive law – lies precisely in the repudiation of any possible identification between party and state. This cannot come as a surprise, since that identification had achieved in the same countries, under previous regulations, perhaps the greatest possible development in the contemporary world. It can be said then that, in the light of some years of experience, the abovementioned provisions have on the whole found a fairly satisfactory level of implementation, even if it would be appropriate to update and verify continuously at an empirical level the correspondence between constitutional statements and praxis, from which some data, if not precisely of blatant denial, at least of contradiction could emerge, at least in the form of indirect party occupation of sectors of the public administration or of an economy still partially mediated by the public sector.

Another peculiarity of the states of this area, which also in this respect were mainly inspired by the German model – even with quite different results in terms of their success – lies in the fact that almost each of them, to the constitutional provisions, added laws consecrated to political parties, in some cases provided for by the respective fundamental laws themselves. This phenomenon, which in part of Western Europe still arouses rejection reactions, in Central and Eastern Europe has instead generalized, with norms in some cases rather penetrating when it comes to the organization and structure of the parties for the purposes of their formal registration as precondition for participation in electoral competitions and the possible disbursement of public funds. Hungary was the first to pass a law on the subject (1989), favoured by the fact that the parties, including opposition parties, were direct protagonists of the transition, followed by Poland (1990), which was also a pioneer in the democratic transition, but where the party system was at the time much more immature. In the wake of these countries, almost all the others adopted a law on the parties in more or less short time, and over time some countries even approved one or even two new laws replacing the previous one (Poland itself in 1997; Bulgaria, 1990, 2001 and 2009, Albania, 1991 and 2000, Croatia 1991 and 1993, Romania 1996, 2003 and 2015, Serbia 1990 and 2009, Slovakia 1990 and 2005, Czech Republic 1991, Slovakia 1990 and 2005, Slovenia 1989 and 1994; Estonia 1994). A common feature of these revisions over time lies in the fact that the first laws, in general, were very liberal, setting minimum conditions and requirements for founding a party (for example, the minimum number of accessions, the procedures for registration, the information on financial sources); while the following regulations became more restrictive and generally somewhat more analytical, since their aims were no longer those of favouring the foundation of the largest possible number of subjects in order to support free pluralist elections, but on the contrary they were based on the need to, above all, tighten up certain funding criteria as a response to opaque phenomena on the financial side.[142] At present, therefore, it has been found that the countries of this area, compared to those who have experienced a totalitarian past but of a non-communist character, have far more intense and detailed legislation on the parties, up to prepare general schemes on the criteria by which the statutes must be drawn up, such as to determine a resemblance between them of the parties on the organizational structure,[143] obviously even when they are very differentiated on the ideological level.

The degree of interference of laws in this area is not uniform, with the extreme cases, for example, of Bulgaria and Hungary. In the first country, the legislation in force is restrictive, particularly in terms of the methods of financing approved by political groups, compensating for a conspicuous and complex supply system through state funds with strict prohibitions on donations, especially by foreign entities. Intervention in matters of internal organization is more limited, although the obligation to hold regular meetings of the top party's organs is imposed, which must be communicated to the court in Sofia as well as personal changes in the highest internal positions or the establishment of new internal organs. It is significant, however, that the omission of acts such as those mentioned above can even lead to the dissolution of a party as a final sanction.[144] The case of Romania is quite similar to this.[145] At the opposite extreme is Hungary, with a lacklustre, essential and quite liberal legislation, especially in terms of internal organization.[146] It is not by

142 B. Kosowska-Gąstoł, P. Borowiec & K. Sobolewska-Myślik, cit., p. 469.

143 F. Casal Bértoa & I. van Biezen, 'Party Regulation and Party Politics in Post-communist Europe', *East European Politics*, Vol. 30, No. 3, p. 302.

144 T. Kostadinova, 'Organizational Structure and Trends in Bulgarian Party Politics', *in* B. Kosowska-Gąstoł, P. Borowiec & K. Sobolewska-Myślik (Eds.), *Organizational Structures*, cit., p. 89.

145 T. Burean & A. Barbus, 'The Internal Organization of Romanian Political Parties', *in* B. Kosowska-Gąstoł, P. Borowiec & K. Sobolewska-Myślik (Eds.), *Organizational Structures*, cit., p. 331: "The Bucharest Court of Justice dissolves political parties which have not held a general meeting for five years; or which have failed to provide candidates for two consecutive local elections (excluding presidential elections), in at least 75 constituencies, a list of candidates for at least one electoral district, or candidates in at least three electoral districts in parliamentary elections." Here the accentuation of the electoral vocation of the parties is evident, alongside the concern for a minimum of internal statutory life, which in turn is not forced to be inspired by excessively democratic canons. It is clear from the most recent law of 2015 that a provision contained in the previous law of 2003 was abolished which went as far as to establish the dissolution of parties that had not obtained at least 50,000 votes at national level in the most recent consultations. Obviously, it is the electoral laws which should serve exclusion objectives of this kind, without draconian measures aimed at eliminating the search for future chances, which must be implicit in the periodicity of the elections and in the reversibility of the related results. It is also noted – *Ibidem*, p. 332 – that it is precisely the law on parties the one which deals with the status of parliamentarians who have left the party for which they were elected (with a relative interference in the issue of the prohibition of a binding mandate). These may leave their original formation, but within the institution of reference they can only act as independent, being inhibited by the use of the name of the party they founded or of the already existing one they have joined.

146 D. Kovarek & G. Soós, 'Cut from the Same Cloth? A Comparative Analysis of the Party Organizations in Hungary', *in* B. Kosowska-Gąstoł, P. Borowiec & K. Sobolewska-Myślik (Eds.), *Organizational Structures*,

chance that the country still maintains a law which was adopted at the dawn of democratization, when a small group of 'proto-parties' managed to play an important role in the round table agreements. The fact that the current Hungarian government has so far refrained from adopting a new law on parties, in years of such a demanding challenge for Magyar democracy, is to be considered a guarantee for pluralism. In any case, it is necessary to recognize for intellectual honesty that only empirical findings 'in the field', in this respect more than others, could make it possible to ascertain what has been the role played in the last decades by the laws on parties in these systems, with which intensity they are really enforced, what the level of their contribution to internal democracy has been, as well as to relations with other subjects, or if by chance these laws have not concurred in engaging the political framework, hindering the entry of outsiders. A partial negative answer to this last aspect can however derive from the emergence of anti-system parties, often with authoritarian, nationalist tendencies, possibly leaning towards compression of the rights of various minorities. These are parties that in some countries could present potential reasons for conflict with certain principles established by the constitutions and – if they are to be rigorous – even with the laws that are being implemented. The survey must therefore remain open.

3.4.2 *The Legislative (and Possibly Constitutional) Regulation of Electoral Systems*

Even in electoral matters, the young democracies of the countries that came out of socialist experience had to learn a lot from the most rooted ones. At least in one respect, however, they have been quite innovative, and this is to be referred to the formation of independent electoral commissions, completely free from the involvement of the executive, which in recent decades have become an increasingly widespread model in the world. Poland has inaugurated this model since 1990.

Regarding the electoral systems in the strict sense, or rather the so-called formula, namely the mechanism of transformation of votes in seats, it must be said that most of the regulations of the considered area has gradually been inspired by a predominantly proportional criterion, or at least not one based on majority mechanisms, and this even if a choice in this direction has not been imposed by an overly constitutional provision. There are, however, cases of the opposite sign, where it was decided to adopt mixed systems but with

cit., p. 186 ("The law does not interfere with party structure, and contains no regulation of internal democracy. Lawmakers apparently believed that the internal life of parties was the business of the parties themselves"). It is significant that such an essential discipline is that laid down by a law still dating from the debut of the democratic experience.

a prevalent majority approach, although the decisions in this direction were characterized by greater uncertainty and contradicted by subsequent corrections.

The widespread option in favour of proportional representation is typical of many young democracies whose fragility is feared. At the beginning of the democratic transitions in these countries, and not only for the obvious fact that the transitional parliaments have often played the role of constituent assemblies, it has been feared that the adoption of majority formulas, in the event of an overwhelming victory of a single party in an electoral consultation, could have led to the establishment of a lasting dominance by that same formation, turning an episodic result into something that, given the weakness of the guarantee institutions, could become difficult to reverse. In many cases, however, the adoption of proportional or non-majority systems has been favoured by the lack of mutual recognition among the parties, or as a form of recognition and guarantee for ethnic and linguistic minorities spread throughout the country, which would have been politically obliterated with the adoption of majority systems based on single-member constituencies.

Even where the preference for proportional-dominated systems is expressed at the constitutional level, it is appropriate at least in some cases to verify how much the electoral laws remain faithful to this prediction. Here the case of Poland is significant, where – as mentioned previously – Article 96 of the Constitution imposes this formula to the election of only the lower house, the *Sejm*, which is clearly prevailing. Well, the Polish electoral legislation, which has remained substantially stable in this respect since 1993,[147] has decided to implement this principle with the adoption of the d'Hondt method in electoral districts of a rather small size and with the additional provision of a national exclusion threshold equal to 5 percent for lists representing individual political parties, and 8 percent for those formed by coalitions of more parties. The combination of these normative data with a political landscape that in the early years of democratization was very fragmented gave rise occasionally to a dispersion of votes which is so strong that it could be compared, though only for limited aspects, to those that would have been obtained in the presence of a majority system.[148] It is still noteworthy, for Poland, a mode of expression of the vote that provides a sort of mandatory individual preference, since the voter cannot vote for a

147 Although an organic electoral code was adopted in 2011, which encompasses the entire discipline on the subject but which on the level of electoral formulas is essentially reproductive of what has already been acquired.

148 A borderline case occurred in the 1993 elections, when 34.5 percent of voters remained without any parliamentary representation, and the first two parties – SLD and PSL – obtained 303 seats in the Diet, equal to 65.9 percent, with just 35.8 percent of votes (*see* data provided by B. Stanley, 'Poland', *in* S. Berglund *et al.* (Eds.), *The Handbook of Political Change in Eastern Europe*, 3rd ed., Cheltenham, Edward Elgar, 2013, pp. 202-203). This situation was approached again in the last legislative elections of 2015, when the 'waisted' votes amounted to 16.6 percent of the total, favouring the triumph of the PiS, which achieved the majority of seats (235 out of 460) with just 37.6 percent of the votes. Such a gap between seats and votes is in fact typical of democracies in which consolidated majority and single-member systems are used.

party symbol, but makes his choice by putting a cross on a square placed alongside an individual chosen candidate on the open list to which he or she belongs. Only in this way is the vote to a party expressed, and the electoral figure thereof, even at national level, results from the sum of individual preferences granted to all its candidates in all of the districts. Being very sporadic, and in any case not regulated by law, the use of primary elections, the composition of the lists takes place according to rather 'vertical' criteria,[149] and the role of voters can only be enhanced by the mandatory expression of a single preference, which sometimes has caused significant alterations with respect to the order of priority established by the internal governing bodies.[150]

The Czech Republic is also among the countries whose Constitution prescribes a proportional system, as regards its Chamber of Deputies. The mechanism is similar to the Polish one, with some differences and changes over time. Among the differences, the fact that the preferential vote is possible and may alter the priority in the allocation of seats only on condition that the candidate reaches a given percentage of preferences, currently set at 5 percent of the votes on the list.[151] The legislation in force in Slovakia is similar, but it uses the Hagenbach-Bischoff quota formula whose effects in practice are much more proportional,[152] within individual forces exceeding the 5 percent exclusion threshold, than in Poland or Czech Republic, greatly easing the distortion in the balance of power between the parties accessing the allocation of seats. A proportional principle also supports political

149 Since 2011, however, a gender quota has been introduced that requires each gender to be represented in a list for not less than 35 percent of its members, yet these proportions are not automatically reproduced in the composition of the assembly, either because there is no additional obligation to alternate between gender within each list, or because the mandatory preferential vote within the open list is the one that ultimately determines the results.

150 As for Poland it is still right to point out that the Senate electoral system – the 'higher' chamber is always elected together with the *Sejm* but a very weakened position – has always distinguished itself from that of the 'lower' but clearly prevailing house. The Senate, as is also clear from the 1997 Constitution, is released from the 'proportional' requirement as a criterion for the allocation of seats imposed instead for the Sejm. This is also the reason why the 100 members of the Senate have long been elected according to the criterion of limited voting in the context of bi or three-member constituencies.

151 Z. Manfeldová, 'The Czech Republic', *in* S. Berglund *et al.* (Eds.), *The Handbook of Political Change*, cit., p. 246, who also refers to a vast modification of the system introduced in 2000, aimed at making it rather selective by increasing the number of constituencies – and thus reducing their size –, a restrictive modification of the divider rule never applied, however, for having been annulled by the Constitutional Court. Only the graduated increase in the access threshold for the representative lists of coalitions, up to 20 percent for those made up of at least four parties, has been saved. Another interesting feature of the Czech electoral law – taken over by Poland only for the European elections – is that the number of seats in each constituency is not allocated according to the respective population, but is calculated after the vote, based on the number of valid votes expressed in each of them. In this way, to be rewarded is not the mere demographic weight, but the actual electoral turnout in individual constituencies.

152 K. Deegan-Krause, 'Slovakia', *in* S. Berglund *et al.* (Eds.), *The Handbook of Political Change*, cit., p. 284. Even in Slovakia, the casting of a preference vote is considered decisive for the allocation of seats as an alternative to the order presented by the open list, on the sole condition that the number of personal preferences expressed exceed 10 percent of the total list votes.

elections in the Baltic countries such as Latvia and Estonia, with national access thresholds of five percent. The same is true for Bulgaria, even if there was a partial experimentation of a majority share, in 2009, which was immediately disavowed.

Then there are countries in which electoral legislation, in particular regarding the transformation of votes into seats, has shown high instability, with frequent changes, either for systemic adaptations made necessary by an empirical process of trial and error, or for reasons of convenience of political forces in power. In these countries the cases in which either a majority or a mixed system was initially in force are more frequent, followed by formulas more oriented towards proportionality. Lithuania was more persistent in this respect, where the law provided half of the seats allocated in single-member constituencies, with a possible second round of ballot, and a second half assigned in multi-member constituencies with the Hare quota.[153] The electoral history of Romania, which has experienced a long period of proportional representation until the Law No. 35/2008 introduced a system based on single-member constituencies for both the Chamber and the Senate.[154] The allocation of seats in constituencies, however, only takes place provided that a candidate reports an absolute majority of votes in a constituency, failing which one proceeds to an attribution through the formula of the highest remains according to a complicated double distribution which takes place firstly in the provincial field and subsequently on a national scale. The need to allocate the seats according to a criterion at least in part proportional imposed the indefiniteness of the total number of seats in both branches of parliament, so that in the 2012 elections as many as ninety-seven deputies and thirty-nine senators were elected with mandates in excess.[155] It is a system that has given rise to complaints about its complication and the difficulty for voters to establish a connection between their vote and the allocation of seats. Therefore, a proportional representation was reinstated with closed lists in 2015, with which it voted in 2016.

An even more acute case of instability of electoral legislation, and perhaps the most extreme of the whole area, is that of Albania, where, until the first years of the present decade, every legislative election was held under a different system. The vivacity of the dispute and the democratic landscape has not gone hand in hand with a widespread persuasion of the actual transparency and authenticity of the electoral process, given that the results of the consultations have almost always been the object of protest even more than

153 Only in 2000 the majority was assigned according to the first-past-the-post the British system, according to K. Duvold & M. Jurkynas, 'Lithuania', *in* S. Berglund *et al.* (Eds.), *The Handbook of Political Change*, cit., p. 165. The proportional share of seats, completely detached from the majority, is assigned with the simple Hare formula of the highest remainders. Because of the frequent run-offs in constituencies, Lithuania is one of the few countries in the area where voting takes place in two rounds.

154 W. Crowther & O.V. Suciu, 'Romania', *in* S. Berglund *et al.* (Eds.), cit., p. 403.

155 www.roaep.ro/prezentare/wp-content/uploads/2013/04/final-report-OSCE.pdf (last accessed September 2018). This report, moreover, criticizes the Romanian system for its lack of guarantees in the field of more general electoral legislation.

in the rest of the Balkan area.[156] Allegations of frauds or findings related at least to irregularities in the proceedings were regularly on the agenda, although it must be said that never an election result, that was recognized as fully authentic or not, gave rise to the establishment of an authoritarian regime that was able to make its dominance irreversible. However, having to identify a trend in this country, from the dawn of democratization in 1990 until today, it consists in a withdrawal of the majority principle in the direction of a growing favour for proportional representation.

The first fully pluralistic elections of 1991 took place with an entirely single-member system. From that moment, for the election of the successive parliaments a mixed system was always adopted with two elements subject to continuous variation: the quota of members reserved for the election with a non-majority mechanism and the access threshold for the parties limited to this quota. What changed was the mix between majority and proportional, but always with a clear prevalence of the first (between 70 and 80 percent of the seats approximately), while the access threshold ranged between two and four percent. The instability of the legislation was exacerbated by the fact that the share of seats distributed through single-member constituencies oscillated between one and two voting rounds of vote (plurality as opposed to majority). The Albanian Constitution of 1998 itself came to incorporate in Article 64 this mixed system, thereby giving at least the impression of a stabilization. Instead, in April 2008 a constitutional amendment was adopted, soon followed by the approval of a new electoral code, with which the legislation on the subject was again binding, but tying it this time to the proportional principle, envisaging multi-member districts linked to the territorial division of the country.[157] These continuous changes with an almost experimental purpose, with an ever more marked trend to abandon the majority system in favour of a proportional one, on the one hand denounce the biased instrumentality used in the matter – although the 2008 amendment with which the majority was in fact rendered unconstitutional was adopted rather consensually – but on the other hand have prevented the country from consolidating a minimum of electoral tradition. Also the direct involvement of the Constitution on the matter must push for reflection. In the case of Albania, the instability of electoral legislation did not meet a limitation in the Constitution, but was itself instrumental in influencing the fundamental law, claiming that this was to shore up the needs of the moment.

Hungary positioned itself immediately on the opposite side of the electoral orientation, compared to Poland or the Czech Republic. This country is known for having opted in

---

156 On this topic see the following paper www.eliamep.gr/wp-content/uploads/2013/04/bn1.pdf (last accessed September 2018).

157 I. Petrela, 'Electoral Systems in Europe and the Case of Albania (with Focus on the Current Electoral Code and General Elections Held in 2009)', *SEE Law Journal*, Vol. 1, No. 1, 2014, www.seelawschool.org/pdf/2_Electoral_systems_in_Europe_and_the_case_of_Albania.pdf (last accessed September 2018).

1990 for a complex mixed system but with a predominance of majority features, with regular elections held every four years until 2010.[158] Almost half of the seats used to be assigned to single-member constituencies, in which only the candidates who had received the absolute majority of votes were elected; otherwise, a second round would take place, to which those who had obtained at least 15 percent of the votes in the college were admitted. There was then a portion of seats allocated in multi-member constituencies – on average seven seats – according to the Hagenbach-Bischoff quotient criterion, but with a further share of seats allocated to national lists, by which a compensation of seats not assigned to the parties both in the single-member constituencies and, through the system of the remains, in the plurinominal ones was carried out. A national exclusion threshold of four percent was set, raised from 1994 to five. This system, which by paradox had been devised between 1989 and 1990 as a compromise between the Communist party still in government and the democratic opposition forces, and had to function as a temporary solution, had time to assert and consolidate itself for six elections in a row, until, following his own election triumph in 2010, Prime Minister Viktor Orbán and his Fidesz party – having collected 68 percent of seats with 52.7 percent of votes – proceeded in parallel not only to the approval of the new Basic Law, but also the adoption of a law of organic modification of the electoral system, which in turn saved its predominant majority approach.

Following these changes, first of all, the total number of members of the unicameral Parliament fell from 386 to 199. Of these, 106 seats are currently attributed to single-member constituencies of plurality type. The remaining ninety-three are assigned in a single national college, applying the d'Hondt method among all the lists that have obtained at least 5 percent of the votes on a national scale with a compensation mechanism. Each list has an electoral number equal to the sum of its votes, the votes obtained by the candidates connected to it that have been defeated in single-member colleges and a share equal to the difference – decreased by one – between the votes obtained and those reported by the best defeated, for each winning candidate.[159] It is therefore a somewhat partial compensation, which in fact, in the last election of 2018 allowed the Fidesz party to obtain over 66 percent of seats with 49.2 percent of votes: a share of elected almost unchanged following a net drop in terms of votes. The majority effects, therefore, seem even stronger than previously, with the addition that citizens not resident in Hungary, being entitled to vote only in the proportional part, further reduce their compensation, increasing the majority effects of the system, which in recent years have constantly rewarded Fidesz. Add to this the conviction of the opposition about a distribution of constituencies such as to favour the current majority.[160]

158 G. Tóka & S. Popa, 'Hungary', *in* S. Berglund, et al. (Eds.), *The Handbook of Political Change*, cit., p. 337.
159 G.F. Ferrari, 'La Costituzione dell'Ungheria', *in* M. Ganino (Ed.), *Codice delle Costituzioni*, cit., 396.
160 *Ibidem.*

4 Territorial Decentralization

Arianna Angeli

4.1 Introduction

In the aftermath of the fall of communist regimes, Central-Eastern, Baltic, and Balkan European countries introduced radical reforms of their territorial-administrative structure. Based on the principle of decentralization, such reforms were aimed at overcoming the highly centralized systems inherited from the socialist period.

Firstly, CEBBE countries re-established "democratic and autonomous local government systems",[1] based on directly elected municipal councils. Secondly, in the context of democratic consolidation and accession to the European Union processes, the countries at stake introduced further reforms.[2]

CEBBE countries opted for different solutions, notwithstanding the influence of common factors, such as a relatively recent origin as nation-state, the presence of national minorities, and the socialist domination. Poland, Czech Republic and Slovakia established administrative regions, which are not endowed with legislative powers. In Romania, Hungary, Bulgaria, and Slovenia the possibility to create administrative regions has been long debated, even if reforms have not been approved yet. Other countries of the area introduced only local self-government institutions, organized on a one/two-tier structure.

The European Union exerted a direct influence on CEBBE candidate countries territorial reforms, within the context of the enlargement process. Regionalization was not included among political criteria for joining the EU. Nonetheless, as for administrative and institutional capacity to effectively implement the *acquis*, the Commission supported candidate countries in introducing a regional-tier of self-government. A specific model was not indicated, in order to allow each member state to opt for the system fitting the most its own political and institutional traditions.[3]

The presence of national minorities widely hampered the development of decentralization processes and historically played a completely different role compared to Western

1 M. Ganino, 'Democrazia e diritti umani nelle costituzioni dei paesi dell'Europa orientale', cit., pp. 145.

2 G. Marcou, 'L'adaptation des structures territoriales face à la politique régionale communautaire', *Revue d'études comparatives est-ouest*, No. 3, 2002, pp. 131 *et seq.*

3 T. Cerruti, 'L'Unione europea alla ricerca dei propri confini. I criteri politici di adesione ed il ruolo dei nuovi Stati membri', cit., p. 173.

European countries.[4] In the latter, minority protection led to ensure the territorial autonomy and to the introduction of an asymmetric territorial organization. Central-Eastern, Baltic and Balkan countries, on the contrary, excluded the possibility to create regions corresponding to territories inhabited by minorities. Separatist fears and a troubled past, in fact, prevented them from introducing forms of regional decentralization to ensure minority protection.[5]

4.2 Origins and Territorial Organization of Nation-States

Territorial reform processes in CEBBE countries were widely influenced by a common historical, economic and social background.

As already mentioned in Chapter I, all the countries at stake were part of multinational empires and had a relatively recent origin. All of them were born as independent nation-states between the end of the nineteenth century and the beginning of the twentieth century, thanks to the weakening and finally the dissolution of the empires.

CEBBE countries inherited from imperial domination a highly centralized territorial structure. The ethnic complexity of the region – mainly derived from arbitrary borders set out by victorious powers at the end of World War I[6] – further exacerbated the need to impose a unitary model and to safeguard the territorial integrity of the state. Decentralization at intermediate and regional level was therefore excluded.

All these countries introduced a centralized system, with a view to consolidate the newly born state. Even in rare examples in which decentralization was formally laid down in constitutions, specific provisions were not actually implemented.

Romania, Serbia, Montenegro and Bulgaria gained their independence (or a high degree of autonomy in the case of Bulgaria)[7] from the Ottoman Empire by the end of the Russo-Turkish War (1877-1878). Territorial arrangements were set out first in the Treaty of Saint Stephen (3 March 1878) and then in the Treaty of Berlin (13 July 1878).[8] Borders defined in the Treaty of Berlin, however, were modified several times in the following years, because

4 A. Angeli, 'Le esperienze di decentramento territoriale nell'Europa centro-orientale', *federalismi.it*, No. 15, 2018, pp. 1-27.

5 G. Marcou, 'L'adaptation des structures territoriales', cit., p. 132.

6 M. Waldenberg, *Le questioni nazionali nell'Europa centro-orientale*, cit., pp. 227-228; J.M. Le Breton, *Una storia infausta. L'Europa centrale e orientale dal 1917 al 1990*, cit.; A. Scottà (Ed.), *La Conferenza di pace di Parigi fra ieri e domani (1919-1920)*, Catanzaro, Rubettino, 2000, p. 521.

7 According to Art. I of the Treaty of Berlin: "Bulgaria is constituted an autonomous and tributary Principality under the suzerainty of His Imperial Majesty the Sultan; it will have a Christian Government and a national militia." In 1885, the autonomous Principality of Bulgaria declared its unification with Eastern Rumelia, and in 1908 it proclaimed itself an independent state.

8 W.N. Medlicott, *The Congress of Berlin and After. A Diplomatic History of the Near Eastern Settlement 1878-1880*, Abingdon, Franck Cass, 1963, pp. 36 *et seq.*

of two Balkan Wars (1912-1913) and World War I. A great instability therefore characterized the Balkan area in the years preceding World War I.

As for Romania, in 1859 the Principalities of Wallachia and Moldova – formally under the suzerainty of the Ottoman Empire – were united under the rule of Prince Alexandru Ioan Cuza. This latter started a wide modernization process and a reform of the administrative system inspired by the French and the Belgian model.[9] The administrative reform led to the introduction of a truly centralized system, in which both communes and counties were not recognized as self-government bodies, but just as public entities. Municipal and county councils were elective, while mayors and prefects were nominated by the central government.[10]

The Constitution of the autonomous Principality of Romania of 1st July 1866,[11] at Article 4, laid down a territorial structure organized into counties, district, and communes. Districts represented just an administrative division; they were headed by a sub-prefect which was nominated by the prefect itself. According to Article 107, the legislation on counties and communes would have been based on the principle of administrative decentralization and it would have ensured the independence of communes. The Kingdom of Romania retained such territorial organization when it gained its independence from the Ottoman Empire in 1878. Territorial enlargements, resulting from the defeat of Central Empires in World War I, strengthened the need to ensure a capillary control of the territory and a uniform implementation of the law. The Constitution of 29 March 1923[12] retained the traditional Romanian two-tier territorial structure, organized into counties and communes. Compared to the previous text, the 1923 Constitution did not make any reference to districts (Art. 4).

As for Bulgaria, it was agreed at the Congress of Berlin that Bulgarian territories would have become an autonomous Principality, under the suzerainty of the Ottoman Empire.[13] On 16 April 1879, the National Assembly approved the so-called Tărnovo Constitution,

---

9 E.S. Tanasescu, 'Local Government in Romania', *in* A.M. Moreno (Ed.), *Local Government in the Member States of the European Union: A Comparative Perspective*, Madrid, INAP, 2012, p. 534.

10 E.S. Tanasescu, 'Les réformes territoriales eu Roumanie', *Revue française de droit administratif*, No. 5, 2015.

11 According to Art. I of the Constitution: "United Romanian Principalities constitute a single indivisible state, named Romania." The text of the 1866 Constitution, in Romanian, www.constitutia.ro/const1866.htm (last accessed September 2018).

12 The text of the 1923 Constitution, in Romanian, www.constitutia.ro/const1923.htm (last accessed September 2018).

13 At the Congress of Belin (13 June-13 July 1878), the creation of a unitary Bulgarian Slavic state in the Balkan peninsula was categorically excluded, in order to avoid the destabilization of the entire region. Therefore, Bulgaria was divided into three parts: the Principality of Bulgaria, in the Northern part of the Balkans, which was a *de jure* vassal state under the suzerainty of the Ottoman Empire; the autonomous *oblast* of Eastern Rumelia, in the Southern part of the Balkans, led by Christian Governor-General appointed by the Sublime Porte with the approval of the Great Powers; and Macedonia, which returned under the control of the Ottomans. L.S. Stavrianos, *The Balkans Since 1453*, cit., pp. 425 *et seq.*

which introduced a three-tier territorial structure, divided into communes, districts and departments (Art. 3). At the municipal level, there were both 'deconcentrated' entities of state administration and 'decentralized' – or 'autarchic' –[14] bodies endowed with limited autonomy. Such 'dual' administrative system represented a common feature of Central-Eastern and Balkan countries, which was inspired by the Napoleonic model.

At the municipal level there was a municipal council and a mayor. The mayor was elected by the council and was at the same time the head of the commune and a Government officer. Districts, or 'sub-prefectures', constituted just administrative units, in charge of public safety and of municipal administrations control. At departmental level there were a departmental council and a prefect. The latter was a representative of the executive in the department and he was in charge of executive, direction, surveillance and control functions.[15]

The 1908 insurrection of the 'Young Turks' was initially aimed at modernizing the country, introducing reforms of the government system, and ensuring all nationalities more autonomy. Despite all these intentions, the revolution deeply weakened the Ottoman Empire from the inside.[16] On 5 October 1908, Bulgaria proclaimed its independence. The Tărnovo Constitution was retained, and it stayed in force until 1947.[17] At the same time, on 6 October 1908, the Austro-Hungarian Empire annexed Bosnia-Herzegovina.

The Principality of Serbia – after five centuries of Ottoman domination, and just after the defeat of the Ottoman Empire in the Russo-Turkish war – was recognized as an independent state at the Congress of Berlin in 1878.[18] In 1882, the Principality was transformed into the Kingdom of Serbia, while Prince Milan IV was proclaimed King of Serbia. The first and the second Balkan War (1912-1913) greatly strengthened the Kingdom of Serbia, who obtained Macedonia, Kosovo and Metohija.

On 29 October 1918, Anton Korošec, Svetozar Pribićević e Ante Pavelić proclaimed the establishment of the State of Slovenes, Croats and Serbs.[19] On 25 November 1918, the

14 F. Bassanini, 'L'amministrazione locale nella Repubblica popolare bulgara', *in* P. Biscaretti di Ruffia, F. Bassanini & M.P. Schlein (Eds.), *L'amministrazione locale in Europa*, Vol. II, Milano, Giuffrè, 1964, pp. 210 *et seq.*

15 Act of 10 May 1922 attributed a special status to the capital city of Sofia. The capital was divided into six urban districts, endowed with their own elective councils and mayors. Sofia was headed by a central municipal council, composed of district councillors elected by the respective councils (3/5) and by district councillors appointed by the Minister of the Interior (2/5). The latter appointed also the mayor of Sofia.

16 A.M. Banti, *Storia contemporanea*, Roma, Donzelli, 1997, p. 224; S. Bianchini, *La questione jugoslava*, Firenze, Giunti, 1999, pp. 23-24.

17 A. Pitassio, *Storia della Bulgaria contemporanea*, Passignano sul Trasimeno, Aguaplano, 2012.

18 W.N. Medlicott, *Congress of Berlin and After. A Diplomatic History of the Near Eastern Settlement 1878-1880*, Oxford, Oxford University Press, 2013, pp. 14 *et seq.*

19 V. Meier, *Yugoslavia: A History of its Demise*, London, Routledge, 2005, p. 51.

new state joined the Kingdom of Serbia, followed by the Kingdom of Montenegro.[20] On 1st December 1918, the new Kingdom of Serbs, Croats and Slovenes was formed, headed by King Peter I Karađorđević.

On 28 June 1921, a new constitution – the so-called Vidovan Constitution –[21] was approved and it introduced a four-tier territorial-administrative structure, organized into *oblasts*, departments, districts and communes (Art. 95, para. 1).[22] *Oblasts* would have been established by law, taking into consideration geographical, social and economic factors, and they would have had up to 800,000 inhabitants (Art. 95, para. 2). *Oblasts* were administered by a *zupan* (or prefect) nominated by the King, who represented also the head of state administration bodies in the *oblast* (Art. 95, para. 4). Territorial self-government entities would have been established by law at the municipal, district and *oblast* level (Arts. 97-101).[23] Territorial organization set out by the Vidovan Constitution was inspired by the French model.

Royal Decree of 26 April 1922 introduced a territorial structure organized into thirty-three *oblasts*, corresponding to the historical regions of the Balkan peninsula.[24] However, the Vidovan Constitution was only partially implemented, and the Kingdom of Serbs, Croats and Slovenes retained for its entire existence a highly centralized administrative structure.

On 20 June 1928, a Serbian-Montenegrin member of parliamentary majority shot five MPs of the Croatian Peasants' Party. A deep political crisis derived from these events. On 6 January 1929, King Alexander I abolished the Vidovan Constitution, dissolved the National Assembly, and imposed its own regime. The King approved a series of acts posing all authorities under his direct control, among whom the Act "On the Royal Power and the Supreme Administration of the State" of 6 January 1929.[25]

20 On 25 November 1918, Vojvodina, which was part of the Kingdom of Croatia and Slavonia, required to be annexed to the Kingdom of Serbia. Analogously, Sirmia, a former region of Vojvodina incorporated into Kingdom of Hungary, required to be annexed to the Kingdom of Serbia.

21 F.R. Dareste & P. Dareste, *Les Constitutions modernes, Europe II*, Paris, Recueil Sirey, 1910.

22 *Cf.* M. Fioravanti, *Lo Stato moderno in Europa*, Roma-Bari, Laterza, 2017.

23 The assembly and the committee were the administrative bodies of the *oblast*. The assembly elected the president (who managed the assembly's work) and the committee (Art. 98). The assembly adopted regulations in the exercise of its own competences (Art. 99), while the committee approved dispositions and instructions to implement them (Art. 100). The prefect assessed the conformity to the Constitution and to laws of *oblast*'s acts and he could refer them to the State Council. The latter had two months to pronounce a judgement. After a two months delay, *oblast*'s acts would have become fully executive.

24 Serbia was divided into fourteen *oblasts*, Bosnia and Herzegovina into six *oblasts*, Croatia into four *oblasts*, Vojvodina into four *oblasts*, Macedonia into three *oblasts*, Slovenia into two *oblasts*, while Montenegro represented one single *oblast*.

25 *The Law on the Royal Power and the Supreme Administration of the State, January 6, 1929*, www.arhivyu.gov.rs/active/en/home/glavna_navigacija/leksikon_jugoslavije/konstitutivni_akti_jugoslavije/zakon_o_kraljevskoj_vlasti.html (last accessed September 2018).

On 3 October 1929, the state changed its name in Kingdom of Yugoslavia (1929-1941) and the administrative division into thirty-three *oblasts* was replaced by a territorial structure articulated into nine *banovinas*.

On 3 September 1931, the King decreed a new Constitution,[26] introducing a three-tier territorial structure, based on *banovinas*, districts and municipalities (Art. 83). Territorial units were at the same time deconcentrated and self-government entities (Art. 84). *Banovinas* were headed by a prefect (*ban*), nominated by the King upon proposal of the Prime Minister (Art. 86).[27]

In Albania, after four centuries of Ottoman domination (1481-1912), the country proclaimed its independence on 28 November 1912. In the first decades of the twentieth century, the new state was characterized by political instability. On 22 November 1913, the *Kanun* (*i.e.* secular legislation in Islamic countries) "On civil administration in Albania" introduced a new territorial organization based on the French model. The territory was divided into eight prefectures[28] led by prefects nominated by the government. Prefectures were in turn formed by sub-prefectures.[29]

The Organic Law "On municipalities" of 1921 radically reformed local government. Villages together with urban and rural municipalities (inhabited by more than 200 families) represented the first level of the territorial structure. Municipal councils and their respective presidents were both directly elected. The Act "On the organization and functioning of municipalities" of 12 January 1928 introduced a further administrative-territorial unit, *i.e.* the commune, composed of several villages. As set out in previous legislation, at the second and third level of the territorial structure there were respectively sub-prefectures and prefectures, which were administered by a prefect nominated by the government and approved by the President (and at a later stage by the King).[30] The number of prefectures, sub-pre-

26 *The Constitution of the Kingdom of Yugoslavia, September 3, 1931 (Octroyed September Constitution)*, www.arhivyu.rs/active/en/home/glavna_navigacija/leksikon_jugoslavije/konstitutivni_akti_jugoslavije/oktroisani_ustav.html (last accessed September 2018).

27 Provinces (*banovinas*) had normative bodies, *i.e.* councils, elected by the people for a four-year term (male suffrage), and executive bodies, *i.e.* committees, elected by the councils among its members (Art. 89). The council adopted regulations, upon proposal of the committee, which were subject to *a priori* review by the State Council, and then enacted by the prefect (Arts. 90-91). As set out in the Constitution, *banovinas* were under the direct control of State authorities (Art. 92). The prefect had the power to annul provincial bodies' acts. Finally, the council could be dissolved with a royal decree, upon proposal of the Minister of Internal Affairs (Art. 93).

28 Berat, Dibra, Durrës, Elbasan, Gjirokastra, Korça, Scutari e Valona.

29 M. Meça, *The evolution of administrative law in Albania and the impact of the decisions of the European Court of Justice in the Albanian legal reforms in administrative justice, Juridical Tribune*, Vol. 4, No. 2, 2014, pp. 187-188.

30 In 1925, the Republic of Albania was proclaimed and a new Constitution adopted. This latter document was inspired by the French Constitutional Laws of the Third Republic. In 1928, Albania became a constitutional monarchy, led by King Zogu.

fectures, municipalities, communes and villages has been modified several times in the following years.[31]

Hungary represents a peculiar case among the countries of the CEBBE area. In 1867, with the *Ausgleich*, the Kingdom of Hungary became one of the two entities composing the Austro-Hungarian Empire, which was headed by the Habsburg monarchy.[32] Act XLII of 1870 and Act XVIII of 1876[33] introduced a new territorial structure for the Kingdom of Hungary and abolished towns' privileges of medieval origin. The institutional organization, as well as the *status*, of territorial-administrative units was unified. The traditional two-tier territorial structure – based on towns/communes and counties administered by elective councils – was retained. Following the defeat in World War I and the collapse of the Austro-Hungarian Empire, in 1918, the Kingdom of Hungary lost part of his territory in favour to neighbouring countries.[34] The territorial structure was not modified, and counties' borders remained unaltered.[35]

At the end of World War I – following the dissolution of the Tsarist Empire and the defeat of Central Empires – Poland and Czechoslovakia became independent. After more than one century of foreign domination, Poland regained its independence in 1918, having to face problems connected to the reunification of the country. The partition of the Polish-Lithuanian Commonwealth (1772-1918) – among the Habsburg monarchy, Russian Empire and Prussia – generated inequalities among different regions, which were inherited by the newly born state at the end of the war. The 1921 Constitution introduced the principle of 'decentralization' and established territorial self-government units organized on three levels (voivodeship, districts and rural/urban municipalities). The constitution was not fully implemented and stating from 1926 the consolidation of an authoritarian regime led to a further centralization of the territorial-administrative system. However, the 1921 Constitution exerted a relevant influence of fundamental laws adopted in Poland in the following years, with a specific reference to the 1992 'small' Constitution and the 1997 Constitution.

Czech and Slovak nations have been subject to foreign domination for long years. The Hapsburg rule nevertheless ensured a certain degree of autonomy to the Czech lands, while

31 www.reformaterritoriale.al/reforma/pse (last accessed September 2018).

32 M. Dicosola, 'Transizione democratica, adesione all'Unione europea e organizzazione territoriale in Ungheria: dalla centralizzazione alla regionalizzazione', *in* A. Torre (Ed.), *Processi di devolution e transizioni costituzionali negli stati unitari – dal Regno Unito all'Europa, atti del Convegno del Devolution Club, Bologna, 24-25 novembre 2006*, Torino, Giappichelli, 2007, pp. 621-633.

33 Z. Szente, 'Hungary. Local Government in Hungary: A Creeping Centralisation?', *in* C. Panara & M. Varney (Eds.), *Local Government in Europe: The 'Fourth Level' in the EU Multi-Layered System of Governance*, London-New York, Routledge, 2013, pp. 151 *et seq.*

34 Hungary ceded: Slovakia and Ruthenia to Czechoslovakia; Transylvania and Banat to Romania; Croatia, Slavonia and Vojvodina to the Kingdom of Serbs, Croats and Slovenes; and Burgenland to Austria. M. Dicosola, *Transizione democratica*, cit., pp. 621-633.

35 Z. Szente, 'Hungary. Local Government in Hungary: A Creeping Centralisation?', cit., p. 151.

the Hungarian authority excluded whatsoever form of self-government for the Slovak counties. The first Czechoslovak Republic was founded in 1918 as a state entity of the 'Czechoslovak' nation. The latter represented a fictitious concept, given that both the Slovak and the Czech nationalities always retained their own identity features, and they never merged into one single nationality. The 1920 Constitution introduced a centralized structure, while recognizing a special *status* to Sub-Carpathian Ruthenia (a region inhabited by a Ruthenian population). However, such special regime was implemented only in part. The 1927 Act "On the administrative organization", which entered into force on 1st July 1928, established four regions (Czech: *země*; Slovak: *krajiny*) – *i.e.* Bohemia, Moravia, Silesia, and Sub-Carpathian Rus – therefore introducing a three-tier territorial-administrative structure. Each region was run by a governor nominated by the central government and by a partially elective territorial diet.

The Baltic governorates of Estonia, Livonia[36] and Courland[37] – corresponding to present-day Estonia and Latvia – benefited from a special status in the Russian Empire. Starting from the last years of the nineteenth century, however, these three governorates were subject to a deep Russification process. With reference to the territorial structure, Estonia, Livonia, and Courland were organized into counties and villages. As in the Kingdom of Poland, also known as 'Congress Poland' (present-day Central-Eastern Poland), Baltic governorates retained their own territorial diet (*Landtag*). The *Landtag* – which was under control of the German nobility – used to elect its own president, who represented the governorate in the Saint Petersburg imperial court. The council was the executive organ of the *Landtag* and it was composed of twelve members.[38] The governor general acted as the head of the administration in the governorate and he was appointed directly by the Tsar among members of the German nobility. Such an office was abolished in 1876.[39]

Estonia and Latvia obtained their independence at the end of World War I, following the dissolution of the Tsarist Empire and independence wars.[40] In Estonia, the 1920 Constitution, at Articles 75-77,[41] introduced for the first time territorial self-government units and retained a two-tier territorial-administrative structure, organized into districts and municipalities. Specific provisions on territorial self-government would have been laid down by law.

36 Estonia and Livonia were annexed to Tsarist Empire following the Great Northern War, as set out in the Treaty of Nystad in 1721.

37 In 1795, Courland became part of the Tsarist Empire following the Third Polish Partition.

38 A. Kasekamp, *A History of the Baltic States*, London, Palgrave, 2018, pp. 51 *et seq.*

39 D.J. Smith (Ed.), *The Baltic States and Their Region. New Europe Or Old?*, Amsterdam-New York, Rodopi, 2005.

40 R. Tuchtenhagen, *Storia dei paesi baltici*, Bologna, il Mulino, 2008.

41 A. Giannini, *Le Costituzioni degli stati dell'Europa Orientale*, Vol. I, cit.

In Latvia, the Constituent Assembly approved a new constitution, the so-called *Satversme*, on 15 February 1922.[42] In the text there was no mention of the territorial structure of the state. Acts "On local government in rural municipalities" and "On local government in urban municipalities" – respectively adopted in 1922 and 1930 – introduced elective councils. Such councils in turn used to elect their own president and a *presidium*, which were in charge of the administration of the municipality.[43]

In the aftermath of World War I, Lithuania was not able to obtain the full control of its territory. Polish armies invaded Vilnius and the surrounding region in 1920. Two years after, in 1922, the newly elected *Sejm* of Wilno (*i.e.* the Diet of Vilnius) required the annexation of the region to Poland. Kaunas became the temporary capital of Lithuania, even if both the 1928 Constitution and the 1938 Constitution continued to consider Vilnius as the official capital of Lithuania.

4.3 Decentralization and Ethno-National Complexity in the Interwar Period

When CEBBE countries gained their independence, the ethnic complexity of the region heavily influenced both the new state system and its consolidation process.[44]

As for the first Czechoslovak Republic, the numeric relevance of the ethnic German population in the Czech lands as well as of the Hungarian minority in Slovakia led to the creation of a common state of the Czechoslovak ('Slavic') nation. It is worth to remember that in Czechoslovakia the ethnic German population outnumbered the Slovak one. The 1920 Constitution[45] ensured a wide protection of national, linguistic and ethnic minorities (Section VI). "Difference in religion, belief, confession or language" would not have represented an obstacle to the access to public offices for any citizen (Art. 128, para. 2). Moreover, the free use of any language would have been ensured to citizen, in private and business relations, as well as in all matters pertaining to religion, in the press and in all publications, or in public assemblies (Art. 128, para. 3).[46]

42 A. Giannini, *Le Costituzioni degli stati dell'Europa Orientale*, Vol. II, cit.

43 F. Loughlin, A. Hendriks & J. Lidström (Eds.), *The Oxford Handbook of Local and Regional Democracy in Europe*, Oxford, Oxford University Press, 2012, p. 598.

44 The possibility to create ethnically homogenous countries was based on a *fictio juris*, far from reality. Minority protection was ensured through international treaties and specific constitutional provisions. S. Mancini, *Minoranze autoctone e Stato: tra composizione dei conflitti e secessione*, Milano, Giuffrè, 1996, p. 73; S. Bartole, 'Internal Ordering in the Unitary State', *in* M. Rosenfeld & A. Sajó, *The Oxford Handbook of Comparative Constitutional Law*, Oxford, Oxford University Press, 2012, pp. 610-612.

45 J. Hoetzel & V. Johachim (Eds.), *The Constitution of the Czechoslovak Republic*, Prague, Politika, 1920.

46 A. Angeli, 'L'evoluzione costituzionale della tutela delle minoranze nazionali nella Repubblica slovacca', *in* A. Di Gregorio & A. Vitale (Eds.), *Il ventennale dello scioglimento pacifico della Federazione ceco-slovacca*, cit., pp. 159 *et seq.*

In negotiations which led to the creation of a common state of Southern Slavs in the Balkan peninsula, different nations requested a high degree of autonomy. Nevertheless, constituents opted for a highly centralized territorial-administrative structure, in order to consolidate the newly born state. On 1st December 1918, the Kingdom of Serbs, Croats and Slovenes was proclaimed. The 1920 Constitution introduced the principle of 'national unitarism' of a single nation with three names. Other ethnic/religious groups – namely Macedonians, Montenegrins, and Muslims – would have had a secondary role.[47]

The 1931 Constitution strengthened the unitary structure of the state and replaced the principle of 'national unitarism' with the 'integral Yugoslavism' (*integralno jugoslavenstvo*) one. As in the already mentioned example of Czechoslovakia, the 1931 Constitution introduced the fictitious concept of the 'Yugoslav' nation.

In the interwar period, one-third of the Polish population was part of a national minority, with specific reference to Ukrainian, Jewish, Belarusian, and German minorities.[48] Discrimination and oppression led all of them to manifest hostility towards the reconstituted Polish state. Furthermore, Ukrainian and Belarusian minorities were subject to an intense process of 'Polonization'.[49]

As already said, in the aftermath of the dissolution of the Tsarist Empire and of the defeat of Central Powers, Romania annexed several new territories, among whom Bukovina (from the lands of the Hapsburg Crown), Banat and Transylvania (which were part of the Kingdom of Hungary) and Bessarabia (from Soviet Russia). Given its new territorial dimension, in the interwar period Romania was defined as 'Greater Romania' (Romanian: *România Mare*).[50] New provinces had been for long time part of multinational empires and they were inhabited by numerous national and religious minorities.[51] Conversely, the Kingdom of Romania up to the end of World War I could have been defined as an ethnically homogeneous country. The only exception was represented by the Jewish minority. In the context of a wider state consolidation process, Greater Romania pursued stability through assimilation policies, which entailed "the homogenisation of the political space, the promotion of the national culture, and the definition of citizenship".[52] The Hungarian

47 Č. Pištan, 'Dalla balcanizzazione alla jugonostalgija: dissoluzione della Repubblica Socialista Federale di Jugoslavia', *Istituzioni del Federalismo*, No. 4, 2014.

48 According to an approximate evaluation, in the Polish Second Republic there were about 5 million Ukrainians (15 percent of the total population), 3 million Jews (10 percent of the population), 1.5 million Belarusians and 800,000 Germans. P.D. Stachura, *Poland, 1918-1945: An Interpretive and Documentary History of the Second Republic*, London-New York, Routledge, 2004, p. 79.

49 A. Roshwald, *Ethnic Nationalism and the Fall of Empires: Central Europe, the Middle East and Russia, 1914-23*, London-New York, Routledge, 2000, p. 164.

50 P. Terruzzi, *La Grande Romania*, Milano, Alpes, 1931; A. Basciani, *La difficile unione. La Bessarabia e la Grande Romania, 1918-1940*, Roma, Aracne, 2007.

51 I. Livezeanu, *Cultural Politics in Greater Romania*, New York, Cornell University Press, 1995.

52 D. Dragoman & B. Gheorghiță, 'Regional Design, Local Autonomy, and Ethnic Struggle: Romania's Syncopated Regionalisation', *Europe-Asia Studies*, No. 2, 2016, pp. 270-290.

minority in Transylvania was the national group such policies hit the most.[53] On 30 August 1940, as set out in the second Vienna Award, Romania had to return Northern Transylvania to Hungary. At the end of World War II, the 1947 Paris Peace Treaty re-established pre-war borders. Nevertheless, the remembrance of forced resettlements and violence towards civilians from both sides, seriously undermined relations between these two countries. Rising fears of secession from the Romanian side and of assimilation from the Hungarian one with reference to the Transylvanian region paved the way for reciprocal suspicion.[54]

In Estonia, the 1920 Constitution laid down specific provisions on national minorities' protection. According to Article 21, members of national minorities would have been entitled to establish autonomous institutions in order to promote their national culture and to provide welfare services. As set out in Article 22, in those areas in which the majority of the population was not Estonian, local self-government institutions were authorized to use the language of the national minority in everyday work. At the same time, every citizen retained the right to use the State official language in its relations with local self-government institutions. Moreover, local self-government institutions had to employ the State language in their relations with State institutions. Finally, citizens of German, Russian, and Swedish nationality were ensured the right to address state institutions in their own language, while the use of the minority language in courts would have been set out by law (Art. 23).

The 1925 Act "On national minorities cultural autonomy" allowed national minorities composed by more than 3,000 persons to establish national-cultural self-government bodies.[55] Such law represented one of the most advanced legislations on minority protection at that time. The cultural council and the cultural government represented respectively the normative and the executive body of national-cultural self-government. Self-government bodies were in charge of the management and supervision of several activities, among whom education, culture, sport, and youth. Such legislation contributed to strengthen the belief that minority protection had to be considered as an individual right, not related to the territory.[56] Citizens were therefore required to declare their national identity and to register in the respective national-cultural council. Both German and Jewish minorities – which were mainly concentrated in towns – benefited from the protection ensured by Article 21 of the Constitution and from the 1925 Act "On national minorities cultural

53 E. Illyés, *National Minorities in Romania: Change in Transylvania*, New York, Columbia University Press, 1982; P. Berteanu, 'Romanian Nationalism and Political Communication: Greater Romania Party (Partidul Romania Mare), A Case-Study', *in* J. Hroch, D. Hollan & G.F. McLean (Eds.), *National, Cultural, and Ethnic Identities: Harmony Beyond Conflict*, Cardinal Station, CRVP, 1998.

54 D. Dragoman & B. Gheorghiță, 'Regional Design, Local Autonomy, and Ethnic Struggle: Romania's Syncopated Regionalisation', cit., 273.

55 According to 1934 census, Estonian population (1.1 million people) was composed by Estonians (88.2 percent), Russians (8.5 percent), Germans (1.5 percent) and Jews (0.4 percent).

56 A. Kasekamp, *A History of the Baltic States*, cit., pp. 107 *et seq.*

autonomy".[57] On the contrary, the Russian and the Swedish minorities – which predominantly inhabited rural areas – where constituted the majority of the population, instead of establishing national-cultural self-government bodies, they elected their own representatives in territorial self-government bodies and benefited from the protection ensured by Article 22 of the Constitution.

In Latvia, despite the lack of a specific legislation on national minorities, in education field the German minority benefited from a similar protection compared to Estonia.[58] In Lithuania, on the contrary, Anastas Smetona authoritarian regime and territorial dispute with Poland prevented the development of any minority protection system.[59]

At the end of World War II, in several CEBBE countries the issue of national minorities dramatically found a solution. As a consequence of Nazi Germany genocidal policies and then of people's forced displacement and resettlement, such countries became more ethnically homogeneous. In Poland, ethnic Germans and Ukrainians were forced to leave the country. In Czechoslovakia, as set out at the Potsdam Conference, ethnic Germans were expelled from the Czech lands. At the same time, Slovakia and Hungary agreed the reciprocal transfer of population. Resettlement of ethnic Slovaks from Hungary could be considered as a voluntary process. On the contrary, the displacement of ethnic Hungarians from Slovakia constituted forced transfer.[60] As laid down in Beneš decrees,[61] German and Hungarian fraternizers were deprived of civil and property rights[62] and of the Czechoslovak citizenship.[63] Moreover, ethnic Hungarians in Slovakia started to be subject to a 'Slovakization' process.

57 *Cultural Autonomy of National Minorities and Cultural Self-Government in the Republic of Estonia*, www.estonica.org/en/Cultural_autonomy_of_national_minorities_and_cultural_self-government_in_the_Republic_of_Estonia (last accessed September 2018).

58 According to 1935 census, the Lithuanian population (1.9 million people) was composed by Lithuanians (75.5 percent), Russians (10.6 percent), Germans (3.2 percent), Jews (4.8 percent), Poles (2.5 percent). A. Kasekamp, *A History of the Baltic States*, cit., p. 106.

59 In 1923, Lithuanian population (2 million people) was composed by Lithuanians (83.9 percent), Jews (7.6 percent), Poles (3.2 percent), Russians (2.7 percent), Germans (1.4 percent). A. Kasekamp, *A History of the Baltic States*, cit., p. 106.

60 I. Gyurcsik & J. Satterwhite, 'The Hungarians in Slovakia', *Nationalities Papers*, Vol. 24, No. 3, 1996, pp. 509-524; M. Mandelbaum, *The New European Diasporas: National Minorities and Conflict in Eastern Europe*, New York, Council on Foreign Relations, 2000; A.J. Rieber, *Forced Migration in Central and Eastern Europe, 1939-1950*, London-New York, Routledge, 2000.

61 Presidential Decrees No. 5/1945, No. 12/1945, No. 108/1945 and Constitutional Decree No. 33/1945.

62 Presidential Decree No. 12/1945 "Concerning the confiscation and reallocation of agricultural properties of German and Hungarian traitors and enemies of the Czech and Slovak nation" [*Dekret prezidenta o konfiskaci a urychleném rozdělení zemědělského majetku Němců, Maďarů, jakož i zrádců a nepřátel českého a slovenského národa*] and Presidential Decree No. 108/1945 "Concerning the confiscation of enemy properties and on the Fund for National Restoration" [*Dekret prezidenta o konfiskaci nepřátelského majetku a Fondech národní obnovy*].

63 Constitutional Decree No. 33/1945 "Concerning the regulation of the Czechoslovak citizenship for persons of German and Hungarian ethnicity" [*Ústavní dekret prezidenta o úpravě československého státního občanství osob národnosti německé a maďarské*].

4.4 The Socialist Period

In new socialist systems of CEBBE countries, the dichotomy between central/local state power bodies (people's councils), on one side, and central/local state administration bodies (executive committees), on the other, replaced the traditional multi-level territorial-administrative structure. Such systems relied on principles of: 'unity of state power' based on elective assemblies, 'socialist legality', 'planned economy', 'democratic centralism' and 'double dependence'. According to the latter, both people's councils and executive committees would have been 'horizontally' accountable to the subject who elected them, and 'vertically' accountable to superior bodies of the same category. In practice, however, the communist party controlled state power bodies, and its organization 'doubled' state institutions at all levels.[64] The intermediate level constituted the most important one, since it supervised the implementation of central orders at local level.

As already mentioned in previous chapters, the socialist state represented a unitary model, with some variations related to different constitutional traditions. SFR of Yugoslavia constituted an exception among CEBBE countries.[65] Basic principles of socialist state were just partially transposed in Yugoslavia. In such model, political and economic self-management led to the actual decay of state structures. The principle of 'unity of state power' was just partially implemented, formally recognizing the difference existing between legislative and constitutional amendment power. 'Democratic centralism' and 'double dependence' were rejected. Instead, the fundamental role of the commune, as a "basic socio-political community", was formally sanctioned in Article 96 of 1963 Constitution. 'Planned economy' was not fully realized, while 'socialist legality' was rigidly imposed, ensuring the protection of ethnic and self-management autonomies, trough constitutional courts. Finally, the principle of 'rotation of political public offices' was introduced.[66]

It is possible to divide the socialist period, considered as a whole, into three different phases common to all the countries at stake.

In a first transitory phase (1945-1948), several elements of the previous systems continued to characterize the new socialist states in Central-Eastern, Baltic and Balkan Europe. In Czechoslovak Republic the territorial structure set out in the 1927 Act was reintroduced, and it stayed in force until the 1949 reform was approved. The territorial organization was not mentioned both in the 1947 Polish 'small Constitution', and in Hungarian 'transitional' constitution (Act I of 1946 "On the State System of Hungary"). In Albania, the territorial structure organized into prefectures and sub-prefectures was retained, while communes

64 M. Ganino, 'Democrazia e diritti umani nelle costituzioni dei paesi dell'Europa orientale', cit., pp. 124, 144.
65 *M. Ganino*, 'Democrazia e diritti umani nelle costituzioni dei paesi dell'Europa orientale', cit., p. 121.
66 P. Biscaretti di Ruffia & G. Franchi (Eds.), *L'amministrazione locale in Europa*, Vol. III, Milano, Giuffrè, 1969, pp. 7-9.

and municipalities were abolished. Then, Act No. 284 of 22 August 1946 modified the number of sub-prefecture and it introduced localities.[67]

In a second phase – also defined by Italian scholars as "the phase of close imitation of the Stalinist model"[68] (1948-1954) – the territorial structure of socialist states was drastically reformed. In particular, the 1952 Romanian Constitution[69] – inspired by the 1936 Soviet Constitution –[70] introduced a three-tier territorial structure, articulated into communes/towns, districts and regions.[71] A new Hungarian Autonomous Region,[72] endowed with its own elective people's council and executive committee, was created (Arts. 57-58).[73]

In Hungary, Article 29 of 1949 Constitution laid down a territorial structure organized into communes/cities, districts and departments. Biggest cities were divided into city districts. Such territorial structure replaced the previous two-tier one, organized into communes/cities and departments.

In Bulgaria, the 1947 Constitution introduced two-tier territorial organization, based on communes and districts. Wider administrative units would have been set out by law (Art. 47). According to this latter provision, Act of 17 September 1949 instituted fourteen departments (each of them composed by six/seven districts) and restored a three-tier territorial-administrative structure.[74]

In Czechoslovakia, Article 123 of 1948 Constitution set out a three-tier territorial structure, organized into regions, districts and communes. In 1949, nineteen regions were established (whose dimension was reduced compared to the previous ones), among whom thirteen Czech regions and six Slovak regions. According to Article 129, the capital Prague benefited from a special status.

In Poland, 1952 Constitution retained a three-tiered structure, based on rural/urban communes, rural/urban districts and voivodeship (Art. 34).

---

67 www.reformaterritoriale.al/reforma/pse (last accessed September 2018).

68 P. Biscaretti di Ruffia & F. Trimarchi & M. Salvati (Eds.), *L'amministrazione locale in Europa*, Vol. I, Vicenza, NeriPozza, 1964, p. 36.

69 www.constitutia.ro/const1952.htm (last accessed September 2018).

70 P. Biscaretti di Ruffia & M. Ganino (Eds.) *L'amministrazione locale in Europa*, Vol. IV, Milano, Giuffrè, 1982, p. 21.

71 The 1952 Constitution replaced the previous territorial structure organized on three levels – *i.e.* communes/circumscriptions, counties, and regions – set out by the 1948 Constitution (Art. 75), www.constitutia.ro/const1948.htm (last accessed September 2018).

72 Composed by three counties: Harghita, Covasna e Mureş.

73 The number of the regions has been reduced from twenty-eight regions, established in 1950, to eighteen regions, in 1952, and finally to sixteen regions, in 1960. E.S. Tanasescu, *Les réformes territoriales en Roumanie*, cit., p. 1.

74 State power bodies in communes and districts, *i.e.* municipal and district people's councils, were elected for a three-year term (Art. 48). Municipal and district committees were executive-administrative bodies of people's councils (Art. 51). Committees were accountable both to people's councils who elected them and to state administration bodies at higher level (Art. 54).

In Estonia, in 1950 the traditional two-tier structure, based on counties and villages, was reformed and thirteen counties were replaced by thirty-nine districts. In 1952, a third tier was added, through the establishment of three departments. However, such further level was abolished just one year after.[75]

In Albania, according to Act No. 1707 of 1953, counties replaced prefectures. The territory was therefore reorganized into counties, districts, localities/villages/towns and the city of Tirana obtained the district status.[76]

Finally, the third phase, also known as "the national way to Socialism"[77] (from 1955 to 1956 on) – which was in theory oriented to introduce solutions closer to each country's constitutional traditions – *de facto* led to a further centralization of the territorial-administrative system.

In Poland, the 1975 administrative reform and 1976 constitutional amendments replaced the traditional three-tier territorial structure (communes, districts and voivodeships) with a two-tier one (communes and voivodeships), abolishing districts. At the same time the number of voivodeships was increased (from 17 to 49) and their competences significantly reduced.

In Romania, the 1965 Constitution reintroduced a two-tier territorial structure, in which cities and communes represented basic administrative units and counties constituted the intermediate level.[78] This new territorial structure replaced the previous three-tiered one, set out in 1952 Constitution. The special regime ensured to the Transylvanian Autonomous Region was therefore abolished. At the same time, the number of ethnic Hungarians in that region started to decrease, as an effect of forced resettlement policies.[79]

In Bulgaria, reforms approved starting from 1959 enlarged communes, while reducing departments' size. Constitutional Act of 7 November 1961 "On the amendment of Articles 18, 19, and 47 of the Constitution" abolished districts. The new Constitution of 9 May 1971, approved by referendum on 16 May that same year, did not introduce any relevant modification. The two-tier territorial structure, organized into communes and departments, was retained (Art. 109). In 1987, twenty-eight departments established through 1959 reforms were reorganized into nine *oblasts*. Reforms approved in late 1980s were part of

75 www.cia.gov/library/readingroom/docs/CIA-RDP80-00809A000700070435-0.pdf (last accessed September 2018).

76 www.reformaterritoriale.al/reforma/pse (last accessed September 2018).

77 P. Biscaretti di Ruffia & G. Franchi (Eds.), *L'amministrazione locale in Europa*, Vol. III, Milano, Giuffrè, 1969, p. 6.

78 The Romanian territorial organization was also set out by Act No. 2 of 16 February 1968 "On the administrative organization of the territory of the Socialist Republic of Romania", which is still in force. Such Act has been amended several times in the years. Act of 2 February 1968 was composed only by ten articles and in the original version laid down a territorial structure organized into thirty-nine counties. www.cdep.ro/pls/legis/legis_pck.htp_act_text?idt=9327 (last accessed September 2018).

79 K. Verdery, *National Ideology under Socialism: Identity and cultural Politics in Ceausescu's Romania*, Berkley, Berkley University Press, 1995.

a wider process. Indeed, twenty-eight departments were abolished with a view to reduce the inefficiency of the bureaucracy at that level and to strengthen people's self-government, both at regional and at communal level.

As for Czechoslovakia, the 1960 Constitution did not introduce any relevant modification to the territorial structure of the country. At a later stage, through the Constitutional Act No. 77/1968 of 24 June 1968 "On the establishment of the federal system in the Socialist Republic of Czechoslovakia" and the Constitutional Act No. 143/1968 of 27 October 1968 "On the Czechoslovak Federation",[80] the Czechoslovak Socialist Republic became a federal state composed by two entities, *i.e.* the Czech SR and the Slovak SR. Constitutional Act No. 77/1968 was based on the right to self-determination of the two constituent peoples, as well as on their equality. A Czech National Council was established, while the number of the members of the Slovak National Council, already introduced by 1960 Constitution, was increased. Constitutional Act No. 143/1968 gave birth to the Czechoslovak Federation, based on the concept of the "three suzerainties"[81] of the Federation and of the Republics. The Federation retained 'exclusive competences' – among whom foreign policy, defence, foreign-exchange reserves, natural resources – and some 'shared' ones. Constitutional Act No. 143/1968 introduced a bicameral parliament, *i.e.* the Federal Assembly, composed by the Chamber of the People and the Chamber of the Nations, as well as the double citizenship. Republics retained a three-tier territorial structure, organized into regions, districts and communes. Finally, a Federal Constitutional Court – whose members would have been elected by the Federal Assembly for a seven years term – was established, together with two other Constitutional Courts at the Republics' level.[82] Such provisions, however, were not actually implemented. In the context of the failure of 1968 reforms and of the starting of the 'normalization' process, Czechoslovakia was radically reorganized through Act No. 125/1970 of 22 December 1970.[83] Czechoslovak FR became a Socialist 'fictitious' Federation, based on the principle of 'centralization of power', under the direct control of the Communist party, which excluded whatsoever form of territorial autonomy.

In Albania, in 1958, the territorial structure of the country was simplified through the abolition of counties and reorganized into districts and localities/villages/cities. The latter could be divided also in urban boroughs. Moreover, in 1967, localities were replaced by

80 www.zakonyprolidi.cz/cs/1968-143 (last accessed September 2018).

81 A. Di Gregorio, 'Lo scioglimento della Cecoslovacchia: aspetti politico-costituzionali', *in* A. Di Gregorio & A. Vitale (Eds.), *Il ventennale dello scioglimento pacifico della Cecoslovacchia*, cit., p. 117.

82 P. Biscaretti di Ruffia, *Introduzione al diritto costituzionale comparato*, cit., pp. 468-469.

83 A. Di Gregorio, 'Lo scioglimento della Cecoslovacchia: aspetti politico-costituzionali', *in* A. Di Gregorio & A. Vitale (Eds.), *Il ventennale dello scioglimento pacifico della Cecoslovacchia*, cit., p. 118.

'unified rural territories'. Such territorial division (districts, unified villages, villages, cities and urban boroughs) remained unchanged up to the end of the 1980s.[84]

As already said, the constitutional evolution of the Republic of Yugoslavia differs in part from the experience of the other CEBBE socialist countries, with reference also to its territorial organization. In a first phase, also known as "the close imitation of the Stalinist model" phase, the 1946 Constitution[85] established six People's Republics, *i.e.* PR of Serbia, PR of Croatia, PR of Slovenia, PR of Bosnia-Herzegovina, PR of Macedonia and PR of Montenegro. The PR of Serbia included in turn the Autonomous Province (*autonomna pokrajina*) of Vojvodina, and the Autonomous Region (*autonomna oblast*) of Kosovo and Metohija (Art. 2). The extremely complex territorial structure of SFR of Yugoslavia was organized on six levels., *i.e.* municipalities (villages and communes), districts, urban districts, cities, departments and regions (Art. 107). Despite the explicit reference to the federal principle, the new Constitution introduced a highly centralized and hierarchical system. The entire state apparatus was under the direct control of the Communist party.

In 1948, friendly relations between the Soviet Union and Yugoslavia rapidly deteriorated, and the latter started to differentiate itself from the Soviet model. The 1953 Constitutional Amendment entirely revised the state structure, both extending the self-management principle to all relevant fields in economic, social and political life, and attributing the communes a primary role.[86] The 1963 Constitution marked the beginning of the third phase of the Yugoslav constitutional evolution. Basic principles underlying the state system were radically reformed and the state changed its name to Socialist Federative Republic of Yugoslavia, *i.e. Socijalistička Federativna Republika Jugoslavija*, SFRJ.[87]

The Constitution established the SFRY Constitutional Court which decided on the conformity of the law to the Constitution and resolved disputes between the Federation and a Republic, between Republics, and between other social-political communities on the territories of two or more Republics (Art. 241). In addition to the Constitutional Court at federal level, the 1963 Constitution established Constitutional Courts at national level, in each of the federated Republics. Starting from 1968, Constitutional Courts were instituted also at provincial level, in the Autonomous Provinces of Vojvodina and Kosovo-Metohija.[88] It is worth to remember that the 1963 Constitution attributed Kosovo-Metohija the status of 'Autonomous Province', or *autonomna pokrajina*, like the AP of Vojvodina (Art. 111).

84 www.reformaterritoriale.al/reforma/pse (last accessed September 2018).

85 http://mojustav.rs/wp-content/uploads/2013/04/Ustav1946.pdf (last accessed September 2018).

86 P. Biscaretti di Ruffia & G. Franchi (Eds.), *L'amministrazione locale in Europa*, cit., p. 6.

87 P. Biscaretti di Ruffia (Ed.), *Costituzioni straniere contemporanee*, Vol. II, cit., p. 122.

88 A. Di Gregorio, 'Il modello interno nella configurazione della giustizia costituzionale nei paesi della ex Jugoslavia', cit., pp. 257-281; Č. Pištan, *Corti costituzionali e processi di transizione democratica. Le esperienze dei Paesi dell'Europa centro-orientale e dell'area ex-sovietica*, Bologna, Archetipolibri, 2012, pp. 37 *et seq.*

A series of constitutional amendments approved between 1967 and 1971 strengthen the autonomous status of federated Republics, Autonomous Provinces and communes. Finally, the 1974 Constitution reorganized the previous text, taking into account the reforms approved starting from 1967.[89] The 1974 Constitution laid down a high degree of autonomy for the six federated Republics and for the two Autonomous Provinces, which were entitled to the same prerogatives of the Republics. The Constitution attributed the Republics "impeditive powers", making them able to block central authorities' decisions in contrast with their own interests. Central authorities' dynamism was therefore reduced, ensuring Republics equal representation in legislative and executive bodies, as well as requiring qualified majorities in voting processes, and attributing each Republic veto powers.[90]

The ethnic complexity of some socialist countries led them to introduce a federal model, while those more ethnically homogeneous opted for a unitary one. The communist doctrine completely rejected the 'horizontal separation of power', while affirming the principle of the 'unity of state power'. At the same time, the official political and legal theory did not fully oppose the principle of the 'vertical separation of power'. A federal model was therefore introduced in the Soviet Union, Czechoslovakia and Yugoslavia. The fictitious nature of constitutional system in socialist countries, however, led scholars to define the socialist federal model as a 'façade' phenomenon. The entire state system in fact always remained under the direct control of the communist party.[91]

4.5 The Re-instalment of Local Self-Government in the Transition Period

By the end of the 1980s, in the aftermath of the fall of communist regimes, CEBBE countries started a transition process towards a new political, economic and social model, which led to the establishment of new democratic systems.[92]

The reintroduction of local self-government played a major role in democratic transitions and led to strengthen the municipal level. On the contrary, due to the role it played during the socialist period in ensuring the control of the territory, the intermediate level resulted drastically weakened. Such level was in some cases suppressed (Slovakia), in some others it became a state administrative unit (Bulgaria, Estonia, Lithuania, Poland, Czech Republic), and in still other cases its competences were drastically reduced (Hungary). Intermediate level functions were therefore attributed to deconcentrated bodies of the

89 P. Biscaretti di Ruffia (Ed.), *Costituzioni straniere contemporanee*, Vol. II, cit., p. 123; P. Biscaretti di Ruffia, *Introduzione al diritto costituzionale comparato*, cit., pp. 512 *et seq.*

90 G. Bognetti, 'Federalismo', *in Digesto Disc. Pubbl.*, Torino, Utet, p. 294.

91 *Ibidem*, p. 293.

92 M. Ganino, 'Democrazia e diritti umani nelle costituzioni dei paesi dell'Europa orientale', cit., p. 113.

state administration or to services under the direct control of ministries. Romania and Latvia represented the only examples in which the intermediate level retained its own role in the transition to a new democratic system.[93]

Democratic principles defined in the context of Western constitutionalism – among whom local self-government – were transposed in Constitutions adopted in the aftermath of the fall of communist regimes.[94] 'Territorial self-government' was included among basic principles in the Constitutions of Albania (Art. 13), Poland (Art. 16), Slovenia (Art. 9), Macedonia (Art. 8), Czech Republic (Art. 6), and Bulgaria (Art. 2). In addition to basic principle's sections, territorial self-government found place also in sections devoted to territorial organization in the Constitutions of Bulgaria (Arts. 135-146), Albania (Art. 113), Poland (Arts. 163 *et seq.*), Macedonia (Art. 116), and Czech Republic (Arts. 99-105). Finally, territorial self-government was solely included in specific sections dedicated to territorial organization in the Constitutions of Romania (Arts. 119-122), Estonia (Arts. 154-160), Slovakia (Arts. 64-71), Hungary (Art. 42), and Croatia (Art. 128).[95]

The accession to the Council of Europe – and then ratification of the European Charter on Local Self-Government – exerted a direct influence on territorial reforms of CEBBE countries.[96] Such reforms were also designed to satisfy the European Union accession criteria. Decentralization processes developed in highly centralized countries, which inherited from their previous systems a 'monolithic' state structure. However, socialist regimes represented just one of the phases which marked the constitutional evolution of these countries. Constitutional traditions of each national experience re-emerged in democratic transition processes – also defined as "back to Europe"[97] processes – which led to the reinstatement of "original"[98] national models. Indeed, as already noticed in previous chapters, constitutions adopted in the interwar period exerted a direct influence on new constitutions approved following the fall of socialist regimes.

Decentralization represented a primary objective of transition processes.[99] As already said, CEBBE countries first of all restored local self-government and strengthened the

93 G. Marcou, 'L'adaptation des structures territoriales', cit., p. 142.

94 M. Ganino, 'Democrazia e diritti umani nelle costituzioni dei paesi dell'Europa orientale', cit., p. 129.

95 *Ibidem*, p. 142.

96 According to Art. 2 of the European Charter on Local Self-Government "The principle of local self-government shall be recognised in domestic legislation, and where practicable in the constitution", https://rm.coe.int/168007a088 (last accessed September 2018).

97 A. Rinella, *La forma di governo semipresidenziale. Profili metodologici e «Circolazione» del modello francese in Europa centro orientale*, Torino, Giappichelli, 1997, p. 257.

98 R. Scarciglia, 'La forma di governo locale e la circolazione dei modelli nell'Europa centro-orientale', *in* R. Scarciglia & M. Gobbo (Eds.), *Nuove tendenze dell'ordinamento locale. Fonti del diritto e forme di governo nell'esperienza comparata*, Trieste, Eut, 2001, p. 143.

99 G. Marcou, 'Adapting Territorial Structure to the European Union's Regional Policy', *Revue d'études comparatives est-ouest*, Vol. 33, No. 3, p. 131; A. Kruglashov, 'Central and Easter Europe Regional Reforms: From Dismantling a Soviet Model to Europeanizing a National One', *in* F. Palermo & S. Parolari, *Regional*

municipal level. Municipal elections were reintroduced and at the same time political parties regained a central position in the political system. Most of the countries at stake[100] opted for a parliamentary system of local self-government. Municipal councils were directly elected by the people, while mayors and executive committees were elected by the respective council. In the following years relations between mayors/executive committees and councils were rationalized, strengthening executives.[101]

In Poland, the first reform of territorial self-government was approved on 8 March 1990.[102] It was followed by municipal elections on 27 May 1990, *i.e.* the first free elections of the post-communist Poland.[103]

Act of 8 March 1990 set out a diversified electoral system. In municipalities with less than 40,000 inhabitants, members of the municipal council would have been elected with a majoritarian system, while in municipalities with more than 40,000 inhabitants municipal councillors would have been elected with a proportional system. Civic Committee Solidarność won municipal elections in May 1990 with 48 percent of valid votes and a voter turnout of 42 percent. The election of mayors by their respective councils marked the beginning of a troublesome phase, characterized by widespread confrontation between heads of executive committees and presidents of municipal councils. Reforms approved between 1992 and 1995 redefined relations between these two municipal bodies, strengthening executives at the expense of assemblies.

In Czechoslovakia, following the Velvet revolution, national committees were replaced by communes, as territorial self-government units. The latter constituted legal entities and were endowed with property rights.[104] 'District offices'[105] were established, as deconcentrated bodies of state administration. At the same time regional competences were re-distributed between municipal and district level.[106]

Dynamics in Central and Eastern Europe. New Approaches to Decentralization, Leiden, Boston, Nijhoff, 2013.

100 Poland, Czechoslovakia, Hungary, Bulgaria, Romania, Croatia, Lithuania and Estonia.

101 R. Scarciglia, 'La forma di governo locale e la circolazione dei modelli nell'Europa centro-orientale', cit., pp. 140 *et seq.*

102 Act No. 16 "On territorial self-government" of 8 March 1990, in http://dziennikustaw.gov.pl/du/1990/s/16/95, (last accessed September 2018).

103 A. Ptak, 'Territorial Self-Government during Poland's Transformation – The significance, evolution and conclusions of *de lege ferenda*', *Studia i Prace Uniwersytetu Ekonomicznego w Krakowie*, No. 12, 2010, pp. 311-321; G. Gorzalek, 'Regional and Local Potential for Transformation in Poland', *Regional and Local Studies*, No. 14, 1998.

104 Act No. 367/1990 "On municipalities"; Act No. 368/1990 "On the elections of municipal representative councils". K. Davey, 'The Czech and Slovak Republics', *in* A. Coulson (Ed.), *Local Government in Eastern Europe. Establishing democracy at the Grassroots*, Aldershot, Edward Elgar Publishing, 1995, p. 42.

105 Act No. 425/1990 "On district offices".

106 G. Filippini, 'Dopo lo scioglimento: la riproposizione del problema della cessione delle competenze statali tra partecipazione all'Unione europea e regionalizzazione interna', *in* A. Di Gregorio & A. Vitale (Eds.), *Il ventennale dello scioglimento pacifico della Federazione cecoslovacca*, cit., pp. 145-148.

In Croatia, the 1990 Constitution (original version, Arts. 129-131)[107] introduced a centralized two-level territorial structure. The territory of the country was organized into municipalities/districts/cities (defined also as 'local self-government') and counties, which were at the same time deconcentrated bodies of public administration and local self-government bodies (Art. 131). The 1990 Constitution instituted also a bicameral Parliament, composed by the Chamber of Representatives and the Chamber of Counties. The latter constituted just a consultative body (Art. 70). Each county elected three representatives in the Chamber of the counties, for a four-year term. The President of the Republic appointed five honorary members and became himself/herself member of the Chamber of the Counties at the end of his/her mandate (Art. 71). Constitutional amendment of 28 March 2001 abolished all these provisions and it introduced a unicameral parliament.

In Albania, Act No. 7572 of 10 June 1992 "On the organization and functioning of self-government", instituted thirty-six districts, forty-four cities and 313 communes (Art. 1). Elective councils operated at district, city and municipal level. Act No. 7608 of 22 September 1992 established twelve prefectures composed by two to four districts. Prefectures were headed by a prefect appointed by the Council of Ministers.[108]

In Estonia, counties were reintroduced on 1st January 1990, as territorial-administrative units whose territory corresponded to Estonian regions of the Soviet period. Both the original and the consolidated version of the 1992 Constitution (Art. 2)[109] define Estonia as a "politically unitary" country and defer to ordinary law the definition of its territorial organization. Article 155 explicitly mentions only rural municipalities and cities, adding that "further local government units shall be established by law".[110] Such provision was implemented through the Act of 2 June 1993 "On the organization of local government"[111] and through Act of 22 February 1995 "On the administrative division of the territory of Estonia".[112] The traditional two-tiered administrative structure, organized into counties and rural/urban municipalities, was reintroduced. However, while rural/urban municipalities constituted local government units, counties represented only deconcentrated bodies of public administration. The latter were headed by a governor appointed by the executive power (Art. 2, para. 2). Several proposals related to the reintroduction of counties as local self-government units, presented in these last years, have not been implemented yet.[113]

107 www.servat.unibe.ch/icl/hr01000_.html (last accessed September 2018).

108 www.reformaterritoriale.al/reforma/pse (last accessed September 2018).

109 www.servat.unibe.ch/icl/en00000_.html (last accessed September 2018).

110 As set out in the original version of the Constitution, the representative body of the local government was the council, which was elected for a three years term. (Art. 156, para. 1). According to the consolidated version of the Constitution, local councils are elected for a four-year term.

111 www.riigiteataja.ee/en/eli/509012014003/consolide (last accessed September 2018).

112 www.riigiteataja.ee/en/eli/518112013003/consolide (last accessed September 2018).

113 'Estonia. Division of Powers', https://portal.cor.europa.eu/divisionpowers/countries/MembersNLP/Estonia/Pages/default.aspx (last accessed September 2018).

The 2016 territorial structure reform, which entered into force between 2017 and 2018, modified counties' and municipalities' borders.[114] The number of municipalities was reduced (from 213 to 79), while the number of counties (15) remained unaltered.

In Lithuania, the Constitution adopted on 25 October 1992 (Art. 11) deferred to ordinary law the definition of the territorial-administrative structure. According to Chapter X "On local government and administration", territorial-administrative units would have been entitled to the right to self-government. Act of 7 July 1994 "On local self-government"[115] initially set out the direct election of municipal councillors and the indirect election of mayors, for a two-year term (then extended to four years).[116] As in the case of Estonia, Act of 19 July 1994 "On territorial-administrative units of the Republic of Lithuania and on their borders" –[117] largely based on the Lithuanian interwar legislation on local self-government – reintroduced two territorial levels, *i.e.* counties and municipalities (Art. 1, para. 3).[118] Municipalities only represented local self-government units, while counties were headed by a governor appointed by the executive power. A new reform, approved on 1st July 2010,[119] abolished counties. Their competences were in part recentralized and in part attributed to local self-government units.[120]

In Latvia, the 1922 Constitution was reintroduced on 21st August 1991. As set out in the fundamental law, 'local government' would have been elected by Latvian citizens (Art. 101).[121] However, the right to elect local assemblies was reserved to Latvian citizen only – and then extended to European Union's citizens – thus excluding the Russian minority members who did not obtain the naturalization. The 1994 Act "On local government"[122] introduced a territorial organization on two levels of 'municipalities' (subsequently amended in 2009). Districts and 'cities of republic significance'[123] constituted the first level of

114 Act No. 788 "On the administrative reform" of 6 June 2016, www.riigiteataja.ee/akt/121062016001 (last accessed September 2018).

115 https://e-seimas.lrs.lt/portal/legalAct/lt/TAD/c18a8ae0f55e11e3b62ec716086f051f?jfwid=5sjolgbam (last accessed September 2018).

116 R. Scarciglia, *La forma di governo locale*, cit., p. 142.

117 https://e-seimas.lrs.lt/portal/legalAct/lt/TAD/TAIS.24729?jfwid=96t6tcwym (last accessed September 2018).

118 Lithuania is organized into ten counties and sixty municipalities.

119 Act No. 248 "On the Abolition of Administrations in Counties of 10 March 2010", https://e-seimas.lrs.lt/portal/legalAct/lt/TAD/TAIS.366902/OaTMnugVPS (last accessed September 2018).

120 *Lithuania. Division of powers*, https://portal.cor.europa.eu/divisionpowers/countries/MembersNLP/Lithuania/Pages/default.aspx (last accessed September 2018).

121 www.servat.unibe.ch/icl/lg00000_.html (last accessed September 2018).

122 Followed by the 1995 Act "On self-government budget" and 1998 Act "On self-government financial resources equalization". *Latvia. Unitary country*, www.oecd.org/regional/regional-policy/profile-Latvia.pdf (last accessed September 2018).

123 According to 1994 Act "On local self-government", Latvia was divided into 26 districts and 7 cities of republic significance.

municipalities, while towns, town's countryside territories and parishes[124] represented the second level.

As for Romania, the 1991 Constitution – in continuity with the socialist one – lays down a territorial-administrative structure organized into counties, cities, and communes (Art. 3, para. 3).[125] The Constitution, Article 1, defines Romania as a 'unitary and indivisible' state. Territorial-administrative units, *i.e.* counties and cities/communes, are legal entities. They are endowed with specific competences separated from the state ones.[126] According to Article 120 "The public administration in territorial-administrative units shall be based on the principles of decentralization, local autonomy, and deconcentration of public services". Local councils and mayors are defined as 'autonomous administrative authorities', who manage public affairs in communes and towns (Art. 121). County councils coordinate the activity of commune and town councils, with a view to carrying out the public services of county interest (Art. 122).

Romania introduced a 'dual system' of territorial administration, in which autonomous administrative authorities operate together with prefects. The latter are appointed by the Government in each county and in the municipality of Bucharest (Art. 123, para. 1). The prefect is the representative of the Government at local level and directs deconcentrated public services of state administration in territorial-administrative units (Art. 123, para. 2). Relationships between the prefect and territorial self-government bodies are not hierarchical (Art. 123, para. 4).

In Hungary, 1990 constitutional amendments reintroduced a two-tier structure,[127] then implemented through Act XLV of 1990 "On local government" and Act XLIV of 1990 "On the election of mayors and representatives of local government". According to Act XLV of 1990, communes – *i.e.* villages, towns, twenty-two urban counties and the capital Budapest, who benefits from a special *status* – represent basic units of local government, while counties constitute the intermediate level. However, local government autonomies result in practice limited by scarce financial resources these authorities are endowed with.[128]

124 *I.e.* Seventy-seven towns, ten town's countryside territories and twenty-four parishes.

125 Constitutional amendment No. 409/2003 of 29 October 2003 radically reformed the text of the Constitution. However, basic features of the Romanian system remained unaltered, with a specific reference to the traditional two-level territorial structure.

126 E.S. Tanasescu, *Les réformes territoriales eu Roumanie*, cit., p. 6.

127 M. Dicosola, *Transizione democratica*, cit., p. 625.

128 M. Dicosola, *Transizione democratica*, cit., p. 629.

4.6 Territorial Decentralization and National Minorities in the Democratic Consolidation Process

The dissolution of communist regimes led to a revival of nationalist tensions and unsolved disputes. As in the interwar period, the presence of national minorities has therefore exerted a direct influence on territorial reforms of CEBBE countries.

It is worth to operate a distinction among countries in which national minorities represent a numerically relevant and territorially concentrated group (*i.e.* Slovakia and Romania with reference to the Hungarian minority, Bulgaria with reference to Turkish minority, Macedonia with reference to Albanian minority), countries in which minorities constitute a numerically relevant but non-territorially concentrated group (even if mostly concentrated in the biggest cities, like in Estonia and Latvia) and ethnically homogeneous countries (Poland, Czech Republic, Hungary, and in some way Slovenia, Croatia, Montenegro, Kosovo and Albania). Serbia represents a peculiar case (*see infra*). After the loss of Kosovo, Hungarians – who are mainly concentrated in the Vojvodina region – constitute the biggest minority of the country, even if they do not represent a numerically relevant group.

In the countries in which national minorities represent a numerically relevant and territorially concentrated group, the possibility to ensure the autonomy of "territorial entities based on an ethno-national identity" –[129] that is to say to establish regions corresponding to territories inhabited by national minorities – was excluded. Fears of separatism still dominate such countries. However, guaranteeing territorial self-government at that level could have represented a solution to ethnic complexity characterizing the area.

In the countries in which national minorities do not represent a territorially concentrated or a numerically relevant group, their presence has not played a major role in territorial reforms started in the context of the democratic transition. The limited territorial dimension of some of these countries also discouraged the establishment of territorial self-government units based on ethno-national identities.

As already seen in Chapter II, in all the countries at stake, national minorities' protection is guaranteed through individual rights. In some cases, collective rights are also ensured, with a specific reference to the right to establish 'non-territorial' minority self-government

129 P. Nikolova & M. Tchimichkian, *Régionalisation et politique régionale en Bulgarie: évaluer le rôle de l'Union européenne, Revue d'études comparatives Est-Ouest*, No. 3, 2008, p. 86.

bodies,[130] the right to elect minority representatives in territorial self-government bodies,[131] and linguistic rights[132] connected to education, relations with public administration and with territorial self-government bodies.[133]

The only exception is represented by Bosnia-Herzegovina, where – given the ethnic complexity of the country – a *sui generis* federal model was introduced through international agreements.[134] Bosnia-Herzegovina is composed by two entities – *i.e.* the Republic of Srpska and the Federation of Bosnia and Herzegovina – and by the Brčko District, which is part of both entities.[135] The Federation of Bosnia and Herzegovina is composed by ten cantons (Bosnian: *kanton*, Croatian: *županije*). Five cantons are inhabited by a Bosniak majority, three of them have by a Bosnian Croat majority, while the remaining two are ethnically mixed. Cantons, in turn, are organized into municipalities. The territory of the Srpska Republic has a one tier territorial structure, divided into municipalities.

As for the countries in which minorities constitute a numerically relevant group, in Slovakia the presence of the Hungarian minority (which represents 8.5 percent of the population)[136] hindered the regional decentralization process.[137] In the debate that preceded the establishment of the regions in 2001, the possibility to introduce a region in the southern part of Slovakia where Hungarians represent the majority of the population has been taken into account, but soon rejected due to separatist fears. That area has been

130 Macedonia (Art. 48 Constitution), Estonia (Art. 50 Constitution), Montenegro (Art. 79, para. 6 Constitution), Lithuania (Art. 45 Constitution), Czech Republic (Art. 25, para. 1 Charter of Fundamental Rights and Freedoms), Slovakia (Art. 34, para. 1 Constitution), Slovenia (with reference only to the Italian and Hungarian minorities, Art. 64 Constitution), Albania (Art. 20, para. 2 Constitution), Kosovo (Art. 59, para. 14 Constitution), Serbia (Art. 79 Constitution).

131 Montenegro (Art. 79, para. 9 Constitution), Serbia (Arts. 77 and 180 Constitution).

132 With only a general mention of cultural, linguistic rights, *etc.*: Latvia (Art. 114 Constitution), Romania (Art. 6 Constitution), Bulgaria (Art. 54 Constitution), Croatia (Art. 15 Constitution).

133 Macedonia (Art. 7 Constitution), Estonia (Arts. 51-52 Constitution), Montenegro (Art. 79, paras. 3-6, 11 Constitution), Poland (Art. 35, para. 2 Constitution), Czech Republic (Art. 25, para. 2 Charter of Fundamental Rights and Freedoms), Slovakia (Art. 34, para. 2 Constitution), Slovenia (with reference only to the Italian and Hungarian minorities, Art. 64 Constitution), Albania (Art. 20, para. 2 Constitution), Kosovo (Art. 59, paras. 3, 6 Constitution), Serbia (Art. 79 Constitution).

134 'The General Framework Agreement for Peace in Bosnia and Herzegovina', Ann. IV, www.osce.org/bih/126173?download=true (last accessed September 2018).

135 S. Keil, 'Federalism and conditionality in Bosnia and Herzegovina', *DPCE*, No. 4, 2008, pp. 1770-1779; G. Venneri, 'Integrazione europea e riforma costituzionale in Bosnia-Erzegovina: oltre il "Paradosso della sovranità"', *DPCE*, No. 4, 2008, pp. 1756-1769; J. Woelk, *La transazione costituzionale della Bosnia ed Erzegovina. Dall'ordinamento imposto allo Stato multinazionale sostenibile*, Padova, Cedam, 2008; F. Palermo, J. Woelk, *Diritto costituzionale comparato dei gruppi e delle minoranze*, Padova, Cedam, 2011; M. Costa, 'Il federalism bosniaco: un'incompleta transizione da "protettorato internazionale" a "democrazia" europea', *federalismi.it*, Special Issue 2, 2018, pp. 1-15.

136 B. Balogová, 'Census: Fewer Hungarians, Catholics – and Slovaks', *The Slovak Spectator*, 5 March 2012.

137 E.L. Paul, 'Perception vs. Reality: Slovak Views of the Hungarian Minority in Slovakia', *Nationalities Papers*, No. 4, 2003, pp. 485-493.

therefore divided among four administrative regions.[138] Similar problems have not emerged in relation to the Roma minority, which represents the second largest minority in Slovakia. Roma population is not concentrated in one single region, but they inhabit the entire Eastern part of the country.[139]

Analogous considerations emerged in Romania, in the context of the (still ongoing) debate on the establishment of region where the Hungarians[140] could represent the majority of the population, corresponding to the counties of Harghita, Covasna and Mureş, in Eastern Transylvania. Fears of Hungarian separatism prevents the adoption of such reform.[141] However, when the Democratic Alliance of Hungarians in Romania (DAHR) – *i.e.* the most important political party representing the Hungarian minority in Romania – entered as junior partner in the governing coalition in 1997, it widely supported the introduction of regional decentralization. DAHR also promoted a better protection of education and cultural rights. In particular, as set out in Act 215/2001 of 23 April 2001 "On local public administration",[142] in territorial-administrative units in which

> "citizens belonging to national minorities represent more than 20 percent of the inhabitants, local public administration authorities shall ensure, in the relations with them, also the use of their mother tongue" (Art. 17).

As already said in Chapter II, in a confirmative referendum held on 8 December 1991, the Hungarian minority voted against the 1991 Constitution. Several provisions were considered by ethnic Hungarians as detrimental to their own rights. Constitutional amendments approved in 2003, this time with the support of the Hungarians, ensured a wider protection to national minorities, with reference to linguistic rights.

In Bulgaria, the Turkish minority constitutes about 8 percent of the population and it is concentrated both in the Southern part of the country, in the provinces of Kardzhali, and in the Northern part, in the provinces of Shumen, Silistra, Razgrad and Targovishte.[143]

---

138 C. Cerreti & N. Fusco, *Geografia e minoranze*, Roma, Carrocci, 2007, pp. 136-141; A. Angeli, 'L'evoluzione costituzionale della tutela delle minoranze nazionali nella Repubblica slovacca', cit., pp. 169-193.

139 'Slovak Republic', www.coe.int/en/web/minorities/slovak-republic (last accessed September 2018).

140 Ethnic Hungarians represent about 6 percent of the population in Romania. www.recensamantromania.ro/wp-content/uploads/2013/07/REZULTATE-DEFINITIVE-RPL_2011.pdf (last accessed September 2018).

141 www.venice.coe.int/webforms/documents/default.aspx?pdffile=CDL(2004)115-e (last accessed September 2018).

142 *Ibidem.*

143 The Turkish minority has been brutally repressed in the liberal period and then subject to forced assimilation in the socialist one. In the 1980s (1984-1989) the assimilation policy was further exacerbated and led about 300.000 Turks to leave the country. J.W. Warhola & O. Boteva, 'The Turkish Minority in Contemporary Bulgaria', *Nationalities Papers*, No. 3, 2003, pp. 255-279; K.R. Ghodsee, *Muslim Lives in Eastern Europe:*

The Constitution explicitly excludes both the possibility to establish "autonomous territorial units" (Art. 2, para. 1), *i.e.* territorial entities based on ethnicity, and the creation of political parties based on ethnic, racial or religious identity (Art. 11, para. 4).[144] According to Judgment No. 4/1992, such political parties should be forbidden only if they promote hatred, violence or support constitutional amendments against territorial integrity and national security.[145]

In Macedonia, the possibility to establish self-government units at intermediate and regional level – corresponding to territories inhabited by the Albanian minority – was excluded due to the fear for the territorial integrity of the state. Ethnic Albanians represent more than 25 percent of the population in Macedonia and they are concentrated in the North-Western part of the country. As already seen in Chapter II, at the end of the civil war, the Ohrid Framework Agreement and constitutional amendments approved in November 2011 ensured a wider protection to national minorities. According to Article 7 of the Constitution, in local self-government units where there is a considerable number of inhabitants belonging to a "nationality" other than the Macedonian one, their language and alphabet are also in official use, in addition to the Macedonian language and Cyrillic alphabet.

As for the countries in which national minorities represent a numerically relevant and non-territorially concentrated group, in Estonia and Latvia, and in some way in Lithuania,[146] the possibility to establish territorial self-government bodies in areas where the Russophone minority is concentrated –[147] *i.e.* in major urban centres – has been categorically excluded. However, in Estonia – in continuity with constitutional provisions on minority protection adopted in the interwar period – Article 50 of the Constitution ensures national minorities the right to establish self-governing agencies. According to Articles 51, para. 2 of the

---

Gender, Ethnicity and the Transformation of Islam in Postsocialist Bulgaria, Princeton, Princeton University Press, 2009.

144 J.P. Stein, *The Politics of National Minority Participation in Post-communist Europe*, Armonk, Routledge, 2000, p. 238.

145 The Constitutional Court has recognized the conformity to the Constitution of the Movement for Rights and Freedoms (MRF), *i.e.* the Turkish minority most important political party. On the contrary, in 2000, the Court declared unconstitutional the United Macedonian Organization – Ilinden. C. Filippini, 'La Costituzione della Bulgaria (1991)', *in* M. Ganino (Ed.), *Codice delle Costituzioni*, cit., p. 3.

146 In Lithuania, the Russian minority constitutes a considerably smaller group compared to the other two Baltic countries.

147 Nowadays, the Russophone minority represents about 5.8 percent of the Lithuanian population, 26.9 percent of the Latvian population and 24.8 percent of the Estonian population. Since 1989, ethnic Russians in the Baltic countries have decreased from 1.7 million people (according to the last Soviet Union census) to 1 million people (among whom 556,000 ethnic Russians in Latvia, in 2017, 321,000 in Estonia, in 2017, and 174,000 in Lithuania, in 2012). www.pmlp.gov.lv/lv/assets/documents/Iedzivotaju%20reģistrs/07022017/ISVN_Latvija_pec_TTB_VPD.pdf (Latvia, last accessed September 2018); www.stat.ee/34278 (Estonia, last accessed September 2018); https://web.archive.org (Lithuania, last accessed September 2018); www.demoscope.ru/weekly/ssp/sng_nac_89.php (last Soviet Union census, accessed September 2018).

Constitution, in localities where at least one-half of the "permanent residents" belong to a national minority, everyone has the right to receive responses from government agencies, local authorities and their officials also in the language of the national minority. In such localities, local authorities may use the language of the majority of permanent residents as their internal working language (Art. 52, para. 2, Constitution). It is worth to stress that the Constitution explicitly refers to 'permanent residents' instead of 'citizens', thus including members of the Russophone minority who did not obtain the naturalization. However, Act "On local elections" of 27 March 2003[148] specifies that foreigners (excluded European citizens),[149] permanently residing on the territory of a municipality, have the right to elect their own representatives in municipal elections (active suffrage), but not right to be elected (passive suffrage), which is reserved only to Estonian and European citizens (Art. 5, para. 2 and para. 5).

In Montenegro, the 2007 Constitution ensures "persons belonging to minority nations and other minority national communities" the right to have local self-government, state and court authorities carrying out proceedings in minority languages, where minorities represent a significant share of the population (Art. 97, para. 5, Constitution). The Constitution recognizes also national minorities the right to be represented in Parliament and in territorial assemblies, where they constitute a significant share of the population (Art. 79, para. 9, Constitution). It is useful to remember that the ethno-national composition of the population of Montenegro is, in theory, extremely complex. In practice, however, it can be difficult to analyse it, given the common linguistic and cultural background that different ethno-national groups do actually share.

Finally, with reference to ethnically homogenous countries, in Hungary territorial self-government played a major role in national minority protection.[150] Act LXXVII of 1993 "On the rights of national minorities" (amended several times in the following years), ensured the latter the right to participate in public affairs through the establishment of

148 www.riigiteataja.ee/en/eli/511072016012/consolide (last accessed September 2018).

149 Active voting rights in municipal elections of European and Estonian citizens are jointly set out in Act of 27 March 2003, Art. 5, para. 1.

150 From an ethnic and linguistic perspective, Hungary can be considered as a relatively homogeneous country: only 6.5 percent of the population is part of a national minority. Nowadays, there are thirteen officially recognized national groups: Romani people (3.2 percent of the Hungarian population), Bulgarians, Greeks, Croats, Poles, Germans, Armenians, Romanians, Ruthenians, Serbs, Slovaks, Slovenians, and Ukrainians. National minorities are not territorially concentrated. It is worth to remember that, on the basis of the Trianon Treaty, Hungary was forced to cede a relevant part of its territory to victorious powers and the ethnic composition of the country resulted simplified. In 1920, about 10 percent of the Hungarian population declared to be part of a national minority. Such simplification was followed by forced replacement of the German and Slovak population, in the aftermath of World War II, and then by assimilationist policies in the socialist period. D. Balázs, 'The Minority Self-Governments in Hungary', *Online Compendium Autonomy Arrangements in the World*, 2016, www.world-autonomies.info/ntas/hun/Documents/Hungary_2016-01-15.pdf (last accessed September 2018).

minority self-governing authorities, that operated together with territorial self-government ones.[151] The 1993 Act was replaced by Act CLXXIX of 2011 "On the rights of nationalities", which has introduced just slightly changes to the previous legislation.[152]

In Poland and Czech Republic, the presence of national minorities was not relevant enough to exert a direct influence on territorial reforms which followed the fall of communist regimes and the start of transition processes. In fact, in Poland, minorities represent about 2-3 percent of the population,[153] while in Czech Republic about 4 percent.[154] Nevertheless, in Czech Republic, reforms of the territorial structure were seriously hampered by the presence of Moravians, who improperly consider themselves as a minority.[155] The fear for Moravian separatism, as a matter of fact, led Czech authorities to exclude the possibility to establish territorial self-government units corresponding to Czech regions of the Hapsburg Empire – *i.e.* Bohemia, Moravia and Silesia – which were endowed with territorial Diets.[156]

As for the Balkans, in the countries which resulted more ethnically homogeneous from the dissolution of the Socialist Federative Republic of Yugoslavia, *i.e.* Slovenia and Croatia, and in Albania, the presence of national minorities played a marginal role in the territorial reform of the state structure.

Finally, in Kosovo, despite the wide protection ensured by the Constitution to national minorities, the possibility to recognize a wider autonomy to Serbian-majority municipalities, in the Northern part of the country, is currently at the heart of the public debate. Such an issue is also at the basis of troubled relations with Serbia.[157] The Serbian minority,

151 C. Filippini, 'La disciplina costituzionale delle minoranze nei Paesi dell'Europa orientale e l'adesione all'Unione europea', *in* M. Ganino & G. Venturini (Eds.), cit., p. 347 *et seq.*

152 A. Di Gregorio, 'Stato, nazione e minoranze in Europa centrale: la tutela minoritaria nell'Ungheria postsocialista', *in* D. Amirante & V. Pepe (Eds.), *Stato democratico e società multiculturale*, Torino, Giappichelli, 2011, pp. 131-153; D. Balázs, *The Minority Self-Governments in Hungary*, cit., pp. 13-14.

153 There are three categories of officially recognized minorities in Poland: nine "national minorities" (Belarusians, Czechs, Lithuanians, Germans, Armenians, Russians, Slovaks, Ukrainians, Jews), four "ethnic minorities" (Karaites, Lemkos, Roma and Tatars) and a "regional linguistic minority", *i.e.* Kashubian. They all represent about 3 percent of the Polish population. Silesian are not officially recognized as a national minority. 'Poland', www.coe.int/en/web/minorities/poland (last accessed September 2018).

154 There are fourteen officially recognized minorities in Czech Republic, *i.e.* Belarusian, Bulgarian, Croatian, German, Greek, Hungarian, Polish, Romani, Russian, Ruskinian, Serbian, Slovak, Ukrainian and Vietnamese minorities. 'Government Council for National Minorities', www.vlada.cz/en/pracovni-a-poradni-organy-vlady/rnm/historie-a-soucasnost-rady-en-16666 (last accessed September 2018); *Cf.* 'Czech Republic', www.coe.int/en/web/minorities/czech-republic (last accessed September 2018).

155 P. Daněk, 'Moravian and Silesian Nationalities: A New Phenomenon in the Ethnic Map of the Czech Lands?', *GeoJournal*, Vol. 30, No. 3, pp. 249-254; L. Petaková, 'Should Moravians be treated as an ethnic minority?', www.radio.cz/en/section/curraffrs/should-moravians-be-treated-as-an-ethnic-minority (last accessed September 2018).

156 M. Mareš, 'Separatist Currents in Moravian Fascism and National Socialism, Fascism', *Journal of Comparative Fascist Studies*, No. 2, 2013.

157 A. Angeli, 'The 2015 Agreements Between Serbia and Kosovo. A Further Step in the Normalization Process', http://radi.unimi.it/?p=1445 (last accessed September 2018).

according to un-official data, represents 7.8 percent of the Kosovar population. In ten municipalities, ethnic Serbians constitute the majority of the inhabitants.[158]

4.7 Recent Reforms of Local Self-Government

The CEBBE countries territorial organization – introduced in the context of democratic transitions – has been amended several times in the following years, in order to address new exigences emerged in the consolidation process of new democratic regimes. Except for Poland, Czech Republic and Slovakia, that established administrative regions, and Serbia, that retained a *sui generis* regional model, the other countries at stake opted for local decentralization only. In Hungary, Romania, Croatia, Albania (at least in part), territorial structure is organized on two levels of self-government, *i.e.* counties and communes.[159] The other countries of the area, that is to say Estonia, Latvia, Lithuania, Slovenia, Montenegro, Kosovo, Macedonia, and Bulgaria, introduced just a one-level system of self-government, corresponding to the commune. In Bosnia-Herzegovina, as already said, the dramatic events that followed the dissolution of the SFR of Yugoslavia, led to adoption of a federal solution guaranteed through international agreements.[160]

As for the Baltic countries, it is possible to highlight a common trend in Latvia and Lithuania, *i.e.* the simplification of the territorial structure through the abolition of the intermediate level. As already mentioned, in fact, democratic transitions led to the reintroduction of local self-government and to strengthening the municipal level. The intermediate level resulted weakened and it was finally suppressed. Economic considerations led these countries to operate such choices – as part of a wider reform of the State organization aimed at public spending reduction – in the context of the accession to the EU.

In 2009, in Latvia, districts were abolished and the territory was reorganized into nine republic cities and 110 municipalities, which represent the one-and-only level of territorial self-government.[161] The Law "On Local Government", adopted on 16 June 2009, sets out specific provisions on local government competences and financial resources, city/municipal councils' and chairpersons' rights and responsibilities, relations between local government and Cabinet/Ministries, as well as with other local government units (Section 1). Councils are representative bodies of republic cities and municipalities (Section

158 http://minorityrights.org/country/kosovo/ (last accessed September 2018).

159 Some authors, within the general category of territorial self-government, use to distinguish between "intermediate" and local authorities. G. Marcou, 'Adapting Territorial Structure', cit., p. 140.

160 'The General Framework Agreement for Peace in Bosnia and Herzegovina, Annex IV', www.osce.org/bih/126173?download=true (last accessed September 2018).

161 Act "On local government" of 16 June 2009, which entered into force on 1st July 2009, and Act "On administrative units and on populated areas" of 18 December 2008, https://likumi.lv/ta/en/en/id/185993-law-on-administrative-territories-and-populated-areas (last accessed September 2018).

3). Local government exert: mandatory autonomous functions, prescribed by law; delegated State administrative functions; and autonomous functions, which are performed as "voluntary initiatives" (Section 6).[162] The city/municipal council appoints and discharges from office (removes from duties) its own chairperson (Section 19 and Section 21, para. 10). The city/municipal chairperson manages the work of the council (Section 25). The Law "On administrative territories and settlements" of 18 December 2008 (Transitional Provision No. 24, para. 1) required the Government to prepare and submit to the *Saeima* a draft law on the establishment of districts by 1st June 2009. However, such a provision has not been implemented yet.

Analogously, Lithuanian counties – which constituted deconcentrated bodies of public administration – were abolished. Nowadays they represent only territorial units for statistical purposes.

Bulgaria constitutes an exception for the entire CEBBE area, considering its demographical and geographical size. In fact, Bulgaria has just one level of territorial self-government, namely the municipality. According to 1991 Constitution, Bulgaria is "a unitary state with local self-government" (Art. 2, para. 1). Its territory is organized into municipalities and *oblasts* (Art. 135). However, municipalities only do represent local self-government units (Art. 136, para. 1). Municipal bodies – *i.e.* the council and the mayor – are elected for a four-year term (Arts. 138-139). The Constitution defines *oblasts* as territorial-administrative units, who carry out *oblasts*' policies, exert deconcentrated state functions, and ensure the correspondence between local and national interests. *Oblasts* are deconcentrated entities run by a governor, appointed by the Council of Ministers, who ensures the implementation of the State's policy, the safeguarding of national interests, law and public order, and exercises administrative control (Art. 143). In 1999, nine *oblasts* established in 1987 were replaced by twenty-eight *oblasts*. The territory of new *oblasts* corresponds to districts introduced by the reforms adopted in 1959.[163] Proposals to create an intermediate level, in between national and local ones, were supported by the Government led by the former King Simeon II (2001-2005). However, such proposals did not lead to the adoption of any reform.

In Hungary, according to the Fundamental Law of 18 April 2011,[164] Article F "Fundamental principles", the territory of the country is comprised of counties and cities/towns/villages.[165] The capital, as well as cities and towns, may be divided into districts. Local governments adopt normative acts (ordinances and decisions), perform autonomous administration, determine their organizational structure, exercise their rights as owner of

162 www.oecd.org/regional/regional-policy/profile-Latvia.pdf (last accessed September 2018).

163 'Government structure', http://countrystudies.us/bulgaria/47.htm (last accessed September 2018).

164 G.F. Ferrari, 'La Costituzione dell'Ungheria', *in* Ganino (Ed.), *Codice delle Costituzioni*, cit., p. 389.

165 Hungary is divided into nineteen departments, 3175 municipalities and the capital Budapest, which in turn is organized into twenty-three districts.

local government properties, determine their budgets, may engage in entrepreneurial activities, decide on the types and rates of local taxes, and are free to associate with other local governments (Art. 32). As set out in Article 33, local governments exercise their competences through local representative bodies. Local councils are headed by a mayor at municipal level and by a president at county level. The latter is elected by the respective council. Local councillors and mayors, instead, are directly elected for a five-year term (Art. 35). According to the Constitution, rules on local government would have been defined by a cardinal act (Art. 31, para. 3). Such provision was implemented through Act CLXXXIX of 2011 "On local government in Hungary".[166] It is worth to remember that reforms adopted starting from 2011 recentralized several competences previously attributed to local government.[167]

In Albania, according to the 1998 Constitution, Articles 108 and 111, communes/municipalities and prefectures are units of local government, they have legal person status and independent budgets. Communes and municipalities are basic units of local government (Art. 108, para. 3). At municipal level, representative bodies, *i.e.* the councils, as well as executive bodies, *i.e.* mayors, are directly elected for a four-year term (Art. 109). The representative body of prefectures, that is the prefectural council, is not directly elected. Municipalities and communes delegate members to the prefectural council in proportion to their population. Moreover, mayors are always members of the prefectural council (Art. 110). Prefectures are administered by the prefect, who is appointed by the Council of Ministers (Art. 114). Act No. 8652 "On the organization and functioning of local government" and Act No. 8653 "On territorial-administrative division of local government units of the Republic of Albania" – they both two adopted on 31 July 2000 – established twelve provinces (corresponding to the twelve prefectures introduced in 1992), sixty-five municipalities and 308 communes.[168] Act No. 115 of 31 July 2014[169] further simplified the territorial structure of the country, that is now organized into twelve provinces and sixty-one municipalities, with a view to improve the efficiency of the system. Difficulties emerged in the context of 2000 reforms – with a specific reference to the mismatch between resources

166 P. Steiner, 'Introduction to the Hungarian Local Government System', www.manorka.net/news/227/94/Introductory-of-the-Hungarian-Local-Government-System (last accessed September 2018).

167 I. Temesi, 'The Swinging Pendulum of Decentralization in Hungary', *in* J. Ruano & M. Profiroiu (Eds.), *The Palgrave Handbook of Decentralisation in Europe*, Cham, Palgrave Macmillan, 2017, pp. 417-441; 'Division of Powers', https://portal.cor.europa.eu/divisionpowers/countries/MembersNLP/Hungary/Pages/default.aspx (last accessed September 2018).

168 O. Mucollari & E. Muharremaj, 'The Judicial Reform, the Effect of Decentralization of Public Services and Good Governance on Combating Corruption', *in* E. Bozheku, G. Spangher & A. Hoxha (Eds.), *La riforma costituzionale ("strutturale") del sistema della giustizia nella Repubblica d'Albania. Riflessioni e confronti con il sistema italiano*, Roma, Edizioni Nuova Cultura, 2017, p. 91.

169 www.reformaterritoriale.al/images/presentations/Ligji_115_2014.pdf (last accessed September 2018).

and competences attributed to local government – still characterize the Albanian territorial-administrative system.[170]

4.8 Administrative Regions in Central-Eastern Europe

At the end of 90s, Poland, Czech Republic and Slovakia – in the context of the democratic consolidation process and of the accession to the European Union – introduced new territorial reforms. The establishment of 'administrative'[171] regions constituted an element of discontinuity in the constitutional evolution of such countries, in the absence of consolidated traditions related to regional decentralization.

Moreover, these three countries represent the only examples in the CEBBE area in which an 'administrative' regional model – inspired to the French system – was introduced in the context of the accession process.[172] As already mentioned, the possibility to establish regions has been considered also in other countries – *i.e.* Romania, Hungary, Slovenia and Bulgaria – where such reforms have not been implemented yet. Finally, Serbia opted for a *sui generis* model of administrative regional decentralization, in line with its own constitutional traditions.

Poland, Czech Republic and Slovakia opted for a 'homogeneous' regional system. Administrative regions are legal entities, they do have directly elected councils, manage their own resources and assets, adopt regulations and act in the interest of the respective territorial community, as set out by law. The possibility to attribute primary legislative powers, as well as policy-making competences, to regions has been categorically excluded. Moreover, there is no hierarchy among different levels of the territorial-administrative structure. It is therefore not possible to consider regions as an intermediate level in between the State and local authorities.

The establishment of regional entities followed the adoption of a new constitution in the case of Poland and required a constitutional amendment in the cases of Czech Republic and Slovakia.

According to the 1997 Polish Constitution, Art. 164, communes are basic units of local government. "Other units of regional government or local and regional government" would have been specified by law. Such provision was implemented though as series of

170 O. Mucollari & E. Muharremaj, 'The Judicial Reform, the Effect of Decentralization of Public Services and Good Governance on Combating Corruption', cit., pp. 89-98.

171 A. Angeli, *La circolazione del sistema francese di decentramento territoriale nell'Europa centro-orientale*, Milano, FrancoAngeli, 2018.

172 G. Marcou, 'L'adaptation des structures territoriales', cit., pp. 162-165; A. Kruglashov, 'Central and Easter Europe Regional Reforms: From Dismantling a Soviet Model to Europeanizing a National One', cit., p. 22; A. Angeli, *La circolazione del sistema francese di decentramento territoriale nell'Europa centro-orientale*, cit.

legislative acts adopted stating from 1998.[173] The latter introduced a three-tier structure, organized into regions or voivodeship, districts and communes, in continuity with the traditional territorial organization of the country, before 1975. At the same time, Poland opted for a 'dual administrative system', in which both self-government bodies and deconcentrated bodies of the public administration operate at regional and district level.[174]

Poland therefore represents the only country of the CEBBE area organized in a three-tier structure of territorial self-government. The other two countries that introduced administrative regions – namely Czech Republic and Slovakia – have no intermediate level in between the municipal and the regional one. In Poland, Act of 24 July 1998 – which entered into force on 1st January 1999 – established sixteen regions, replacing the previous forty-nine regions introduced through Act of 28 May 1975. The denomination of new regions, in continuity with Polish historical traditions, coincides in part with the Second Republic one. Regions established in 1975, instead, took their name from small- or medium-sized towns situated in proximity to their centres, that became regional capitals. Moreover, new regions' territorial size was increased, compared to the previous one. The main purpose of such reform was to make regions more competitive in the context of the accession process, and to ensure them an easier access to EU structural and cohesion funds.[175]

The 1992 Constitution defines Czech Republic as a unitary state (Art. 1), who ensures "the right to self-government of autonomous territorial units" (Art. 8). Czech territorial structure is organized into two levels: regions, that are "higher territorial self-governing units", and municipalities, that are the "basic territorial self-governing units" (Art. 99). The 1992 Constitution in the original version mentioned only "higher territorial self-governing units". Constitutional Amendment No. 347/1997 introduced the denomination "regions" (Czech: *kraj*) for higher territorial self-governing units.[176] Act No. 129/2000 "On regions (establishment of regions)" – which implemented both the Constitution and Constitutional Amendment No. 347/1997 – lays down specific provisions on the organization and competences of regional bodies and it entered into force on 1st January 2001.[177]

173 Act of 24 July 1998 "On the introduction of the territorial division of the State into three levels"; Act of 5 June 1998 "On voivodeship self-government"; Act of 5 June 1998 "On the administration in the voivodeship"; Act of 5 June 1998 "On district self-government". Elections of territorial self-government representative bodies were held that same year and the new territorial system started to operate on 1st January 1999.

174 M. Kozlowska, 'Aspetti costituzionali ed amministrativi del decentramento dello Stato unitario polacco', www.issirfa.cnr.it (last accessed September 2018).

175 C. Filippini, *Polonia*, cit., pp. 92-93.

176 Constitutional Act No. 347/1997 of 3 December 1997 "On the establishment of higher territorial self-government units and amendment of the Constitution of Czech Republic, as amended by Constitutional Act No. 176/2001". www.usoud.cz/fileadmin/user_upload/ustavni_soud_www/Pravni_uprava/AJ/347_1997_EN.pdf (last accessed September 2018).

177 Act No. 129/2000 of 12 April 2000 "On regions (establishment of regions)", subsequently amended by Act No. 273/2001, Act No. 320/2001, Act No. 450/2001 and Act No. 231/2002.

Czech territory is organized into fourteen regions, included the city of Prague, which benefit from the *status* of capital, region and municipality.[178]

In Slovakia, according to the 1992 Constitution in the original version, the commune represented the basic unit of territorial self-government, while higher territorial self-government units and their bodies would have been defined by law (Art. 64, para. 3). Such provision was implemented several years after. Between 1993 and 1996, the Slovak territorial structure was organized on two levels, *i.e.* districts and municipalities.[179] The establishment of regions required a constitutional amendment, which was approved on 8 March 2001. Finally, on 4 July 2001, the Slovak National Council approved the Act "On higher territorial self-government units (regional self-government)",[180] which established eight administrative regions. Act No. 302/2001 lays down only basic elements of regional self-government institutional structure, while specific provisions are set out in other legal texts.[181]

As already said, regional self-government issue has been widely debated also in other Central and Eastern European countries, in the aftermath of the fall of communist regimes.

The Treaty of understanding, cooperation and good neighbourliness, signed on 16 September 1996[182] with Hungary, encouraged Romania to start a debate on the introduction of regional decentralization. In the Treaty, the inviolability of the common border, as defined in the Paris Peace Treaty of 1947, was re-affirmed (Art. 4), and mutual protection of national minorities restated (Preamble and Art. 15).

In 2011, considering difficulties experienced by Romania in having access to European structural funds, the possibility to introduce regional decentralization re-emerged in the public debate. That same year, the governing coalition, composed by the Democratic-Liberal Party and the Democratic Union of Hungarians in Romania (DUHR), presented a project to reform the territorial-administrative structure of the country. In the project, the governing coalition proposed to unify forty-one existing counties into eight macro-counties, corresponding to development regions, plus the capital city of Bucharest. Such project was rejected by the oppositions, as it would have introduced a regional level without requiring the amendment of the Constitution. At the same time, the project was not fully

178 Act No. 131/2000 of 13 April 2000 "On capital Prague".

179 J. Nemec, P. Bercik & P. Kuklis, 'Local Government in Slovakia', *in* T. Horváth (Ed.), *Decentralization: Experiments and Reforms*, Budapest, Local Government and Public Service Reform Initiative, 2000, pp. 301 *et seq.*

180 Act No. 302/2001 of 4 July 2001 "On self-government of higher territorial units (regional self-government)", www.slov-lex.sk/pravne-predpisy/SK/ZZ/2001/302 (last accessed September 2018).

181 Among whom the Act "On properties of higher territorial units", the already mentioned Act "On regional elections", Act "On salaries and wages of the presidents of higher territorial units", Act "On territorial self-government budget rules", *etc.*

182 https://treaties.un.org/doc/Publication/UNTS/Volume%201966/volume-1966-I-33604-English.pdf (last accessed September 2018).

supported also by the DUHR[183] (junior coalition partner), considering that the Hungarian minority is manly concentrated in the Eastern part of Transylvania and that it represents the majority of the population in three counties only (Harghita, Covasna and Mureş), also known as Székely Land.[184] The establishment of macro-counties would have led to the unification of three Hungarian-majority counties with other three Romanian-majority counties (Braşov, Alba e Sibiu), thus reducing the political relevance of ethnic Hungarians. The DUHR therefore presented an alternative project, which would have led to the establishment of sixteen macro-counties, and to the creation of a Hungarian-majority region. The latter would have corresponded to the Hungarian Autonomous Region of the socialist period, for long-time contended between Romania and Hungary. Both two projects did not receive enough support, and they were soon abandoned, due to the fear of ethnic tension revival in the Székely Land.[185]

On 6 February 2013, Social-Democratic Party presented a new bill "On the establishment, organization and functioning of regions",[186] inspired by the Polish regional model, that would have required the amendment of the Constitution. Regions would have been established as legal entities, endowed with an elective council and a pluriannual budget. Constitutional amendments should have been approved by the Parliament in 2013, and then through a confirmative referendum. Such a project would have represented a solution to the impellent need to introduce regional decentralization in Romania, through a more inclusive process compared to the previous attempts.[187] However, the reform process did not come to an end, and the confirmative referendum – initially scheduled for 25 May 2014 and then postponed to the end of 2015 – did not take place. On 5 November 2015, Prime Minister Victor Ponta resigned. The technocratic cabinets that followed (led by

183 L. Stroie, *Emil Boc, Comasarea judetelor poate fi facuta fara revizuirea Constitutiei* [Emil boc: The union of counties can be made without constitutional amendment], www.ziare.com/emil-boc/stiri-emil-boc/emil-boc-comasarea-judetelor-poate-fi-facuta-fara-revizuirea-constitutiei-1100581 (last accessed September 2018), 11 July 2011; J. Benedek & H. Bajtalan, 'Recent Regionalisation Discourses and Projects in Romania with Special Focus on Székelyland', *Transylvanian Review of Administrative Science*, No. 44, 2015, pp. 23-41; D. Dragoman & B. Gheorghiţă, *Regional Design*, cit., p. 279.

184 'The 2011 Population and Housing Census', www.recensamantromania.ro/en (last accessed September 2018).

185 D. Dragoman & B. Gheorghiţă, *Regional Design*, cit., p. 281.

186 *Lege privind infiintarea organizarea si functionarea regiunilor* [Act on establishment, organization and functioning of regions], http://adrvest.ro/attach_files/legea_regiunilor.pdf (last accessed September 2018). Cf. C. Fierbinteanu, *Proiect de lege: România, împărţită în 8 regiuni. Unde vor fi capitalele regiunilor* [Draft law: Romania, divided into 8 regions. Where are the capitals of the regions], www.mediafax.ro/politic/proiect-de-lege-romania-impartita-in-8-regiuni-unde-vor-fi-capitalele-regiunilor-10547169 (last accessed September 2018), 6 February 2013; *Proiect de lege: Romania, impartita in 8 regiuni, cu buget multianual* [Draft law: Romania, divided into 8 regions with a multiannual budget], www.ziare.com/politica/lege/proiect-de-lege-romania-impartita-in-8-regiuni-cu-buget-multianual-conduse-de-consilii-regionale-1217185 (last accessed September 2018), 6-2-2013.

187 M. Ganino, 'La Costituzione della Romania (1991)', *in* M. Ganino (Ed.), *Codice delle Costituzioni*, cit., pp. 253-254.

Sorin Cîmpeanu and by Dacian Cioloş) did not politically support the reform project and the constitutional amendments.

4.8.1 *The Case of Serbia*

The dissolution of the Union of Serbia and Montenegro – together with the ethnic complexity that historically characterized the Balkan area – greatly contributed to shape nowadays territorial structure of Serbia.

The 2006 Constitution,[188] in continuity with the previous texts, guarantee the autonomy of the two Serbian provinces, or *pokrajine*, of Vojvodina and Kosovo-Metohija (Art. 182). The latter is predominantly inhabited by an Albanian population and is no more *de facto* under the control of Serbian authorities. In Vojvodina, instead, there is a relevant Hungarian minority.[189] Serbia opted for an 'administrative' regional model and for an 'asymmetric' system. Firstly, regions do not exercise primary legislative powers, but they are entitled to adopt secondary legislation. Secondly, the regional system does not cover the entire territory of the country.

Autonomous Provinces are self-government units of 'regional relevance'. According to the Constitution, APs "have the *status* of legal entities" (Art. 176, para. 2), enact decisions and other acts in the exercise of their competences (Art. 185), and are administered by an elective council (Art. 180). APs regulate the matters of provincial interest in the fields of: urban planning and development, agriculture, forestry, hunting, fishery, tourism, environmental protection, industry and craftsmanship, roads, river and railway transport, education, sport, culture, health care and social welfare, and they ensure the exercise of human and minority rights (Art. 183). APs own autonomous financial resources to exercise their competences (Art. 184), and adopt their own statute, that is subject to the prior approval of the National Assembly (Art. 185). Constitutional Court judges on the conformity of provincial decisions to the Constitution and to the laws – upon request of the Government – prior to their entry into force (*a priori* review). Moreover, the Constitutional Court safeguards the provincial autonomy – upon request of the AP itself, in the exercise of provincial competences – from local self-government units' and central authorities' interference (Arts. 186-187).

Judgement of the Constitutional Court No. 353/2009 of 10 July 2012 declared Act No. 99/2009 "On the competences of the Autonomous Province of Vojvodina" partially not compliant to the Constitution. Such judgment greatly limited the autonomy of the AP of

188 www.ius.bg.ac.rs/prof/materijali/martan/Ustav_Srbije.pdf (last accessed September 2018).

189 Vojvodina has a population of 1.9 million people. The 66 percent of the inhabitants are ethnic Serbs, while the Hungarian minority represents the 13 percent of the population. D. Vukmirović (Ed.), *Ethnicity. Data by municipalities and cities*, Beograd, Statistical Office of the Republic of Serbia, 2012.

Vojvodina, stating that "while Serbia recognize the principle of territorial decentralization, it still remains a unitary country".[190]

As laid down in the Constitution, Article 185, on 22 May 2014 the Assembly of the AP of Vojvodina approved its own statute.[191] In the latter, the AP is defined as "an autonomous territorial community of the Republic of Serbia in which citizens shall exercise their right to provincial autonomy, in conformity with the Constitution and law" (Art. 1). The assembly represents the highest authority of the Autonomous Province, it adopts normative acts (Art. 30), is composed by 120 members directly elected for a four-year term (Arts. 32, paras. 1 and 34, para. 1). The provincial government is the executive authority of the AP, it is accountable to the assembly (Art. 44) and is composed by a president, one or more vice-presidents and its members (Art. 46).

The statute of Vojvodina ensures the protection of national minorities/national communities – with a specific reference to the right to self-government in the fields of culture, education, information and official use of the language/alphabet – through elective national councils (Art. 23). In addition to Serbian language and Cyrillic alphabet, Hungarian, Slovak, Croatian, Romanian and Ruthenian languages and their respective alphabets are in official use in public bodies of AP of Vojvodina (Art. 24).

190 M. Dicosola, 'Serbia – La Corte costituzionale stabilisce i limiti dell'autonomia della Vojvodina', *DPCEonline*, No. 4, 2012, p. 4.

191 www.skupstinavojvodine.gov.rs/Strana.aspx?s=statut&j=EN (last accessed September 2018).

5 Constitutional Justice and Judicial Power. The Role of Constitutional Courts in the Processes of Democratization and Europeanization[1]

Čarna Pištan

5.1 Introduction

The constitutional justice, intended as judicial review of legislation, has been introduced in almost all countries of Central and Eastern Europe and post-Soviet Union sphere during the initial phase of democratic transition of the early 1990s. The general proliferation of constitutional review in the post-communist region has been often described as one of the most spectacular features of the transition from socialism to democracy, and as one of the most revolutionary aspects of the great 1989-1990 regime change.[2] This is because, as many authors have observed, systems of constitutional justice were established in countries which in their past were familiar with the principle of legality, but had no previous traditions of constitutionalism and constitutional jurisdiction.[3] Certainly, the establishment of constitutional review at the beginning of the democratic transition represented an absolute novelty in several countries of the area; however, some countries of the region had experienced in their constitutional history some limited forms of judicial review. For this reason, more impressive than the mere emergence of systems of constitutional justice in the post-communist sphere in the early 1990s has been the formidable role played by constitutional adjudication bodies in the processes of democratization and Europeanization of their renewed legal orders.

1 The research conducted for this chapter was carried out at the *Center for Constitutional Studies and Democratic Development* (CCSDD) under the support of George Lawrence Abernethy Endowment.

2 *See* W. Sadurski, 'Postcommunist Constitutional Courts in Search of Political Legitimacy', *European University Institute Law Working Paper*, No. 11, 2001, p. 1.

3 *See* C. Boulanger, 'Europeanization Through Judicial Activism? The Hungarian Constitutional Court's Legitimacy and the "Return to Europe"', *in* W. Sadurski, A. Czarnota & M. Krygier (Eds.), *Spreading Democracy and the Rule of Law? The Impact of EU Enlargement on the Rule of Law, Democracy and Constitutionalism in Post-Communist Legal Orders*, Dordrecht, Springer, 2006, p. 264.

This chapter focuses on the reconstruction of the current systems of constitutional justice in Central and Eastern, Baltic and Balkan European countries (CEBBE) under two perspectives. On the one hand, it firstly examines the historical precedents of constitutional review in the region, and then focuses on the (re)birth of constitutional justice in the phase of democratic transition. In this sense, it investigates, in particular, the dominant model of constitutional review in the CEBBE countries, and the normative framework regulating the composition, organization and powers of constitutional adjudication bodies. The aim of such analysis is to identify the different features that have shaped the current systems of constitutional review, *i.e.* to verify if the CEBBE countries have simply imported one of the traditional models of constitutional justice, or if they are still influenced by their historical precedents of constitutional review, as well as to identify the innovations that the most recent proliferation of constitutional review in Europe has introduced. On the other hand, the chapter focuses on the evolution of Constitutional Courts' case law with the aim to investigate the role assumed by constitutional adjudication bodies firstly in the process of democratization, and more recently in the process of Europeanization of CEBBE region. Finally, the chapter provides for a general overview of the judicial systems of CEBBE countries, as in several cases constitutional adjudication bodies are perceived as part of judicial power.

5.2 Historical Precedents of Constitutional Review

Undoubtedly, the general openness of CEBBE countries to constitutional jurisdiction dates back to the great regime change, which was experienced by all countries of the region following the fall of socialism. Nonetheless, at the beginning of democratic transition not all CEBBE countries were in the same position with respect to constitutional justice. In some of these countries, the first attempts aimed at introducing limited forms of constitutional review date back to the pre-socialist period or, rather, to these countries' socialist past.

As far as the pre-socialist period is concerned, several scholars have already emphasized that since the nineteenth century the whole area of Central and Eastern Europe represented an immense receptacle of legal models and institutions of Western origin, largely thanks to the deep and lasting bonds which unified the legal cultures of that period.[4] Similar considerations are also valid for constitutional models, and therefore for the emergence of the idea of constitutional review. In fact, in the nineteenth century the area of today's CEBBE countries was marked by several historical precedents of constitutional review,

4 *See* G. Ajani, *Fonti e modelli nel diritto dell'Europa orientale*, Trento, Centro stampa dell'Università degli studi di Trento, 1993, p. 91.

mainly of French origins,[5] while the interwar period saw some first attempts aimed at introducing the traditional models of constitutional justice in the region.

The first example of this trend can be found in the 1866 Constitution of Romania, which established the principle of constitutional supremacy, but remained silent to the prediction of any mechanism aimed at its protection. Nevertheless, between 1912 and 1923, in the absence of any specific constitutional provisions, an ephemeral form of constitutional review was established by the case law. More precisely, the Tribunal of Ilfove in one first decision of 9 February 1912 refused to apply to the case under consideration legislative norms contrary to the Constitution,[6] while in the most famous *Bucharest Tram Company case* of 16 March 1922, the Court of Cassation and Justice affirmed that the power to perform constitutional review, although not expressly established by the Constitution, belonged to all judges, as it originated from the duty of judges to apply the law and, above all, the Constitution.[7] The 1912 decision pronounced by the Court of Cassation and Justice has been often described as the Romanian *Marbury v. Madison*.[8] In fact, with this decision Romania implemented the US model of constitutional justice in a period in which the idea to emulate the American system of judicial review was contended in very few Western European countries. The 1912 decision remains important also for the future development of constitutional justice in the Romanian legal system. For example, it is still invoked by national scholars as a source which justifies the current existence of constitutional review in the country.[9]

---

5 *See, e.g.*, the 1791 Constitution of Poland had empowered the Senate with the competence to exercise a mandatory *ex ante* review of draft legislation. Its decisions on unconstitutionality of draft legislation had the effect to suspend its entering into force, which had to be re-examined by the Chamber of Deputies. This solution should be read in the light of the particular Polish political system of the time, known as Nobles' Democracy, as well as in terms of the traditional relationship between the Polish legal system and the French legal order. The French legal thought influenced the Polish legal solutions also in the interwar period and for this reason they could not culminate in the acceptance of one of the traditional models of constitutional justice. Accordingly, the Polish Constitutions of 1921 and 1935 reconfirmed the Senate as a body which had the power to exercise an *ex ante* review of legislation. *See* Č. Pištan, *Tra democrazia e autoritarismo. Esperienze di giustizia costituzionale nell'Europa centro-orientale e nell'area post-sovietica*, cit., 2015, p. 64.

6 *Cf.* N. Păun, 'Il modello romeno nel periodo interbellico', *in* P. Fornaro (Ed.), *La tentazione autoritaria. Istituzioni, politica e società nell'Europa centro-orientale tra le due guerre mondiali*, Soveria Mannelli, Rubettino, 2004, p. 165.

7 It is interesting to note that the 1912 decision of the Court of Cassation and Justice was adopted following some consultations with French legal experts in a historical moment in which France denied a similar jurisdiction to its judges. *See* H. Schwartz, *The Struggle for Constitutional Justice in Post-Communist Europe*, Chicago University of Chicago Press, 2000, p. 17.

8 *See* G. Conac, 'O anterioritate română: controlul constituționalității legilor în România de la începutul secolului XX până în 1938' (A Romanian antithesis: the constitutional review of legislation in Romania from the beginning of the 20th century until 1938), *Revista de Drept Public*, No. 1, 2001, p. 2.

9 *See* I. Muraru, 'Câteva considerații teoretice privind efectele juridice ale unor decizii date în contencios constituțional' (Some theoretical considerations on the legal effects of some decisions of the constitutional litigation), *Revista Română de Drept Privat*, No. 2, 2012, p. 171.

However, the 1912 Romanian diffuse system of judicial review was subjected to some changes with the adoption of the 1923 Constitution. On the one hand, the Article 103 of the Constitution formalized the well-established judicial practice, but limited the power to perform an *ex post* review of legislation to the Court of Cassation; on the other hand, the Article 76 of the Constitution introduced a new body, the Legislative Council, which was structurally part of the Council of State, and was authorized to perform an *ex ante* review in the form of advisory opinions on the constitutionality of legal acts prior to their promulgation.[10] The Romanian 1923 solution had many points in common with proposals already advanced in France. Evidently, the constant reference of the Romanian legal system to the evolution of the French legal thought was decisive in this phase, bringing to fulfilment both the (rejected) proposal advanced during the French Third Republic, which reserved the power to perform an *ex post* review to the Court of Cassation, and the introduction of an *ex ante* norm control, which was performed in France by the *Conseil d'Etat* since 1848.[11]

However, the most relevant historical precedent of constitutional justice in CEBBE region is given by the 1920 Constitution of Czechoslovakia, which was inspired by the rule of law and permeated by the influences of German constitutionalism. The 1920 Czechoslovak Constitution announced the creation of the first European Constitutional Court (introduced a few months earlier than the Austrian one). The Czechoslovak attempt

10 *See* A.N. Gane, 'Le Conseil législatif en Roumaine', *Bulletin de la Société de législation compare*, Vol. 58, No. 7-9, 1929, pp. 506-516.

11 At the beginning of the twentieth century, the French solution was imitated by other countries of Central and Eastern Europe. For example, in Serbia, the 1903 Constitution created the Council of State, which in addition to perform competences related to administrative justice had the power to adopt opinions on the constitutionality of draft legislation. The events in the rest of the neighbouring territories should be read, instead, in the light of the Habsburg experience. In this sense, the two regions of Slovenia and Dalmatia, as members of the Austro-Hungarian Empire, experienced the jurisdiction of the *Reichsgericht*. The Court of the Empire was configured as a judge of conflicts, capable of guaranteeing the equality of rights formally recognized to the member countries of the Empire, and as the maximum guarantor of fundamental rights. As pointed out by A. Zorzi Giustiniani, *Norme costituzionali e regolamentari sulla Corte costituzionale jugoslava*, cit., p. 50, in the framework of the protection of fundamental rights of Slovenian and Dalmatian citizens, as well as of the rights formally recognized to Slovenia and Dalmatia, the limited competences of constitutional review exercised by the *Reichsgericht* did not prove to be completely satisfactory in the practice. In other words, what has been the real impact of the activities of the Vienna Tribunal on the above mentioned member countries remains difficult to establish. However, the ruling classes, jurists and politicians of the time had have certainly the opportunity, if not to petitioned it, to appreciate its competences and reflect on its functions. The subsequent events in the Balkans saw the emergence of the first Yugoslavia, which 1921 and 1931 Constitutions remained in silence with respect to any kind of mechanism aimed at controlling the legislative power. Nevertheless, the Yugoslav legal scholars of the time had proven to be particularly sensitive on the topic of judicial review, and thanks to the spread of comparative studies some authors have shown a particular scientific interest in foreign models, especially the US system of judicial review. *See* A. Djordjević, 'Ruzveltova reforma Vrhovnog suda' (Roosevelt's reform of the Supreme Court), *Arhiv za pravne i društvene nauke*, No. 4, 1937, p. 67 and L. Pitamic, 'Ustavnosudska kriza u Sjedinjenim Državama Amerike 1937 godine' (The 1937 constitutional and judicial crisis in the United States), *Arhiv za pravne i društvene nauke*, No. 12, 1938, p. 76.

to introduce a system of constitutional justice was thus contemporary to the much more fortunate experience of the neighbouring Austria, and was influenced by the same theories of Hans Kelsen and the Vienna School.[12] In accordance to the Kelsenian model of constitutional justice, the Czechoslovak Constitutional Court was composed of seven judges, designated on the basis of a mixed system (three by the President of the Republic on the proposal of the parliament and the government, two by the Supreme Court and two by the Supreme Administrative Court). It was competent to carry out an *ex post* abstract norm control, which could be initiated by the supreme courts of the country (the Supreme Judicial Tribunal, the Supreme Administrative Court and the Electoral Tribunal), and legislative assemblies (Chamber of Deputies, Senate and the Parliamentary Assembly of Ruthenia). The Court's decisions were adopted at public hearings and were final and void from the day of their publication.[13] The constitutional adjudication body started to perform its activities on 17 November 1921 and until 1941, when it ceased to exist, it adopted sixty-five decisions.[14]

Although the Czechoslovak Constitution affirmed the exclusive competence of the Constitutional Court to perform the constitutional review of legislation, the Supreme Administrative Court also had some limited powers in the field of constitutional justice, as it had the power to decide on individual complaints. According to some scholars, such institutional design stemmed from the attempt to unite the two traditional Western prototypes of constitutional justice while drafting the 1920 Constitution, with the result that the constitutional review was inspired simultaneously by both the Austrian model and the American model.[15]

Further attempts aimed at introducing the judicial review in CEBBE sphere can be found in the Baltic area. For example, in Estonia, debates concerning the establishment of a constitutional court date back to the period of the adoption of the 1938 Constitution, but a constitutional adjudication body was not included in the final constitutional text. In Latvia, a proposal aimed at creating a State Court with the dual competence of reviewing the constitutionality of laws and the legality of governmental and presidential acts was put

12 A. Di Gregorio, 'La transizione in Cecoslovacchia. Principali profili di diritto costituzionale', *in* S. Gambino (Ed.), *Costituzionalismo europeo e transizioni democratiche*, cit., p. 250.

13 *Cf.* L. Cutler, H. Schwartz, 'Constitutional Reform in Czechoslovakia: E Duobus Unum?', *University of Chicago Law Review*, Vol. 58, No. 2, 1991, p. 511.

14 C.J. Přibán, 'Judicial Power vs. Democratic Representation. The Culture of Constitutionalism and Human Rights in the Czech Legal System', *in* W. Sadurski (Ed.), *Constitutional Justice, East and West. Democratic Legitimacy and Constitutional Courts in Post-Communist Europe in a Comparative Perspective*, The Hague, Kluwer Law International, 2002, p. 373.

15 C.D. Malová, 'The Role and Experience of the Slovakian Constitutional Court', in W. Sadurski (Ed.), *Constitutional Justice, East and West. Democratic Legitimacy and Constitutional Courts in Post-Communist Europe in a Comparative Perspective*, cit., p. 351.

forward in 1934. It requested an amendment to the 1922 Constitution, but the proposed amendment did not reach the necessary majority of two-thirds of votes of the Parliament.

In the socialist period, CEBBE countries generally rejected the judicial review of legislation due to its fundamental incompatibility with the ideology of the socialist legal system: the idea of withering away of the state and the law; the particular communist concept of the Constitution, and the socialist basic principles, such as the unity of state power, democratic centralism, and the dogma of absolute supremacy of the representative assembly. The constitutional review was, therefore, considered as illegitimate in the case it was exercised by a constitutional court, as well as in the case it was carried out by ordinary judiciary and the supreme court. In fact, socialist states perceived as inconceivable empower a body different from the representative assembly with the competence to review the content of the laws adopted by the supreme representative body.[16] However, this does not mean that the concept of constitutional review was totally unknown to socialist states, but only that it was conceived in a totally different manner from liberal states. The rejection of the idea of constitutional review practiced by an extra-parliamentary body led to the acceptance of the political type of review, as the only type of legitimate constitutional review, according to which the review of constitutionality of legislation was performed by the representative assemblies, or by a more restricted bodies, which formed part of the supreme representative body.[17]

The only exception to this trend is given by Yugoslavia, which had introduced in its 1963 Constitution (and confirmed by the 1974 Constitution) a complex system of constitutional courts at the federal, republican and provincial levels. From the formal perspective, the Yugoslav socialist system of constitutional justice incorporated all the characteristic features of the Austrian model. The Federal Constitutional Court (as well as the other republican and provincial courts, which were modelled in correspondence to the latter) was equipped with all essential requisites necessary to compose the classical Kelsenian *Verfassungsgerichtsbarkeit*. At the same time, the Yugoslav system of constitutional review imported several elements from the Italian and German systems, and introduced also some innovative aspects.[18] From a substantial perspective, the Yugoslav variant of the European-

16 *See* D. Roussillon, 'Le problème du contrôle de la constitutionnalité des lois dans les pays socialistes', *Rev. dr. Publ. Sc. pol.*, No. 1, 1977, p. 61.

17 *See* P. Biscaretti di Ruffia, 'Il problema del controllo di costituzionalità delle leggi negli "stati socialisti" europei', *in Scritti in onore di Vezio Crisafulli*, Vol. I, Padova, Cedam, 1985, p. 364.

18 The Federal Constitutional Court – composed of eleven judges elected by the Federal Assembly on the proposal of the Presidency of the Republic – was competent to exercise both the review of constitutionality of laws and the review of constitutionality and legality of other general normative acts. As a rule, the Court was competent to review normative provisions already in force, but it could also review, as in the German system, legislation and other normative acts, which have lost their legal force, provided that no more than one year has elapsed from the date when they went out of force. Further, the Court was endowed with extensive competences of decision-making, such as the power to decide *ultra petitum*. The Federal Court exercised an *ex post* abstract norm control, which was characterized by a broad range of figures being

Kelsenian model of constitutional justice remained a limited experiment of judicial review as the the effects of constitutional courts' decisions were limited.[19]

The reasons which led the framers of the Yugoslav Constitution to introduce the articulated system of constitutional courts, although often attributed to the federal character

---

authorize to commence the proceeding, including public and social bodies, and the Court *ex-officio*. It also exercised the concrete review, which, however, remained limited as only the Supreme Court, and not also other ordinary courts had the power to refer constitutional questions to the Constitutional Court. The Yugoslav system introduced also the direct access of citizens to the Court against individual acts, which was modelled on the basis of the German system, albeit it was never completely regulated, and in the practice issues concerning individual acts continued to be decided by the Supreme Court. The other powers of the Federal Court included the resolution of inter-states disputes and conflicts between judicial and political-administrative bodies, which discipline was based on the Art. 93 of the *Grundgesetz*. Finally, the Court was empowered by some additional competences, which were not derived from the Austrian model (or its German and Italian sub-models), and which can be thus defined as innovative: the power to decide on *actio popularis* with which 'everybody' could appeal to the Court to declare laws and other normative acts invalid on the grounds that they violate the Constitution; provided binding interpretations of the Constitution, and monitor the execution of the principles of constitutionality and legality, including reporting to the Federal Assembly any kind of observed unconstitutionality and legality through the formulation of opinions and proposals. Especially with the 1974 Constitution, the principles of constitutionality and legality assumed an unprecedented importance. This was also confirmed by the special chapter the Constitution dedicated to the two principles. For an ultimate reconstruction of the Yugoslav socialist system of constitutional justice *see* Č. Pištan, *Tra democrazia e autoritarismo. Esperienze di giustizia costituzionale nell'Europa centro-orientale e nell'area post-sovietica*, cit., p. 117.

19 In particular, decisions on unconstitutionality of normative acts had different effects depending on whether they referred to legislation or sublegislative acts. In the case of unconstitutionality and illegality of sublegislative acts, the Federal Court (as well as the republican and provincial courts) had the possibility to adopt different decisions, which might imply, depending on a temporal effects, the annulment or abrogation of the disputed sublegislative act. Decisions which established the annulment of sublegislative acts were considered as declaratory and had *ex tunc* effects, whilst decisions which provided for the abrogation of sublegislative acts were considered as constitutive and had *ex nunc* effects. The decision on whether proceed with the annulment or abrogation of disputed sublegislative acts was a discretionary choice of the Court, which was, however, obliged to consider the seriousness of the violation of the Constitution and law, the rights of citizens and social organizations, the legal relationships which were established on the basis of disputed sublegislative acts, and the principle of legal certainty. When, on the other hand, the Court declared the unconstitutionality of legislation, it could not directly struck it down, as it was limited to ascertain its non-conformity with the Constitution by adopting a declaratory decision and notify this decision to the legislative assembly. The declaratory decision obliged the representative assembly to change the law in line with the Constitution within a term of six months (extendable to other six months) from the day when the Constitutional Court decision was published. If the legislative assembly failed to bring the law into conformity with the Constitution within that deadline, that law went out of force, but only after the adoption by the Court of a second declarative decision aimed at ascertaining that the legal rules, by virtue of the inertia of the assembly, ceased to exist. The second decision had *erga omnes* and *ex nunc* effects, and it was binding from the day of its publication. In this way, the Yugoslav system had extended and made mandatory an instrument already introduced by the Austrian Constitution, namely the temporal deferral of the effects of decisions on unconstitutionality, with the difference that in Austria it is not imperative, while in the Yugoslav system it became the rule. Of course, in the latter case the temporal limitation of constitutional courts' decisions was introduced as it was considered in line with the principles of the unity of state power, and the absolute supremacy of the parliamentary assembly. *See* A. Djordjević, *Ustavno pravo* (Constitutional Law), Beograd, Savremena Administracija,1978 e V. Čok, *Vrste i dejstvo odluka ustavnih sudova* (Types and effects of Constitutional Courts' decisions), Beograd, Institut za uporedno pravo, 1972.

of the Yugoslav state,[20] should be more properly ascribed to the political-economic system of self-management, which marked the Yugoslav version of socialism.[21] Thus the main reason of the establishment of the Yugoslav variant of constitutional justice should be ascribed to political reasons as it was aimed at the full realization of the system of self-management. The latter led to the decentralization of the normative activity, and as a consequence to the proliferation of a very high number of sublegislative acts, which had to be coordinated and harmonized with both the legislation and the constitution. Similar assumptions had been fully confirmed in the practice, which showed that the main function of the Federal Court (as well as the republican and provincial courts) was not the constitutional review of legislation, but the review of constitutionality and legality of sublegislative acts. For this reason, constitutional courts established in Yugoslavia cannot be described as real constitutional adjudication bodies, but rather as bodies that primarily performed functions of administrative justice. Although the Yugoslav system represented a limited system of constitutional justice, it showed an attractive force in other European socialist countries. On the example of Yugoslavia, Czechoslovakia (re)introduced the Constitutional Court in 1968 (but did not became active in practice), Poland created a Constitutional Tribunal in 1982, and Hungary a Constitutional Council of Law in 1983.[22]

---

20 *See* P. Biscaretti di Ruffia, 'Il problema del controllo di costituzionalità delle leggi negli "stati socialisti" europei', cit., p. 368.

21 *See* T. Vasiljević, 'Neka pitanja metoda i tehnika pripremanja pravnih propisa' (Some questions on the method and techniques for drafting legal documents), *Arhiv za pravne i društvene nauke*, No. 4, 1964, p. 373, and V. Šimić, 'Problemi zakonodavstva i izgradnje pravnog sistema' (Problems of legislation and construction of the legal system), *Arhiv za pravne i društvene nauke*, No. 4, 1964, p. 313.

22 As in the Yugoslav system, the election of constitutional judges was demanded to representative assemblies. In all cases, constitutional adjudication bodies exercised both the review of constitutionality of laws and the review of constitutionality and legality of sublegislative acts. Furthermore, they all performed the abstract review (everywhere characterized by a broad range of figures authorized to initiate the proceeding), and with the exception of Hungary, the concrete review, which as in the Yugoslav case remained limited in Poland, but not in Czechoslovakia. Finally, in all of these countries the decisions of constitutional adjudication bodies were subjected to temporal limitations. Poland and Hungary were even less courageous than Yugoslavia as in both countries the only effect of decisions on unconstitutionality of legislation and decisions on unconstitutionality and illegality of sublegislative acts was to request the body that had adopted the disputed act to conform it to the Constitution, or override the decision adopted by the constitutional adjudication body. *See* A. Zorzi Giustiniani, *Norme costituzionali e regolamentari sulla Corte costituzionale jugoslava*, cit., p. 81. On the role of the Polish Constitutional Tribunal in the last years of the socialist period (1986-1989) *see* J. Sawicki, *La funzione normativa nell'esperienza della Polonia. Continuità e mutamenti nella trasformazione della forma di Stato e di governo*, cit., pp. 43-61.

5.3 (Re)Birth of Constitutional Justice in the Context of Democratic Transition

The formal and legal premises for the introduction of the modern constitutional review in the sphere of CEBBE countries were created only with the collapse of the socialist state and the consequent process of transition to democracy, when in the framework of radical constitutional reforms and by accepting one of the cardinal principles of Western constitutionalism, all countries of the area had introduced in their new (or renewed) Constitutions a system of constitutional justice.[23] The post-communist regime transformation was marked by the imitation of political and economic models and institutions belonging to the Western legal tradition, which were quickly transplanted during the new constitution-making process of the 1990s. Unsurprisingly, the same path was followed in the establishment of constitutional adjudication.

During the constitution-making process (or approval of amendments to existing Constitutions) of the early 1990s, the traditional models of constitutional review started to rapidly circulate throughout the sphere of CEBBE countries, and systems of constitutional justice were incorporated in constitutional texts, largely imitating those realized in the consolidated Western democracies. Between the two traditional models of constitutional justice, the framers of new (or renewed) constitutions in CEBBE countries did not show particular interest in the US system of judicial review, having preferred focus their attention on the European-Kelsenian model and, in particular, on its German, Italian, Spanish, and Portuguese sub-models. In addition, some countries were also inspired by the French variant of constitutional review. The result was a spectacular proliferation of specialized body typically called constitutional courts (or tribunals), with the competence of carrying out constitutional review. This occurred not only in countries with some limited historical precedents of judicial review, but more generally in the whole CEBBE area.[24]

---

23 *See* G. de Vergottini, 'Foreword', *in* G. de Vergottini (Ed.), *Giustizia costituzionale e sviluppo democratico nei paesi dell'Europa centro-orientale*, Torino, Giappichelli, 2000, p. 2.

24 The reasons for the wide adoption of the European model of constitutional justice as opposed to US-style judicial review have been explained by several authors and are generally related to both international and domestic factors. According to H. Schwartz, *The Struggle for Constitutional Justice in Post-Communist Europe*, cit., p. 24, it was very natural that the Central and Eastern European countries opted for the European model of concentrated review. After all, they have the same civil law traditions as Western European countries and, hence, little familiarity with the US system of judicial review. According to L. Sólyom, The Role of Constitutional Courts in the Transition to Democracy, with Special Reference to Hungary', *International Sociology*, Vol. 18, No. 1, 2003, p. 135, the post-communist choice of a concentrated model of judicial review and the consequent growth of constitutional courts throughout the CEBBE countries was a direct consequence of the fact that these countries had just emerged from a period of authoritarian rule. As the precedent waves of constitutional justice in Western Europe demonstrate, constitutional courts appear historically after the experiences of authoritarian regimes and during the creation of a new democratic order. For example, this was the case of the first generation, the Italian and German Constitutional Courts,

The only country partially influenced by the US model of decentralized (or diffuse) concrete review was Estonia, where all national courts are authorized to consider the constitutionality of legislation and to not apply legal provisions that, in their opinion, are unconstitutional; however, the only body with the power to annul laws in conflict with the Constitution is the Constitutional Review Chamber, which is structurally a part of the national Supreme Court. According to some authors, the Constitutional Review Chamber could be assimilated to a constitutional court since it exercises all the powers normally attributed to the latter.[25]

Although the choice of setting up constitutional courts can be considered as a common feature of CEBBE countries, the emergence of new systems of judicial review has followed two different paths. In fact, there is the necessity to distinguish between countries which had experienced in their pre-socialist and / or socialist past limited forms of constitutional review, and the rest of CEBBE legal systems which experienced in their national history only forms of political review of legislation.

In the first case, the introduction of constitutional courts was not subjected to particular debates, with the consequence that their establishment occurred very quickly. Furthermore, in all these cases, in addition to importing foreign models, countries have found further inspirations in their national traditions. As a result, the rebirth of constitutional justice

established in the 1950s, following the fascist and Nazi regimes, and of the second generation, the Spanish and Portuguese Constitutional Courts, created in the 1970s, following the fall of Francoism and Salazarism. The countries of Central and Eastern Europe followed this path, establishing the third generation of constitutional courts during the initial phase of democratic transition as part of their anti-authoritarian reforms. Consequently, the general creation of constitutional courts through the post-communist region represented a clear break from past political arrangements and served as a 'trademark' or 'proof' of the democratic character of the country and a sort of patent of international recognition. *See* M. Verdussen (Ed.), *La Justice Constitutionnelle en Europe Centrale,* Paris-Bruxelles, Bruylant, 1997, p. 233. *See also* R. Teitel, 'Transitional Jurisprudence: The Role of Law in Political Transformation', *Yale Law Journal,* Vol. 106, No. 7, 1997, p. 2033, and S. Bartole, *Riforme costituzionali nell'Europa centro-orientale. Da satelliti comunisti a democrazie sovrane*, Bologna, Il Mulino, 1993, p. 193. Another argument that explains the victory of the centralized review and the consequent hostility towards the decentralized review in the new post-communist democracies was proposed by J. Ferejohn & P. Pasquino, 'Deliberative Institutions', *in* W. Sadurski, *Constitutional Justice, East and West: Democratic Legitimacy and Constitutional Courts in Post-Communist Europe in a Comparative Perspective*, cit., p. 22, who related it to the generalized distrust of the ordinary judiciary that was perceived during the former regime as an obedient servant of the communist authorities. A final reason for establishing constitutional courts through the CEBBE region was pointed out by B. Ackerman, 'The Rise of World Constitutionalism', *Virginia Law Review*, Vol. 83, No. 7, 1997, p. 776, who related it to the desire especially of Central and Eastern European countries to ally with the rest of Europe by meeting democratic criteria – which would facilitate their accession first to the Council of Europe and then to the European Union. This claim was criticized as unfounded by W. Sadurski, 'Legitimacy and Reasons of Constitutional Review After Communism, in W. Sadurski (Ed.), *Constitutional Justice, East and West: Democratic Legitimacy and Constitutional Courts in Post-Communist Europe in a Comparative Perspective*, cit., p. 172, who emphasized that the idea of establishing constitutional courts, even if supported and encouraged by the Council of Europe, has not been particularly important during the European Union accession negotiations.

25 *See* W. Sadurski, 'Postcommunist Constitutional Courts in Search of Political Legitimacy', cit., p. 3.

should be necessarily read in these cases in the light of national historical precedents of constitutional review. For example, in Czechoslovakia the 1991 approval of constitutional amendments to the 1986 socialist Constitution resulted in the establishment of a new Federal Constitutional Court, which was marked by three different features: return to a centralized system of judicial review since it was already experienced in the pre-socialist period; continuity with the system formally introduced during the socialist regime as the Court's decisions on unconstitutionality remained subjected to temporal limitations; transplantation of the foreign model as the constitutional complaint was introduced on the example of the German sub-model of constitutional review.[26] Although the institutional life of the new Federal Court was rather short (in all eleven months) due to the subsequent dissolution of the Czechoslovak federation, the choice to maintain constitutional courts was subsequently reconfirmed by both the Czech Republic and Slovakia with the adoption of their new constitutions in 1992.

An another example is given by Romania, where contrary to the Czechoslovak experience, the country could count only on the precedent of constitutional review derived from its pre-socialist past. Accordingly, in the decision No. 4 of 14 January 1991, adopted at the beginning of a democratic transition, for the second time in the history of the country the Court of Cassation by relaying on the pre-socialist case law and the 1923 Constitution held to be the only body authorized to exercise the review of constitutionality of legislation.[27] Following the adoption of the new 1991 Romanian Constitution, this first post-socialist experience of constitutional justice has been replaced by the introduction of a constitutional court, strongly influenced by the French variant of constitutional review.

The experience of new states emerged from the Yugoslav dissolution was different as in all of these cases, the previous socialist system of constitutional review was only partially renewed.[28] As has been observed, Western models have circulated in this area mediated by the internal socialist model, which had already assimilated the basic connotations of

26 *See* A. Di Gregorio, 'La transizione in Cecoslovacchia. Principali profili di diritto costituzionale', cit., p. 250.

27 Cfr. M. Criste, 'Un contrôle juridictionnel des lois en Roumanie? Décision du 14 janvier 1991 de la Cour suprême de justice', *Rev. française de Droit constitutionnelle*, No. 9, 1992, p. 179.

28 This applies not only to Slovenia, Croatia and Macedonia, but also to Bosnia-Herzegovina. In the latter case, the 1995 Dayton Constitution has been drafted by imitating the Anglo-Saxon model, and was adopted according to an externally imposed procedure, and finally inserted into an international treaty. Nonetheless, its framers preferred maintain a constitutional court with the exclusive competence of exercising constitutional review, precisely because it was a body already known by the country. As for Serbia and Montenegro, the 1992 Constitution of the Yugoslav Federation continued to provide for a Federal Court, while the Constitutions of the two federated republics, adopted in 1990 and 1992 respectively, maintained the republican constitutional courts. It was only with the entry into force of the 2003 Constitutional Charter of the State Union of Serbia and Montenegro that the Federal Court finally ceased to exist. The subsequent dissolution of the union between Serbia and Montenegro led the two countries to adopt new constitutions in 2006 and 2007 respectively. The new constitutions have only partially renewed the previous system of constitutional justice by mantaining, as in other post-Yugoslav states, multiple elements of the previous Yugoslav socialist model.

the Kelsenian system. What the process of democratization most properly required in this area was to import from Western Europe the new aims that constitutional courts would have to assume in the context of a new democratic order.[29] Similar considerations are valid also in the case of Poland, where the old socialist system of constitutional justice was maintained since the 1997 Constitution, which finally introduced several innovations in relation to constitutional review.

By contrast, in Hungary the 1989 constitutional reform introduced important novelties in the field of constitutional justice, starting from the creation of the Constitutional Court. However, the most recently adopted 2011 Fundamental Law has deeply changed the system of constitutional review originally introduced in 1989 by significantly reducing the powers of the constitutional adjudication body.

In countries without previous traditions of constitutional justice, it was only in a period of a democratic transition that the basis for the genesis of judicial review of legislation were laid down. Thus in these cases, the introduction of constitutional courts represented an absolute novelty. However, not always the creation of constitutional courts occurred here without debates and discussions. For example, in Bulgaria, a faction of the former Socialist Party was opposed to the creation of the constitutional court by arguing that the constitutional review should be exercised by the supreme court, and that the parliament should have the power to reject its decisions.[30] Even in the Baltic sphere the establishment of constitutional courts encountered some resistance, so much so that the new legislation on judicial system had initially attributed the competence to exercise the judicial review of legislation to the national supreme courts. The latter choice has been maintained until today only in Estonia. Lithuania and Latvia opted instead for the introduction of constitutional courts in 1992 and 1996 respectively. Nonetheless, once the Latvian Constitutional Court was created it was only the President of the Republic who admitted that it represents a proof of a democratic development of the country, and the crown of the judicial system. Proposals aimed at empowering the supreme court with a judicial review were revived in 1999 by a government that attempted to cancel the constitutional court from the national legal system. The attempt has been, however, strongly rejected by almost all Latvian political and academic world.[31]

A common feature of all CEBBE countries is given by the almost total absence of debates concerning the democratic legitimacy of constitutional courts, an issue that in Western Europe was originally imposed with particular vigor. The issue that has, instead, greatly affected CEBBE countries concerned the legal nature of constitutional courts, that is

29 *See* A. Di Gregorio, 'Il modello interno nella configurazione della giustizia costituzionale nei paesi della ex Jugoslavia, ovvero delle ascendenze socialiste', cit., p. 260.

30 V.I. Ganev, 'The Bulgarian Constitutional Court, 1991-1997: A Success Story in Context', *Europe-Asia Studies*, Vol. 55, No. 4, p. 599.

31 *See* R. Apsîtis, 'Introduction', www.satv.tiesa.gov.lv (last accessed January 2018).

whether these bodies should be defined as part of judicial power, or *sui generis* bodies. The different outcomes of this debate led to the different placements of constitutional courts in national constitutions. In fact, in many cases constitutional courts do not seem to constitute autonomous and independent bodies as they are included in parts of constitutions dedicated to the judicial power (Czech Republic, Slovakia, Slovenia, Latvia), or in a specific sub-chapter inserted inside the chapter on "courts and tribunals" (Poland). In other cases, constitutional courts have been included, in line with the Western European solution, in separate and autonomous constitutional chapters (Hungary, Lithuania, Romania, Bulgaria, Croatia, Bosnia-Herzegovina, Serbia, Montenegro, Macedonia, Albania). The particular position of constitutional courts inside Constitutions led some observers to define the constitutional adjudication bodies of CEBBE countries as integral parts of the judicial power.[32] Nevertheless, this position appears to be only formal since the constitutional framework establishes everywhere a series of guarantees aimed at ensuring the independence of the constitutional adjudication bodies. This more realistically defines completely independent constitutional courts from the judicial power.

5.4 Constitutional Courts' Normative Framework

In all CEBBE countries the normative framework regulating constitutional courts has been set by constitutions only in broad terms, while the detailed discipline on their composition, organization, functioning and powers is contained in different types of laws (constitutional, organic, ordinary), which implement constitutional provisions (or alternatively in the rules of procedure).

Overall, this regulatory framework has been marked by considerable dynamism, as it has undergone many changes and adjustments over the time. These changes have had a certain impact on the functioning of constitutional courts, as well as on determining the results they have achieved in practice.

5.4.1 *Composition, Organization and Functioning*

The normative framework on composition, organization and functioning of constitutional courts places particular emphasis on their autonomy by providing for a large set of guarantees of independence. This includes guarantees which can be usually found in systems of constitutional justice in Western Europe: financial, administrative and organizational autonomy, protection of seat, power of self-regulation, specific methods of selection of

32 *See* O. Fiss, 'Judiciary Panel: Introductory Remarks', *Yale Journal of International Law*, Vol. 19, No. 1, 1994, p. 219.

constitutional judges, stringent requirements for their appointment or election, and a series of rights and duties, incompatibilities and prerogatives resulting from judges designation. In principle, constitutions require that candidates to the office demonstrate an adequate legal preparation, or that they are well-known jurists, university professors with a law degree, and have an adequate experience in the legal profession.[33]

As regards the modalities for the designation of constitutional judges, several different types can be found. Some countries have preferred the mixed system, whereby the designation of judges is shared between different bodies, such as parliament, president of the republic and national supreme courts (Bulgaria, Romania, Serbia and Bosnia-Herzegovina).[34] In other countries, the appointment of constitutional judges has been assigned to the president of the republic on the proposal (or consensus) of the parliament (Czech Republic, Slovakia and Albania), while the rest of the countries have introduced the parliamentary election of constitutional judges. Some legal scholars have thus argued that the link between parliaments and constitutional courts seems very close, which can potentially lead to undermining the independence of constitutional adjudication bodies. According to this view, the choice of the parliamentary election of constitutional judges, although apparently inspired by the traditional Kelsenian model (*i.e.* the German and Portuguese sub-models), should be considered more properly as a residue of the previous socialist system. In fact, in the case of Poland, Hungary, Slovenia, Croatia, Montenegro, and Macedonia the parliamentary election of constitutional judges was introduced by the past socialist regime – a choice that was then reconfirmed in the post-socialist period.[35]

The close link between constitutional courts and parliaments, underlined negatively by some legal scholars, should be downsized or mitigated for at least three reasons. First, where this type of election has been introduced, several countries request the absolute or qualified majority for the election of constitutional judges with the aim to ensure the greatest possible degree of unanimity.[36] Second, in most countries the parliamentary election of constitutional judges follows a quite complex procedures as it usually requests a prior

33 *See, e.g.*, Czech Republic (Art. 84 Constitution); Hungary (section 6, letters a)-c) Law on the Constitutional Court); Poland (Art. 194 Constitution).

34 Due to the particularities of the transition process in Bosnia-Herzegovina, the criteria for designation of constitutional judges are quite singular: four members of the Constitutional Court are selected by the House of Representatives of the Federation and two members by the Assembly of the *Republika Srpska*. The remaining three members are selected by the President of the European Court of Human Rights after consultations with the Presidency. The judges selected by the President of the European Court of Human Rights shall not be citizens of Bosnia-Herzegovina or any neighbouring state (Art. VI Dayton Constitution).

35 *See* M. Mistò, 'La giustizia costituzionale nei paesi dell'Europa centro-orientale9', *in* M. Olivetti & T. Groppi (Eds.), *La giustizia costituzionale in Europa*, Milano, Giuffrè, 2003, p. 302.

36 *See, e.g.*, in Hungary (Art. 24, para. 4 Fundamental Law) and Croatia (since 2010) (Art. 126 Constitution) a two-thirds majority of all members of the parliament is required; in Slovenia (Art. 163 Constitution) the absolute majority of all members of the parliament is requested, *etc.*

proposal of other institutional bodies.[37] Third, the strong guarantees accorded to constitutional judges (such as the long term in office often accompanied by the prohibition of re-election) are aimed at guaranteeing their full independence from external influences.[38]

Besides the modalities of the selection of constitutional judges, the normative framework on constitutional courts generally provides that judges are independent in exercising their competences, enjoy the same immunity as the members of the parliament,[39] are not responsible for the opinions expressed and votes given in exercising their functions, and

37 *See, e.g.*, Macedonia requires the prior proposal of the President of the Republic and the Judicial Council (Art. 19 Constitutional Court Act); Lithuania, the prior proposal of the President of the Republic, President of the Parliament and President of the Supreme Court (Art. 103 Constitution); Latvia, the prior proposal of the Parliament, Council of Ministers and Supreme Court (Sect. 4 Constitutional Court Act), *etc.*

38 In the practice, the parliamentary election of constitutional judges did not create particular problems in relation to their selection and independence at least until recently, when some issues have invested three countries: Croatia, Hungary, and Poland. In Croatia, the initial constitutional provisions had established that the absolute majority of votes of the members of parliament is required for the election of constitutional judges. Following the 2010 constitutional reform this has been replaced by the requirement of a two-thirds of votes of the members of parliament. However, between 2010 and 2015 the office of three judges has expired and the practice has shown that the newly requested two-thirds majority may be difficult to achieve since the parliament was unable to elect new judges. The Constitutional Court thus carried out its activities in a restricted composition of ten judges. The situation has risked to provoke the complete paralysis of the Court as the office of other five judges has expired in 2016. *See* B. Smerdel, 'Ustav RH nakon ustavnih promjena 2010 godine' (The Constitution of the Republic of Croatia following the 2010 constitutional changes), *Hrvatska pravna revija*, Vol. 10, No. 9, 2010, pp. 1-8. In Hungary, the Constitutional Court was originally composed of fifteen judges. Following the 1994 constitutional reform, this number was reduced to eleven on the request of the Constitutional Court due to some problems in functioning with the number of judges originally introduced. Nevertheless, the 2011 Fundamental Law has re-established the original number of fifteen judges. Moreover, although the majority of two-thirds of votes of the members of parliament for the election of constitutional judges has been reconfirmed, this guarantee is today purely formal since following the most recent 2018 general elections the government is continuing to maintain its super majority of two-thirds of parliamentary seats. Finally, in Poland, the 1997 Constitutional Tribunal Act has been replaced in 2015 with a new Constitutional Tribunal Act. The latter contained a transitional provision which allowed the parliament to elect five constitutional judges, whose office would expire by the end of 2015. The move represented an attempt of the government to elect new judges close to the executive before the general elections of 25 October 2015 took place. However, this replacement was not recognized by the President of the Republic, and following the 2015 parliamentary elections, the newly elected government, which can now count on the absolute majority of the seats in the *Sejm*, has firstly amended the 2015 Constitutional Tribunal Act, and then cancelled the appointment of five constitutional judges, which were selected prior to the 2015 general elections. As a result, the *Sejm* elected five new constitutional judges on 2 December 2015, but the day after the Constitutional Tribunal adopted the decision No. K 34/15, which established as valid three of five appointments of 8 October 2015. On 9 December 2015, the Constitutional Tribunal adopted the decision No. K 35/15, which further contested the appointments of the three judges elected on 2 December 2015. Following the opinion of the Venice Commission and the EU pressures, a new Constitutional Tribunal Act has been adopted on 22 July 2016, which, however, still contains some limits to the functioning of the constitutional adjudication body. *See* A. Angeli, 'Polonia. Le derive di una democrazia (quasi) maggioritaria: tra rischio di paralisi dell'organo di giustizia costituzionale e dualismo giuridico', *federalismi.it*, No. 17, 2016; J. Sawicki, 'Prove tecniche di dissoluzione della democrazia liberale: Polonia 2016', *Nomos*, No. 1, 2016, pp. 1-24.

39 *See, e.g.* Slovakia (Art. 136 Constitution); Croatia (Art. 127 Constitution); Slovenia (Art. 167 Constitution); Serbia (Art. 173 Constitution); Bulgaria (Art. 147 Constitution), *etc.*

cannot be prosecuted or arrested without a decision adopted by the constitutional court, nor can be detained or subjected to other limitations of personal liberty without the consent of the court, except in the case of been caught in the act of committing a criminal offence.[40] The office of constitutional judges is generally incompatible with the membership in political parties or movements, other public paid positions with the sole exception of university teaching and scientific research.[41]

As regards the internal organization, it is generally established that the most important decisions should be taken in plenary sessions, while the principle of collegiality does not apply for matters of minor importance which are decided in restricted sessions. The decisions adopted by the plenum or restricted sessions should be voted by the majority of the members, or by the majority of those present. In many cases, judges can express dissenting and / or concurring opinions, which are published together with the majority decision.[42]

Finally, the Estonian system of constitutional justice presents itself as a more complex. In fact, if the Constitutional Review Chamber normally deals with issues relating to the constitutionality of legislation, there are some circumscribed hypotheses in which it is up to the plenum of the Supreme Court to deal with constitutional review: the first concerns the case in which at least one member of the Constitutional Review Chamber expresses a dissenting opinion; the second concerns the case in which the ruling of the Supreme Court is requested for changing previous practices of interpretation or decision-making; the third was initially identified by the case law (Dec. No. 10 of 22 December 2000), and then included in the 2002 Supreme Court Act, which provides that an issue of constitutional legitimacy should be referred to the Supreme Court when one of the Chambers of which the latter is composed held that an international treaty, relevant for the solution of the case, is unconstitutional.[43]

5.4.2 Competences and Parameter of Constitutional Review

The constitutional courts of CEBBE countries have been empowered with a plurality of competences which generally reflects the powers exercised by constitutional courts in the Austrian, German, Italian, Spanish, Portuguese and (in some cases) French systems of

40 *See* Poland (Art. 196 Constitution); Hungary (Art. 24, para. 8 Constitutional Court Act); Slovakia (Art. 136 Constitution); Albania (Art. 126 Constitution), *etc.*

41 *See* Czech Republic (Art. 4 Constitutional Court Act); Croatia (Art. 10 Constitutional Court Act); Serbia (Art. 173 Constitution), *etc.*

42 Slovenia (Art. 25 Constitutional Court Act); Lithuania (Art. 55 Constitutional Court Act); Czech Republic (Art. 13 Constitutional Court Act); Croatia (Art. 27 Constitutional Court Act), *etc.*

43 *See* Č. Pištan, 'I sistemi di giustizia costituzionale nei paesi dell'Europa centro-orientale e dell'area post-sovietica', *in* L. Mezzetti (Ed.), *Sistemi e modelli di giustizia costituzionale*, Vol. II, Padova, Cedam, 2011, p. 203.

constitutional justice. At the same time, constitutional adjudication bodies of CEBBE countries also differ from their Western European counterparts in that they have even more powers and are accessible to myriad political actors. Most of these powers are borrowed from their Western European counterparts; some are drawn from national traditions while other powers can be defined as really innovative (or original) since they cannot be ascribed to either the Western European systems of constitutional justice or to the limited systems of judicial review experienced by some CEBBE countries in their past. As a result, the powers of constitutional courts of CEBBE countries can be easily distinguished into three different groups.

The first group includes powers which should be ascribed to the European model. The latter has been imported throughout the CEBBE countries in a broad manner since (with the exception of a small number of cases) the most recently formed constitutional courts can often exercise all of the variants of Western European constitutional courts' powers. Accordingly, the most significant power of these courts is that of *a posteriori* abstract review (that is, the review of laws already enacted), characterized by a broad range of political figures being authorized to initiate the proceeding: the president of the republic, the government (the prime minister or even single minister), and a group (defined by number or percentage) of parliamentarians.[44] In many cases the power of initiative is further extended to various other bodies, such as the constitutional court *ex officio*,[45] national supreme courts,[46] the ombudsman,[47] the prosecutor general,[48] the chancellor of justice,[49] local governments,[50] trade unions and / or religious organizations.[51] Certainly, legislative majorities would have no incentive to challenge their own handiwork before the court, but if presidents and members of the minority opposition have the right to challenge laws, it undoubtedly encourages political adversaries to use the court to resolve their disputes.[52]

Where countries were also inspired by the French variant of constitutional review, constitutional courts can perform an *a priori* abstract review (that is, before the promulga-

44 Slovakia (Art. 130 Constitution); Lithuania (Art. 65 Constitutional Court Act); Czech Republic (Art. 64 Constitutional Court Act), Albania (Art. 134 Constitution), *etc.*

45 Montenegro (Art. 150 Constitution); Croatia (Art. 128 Constitution); Macedonia (Art. 12 rules of procedures), *etc.*

46 Bulgaria (Art. 150 Constitution).

47 Czech Republic (Art. 64 Constitutional Court Act); Croatia (Art. 128 Constitution); Poland (Art. 191 Constitution), *etc.*

48 Poland (Art. 191Constitution); Hungary (Art. 24, para. 7 Fundamental Law); Bulgaria (Art. 150 Constitution); Latvia (Art. 17 Constitutional Court Act), *etc.*

49 Estonia (Art. 6 Supreme Court Act).

50 Poland (Art. 191 Constitution); Latvia (Art. 17 Constitutional Court Act); Estonia (Art. 6 Supreme Court Act); Slovenia (Art. 160 Constitution); Croatia (Art. 128 Constitution); Serbia (Art. 167 of the Constitution), *etc.*

51 Albania (Art. 134 Constitution); Serbia (Art. 168 Constitution); Poland (Art. 191 Constitution), *etc.*

52 *See* H. Schwartz, *The Struggle for Constitutional Justice in Post-Communist Europe*, cit., p. 19.

tion of laws). This type of review could result problematic especially in new democracies. When constitutional courts strike down a law that has not yet become effective they often provide indications to the legislative body on how it should be revised. As such, the preventive norm control may easily develop into political battle between the legislative and executive levels. On the other hand, this type of review can also have positive effects as it allows a quick resolution of problematic situations, and can be useful especially in reviewing the conformity of international treaties prior to their ratification to the constitution.[53] An example of a CEBBE country, which has more closely adhered to the French variant of constitutional review is given by Romania, where in fact the Constitutional Court carries out an *ex ante* abstract review of legislation, parliamentary standing orders, drafts constitutional amendments, and international treaties prior to their ratification (Art. 146 of the Constitution). The Romanian Constitutional Court performs also the *ex post* review, but only in the form of concrete review. In all other CEBBE countries, the preventive norm control coexists with the *ex post* abstract norm control, and is mainly exercised against international treaties prior to their ratification.[54] However, there are cases in which the *ex ante* review has been extended to both not ratified international treaties and national legislation,[55] or in which the *ex ante* review includes only national legislation not yet entered into force.[56]

With the exception of Bulgaria, the abstract review has generally accompanied a concrete review which is typically initiated by all ordinary courts if they are faced with doubt concerning the constitutionality of a legal provision that has to be applied in a pending individual case.[57] If this is the general trend, the discipline of the concrete norm control in

53 *See* H. Steinberger, *Models of Constitutional Jurisdiction*, Council of Europe Press, Strasbourg 1994, p. 51.

54 Czech Republic (Art. 87 Constitution); Slovakia (Art. 125 Constitution); Slovenia (Art. 160 Constitution); Bulgaria (Art. 149 Constitution); Albania (Art. 134 Constitution); Lithuania (Art. 105 Constitution); Latvia (Art. 16 Constitutional Court Act).

55 Hungary (Art. 24, para. 2, letter a) Fundamental Law); Poland (Art. 122 Constitution); and Estonia (Arts. 5-6 Supreme Court Act).

56 Serbia (Art. 169 Constitution); Bosnia-Herzegovina (Art. IV, para. 3 Constitution). In Bosnia-Herzegovina, the Constitutional Court is empowered to exercise the ex post norm control. However, it can also decide on the constitutionality of draft laws (or other parliamentary acts) if they has been declared or voted by the majority of the members of the Parliament as "detrimental to the vital interests" of one of the constituent peoples, and only if the legislative body has exhausted all the other legal remedies. According to Z. Miljko, *Ustavno pravo Bosne i Hercegovine* (Constitutional Law of Bosnia-Herzegovina), Zagreb, Hrvatska sveučilišna naklada, 2006, p. 314, such solution represents an interference in the legislative power that in any case should be avoided.

57 *See* Czech Republic (Art. 95 Constitution); Slovakia (Art. 101 Constitution); Hungary (Art. 24 Fundamental Law); Lithuania (Art. 101 Constitution); Slovenia (Art. 160 Constitution); Montenegro (Art. 150 Constitution); Serbia (Art. 63 Constitutional Court Act); Bosnia-Herzegovina (Art. VI, para. 3, letter c) Dayton Constitution), and Albania (Art. 101 Constitution). Initially, the concrete norm control was limited in Croatia and Poland. In particular, in Croatia, ordinary courts could not refer directly constitutional issues to the constitutional court, but had firstly to invest the supreme court, as the latter was the only body with the power to refer cases directly to the constitutional court. Similarly, in Poland, ordinary courts had to

Estonia appears more complex, as the concrete review is exercised not exclusively by the Constitutional Review Chamber, but all national courts, which are authorized to consider the constitutionality of legislation and to not apply any legal provision that, in their opinion, are unconstitutional. In this case the decision on unconstitutionality will have *inter partes* effects. However, Estonia is also a civil law country, and therefore it is not familiar with the principle of *stare decisis*. For this reason, in the case in which the ordinary court refuses to apply to the concrete case a law deemed unconstitutional, it should invest on the issue the Constitutional Review Chamber since the latter represents the only body with the power to annul unconstitutional acts and adopt rulings with *erga omnes* effects. Furthermore, in order to avoid conflicts between judgments, the 2002 Supreme Court Act states that the parties involved in the trial before an ordinary court can appeal against the decision of the latter, but only once the Constitutional Review Chamber has adopted its decision with *erga omnes* effects.

Finally, in Macedonia the concrete norm control is similar to the Estonian solution. Although the country established a centralized system of constitutional justice, the concrete norm control is regulated by the 1995 Law on the judicial system, which states that in the hypothesis in which an ordinary court considers that the law to be applied to the concrete case is in contrast with the Constitution, the case must be decided by not applying the contested law and applying the Constitution. The decision produces *inter partes* effects. Only if the ordinary court finds impossible to apply the Constitution directly it is obligated to suspend the proceedings and to refer the case to the Constitutional Court.

In addition to a concrete review that allows individuals indirect access to constitutional adjudication bodies, with the sole exceptions of Romania and Bulgaria, the rest of CEBBE countries have introduced the mechanism of constitutional complaint, according to which citizens are allowed direct access to constitutional courts to complain against violations of their fundamental rights. The constitutional complaint is generally modelled on the German example, and can be used against acts implementing the legislation (courts' judgments or administrative acts), and in some cases also against laws. The admissibility requirements include the immediacy and personality of the violation and the exhausting of all legal remedies foreseen by the national legal order. The admissibility of the constitutional complaint mainly involves the annulment of the contested legal act.

---

refer constitutional questions alternately to the president of the supreme court, to the president of the High Administrative Court, to the ministers or other central bodies, as they represented the only bodies which had the power to address constitutional issues to the Constitutional Tribunal. This initial discipline was inherited in both countries by the past socialist system, and was permanently abandoned in Poland with the 1997 Constitution and in Croatia with the adoption of the new 1999 Constitutional Court Act. *See* J. Crnić, 'Pokretanje postupka za ocjenu ustavnosti i zakonitosti pred Ustavnim sudom' (Initiating the review of constitutionality and legality before the Constitutional Court), *Slobodno poduzetništvo*, No. 8, 2001, p. 93.

The above mentioned normative framework shows that, in accordance with the Western European systems of constitutional justice, almost all CEBBE countries resemble the mixed systems of judicial review, endowing their constitutional courts with a double function: the review of law and the protection of human rights. One exception is Bulgaria, which preferred the traditional Kelsenian model of abstract review that originally did not provide for either concrete norm control or the mechanism of constitutional complaint. This was also the case of Latvia, at least until 2002, when both the concrete norm control and the constitutional complaint were introduced. On the contrary, Romania is the only CEBBE country in which the only type of *a posteriori* review is given by the concrete norm control.

Further, like their Western European counterparts, Constitutional Courts of CEBBE countries perform a wide number of other powers[58]: the review of constitutionality of political parties[59]; the resolution of jurisdictional disputes between the highest institutions of the state[60] and / or between local and central authorities[61]; the impeachment of the president of the republic[62]; individual ministers, judges and other executive officials,[63] the members of the parliament, and supreme court[64]; the president's permanent or temporary capacity[65]; the constitutionality of presidential elections[66]; the constitutionality of parlia-

58 *See* G.F. Ferrari, 'Le forme di controllo di costituzionalità "anomale", Diritto pubblico comparato e europeo', No. 1, 2000, p. 351; S. Baldin, *Le "altre" funzioni delle corti costituzionali. Modelli europei e recezioni con particolare riferimento all'Est europeo*, Trieste, EUT, 2000.

59 Bulgaria (Art. 149, No. 5) Constitution); Romania (Art. 146, letter k) Constitution); Poland (Art. 188 Constitution); Croatia (Art. 129 Constitution); Slovenia (Art. 160 Constitution); Macedonia (Art. 110 Constitution); Albania (Art. 134 Constitution); Serbia (Art. 167 Constitution); Montenegro (Art. 149 Constitution); whilst in the Czech Republic (Art. 87 Constitution), and in Slovakia (Art. 129 Constitution) constitutional courts have not the power to directly decide on the constitutionality of political parties, but on decisions on dissolution eventually adopted by the government.

60 Poland (Art. 189 Constitution); Croatia (Art. 128 Constitution); Romania (Art. 146 Constitution); Bulgaria (Art. 149 Constitution), and Hungary (Art. 36 Constitutional Court Act).

61 Hungary (section 36 Constitutional Court Act); Slovenia (Art. 160 Constitution); Czech Republic (Art. 87 Constitution); Slovakia (Art. 126 Constitution); Montenegro (Art. 149 Constitution); Serbia (Art. 167 Constitution); Macedonia (Art. 110 Constitution), and Albania (Art. 131 Constitution).

62 Slovenia (Art. 63 Constitutional Court Act); Croatia (Art. 128 Constitution); Czech Republic (Art. 65 Constitutional Court Act); Slovakia (Art. 129 Constitution); Bulgaria (Art. 103 Constitution); Albania (Art. 130 Constitution); Romania (Art. 95 Constitution), and Hungary (Art. 35 Constitutional Court Act).

63 Slovenia (Art. 63 Constitutional Court Act), and Croatia (Art. 128 Constitution).

64 Lithuania (Art. 74 Constitution), and Serbia (Art. 155 Constitution).

65 Poland (Art. 131 Constitution); Romania (Art. 144 Constitution); Slovakia (Art. 105 Constitution); Bulgaria (Art. 97 Constitution); Albania (Art. 91 Constitution), and Lithuania (Art. 107 Constitution).

66 Romania (Art. 144 Constitution); Bulgaria (Art. 149 Constitution); Slovakia (Art. 109 Constitution); Albania (Art. 131 Constitution); Croatia (Art. 125 Constitution), and Lithuania (Art. 107 Constitution).

mentary elections[67]; loss of electoral mandates[68]; the constitutionality of referendums,[69] as well as on the compliance with the conditions for the exercise of the legislative initiative by citizens.[70]

The second group of powers include those recovered from countries historical precedents of constitutional justice. The most important example is given by the former Yugoslav republics, where several elements of the previous Yugoslav system of constitutional justice have become an integral part of the current systems of constitutional review. The continuity with the past can be detected, in particular, in the power of constitutional courts to exercise not only the review of constitutionality of laws, but also the review of constitutionality and legality of other normative acts (Slovenia, Croatia, Macedonia, Serbia, and Montenegro); to decide on *actio popularis* – the process of abstract, de-individualized constitutional complaint, according to which everybody (even foreigners) can appeal to the court to declare laws invalid on the grounds that they violate the constitution (Montenegro, Macedonia, Croatia, Slovenia, Serbia, and Montenegro); in the permanence of the courts' power to act on their own motion (Croatia, Macedonia, Serbia, Slovenia, and Montenegro); in the courts' power to decide on legal acts, which have lost their legal force, provided that no more than one year has elapsed from the date when they went out of force (Croatia, Serbia, and Montenegro); in the courts' possibility to decide *ultra petitum* (Slovenia, Macedonia, Croatia, Serbia, and Montenegro), and in monitoring the execution of constitutionality and legality, and reporting to the national parliament about any kind of observed unconstitutionality and legality (Croatia, and Montenegro).[71]

Some elements of the Yugoslav socialist system continue to survive not only in the new states emerged from the dissolution of Yugoslavia, but also in other CEBBE countries. For example, the power to decide on *actio popularis* could be found in Hungary (up to 2012), and in Slovakia (up to 2001), which represents two countries that were influenced by the Yugoslav system in the socialist period. The power to provide binding interpretation of the constitution, which paradoxically did not survive in the countries of the former Yugoslavia, is still present in Hungary, Slovakia, and introduced in the period of democratic transition in Albania and Bulgaria. In Hungary and Czech Republic courts maintained the power to act on their own motion, while in Poland (up to 1997) the Constitutional Tribunal could report and inform the national parliament about any kind of observed

67 Croatia (Art. 125 Constitution); Bulgaria (Art. 149 Constitution); Slovakia (Art. 129 Constitution); Albania (Art. 131 Constitution), and Lithuania (Art. 105 Constitution).

68 Slovenia (Art. 82 Constitution); Czech Republic (Art. 87 Constitution); Slovakia (Art. 124 Constitution); Albania (Art. 131 Constitution) and Bulgaria (Art. 72 Constitution).

69 Croatia (Art. 128 Constitution); Slovenia (Art. 67 Constitutional Court Act); Hungary (Art. 33 Constitutional Court Act); Romania (Art. 146 Constitution), and Slovakia (Art. 129 Constitution).

70 Romania (Art. 146 Constitution).

71 *See* A. Di Gregorio, *Il modello interno nella configurazione della giustizia costituzionale nei paesi della ex Jugoslavia, ovvero delle ascendenze socialiste*, cit., p. 258.

unconstitutionality within the legal system. In several other cases courts' can perform also the review of constitutionality and legality of sublegislative acts (Czech Republic, Slovakia, and Poland).

Finally, some courts have expanded powers in other areas, as they exercised some additional competences unknown to both the European-Kelsenian model and the countries' historical precedents of constitutional review. Under these additional powers, courts can exercise the legislative initiative and declare the unconstitutionality of legislative omissions (Hungary up to 2012), as well as provide binding interpretation of the constitution in connection with the EU law (Estonia since 2002). However, the most innovative and courageous competence is given by the courts' power to review the conformity of national normative acts with ratified international treaties and conventions, which can be usually activated by the same subjects authorized to initiate the proceeding of abstract norm control, and by courts *ex officio*. The difference with the other types of reviews is given by the fact that the parameter in this case is given by international treaties (or conventions).[72]

In fact, the establishment of different types of review (constitutionality, legality and compliance of national legal acts with ratified international treaties) has had a direct impact on the discipline of justiciable acts, and the parameter of constitutional review. In particular, it led to an extension of justiciable acts, meaning that the constitutional review can be exercised in relation to both primary and secondary legislation. This has been followed by an extension of the parameter, which in almost all cases includes not only constitutions, but also other sources of law (constitutional laws, organic laws, ordinary laws, and ratified international treaties).[73]

---

72 The power to review the conformity of national normative acts with ratified international treaties has been expressly recognized in Poland (Art. 188 Constitution); Hungary (Art. 24, para. 2 Fundamental Law); Slovenia (Art. 160 Constitution); Albania (Art. 131 Constitution); Bulgaria (Art. 149 Constitution); Slovakia (Art. 124 Constitution); Serbia (Art. 167 Constitution); Montenegro (Art. 144 Constitution); Bosnia-Herzegovina (Art. II, para. 2 Constitution), and Latvia (Art. 16, No. 6) Constitutional Court Act). In Croatia, it was the Constitutional Court, which has established its competence to review the conformity of national legislation with ratified international treaties (*see* Constitutional Court of Croatia, decision U-I-745/99 of 8 November 2000). In other legal orders, where this type of review has not been expressly provided, the courts' case law shows that international conventions on human rights have been widely used as interpretative criteria of national constitutional provisions. This trend can be found in Estonia (*see* Constitutional Review Chamber, Dec. No. 2-4-1-1-96 of 1 April 1996), and Lithuania (*see* Constitutional Court, Decision of 13 February 1997).

73 *See* Č. Pištan, *Tra democrazia e autoritarismo. Esperienze di giustizia costituzionale nell'Europa centro-orientale e nell'area post-sovietica*, cit., p. 222.

5.5 EFFECTS OF DECISIONS

The decisions of constitutional courts are everywhere final, void, and unappealable with *erga omnes* effects. The temporal effects of judgments generally follows the Austrian model, which already in the Kelsen's view envisaged the cassation of unconstitutional norms from the moment the decision has been published, or after a short period of *vacatio*; in some cases, courts may decide to differ the effects of their decisions to an another date. At the same time, it is specified that rulings on unconstitutionality may also have limited retrospective effects.

However, according to the initial design in some CEBBE countries decisions on unconstitutionality were subjected to several limits. For example, in Poland, until the adoption of the 1997 Constitution, the 1992 "Little Constitution" established in continuity with the previous socialist period that rulings on unconstitutionality of legislation had only procedural effects, obliging the parliament to review the law, or to overrule the decision adopted by the Constitutional Tribunal by a majority of two-thirds of votes. Similarly, in Romania until the 2003 constitutional reform the Court's judgment resulting from the *ex ante* abstract norm control could be rejected by a two-thirds majority of votes of the parliament.

The socialist rule according to which constitutional courts' decisions on unconstitutionality were subjected to temporal limitations, originally introduced by the Yugoslav system, has survived in the sole Slovakia (Art. 125 Constitution), where it continues to be valid in the case of judgments on unconstitutionality. Accordingly, political authorities that passed laws or other normative acts found to be unconstitutional by the Court are obliged to conform them to the Constitution no later than six months following the finding of the Court. In the case of inertia of the body which adopted the disputed law or other normative act, the latter ceased to have effects at the end of six months.

Some final observations should be made in relation to countries emerged from the dissolution of Yugoslavia, where in several cases the difference between abrogation / annulment of unconstitutional acts is still present. In particular, Croatia (Art. 130 Constitution) and Slovenia (Art. 160 Constitution) have preserved the distinction between two hypotheses: in the case of the decision on unconstitutionality of laws, the judgment has *ex nunc* effects, while in the case of a decision of unconstitutionality / illegality of other normative acts, the judgment has, at the discretion of the court, *ex nunc*, or *ex tunc* effects. A similar solution is also established in Macedonia, where, however, the double sanction exists also in the case of legislative acts. According to the Art. 112 of the Macedonian Constitution, the Court can abrogate or annul the law if it establishes that the latter is not in conformity with the Constitution and can abrogate or annul other normative acts if it establishes their non-conformity to the Constitution and the law.[74]

5.6 Evolution of Case Law

The normative framework on constitutional courts clearly shows that in CEBBE countries political actors have preferred to equip their constitutional adjudication bodies with a wide range of powers. This resulted in the creation of potentially powerful constitutional courts which are, at least formally, capable of influencing multiple aspects of their renewed constitutional orders. Of course, this trend might seem at first incomprehensible, especially if one considers the period in which constitutional courts were established. The post-socialist transition was marked by an epochal regime change and reconstruction, which required deep political, economic and social transformations. In this situation, one could have expected that newly elected democratic legislatures, the governments of the day or the directly elected presidents would have liked to preserve their powers. Instead, politicians endowed courts with a broad range of powers, the active use of which might have a great impact upon different branches of government. Undoubtedly, in the absence of cultural traditions that support a judicial review, some political actors might not have comprehended the ramifications of giving courts such functionality, and not all of them may want such institutions to become so powerful. As it has been pointed out, the main aim of political actors was to use constitutional courts as key institutions in realizing their interests.[75] Constitutional courts have been thus endowed with a broad range of competences, while the particularly extensive direct access to courts was aimed at ensuring the stable access of politicians to constitutional adjudication bodies.

---

74 The main difference between abrogation and annulment is given by the different effects that decisions have (*ex nunc* / *ex tunc*). However, given that the term abrogation always implies *pro futuro* effects, it should be pointed out that in both Slovenia and Croatia constitutional courts can also adopt decisions with retrospective effects. It follows that decisions on unconstitutionality of legislative acts can have also limited retrospective effects, which is fundamental in the case of the concrete norm control. This leads to the conclusion that in Croatia and Slovenia the distinction between abrogation and annulment appears only tendential, and that it would be, therefore, more convincing to argue that even decisions on unconstitutionality of legislation may imply the annulment of the unconstitutional legislative act. In other words, it would be more correct to assert that in both countries there are two different types of cassation decisions: the first, on unconstitutionality of laws, which except for the limited retrospective effects will have *ex nunc* effects; the second, on unconstitutionality/illegality of sublegislative acts which, depending on the case, will have *ex tunc* or *ex nunc* effects. *See* Č. Pištan, 'La giustizia costituzionale nell'Europa centro-orientale: le esperienze della Croazia, Slovenia, Polonia, Ungheria', *in* L. Mezzetti (Ed.), *Sistemi e modelli di giustizia costituzionale*, cit., p. 393.

75 C. Thorson, 'Why politicians want constitutional courts: the Russian case', *Communist and Post-Communist Studies*, Vol. 37, No. 2, 2004, p. 189.

Contrary to the wishes of many politicians these new constitutional courts have assumed a central role in the democracy-building process. They not only survived the attacks of national politicians but, at times, have imprinted their visions of the new constitutional order by aggressively challenging national legislators. Even if criticized, their decisions were implemented. Moreover, the new courts have shown the ability to re-transform themselves, assuming new, influential roles during the following processes of democratic consolidation and, where applicable, Europeanization. This trends are all well reflected in the evolution of their case law.

Looking back at more than three decades of constitutional court activities in CEBBE countries, one can describe their case law as an evolutionary process of gradual change that can be distinguished in two different phases. The first one goes back to the early 1990s and lasted into the first few years of the 2000s, when the second phase started, which is still ongoing. During the first decade of their institutional life, constitutional courts primarily dealt with large-scale structural reform related to the transition and its political, economic and social transformation. Moreover, this initial phase was characterized by courts' excessive intervention in the resolution of political conflicts between different branches of government, which were reduced only at the end of the 1990s in favour of a more daily approach to constitutional questions. This was possible thanks to the approval of several constitutional reforms, or new constitutions, which better clarified the separation of roles between political branches of government. As a consequence, since the beginning of the new millennium, constitutional courts' case law has gradually changed. In fact, constitutional courts have progressively left the transitional period behind and concentrated their activities on the protection of human rights. Further, with the accession of some CEBBE countries to the EU, constitutional courts have shown that they can turn into important actors of the process of 'Europeanization'.

The nature of Constitutional Courts of CEBBE countries is thus well reflected in the issues with which they have dealt, and it can be defined as a 'chameleonic nature' due to these courts ability to transform and re-transform themselves and assume new and multiple roles in accordance with the development of their political and legal systems. They firstly acted as main actors of the process of democratization and active political players and arbiters of political conflicts, and then transformed themselves in promoters of fundamental rights and important actors of the European integration process.[76]

76 The attempt to classify the evolution of constitutional courts' case law in two different phases corresponding to two different temporal periods is especially valid for the countries of Central and Eastern Europe and the Baltic area. As far as the Balkans are concerned, in Croatia, for example, during the first decade of the institutional life of the new Constitutional Court, the country remained an authoritarian regime. Although the Court adopted some important decisions, it could not be defined in this period as a really independent body. More specifically, the main task of the Constitutional Court was to exercise the review of constitutionality and legality of other normative acts, thus presenting itself, in continuity with the previous socialist

5.6.1 The First Phase (1990-2000): The Process of Democratization

The appearance of constitutional adjudication bodies on the post-communist scene led to their effective involvement in a series of highly contentious issues related to the democracy-building process. Some examples of typical transitional issues with which courts dealt simultaneously included the dismantling of communist-era laws as well as reviewing the constitutionality of the newly passed laws, which concerned matters ranging from property restitution, economic and social policy to past injustices and communist political crimes. In fact, the access to the courts is very easy (almost all countries give the authority to challenge legislative actions to a wide range of political agents, including the parliamentary minorities or even to 'everybody' if the *actio popularis* is envisaged), and basically all political and legal problems of the transition ended up in the courts and had to be decided. As a result, CEBBE countries initially saw a very high number of abstract review cases.

Constitutional courts responded to these challenges by showing from their inception an extraordinary judicial activism. They frequently struck down not only particularly controversial enacted legislation but also many new laws passed by the newly elected parliaments – even if the law's adoption was vital to the executive branches of government. Significant provisions of laws on abortion, the death penalty, lustration, the criminal prosecution of former communist officials responsible for crimes against the people during the communist period, economic austerity measures, fiscal policy and the indexation of pensions have all been invalidated.[77]

---

period, as a body of administrative justice. *See also* S. Barić, 'The Transformative Role of the Constitutional Court of the Republic of Croatia: From the ex-Yu to the EU', *Analitika Working Paper*, No. 6, 2016, p. 3. Similar conclusions are also applicable to Montenegro and Serbia, where, among others, the current constitutional courts have been established in 2006 and 2007 respectively. Finally, neither in Bosnia-Herzegovina, the evolution of Constitutional Court's case law cannot be compared to the countries of Central and Eastern Europe due to the particularly difficult transition process experienced by this country.

77 *See, e.g.*, capital punishment was declared unconstitutional by constitutional courts in Lithuania, Albania, Ukraine and Hungary (*see* the Hungarian Constitutional Court decision No. 23/1990 of 31st October 1990), while important aspects on abortion law have been struck down by the Polish and the Hungarian Constitutional Courts (*see* the Polish Constitutional Tribunal decision No. K. 26/96 of 28th May 1997, and the Hungarian Constitutional Court decision No. 64/1991of 17th December 1991). In another group of cases related to the economic transition, the Polish Tribunal readily invalidated the newly adopted pension law that restricted old-age and disability benefits for pensioners by emphasizing how pensions and social security rights deserve strong and equal protection (*see* the Polish Constitutional Tribunal decision No. K. 14/91 of 11th February 1991). Later, the same Tribunal ruled that a 1995 law that would suspend the indexation of pensions in the fourth quarter of 1996 was unconstitutional (*see* the Polish Constitutional Tribunal decision No. K. 8/96 of 17th July 1996), whilst in another decision it overturned a number of provisions of the 1991 tax statute (*see* the Polish Constitutional Tribunal decisions No. K 8/97 of 16 December 1997 and K 8/96 of 17 July 1996). Similarly, the Croatian Constitutional Court invalidated in 1998 a provision of the 1993 Code on Equating Retirement Incomes on the basis that the code demanded that pensions increase relative to changes in the cost of living rather than relative to the increase in average

For example, in Poland from 1990-1997, of some fifty-two statutes reviewed by the Tribunal, forty were found unconstitutional.[78] The Hungarian Court was even more aggressive: from 1990-1995 it found 273 national laws unconstitutional and, in general, during the transition period the Court struck down nearly one law out every three that came before it. In addition, the same Court frequently used its substantial powers to order the parliament to pass new laws on a wide range of topics.[79] Consequently, some commentators described the Hungarian Constitutional Court as one of the most active and powerful Courts in the world, Hungarian politics of the 1990s as Court-centred politics and the Hungarian political system during the first years of the transition as 'Courtocracy'.[80]

The strong judicial activism exercised by constitutional courts is thus well known and a lot has been written for and against it. Several scholars have uncritically exalted the activist role of some of these courts often described them as a "flagship of the rule of law and constitutional faith in the emergent Eastern European democracies" as well as "promoters and defenders of the values of constitutionalism, the rule of law and human rights in political and legal environments contaminated by legal nihilism and marked by disregard for individual rights and the lack of a tradition of *Rechtsstaat*."[81] On the contrary, other authors have criticized the activities of 'over-prestigious' courts of CEBBE countries. For example, it has been argued that overconfidence in constitutional courts might diminish the power and prestige of legislatures,[82] and that courts have no right to decide on complex legal and political problems by invoking abstract constitutional principles (such as equality, freedom, justice, the rule of law, non-retroactivity or vested rights) and neglecting to

---

incomes. In Bulgaria, the Court successfully prevented a government action supported by an absolute majority in parliament from raising taxes by decree (*see* the Bulgarian Constitutional Court decision No. 17/95 of 3 October 1995). In deciding several similar cases, the Hungarian Constitutional Court struck down important aspects of a number of laws that were meant to constitute a package of austerity measures introduced by the government in 1995. In one of its most controversial decisions, the Court struck down 26 different provisions of the Austerity Package Act passed by the parliament to reduce the increasing fiscal burden of the welfare state (*see* the Hungarian Constitutional Court decision No. 43/1995 of 30th June 1995 on social security benefits). In dealing with issues of privatization, the same Court held that several parts of the compensation law that regulated re-privatization (that is, compensation) of formerly confiscated property were unconstitutional. Most of the courts' rulings have had serious financial and budgetary consequences, but even if criticized, they were both followed and respected. *See* W. Sadurski, 'Postcommunist Constitutional Courts in Search of Political Legitimacy', cit., p. 4, and B. Bugaric, 'Courts as Policy-Makers: Lessons from Transition', *Harvard International Law Journal*, Vol. 42, No. 1, 2001, pp. 247-288.

78 *See* H. Schwartz, *The Struggle for Constitutional Justice in Post-Communist Europe*, cit., p. 24.

79 *See* K.L. Scheppele, 'Post-Soviet Europe Constitutional Negotiations: Political Contexts of Judicial Activism in Post-Soviet Europe', *International Sociology*, Vol. 18, No. 1, 2003, p. 223.

80 *See* K.L. Scheppele, 'Democracy by Judiciary (Or Why Courts Can Sometimes Be More Democratic Than Parliaments)', Paper prepared for the conference on Constitutional Courts, Washington University, 1-3 Nov. 2001 *See also* S. Zifcak, 'Hungary's Remarkable, Radical, Constitutional Court', *Journal of Constitutional Law in Eastern and Central Europe*, Vol. 26, No. 3, 1996, p. 26.

81 *See* W. Sadurski, 'Postcommunist Constitutional Courts in Search of Political Legitimacy', cit., p. 7.

82 *See* S. Holmes, 'Back to the Drawing Board', *East European Constitutional Review*, Vol. 2, No. 1, 1993, p. 21.

consider, on the other hand, the economic consequences of their decisions.[83] For example, the Hungarian Court not only decided on the basis of general principles found in the Constitution but elaborated a doctrine of an 'invisible constitution', described as a system of dogma, principles and methodology drawn from contemporary constitutional thinking in leading national and international courts around the world, including the US Supreme Court.[84]

However, not all CEBBE countries' constitutional courts have dealt with national legislation in a manner contrary to the wishes of governing parliamentary majorities or by aggressively challenging the legislator. For example, the decisions of the Czech Constitutional Court were often aligned with the feelings of parliamentary majorities and governments of the day. In other cases, courts maintained an approach of self-restraint, preferring not to intervene in the choices of political branches of government.

5.6.1.1 Transitional Justice

Different courts' approaches towards transitional issues are particularly evident in the case law concerning two basic aspects of transitional justice: lustration measures, and the punishment of past political crimes (which raised the problem of retroactive criminal legislation).

Among the first transitional justice issues with which constitutional courts had to deal one can find the lustration laws, which contained several measures aimed at limiting the participation of former communists, and especially informants of the communist secret police, in the successor governments or even in civil service positions. Lustration measures have been adopted in several countries of the area. However, in most cases, these measures did not lead to particularly incisive purges, or had only symbolic effects since they were not implemented in practice. The only exception is given by the Czech Republic, where the number of people involved in lustration was significant. In several CEBBE countries constitutional courts decided on the constitutionality of lustration laws, and with the sole exception of the Czech Republic, laws on lustration were struck down (or substantially weakened).[85] It is very interesting to compare the orientations adopted by the Czech and

---

83 *See* B. Bugaric, 'Courts as Policy-Makers: Lessons from Transition', cit., p. 21.

84 H. Schwartz, *The Struggle for Constitutional Justice in Post-Communist Europe*, cit., p. 82.

85 *See, e.g.*, lustration laws were declared unconstitutional or partially unconstitutional in Albania, Bulgaria, Poland, Hungary, and more recently in Macedonia (*see* Constitutional Court of Albania, decision of 21st May 1993; Constitutional Tribunal of Poland, Dec. No. K39/1997; K24/1998; K7/2001; K44/2002; K31/2004; Constitutional Court of Bulgaria, Dec. No. 8 of 8th July 1992; Constitutional Court of Macedonia, decision of 24th March 2010). These rulings on unconstitutionality have not, however, precluded the adoption of entirely new lustration laws in Bulgaria and Albania in 2006 and 2009 respectively. As a result, in Albania, the Constitutional Court considered also the new lustration law unconstitutional, probably thanks to critics provided by the Venice Commission, which considered the lustration as a potential and serious threat to the guarantee of human rights. In the Polish legal system, the lustration law was changed two times by the

Hungarian Courts on lustration measures, as the two Courts proposed completely opposite solutions.

In the case of the Czech Republic, a radical version of lustration law was adopted in 1991 and thus in a period prior to the dissolution of Czechoslovakia. The Czechoslovak Federal Court was thus the first court that had the opportunity to rule on the lustration law. In the *Lustration I case* (Dec. No. 14/1992) it found the whole lustration procedure acceptable mainly because it was temporary and transitional. The latter decision remains important as the Federal Court took the opportunity to explain why the previous socialist legal order could not be considered 'legitimate' even though it was 'legal'. It based its explanation on the so-called 'theory of values', which is profoundly different in the two legal systems (socialist and democratic), meaning that different values end up filling same formal legal principles (such as the principle of equality or legal certainty), with opposite meanings. In the opinion of the Federal Court, the respect of the continuity with the old system of values would lead to the rejection of the new system of values and, therefore, every state, especially if it has been forced to experience for more than forty years violations of human rights by the totalitarian power, has the right to establish a democratic order, introducing also legislative measures which allow to avoid the risk of possible revivals of totalitarianism, or at least should try to limit this risk. Following the break-up Czechoslovakia, the lustration law was applied subsequently in the Czech Republic (but not in Slovakia). In 2000 the parliament expanded *de facto* the lustration process *sine die*, and in the *Lustration II case* (decision No. Pl. US 9/01), the Czech Court found the law constitutional again. In particular, it provided for its own interpretation of the process of democratization - which duration is unpredictable - and the meaning of consolidated democratic state by relaying on the case law of the ECtHR concerning the principle of 'a democracy able to defend itself'. At the same time, the Court argued that it cannot establish in which period the democratic process would be finished, thus concluding that lustration measures still served their purpose of protecting the democratic state against the return of totalitarianism.[86]

The solution adopted by the Hungarian Constitutional Court was profoundly different. In particular, it found the 1994 lustration law unconstitutional on various grounds by relaying on the argument that a successful transition to a democratic system does not need a change of public administration personnel through lustration.[87] In fact, the Court made

parliament in 2007, and the Constitutional Tribunal then intervened again in order to invalidate a series of provisions concerning the 2007 changes (*see* Constitutional Tribunal of Poland, Dec. No. K2/2007 of 12 May 2007). *See also* N. Letki, 'Lustration and Democratization in East-Central Europe', *Europe-Asia Studies*, Vol. 54, No. 4, 2002, pp. 529-552.

86 On the evolution of both the Czechoslovak and Czech Constitutional Courts' case law in the first years of democratic transition *see* A. Di Gregorio, *La transizione in Cecoslovacchia. Principali profili di diritto costituzionale*, cit., p. 257.

87 Constitutional Court of Hungary, Dec. No. 60/1994.

it clear that the legitimacy of the lustration law should not be judged by referring to the unusual circumstances of transition, but, rather, according the principles applicable to a democratic state based on the rule of law.

This difference in constitutional courts' decisions on lustration laws was basically a result of each court's attitudes towards the past regime. Thus, in the Czech Republic, the Court approach on lustration was strictly related to the orientations adopted in its very first decision, the *Lawlessness case* (decision No. Pl. US 19/93), when it declared the constitutionality of the 1993 Law on the Illegality of the Communist Regime and Resistance to It. The law described the communist regime existing between 1948 and 1989 as 'criminal, illegitimate and reprehensible' and the Communist Party of the CSSR a 'criminal and reprehensible' organization, whereas the resistance to this regime was deemed 'legitimate, just and honourable'. Further, the law suspended the statute of limitations for crimes committed from 1948 to 1989, which had not yet been prosecuted for political reasons. In its decision, the Court recalled and enforced the so-called 'theory of values', already introduced by the Czechoslovak Court in the *Lustration I* case. Accordingly, the Czech Court rejected the principle of formal legality, referring to the experience of the Weimar Republic, and emphasized the illegality of the communist regime. In the view of the Court, even while there is a continuity of 'old laws', there is also a discontinuity of values between the socialist regime and the new democratic state.

By contrast, in the view of the Hungarian Court, the revolution in Hungary had a legal nature since it was achieved without dissolving the old legal relationships but by preserving legal continuity with the prior regime. In particular, it introduced the theory of a 'revolution under the rule of law',[88] according to which the rule of law has been viewed largely as consisting of legal certainty. In sum, while in the Czech Republic the priority was given to substantive justice, which allowed the Court to declare both the illegality of the communist regime and the constitutionality of lustration measures, in Hungary the principle of legal certainty and, hence, the principle of legal continuity with the past were more important than subjective justice. In other words, in contrast to its Czech counterpart, the Hungarian Court preferred to emphasize the formal aspect of the rule of law – that is, the legality of the regime change – rather than the necessity of a legal break or discontinuity. By invoking these principles, the Hungarian Court not only declared lustration unconstitutional but, in one of its first decisions, readily struck down the 1992 Zetenyi-Takacs Law that, as in the Czech case, extended the statute of limitations for all crimes not prosecuted in the Soviet era for political reasons.

These different approaches of the two courts can be found also in the area of denationalization. Basing its arguments on the illegitimacy of the socialist regime, the Czech Court

88 *See* L. Sólyom & G. Brunner, *Constitutional Judiciary in a New Democracy: the Hungarian Constitutional Court*, Chicago, The University of Michigan Press, 2000, p. 214.

had considered the return of property confiscated by the old socialist regime as an elimination of the illegitimate transfer of ownership, and as a duty of the present state to rebuild the original structure of the property, recognizing at the same time that the criteria regarding the type of property which should be returned should be established by the parliament. On the contrary, by relaying on the formal legality of the communist period, the Hungarian Court was able to introduce the principle of novation, affirming the loss of the property confiscated by the former regime.

5.6.1.2 Resolution of Political Conflicts

The first decade of the constitutional courts' institutional life was further characterized by their excessive involvement in solving political conflicts, thus assuming the role of arbiters and mediators of the struggles occurred between various branches of government. More precisely, both intra-executive and executive-legislative conflicts occurred frequently in almost all CEBBE countries and were in large part a direct consequence of the ambiguous constitutional design related to the prerogatives of presidents and governments.[89] In other words, vague constitutional provisions that affected president-cabinet relations served as the terrain on which political incumbents struggled to expand and define their influence. In all of these experiences, national presidents attempted to increase the scope of their powers in many policy areas, such as defence, internal security and international relations, by broadly interpreting their powers, which frequently produced tensions with cabinets and prime ministers that accused presidents of transgressing their constitutional authority, and which sometimes also involved the legislative power.[90]

Equipped with a broad jurisdiction and especially with the power to give universally binding interpretations of national constitutions, constitutional courts have provided an effective political check on other branches of government, even in some of the most explosive conflicts over inter-branch struggles. In concrete political terms, courts were obliged to both survive attacks by other branches of government and actively check improper encroachments by those entities. Consequently, the major challenge for constitutional courts has been to fulfil their responsibilities as arbiters of political disputes without being used as an alternative venue for political manoeuvring. Obviously, one of the biggest threats to this was the risk of court decisions being politicized by various actors.

Among the parliamentary systems, courts involvement in political disputes was particularly marked in Hungary and Slovakia, although it can be found also in Estonia and

89 *See* J. de Raadt, 'Contestable Constitutions: Ambiguity, Conflict, and Change in East Central European Dual Executive Systems', *Communist and Post-Communist Studies*, Vol. 42, No. 1, 2009, p. 82.

90 *See* O. Protsyk, 'Politics of Intra-Executive Conflict in Semi-Presidential Regimes in Eastern Europe', *East European Politics and Society*, Vol. 19, No. 2, 2005, p. 138.

Latvia.[91] Despite the fact that Hungary introduced a 'pure parliamentary' system, a form of dual executive emerged in the early 1990s mainly due to the ambiguities of the Constitution in outlining the relationship between president and prime minister, especially in the areas of defence and foreign affairs.[92] However, in two important decisions, the Constitutional Court clearly defined the limits of presidential powers by interpreting them in line with the Article 30A of the Hungarian Constitution (of 1949 as amended in 1989), and these decisions were never contested. In both rulings, the Court justified its orientations by using legal and not political arguments. In particular, it based its decisions on a coherent system of principles related to the parliamentary form of government, which made it difficult for political actors to argue that the Court had decided the cases politically.[93]

The role played by the constitutional court in solving major political disputes between president and prime minister was largely different in Slovakia. In its decision of 2nd June 1993 the Court relied on several arguments that did not sit well with the parliamentary system of government since it placed the head of state in the context of the executive power.[94] In particular, it asserted not only the supremacy of the president over the cabinet but also bestowed executive power upon the head of state. Showing great difficulties to remain outside the political struggles, from 1994 to 1998 the Constitutional Court ruled sixteen times against the government and in favour of the president. These Court's orientations were likely based on the concentration of power in the prime minister within the Slovak parliamentary regime, and therefore the Court ruled on several occasions against the cabinet and in favour of the president. The government responded by criticizing the

---

91 An exception is the Czech Republic since, in this case, the power struggles did not occur during the first decade of Constitutional Court activities. Here, the new democratic elite had undertaken immediately, and with broad public consensus, ambitious political and economic reforms in order to quickly achieve European standards and European Union integration. After an initial period in which the Czech Court had to deal with issues related to the past injustices, it focused its activities on protecting human rights. *See* A. Di Gregorio, 'La transizione in Cecoslovacchia: principali profili di diritto costituzionale', cit., p. 276. However, the situation for the Czech Court became particularly complicated during the second decade of its activities and, in particular, in 2003 when Vaclav Klaus was elected as president of the Republic. In fact, the newly elected president was notorious for his criticism of the Constitutional Court's activism, and since in the same period, the term of office of nine constitutional judges had expired, he had the opportunity to put forward new candidates to the upper house of the parliament. The Senate's reluctance towards the presidential nominees led to hostilities between Klaus and the upper house of the Czech Parliament, and resulted in the paralysis of the Constitutional Court due to an insufficient number of justices on the bench. The Court finally resumed its activities in 2005, when the new elections gave the majority to the president's party in the Senate. For more, *see* K. Leich & W. Sadurski, 'Constitutional Courts of Central and Eastern Europe: Between Adolescence and Maturity', *Journal of Comparative Law*, Vol. 3, No. 2, 2008, p. 227.

92 *See* P.H. O'Neill, 'Hungary: Political Transition and Executive Conflict: The Balance or Fragmentation of Power', *in* R. Taras (Ed.), *Postcommunist Presidents*, Cambridge, Cambridge University Press, 1997, p. 201.

93 Constitutional Court of Hungary, Dec. No. 48 of 26th September 1991. *See also* G. Szoboszlai, 'Parliamentarism in the Making: Crisis and Political Transformation in Hungary', *in* A. Lijphart & C. Waisman (Eds.), *Institutional Design in New Democracies*, Boulder, Westview Press, 1996, p. 129.

94 *See* P. Kresak, 'The Government Structure in the New Slovak Republic', *Tulsa Journal of Comparative and International Law*, Vol. 4, No. 1, 1996, p. 27.

Court and describing it as the 'sick element' of Slovakia's political scene.[95] In general, the decisions unfavourable to the ruling party were followed by attempts to undermine the Court's prestige and limit its independence. But although the government has tried to strike back at the Court in various ways, it has also complied with its rulings.[96] Nonetheless, after this negative experience, Slovakia amended its Constitution firstly on 14 January 1999, and then on 23 February 2001, by introducing the popular election of the president, which has reduced the political struggles in the country.[97]

The orientations adopted by the Latvian Constitutional Court and the Estonian Constitutional Review Chamber were still different. In both cases, the constitutional adjudication bodies preferred to exercise judicial restraint, not intervening in political conflicts in order to prevent political attacks.[98]

---

95 T. Haughton, *Constraints and Opportunities of Leadership in Post-Communist Europe*, Burlington, Ashgate, 2005, p. 95.

96 S. Zifcak, 'The Battle Over Presidential Power in Slovakia', *East European Constitutional Review*, Vol. 1, No. 1, 1995, p. 61.

97 Similar implications are traceable also in Albania. In this case, constitutional judges were strong supporters of the president, and have practically rubber-stamped everything that the president did without adopting really independent decisions. A significant struggle between different branches of government and the Constitutional Court occurred, however, when the Court ruled on the parliamentary decision on the removal of the prosecutor general. The Court argued that the removal procedure was not in line with the Constitution, but it did not re-establish in the office the removed prosecutor (*see* the Constitutional Court of Albania, Dec. No. 75 of 19th April 2002). The only effect of the decision was on the interpretative level, binding the parliament to adopt in the future new rules on the removal procedures of the highest offices of the State. However, the reaction of political bodies was marked by strong criticism of the Constitutional Court: the President of the Republic invited the parliament to reduce the powers of the Constitutional Court, declaring himself in favour of its suppression, or the devolution of its functions to the supreme court; the president of the Parliament presented his resignation, motivating this decision with the need to defend the prestige, dignity, morality and autonomy of the legislative body; the parliamentary committee on legal affairs considered itself competent to declare the unconstitutionality of Constitutional Court's decisions, recommending to the parliament not to implement what was established by the constitutional adjudication body, an invitation that the parliament readily accepted by refusing to implement the Court's decision. The case is emblematic because it emphasized the failure of Albanian political bodies to recognize and respect the decisions of the constitutional adjudication body. *See* Č. Pištan, 'Le Corti costituzionali dell'Europa centro-orientale: arbitri di conflitti politici o promotori di diritti fondamentali?', *Percorsi costituzionali*, No. 2-3, 2010, p. 205.

98 An example of this trend can be found in Estonia in the early 1990s. The Constitution establishes the parliamentary election of the president of the Republic and delimites the presidential powers by reducing them to ceremonial powers, but the Parliament attempted to adopt a series of laws in order to further reduce president's functions, which led the head of state to petition several times the Constitutional Review Chamber. Although the latter has generally accepted the petitions, it has never ruled in favour of one or the other constitutional body (*see* Estonian Constitutional Chamber, judgment of 13th June 1994). For a contrary opinion *cf.* V. Pettai, 'Democratic Norm Building and Constitutional Discourse Formation in Estonia', *in* A. Czarnota, M. Krygier & W. Sadurski (Eds.), *Rethinking the Rule of Law after Communism*, Budapest, CEU Press, 2005, p. 96, who argues that the Constitutional Review Chamber generally ruled in favour of the head of state, which discourage further political attempts aimed at reducing presidential powers.

Within semi-presidential systems, the involvement of constitutional courts in political conflicts has been particularly marked in Poland, Romania and Bulgaria, although some minor interventions can be also found in Lithuania. If compared to parliamentary systems, conflicts between presidents and prime ministers in semi-presidential regimes tend to assume more serious character. In fact, semi-presidential systems are characterized by a dual executive, and political conflicts are here usually defined as struggles for the control of the executive power.[99] For these reasons, any conflict within the dual executive can be considered a potential threat to political effectiveness and stability, especially in still fragile democracies.

Poland represents a good example of this, since the 1992 "Little Constitution" was particularly deficient in defining the limits of presidential involvement in executive matters; the ambiguities of constitutional provisions, and an unusual overlapping of competences within the dual executive in the sphere of foreign policy and defence under the Wałęsa presidency led to continues clashes between the president and prime ministers.

Although the Constitutional Tribunal was called several times to resolve political conflicts, its initial approach clearly showed that it avoided to play a mediating role among different branches of government.[100] The reason for this orientation laid in two orders of issues: on the one hand, the "Little Constitution" represented a transitional constitutional text; on the other, the Constitutional Tribunal was probably influenced by the fact that in this period the *Sejm* could override its rulings since until the adoption of the 1997 Constitution the Tribunal's judgments on unconstitutionality produced only procedural effects, obliging the parliament to reexamine the legislative act.

Nonetheless, in one second moment, the Polish Constitutional Tribunal assumed a new role of an effective arbiter of political struggles.[101] In particular, following the adoption of the 1997 Constitution, the most controversial elements of the Polish form of government were eliminated, and the president-government-parliament triangle began to operate more efficiently. At the same time, the Constitutional Tribunal adopted a more aggressive approach in reviewing the constitutionality of laws, definitively abandoning the previous practice of avoiding controversial issues, having eliminated the new Constitution the limits concerning the effects of its decisions.

---

99 *See* O. Protsyk, 'Politics of Intra-Executive Conflict in Semi-Presidential Regimes in Eastern Europe', cit., p. 138.

100 *See* A. Krok-Paszkowska, 'Poland', *in* R. Elgie (Ed.), *Semipresidentialism in Europe*, cit., 167.

101 *See, e.g.*, in the Dec. No. OTK-ZU 1/95, the Constitutional Tribunal ruled on the ministerial counter-signature, which was foreseen by the "Little Constitution" as a general rule applicable to all presidential legal acts (the exception was given by twenty types of acts expressly listed). In practice, this requirement was used only in the case of legislative acts, but the Constitutional Court ruled against such a practice by restoring the requirement of the ministerial counter-signature for presidential acts in line with the provisions of the Constitution.

In Romania, the evolution of the semi-presidential system during the first decade of democratic transition was marked by the pre-eminence of the president over the prime minister and a parallel involvement of the Constitutional Court in political struggles.[102] The orientations held by the constitutional adjudication body were of two types: on the one hand, the Romanian legal system of the first years of the transition remained semi-authoritarian. This subjected the Court to the President, and led it to approve every presidential action[103]; on the other hand, the Court has shown a rather aggressive attitude towards the Parliament, although the effects of its rulings remained limited until the 2003 constitutional reform.[104]

Bulgaria represents an another case in which the Constitutional Court exercised an important role in political processes. However, it often ruled in favour of the president. Moreover, since the presidency in Bulgaria has more limited powers than its counterparts in other semi-presidential regimes, the Court has been an important institution for the president. In fact, the president relied heavily on the Court's ability to mediate conflicts and to confirm the autonomy of the presidency within the executive. The fact that the president has petitioned the Court a few times does not reflect what has happened in practice. This is because, especially in periods of cohabitation, the president preferred to avoid petitions since the legislation voted by the majority was challenged before the Court by the parliamentary opposition. Without any doubt, the Court's case law has finished to expand the presidential powers: on two occasions, by ruling on the constitutionality of presidential decrees, the Constitutional Court decided against the petitioners and in favour

102 *See* C. Weber, 'Constitutionalism as a Vehicle for Democratic Consolidation in Romania', *in* J. Zielonka (Ed.), *Democratic Consolidation in Eastern Europe: Volume 1, Institutional Engineering*, cit., p. 156.

103 H. Schwartz, 'Eastern Europe's Constitutional Courts', *Journal of Democracy*, Vol. 9, 1998, p. 113.

104 An example of the first trend is given by the attempt to remove the President from his office due to serious violation of the 1994 Constitution. The attempt was, however, rejected by the Parliament following the negative opinion of the Constitutional Court. A second example of the same trend dates back to 1999 and concerned the presidential decree on the removal of the Prime Minister. The latter petitioned the Constitutional Court against this decree, which was perceived as unconstitutional also by the majority of Romanian legal scholars, but the Court, through its president, declared its incompetency to rule on the constitutionality of presidential decrees. An example of the second trend can be found in the case on the review of constitutionality of the 1994 parliamentary standing orders. It was requested by the presidents of the Chamber of Deputies and the Senate after the standing orders were adopted. In the Dec. No. 87/1994, of some 213 provisions of the parliamentary orders of the Chamber of Deputies, 25 were found as unconstitutional, and of some 184 provisions of the parliamentary orders of the Senate, 29 were found as unconstitutional. Following this decision, the two chambers of the Parliament have amended the disputed provisions in line with the indications offered by the constitutional adjudication body, thus demonstrating the acceptance of a significant limitation of their autonomy and the decision of the Constitutional Court. Additionally, the Court took the opportunity to define the role of the Head of State in the Romanian semi-presidential regime. It argued that parliamentary committees could not oversee the president's activities or request the president to appear before it without violating the constitutionally established relationship between president and parliament. In sum, the ruling demonstrates that the Court has taken its role seriously, issuing decisions not inspired by any political motive.

of the president; in other cases, the Court proposed interpretations of the Constitution favourable to the president.[105] Scholars, however, are unanimous in sustaining that the Court ensured to the president a sphere of prerogatives that went far beyond the constitutional provisions. However, in a second moment, the acquired balance within the dual executive has led to the primacy of the prime minister, thus increasing the contradiction between the strong legitimacy that the popular election ensures to the president and the limited presidential powers concretely assigned by the Constitution. At the same time, it has been pointed out that the case law favourable to the president led to questioning the independence of the Court in the first years of transition; however, these initial approaches adopted by the Court could be also interpreted in the light of the campaign promoted by the Socialist Party against the constitutional adjudication body. The campaign was aimed at diminishing the influence of the Court as well as at 'purging' the Court since some judges were considered as political opponents. In this light, the Constitutional Court's case law can be read as an attempt to assert its autonomy against the parliament and government, which were dominated by the Socialist Party, and the decisions favourable to the President should be understood as a sort of temporary alliance between the Court and the President (especially until 1995), which proved to be rather profitable since the Court had managed to preserve its autonomy.[106]

5.6.2 *The Second Phase (Since 2000): Protection of Fundamental Rights*

The involvement of constitutional courts in transitional justice issues as well as in the resolution of political conflicts has diminished at the end of the first decade of their insti-

105 A first example is given by the Dec. No. 6/1993, which affirmed that the decree of appointing the head of the National Investigation Service needed the signature of the president, as the sole approval by the Council of Ministers was not sufficient. In the Dec. No. 25/1995, the Court proposed a rather forced interpretation of the Art. 92 of the Constitution so as to ensure to the president a power to intervene in the course of the electoral campaign in favour of some political forces. In the Dec. No. 4/1995, the Court declared the unconstitutionality of one parliamentary resolution, which required that candidates designated by the President to diplomatic corps should receive also the parliamentary approval; in the Dec. No. 13/1996, the Court declared the unconstitutionality of an another parliamentary resolution, which established the necessity of the ministerial counter-signature for presidential decrees judges appointments. In particular, the Court stated that the counter-signature had no general character, therefore in the absence of specific constitutional provisions presidential acts do not need a ministerial counter-signature. *See* V.I. Ganev, 'Bulgaria', *in* Elgie (Ed.), *Semi-presidentialism in Europe*, cit., p. 139.

106 Lithuania represents an exception as in this case the relations within the dual executive have been marked by a peaceful coexistence. The few conflicts that occurred in the country did not involve the Constitutional Court. Nevertheless, the latter had the opportunity to limit presidential powers, thus confirming the parliamentary dynamics of the form of government. *See* Constitutional Court of Lithuania, Decision of 10 January 1998. *See also* Urbanavicius, 'Lithuania', *in* R. Elgie (Ed.), *Semi-presidentialism in Europe*, cit., p. 156. For a contrary opinion *see* M. Mazza, 'La Costituzione della Lituania (1992)', *in* M. Ganino (Ed.), *Codice delle Costituzioni*, cit., p. 111.

tutional life. This period was marked in some cases by the adoption of entirely new constitutions (Poland in 1997 and Albania in 1998) or by the adoption of a series of constitutional amendments (Slovakia in 1999 and Croatia in 2000) that had changed the form of government by reducing presidential powers. As a result, the involvement of constitutional courts in solving political conflicts and in transitional justice issues was reduced.

With the opening of the second decade of their activities, constitutional courts have gradually changed their role: from active policymakers and arbiters of political conflict, they transformed themselves into protectors of fundamental rights and freedoms. Certainly, this is not to say that during the first phase of their activities, courts did not render decisions on human rights protection. As the evolution of their case law clearly demonstrates, courts have adopted many decisions that have shaped economic and political reforms during the 1990s, deciding many cases related to social and economic rights but not those involving classic political and civil rights. On the contrary, since the early 2000s, not only have transitional issues and political disputes been replaced by case law on the protection of human rights, but political and civil rights issues raised by individual citizens have become an important part of Constitutional Courts' dockets.

The increasing involvement of Constitutional Courts in human rights issues was possibly due to the fact that almost all CEBBE countries allowed citizens direct and indirect access to their national Courts. Indeed, constitutional adjudication bodies can perform concrete norm control and, most importantly, they can rule on individual petitions filed by citizens who believe that their constitutional rights have been violated by a legislative, judiciary and / or an administrative decision. Additionally, in many cases courts can review the conformity of national legislation with international conventions on human rights. Accordingly, following the enlargement of the Council of Europe to the East, the courts' case law on human rights often refers to these international documents, especially the European Convention on Human Rights (ECHR) and the case law of the European Court on Human Rights (ECtHR).[107]

5.6.2.1 The Process of Europeanization

After the regime transformation in the 1990s, the second major challenge faced by the CEBBE countries has been 'Europeanization'.[108] The European integration process affected and profoundly changed the institutional and legal framework of these countries as it requested in the pre-accession period a gradual harmonization of their legal systems with European one and, after the enlargement of the European Union towards several CEBBE

107 *See* O. Pollicino, *Allargamento dell'Europa a Est e rapporto tra Corti costituzionali e Corti europee*, Milano, Giuffre, 2010.

108 *See* Z. Kuhn, 'The Application of European Law in the New Member States: Several (Early) Predictions', *German Law Review*, Vol. 6, No. 3, 2005, p. 563.

countries, the direct applicability and the unconditional primacy of EU law over national legislation. Even if CEBBE countries, which became EU Member States following the EU enlargements of 2004, 2007 and 2013, adapted their national Constitutions for the EU membership, the so-called 'Euroamendments' had not completely solved the issues concerning relations between the European and national legal orders and, in particular, the relations between national legislation and EU law. Moreover, the often imprecise European clauses were introduced in countries that had just regained their sovereignty and were supposed to coexist with constitutional documents that guaranteed a high level of protection to the principles of sovereignty and the supremacy of national Constitutions.[109]

The EU enlargement process thus created a totally new sphere of reality – in which constitutional courts have readily reserved for themselves a new, important role, completing their transformation: from post-communist courts they became European courts with an active role in solving issues concerning the relationship between the national and EU constitutional orders and, in particular, the relations between domestic legislation and the accumulated body of EU law, the *acquis communautaire*. More precisely, constitutional courts undertook a fundamental role in both the pre-accession and post-accession phases, acting at the same time as the engine and the brake of Europeanization.

During the pre-accession phase, constitutional courts had generally shown a very pro-European character by widely referring in their decisions to the *acquis communautaire* as well as to the case law of the European Court of Justice (ECJ), although in this period EU law did not formally have binding force in the candidate countries. Perhaps the main example of this Euro-friendly attitude is the Polish Constitutional Tribunal, which expressly stated that the European integration process obliged Poland to ensure that future legislation is compatible with EU law. This obligation, according to the Tribunal, also implied the duty to interpret the existing national legislation in a way that ensured the greatest possible degree of compatibility.[110]

---

109 *See* A. Albi, *EU Enlargement and the Constitutions of Central and Eastern Europe*, cit. On the relations between Constitutional Courts and supranational Courts *see* G.F. Ferrari (Ed.), *Corti nazionali e Corti europee*, cit.

110 Polish Constitutional Tribunal, Dec. No. K 15/97. Similarly, in the *Škoda Auto case*, the Czech Constitutional Court emphasized that both the Treaty of Rome and the EU Treaty derive from the same values and principles as Czech constitutional law, therefore the interpretation of EU law by European bodies is valuable for the interpretation of the corresponding Czech rules. Moreover, in the *Milka Quota case*, the same Court rejected the idea that EU law could not be applied because at that time it was not binding; the Court argued instead that primary EU law was not foreign law for the Constitutional Court, but to a wide degree it penetrated into the Court's decision-making – particularly in the form of EU law general principles. *See* the Czech Constitutional Court, *Škoda Auto case*, decision No. US 31/97-35 of 29 May 1997, and the *Milka Quota case*, Dec. No. Pl ÚS 5/01 of 16 October 2001. The need to consider the general principles of EU law or to assess domestic legal acts in light of EU law was further emphasized by the Latvian Constitutional Court, and the Estonian Constitutional Review Chamber. *See, e.g.*, the Latvian Constitutional Court Dec. No. 200-03-01, and the Estonian Constitutional Review Chamber Dec. No. III-4/A-5/94.

On the contrary, the Hungarian Constitutional Court opted in the pre-accession context for a more aggressive approach towards EU law. In its *Europe Agreement* decision, the Court found that the direct applicability of EU secondary law, qualified as foreign law, would constitute a violation of the constitutional provisions that protect national sovereignty and therefore would require an authorizing constitutional amendment.[111]

After the EU enlargement to the East, constitutional courts encountered the same challenge previously faced by the constitutional courts from the old EU Member States, related to the issue of the unconditional primacy of EU law over national legislation (including the constitution). Inspired by their Western European counterparts, which did not unconditionally accept the view of the ECJ that accorded absolute primacy to EU law and, in particular, by the two fundamental cases of the German Federal Constitutional Court, *Solange II* and *Maastricht* decisions, courts gradually substituted their previous pro-European attitude with a more hostile approach. By not accepting that any source of law might prevail over the national constitution, these courts have elaborated a series of reservations against an absolute primacy of EU law in order to safeguard the superiority of their national constitutional values.

The first post-accession decision was pronounced by the Hungarian Constitutional Court. In the *Surplus Act case*, the Court found a national law implementing EU regulations on surplus sugar stock of agricultural products retroactive and thus unconstitutional, although the provisions of the Surplus Act, adopted by the Hungarian parliament, were identical to the provisions of the EU regulations. Therefore, the Hungarian Court indirectly attacked the EU regulations on the surplus sugar stock by simply disregarding that the obligation resulted from Hungary's membership in the EU and solved the case by situating it in a domestic context. Moreover, in the view of the Hungarian Court, constitutional principles could prevail over Hungary's obligations resulting from EU membership and could operate as a limit to the process of European integration.[112]

Other important indications concerning the relations between the national and EU legal orders were given by the Polish Constitutional Tribunal in its two famous decisions:

111 *See* Constitutional Court of Hungary, Dec. No. 30/1998, (VI 25) AB. *See also* J. Volkai, 'The application of the Europe Agreement and European Law in Hungary: The judgment of an activist Constitutional Court on Activist Notions', *Harvard Jean Monnet Working Paper*, No. 8, 1999, p. 9, and W. Sadurski, 'Solange, Chapter 3: Constitutional Courts in Central Europe – Democracy – European Union', *EUI Working Paper*, No. 40, 2006.

112 *See* the Hungarian Constitutional Court, *Surplus Act* case, judgement No. 17/2004 (V.25.) AB. Again, similar outcomes can be detected in the Czech Republic. In the *Sugar Quotas* case, the Czech Court basically recognized that the EU has an autonomous legal order that is applicable in the Czech Republic and prevails over all provisions of the Czech legal order, with the exception of fundamental elements of the rule of law and the foundations of the Czech Republic's state sovereignty. According the Court, acceptance of the EU principles is not unconditional, therefore it reserved for itself the authority to decide in situations where EU norms might be in conflict with the Constitution's fundamental core. *See* the Czech Constitutional Court, *Sugar Quotas* case, judgement No. Pl. US 50/04 of 8 March 2000.

the *Treaty Accession case* (Dec. No. K 18/4 of 11 May 2005), and the *European Arrest Warrant* (Dec. No. P. 1/05 of 27 April 2005). In the Treaty Accession case, the Polish Tribunal took the opportunity to further clarify its previous position towards EU law and clearly excluded any possibility of the ultimate supremacy of EU norms over constitutional norms. In the Tribunal's view, the accession of Poland to the EU did not undermine the supremacy of the Constitution over the whole legal order in the context of the sovereignty of the Republic of Poland. The norms of the Constitution, being the supreme act that is an expression of the nation's will, would not lose their binding force or change their content by a mere irreconcilable inconsistency between these norms and any EU provision. In addition, the Tribunal felt it necessity to add that in case of conflict between EU law and constitutional norms, the nation, as the sovereign, would need to decide whether to amend the Constitution, cause modification within the EU prevision or, ultimately, on Poland's withdrawal from the EU. Nevertheless, the Tribunal hastened to explain that any conflicts between EU and domestic law are to be placed in the background of the general principle of consistent interpretation between domestic and EU law.

In the second case, the Constitutional Tribunal took a less aggressive attitude. Although it found in the national legislation implementing the EU directive on the European arrest warrant an opposition to Article 55 of the Polish Constitution (which at the time prohibited the extradition of Polish citizens), the Court accepted indirectly the supremacy of EU law, indicating the constitutional revision as the only way out for the resolution of the conflict in order to make Art. 55 of the Constitution compatible with European secondary legislation.[113] However, it is also interesting to note that in its *European Arrest Warrant* decision, the Czech Constitutional Court opted to solve the case differently – that is, on the basis of the principle of consistent interpretation between national and EU legislation.[114]

On the contrary, the Estonian Review Chamber and the Lithuanian Constitutional Court preferred to maintain a broadly pro-European approach even in the post-accession period. In the Estonian case, the Constitutional Review Chamber clearly accepted the ultimate supremacy of EU law. In the view of the Chamber, the Constitution is applicable only when in conformity with EU law or when regulating the relationships that are not governed by EU law. Those constitutional provisions that are not compatible with EU law should be considered inapplicable and suspended.[115] On the other hand, the Lithuanian

---

113 *See* K. Kowalik-Banczyk, 'Should We Polish It Up? The Polish Constitutional Tribunal and the Idea of Supremacy of EU Law', *German Law Journal*, Vol. 6, No. 10, 2005, pp. 1360-1361; D. Leczykiewicz, 'Case Note on the Judgment of 27 April 2005 of the Polish Constitutional Tribunal', *Common Market Law Review*, Vol. 43, No. 4, 2006, p. 1187.

114 Constitutional Court of the Czech Republic, Dec. No. Pl. US 66/04 of 3 May 2006.

115 *See* Constitutional Review Chamber of Estonia, Opinion, No. 3-4-1-3-06 of 11 May 2006. *See also* A. Albi, *Supremacy of EC Law in the New Member States: Bringing Parliaments into the Equation of 'Co-operative Constitutionalism'*, cit., p. 45.

Constitutional Court was the third European Court to exercise the reference for a preliminary ruling on the basis of Article 234 of the Treaty on the Functioning of the EU, and referred a case already underway to the ECJ in order to question it against the interpretation of EU law.[116] The case concerned the EU directive 2003/54/CE of 26 June 2003 concerning common rules for the internal market in electricity.

Other significant decisions on the relationship between domestic and EU legal orders were pronounced more recently by the Latvian and the Czech Constitutional Courts when they were called to decide on the constitutionality of the Lisbon Treaty (2007) prior to its ratification. The Latvian Court found the Treaty of Lisbon not in conflict with the constitutional principle of national sovereignty, since the new treaty provided for respecting the identity and sovereignty of the member states and does not contain any norm that would confirm that the EU claims to become a federal state.[117]

In the Czech case, the Lisbon Treaty saga needs more attention, as the Court has ruled twice on its constitutionality. In the *Lisbon Treaty I case* (Dec. No. Pl. ÚS 19/08 of 26 November 2008), the Court stated that the parts of the Lisbon Treaty that the applicant (the Senate) contested were in fact consistent with the Czech Constitution. The Court showed a very pro-European approach, emphasizing the necessity of EU integration in the globalized world as well as the need of close cooperation and further integration. It further observed that the transfer of certain state competences that arise from the free will of the sovereign, and continue to be exercised with the sovereign's participation in a manner that is agreed upon in advance, is not a conceptual weakening of the sovereignty of a state but, on the contrary, paves the way for resorting to the concept of 'pooled sovereignty'. However, the Court also referred to its previous decisions on the limits to constitutional amendments, and made it clear that any transfer that would deprive the Czech Republic of its status as a sovereign state should be prohibited. Thus, according to Court, the transfer of sovereign powers under the Constitution is conditional at two levels: the formal level, as outlined in Article 1 of the Constitution, which protects the foundations of the state sovereignty of the Czech Republic; and the substantial level, which is reflected through the fundamental core of the Constitution. The Court then drew inspiration from the *Solange II* and *Maastricht* decisions of the German Constitutional Court, and added that the concept of sovereignty, interpreted in the context of Articles 1 and 10a of the Constitution, clearly shows that there are certain limits to the transfer of sovereignty, but that these limits should be left primarily to the legislature to specify since this is *a priori* a political question. Therefore, the Constitutional Court should interfere only in exceptional cases, in which it would operate as an *ultima ratio* and review whether an act of the EU had exceeded the limits of powers transferred to it by the Czech Republic. Finally, the

116 *See* Constitutional Court of Lithuania, Decision of 8 March 2007.

117 *See* Constitutional Court of Latvia, Dec. No. 2008-35-01 of 7 April 2009.

Court concluded that the Treaty of Lisbon does not have such consequences, since it confirms that the constitutional *Kompetenz-Kompetenz* – that is, the power to amend EU primary law – remains with the member states, which may at any time withdraw from the EU. Consequently, according to the Court, even after the Lisbon Treaty enters into force, the EU will not acquire the power to create its own new competences and the member states will still remain the 'Masters of the Treaties'.[118]

In its first decision on the Lisbon Treaty, the Czech Constitutional Court clearly used the *Bundesverfassungsgericht* as its guide. Of course, the Court could only cite the *Solange II* and *Maastricht* decisions since the German Constitutional Court had not yet adopted its famous Lisbon Treaty decision. Thus, the most interesting characteristic of the *Lisbon Treaty II case* (Dec. No. Pl. ÚS 29/09 of 3 November 2009) is the way the Czech Court distanced itself from the decision on the Lisbon Treaty of the German Constitutional Court. In particular, in its second decision on the Lisbon Treaty the Court reinforced that the Czech Republic had opted for a notion of sovereignty that can be pooled among states, specifying that this does not entail a loss but instead can reinforce sovereignty. Additionally, it refused to authoritatively define the notion of 'the substantive limits to transfers of competences' as well as to create a list of state competences that cannot be transferred to the EU, despite being demanded by the petitioner (a group of senators). The Court instead stated that "these limits should be left primarily to the legislature". Moreover, the Court clearly criticized the petitioner for having being inspired by the judgment of the German Constitutional Court, which provided for such a list of competences in its decision. Nevertheless, the Czech Constitutional Court again sent a clear message: even if only as an *ultima ratio*, it is ready to transform itself into the arbiter over questions of whether the EU exceeds its competences or not.[119]

In actual fact, it was not just a message since in the more recent *Landtová case* (Dec. No. Pl. ÚS 5/12 of 31 January 2012), the Czech Court has declared *ultra vires* the ECJ ruling of 22 June 2011 (C-399/09). The latter dealt with the interpretation of EU regulation 1408/71, and was adopted in response to a submitted request for a preliminary ruling, which was raised in the context of the dispute between Mrs. Landtová, a citizen of the Czech Republic, residing in that member state, and the Czech social security institution. It concerned an alleged discriminatory pension scheme in the Czech Republic that resulted

118 *See* A. (Ton) van den Rink, 'The Czech Constitutional Court and the Treaty of Lisbon, *Tijdschrift voor Constitutioneel Recht*, No. 3, 2010, pp. 315-321. *See also* P. Bříza, 'The Czech Republic: The Constitutional Court on the Lisbon Treaty Decision of 26 November 2008', *European Constitutional Law Review*, Vol. 5, No. 1, 2009, pp. 143-164.

119 *See* J. Komarek, 'The Czech Constitutional Court's Second Decision on the Lisbon Treaty of 3 November 2009', *European Constitutional Law Review*, Vol. 5, No. 3, 2009, pp. 345-352. *See also* O. Pollicino, 'Qualcosa è cambiato? La recente giurisprudenza delle Corti costituzionali dell'est vis-à-vis il processo di integrazione europea', *Il diritto dell'Unione europea*, Vol. 17, No. 2, 2012, pp. 765-788.

from the dissolution of Czechoslovakia. In dealing with the *Landtová case*, the Czech Court responded in an excessively aggressive manner to the ECJ, arguing that the EU has no competence in social security matters, since under the Article 10 of the Czech Constitution this remains an exclusive competence of the Czech State. As a result, an excess of the Luxembourg Court and a conduct *ultra vires* occurred. In arguing that it will not implement the ECJ judgment, the Court summarized its previous case law on the relationship between national law and EU law and above all emphasized the thesis under which constitutional courts maintain their role of supreme guardians of constitutionality even in the realms of the EU and even against potential excesses on the side of EU institutions. However, the Court was not defending the fundamental core of the Constitution but the agreement concluded with the EU at the time of accession, forgetting in its decision some key principles of the EU law, such as the prohibition of non-discrimination. It has been thus argued that giving the Solange doctrine in the hands of the Czech Court meant letting 'children play with matches'.[120]

Finally, in Hungary, the Constitutional Court ruled on 30 November 2016 (Dec. No. 22/2016 (XII. 5.) AB) on the EU's refugee relocation system scheme and its application in Hungary by threatening not to apply the relevant EU law. In doing this, the Court provided for an interpretation of the Constitution, which unequivocally states that the protection of constitutional identity, which derives from the Hungarian historical Constitution, cannot be questioned by the needs of EU integration.[121]

5.7 Judicial Power

As far as the judiciary system is concerned, constitutions of CEBBE countries establish the independence and autonomy of the judiciary, as well as the separation of the judicial power from other state's powers.[122] To this end, constitutions regulate judges' immunity (usually similarly to the parliamentary immunity),[123] and immovability, and in specific cases the incompatibilities with the office.[124] The Bulgarian Constitution further establish the

120 J. Komarek, 'Playing with Matches: The Czech Constitutional Court's Ultra Vires Revolution', *VerfBlog*, 22 February 2012.

121 *See* G. Halmai, 'The Hungarian National(ist) Constitutional Identity', *Quaderni Costituzionali*, No. 1, 2017, p. 154, who describes the Constitutional Court's interpretation of constitutional identity as "unconstitutional constitutional identity".

122 Bulgaria (Art. 117 Constitution); Croatia (Art. 115 Constitution); Czech Republic (Art. 81 Constitution); Lithuania (Art. 98 Constitution); Macedonia (Art. 62 Constitution); Polonia (Art. 123 Constitution); Romania (Art. 123 Constitution), *etc.*

123 Bulgaria (Art. 132 Constitution); Croatia (Art. 119 Constitution); Lithuania (Art. 114 Constitution); Macedonia (Art. 100 Constitution), *etc.*

124 Czech Republic (Art. 82 Constitution); Estonia (Art. 147 Constitution); Romania (Art. 124 Constitution); Slovenia (Art. 134 Constitution), *etc.*

necessity of a creation of a separate budget for the judiciary (Art. 117 Constitution). Specific limitations to the criminal prosecution of judges are established in Constitutions of Estonia (Art. 153 Constitution) and Lithuania (Art. 116 Constitution).

In principle, constitutions distinguish between ordinary courts, which deal with disputes in civil and / or criminal cases, and specialized courts.[125] Most of CEBBE judicial systems are inspired by the French model, as they structure is divided into three tiers. Courts of first instance may be local (district or municipal courts), and regional (but only in specific cases provided for by law); courts of second instance include regional courts, which are competent to decide on appeals against decisions adopted by local courts. At the top of the judicial system there is the supreme court, which is modelled in several cases on the basis of the German Federal Court of Justice, which means that it operates as a revision court,[126] whereas other countries have implemented the French model.[127]

Moreover, some CEBBE countries have provided for the establishment of a Supreme Administrative Court: Bulgaria, Poland, and more recently the Czech Republic (established by the Act No. 150/2002), and Croatia (established on 1 January 2012). Both in Czech Republic and Croatia, the creation of the supreme administrative courts has reduced the spectrum of constitutional courts' justiciable acts. In the first case, the Supreme Administrative Court has replaced the Constitutional Court in reviewing individual and concrete administrative acts, as well as in deciding on jurisdictional disputes; however, the Constitutional Court may still review the secondary legislation. In the second case, the 2010 Administrative Disputes Act introduced a formal criterion for dividing the competences between the Constitutional Court and the High Administrative Court; in this sense, the latter has the power to rule on all the general acts adopted by the bodies of local and regional self-government and public legal persons (regardless the content of these acts), while the review of all other normative acts remain under the jurisdiction of the Constitutional Court, including the statutes of local and regional authorities.[128]

---

125 This is for example the case of Croatia, where the 2018 Courts Act specifies that the judicial power is exercised by both regular and specialized courts. Regular courts are municipal courts, county courts and the Supreme Court of the Republic of Croatia. Specialized courts are misdemeanour courts, commercial courts, the High Misdemeanour Court of the Republic of Croatia, the High Commercial Court of the Republic of Croatia and the Administrative Court of the Republic of Croatia.

126 *See, e.g.*, Estonia, Chapter XVIII Constitution.

127 *See, e.g.*, Romania, Chapter VI Constitution. On the judicial system of the CEBBE countries *see also* C. Dallara, *Democracy and Judicial Reform in South-East Europe*, Dordrecht, Springer, 2014, and Z. Kühn, *The Judiciary in Central and Eastern Europe: Mechanical Jurisprudence in Transformation?*, Leiden, Brill, 2011.

128 J. Omejec & S. Banić, 'Diferencijacija propisa i općih akata u budućoj praksi Ustavnog suda i Upravnog suda u povodu zakona o upravnim sporovima' (Differentiation of regulations and general acts in the future practice of the Constitutional Court and the Administrative Court on the basis of the administrative disputes law), *Zbornik pravnog fakulteta u Splitu*, No. 2, 2012, p. 317.

Furthermore, several constitutions of CEBBE countries provide for the establishment of a body, differently denominated and composed, but which exercises the competences of the high council of the judiciary.[129] Finally, as regards to the prosecutor general, the Polish and Romanian Constitutions explicitly provide for its dependency on the minister of justice, while the Bulgarian, Romanian and Hungarian Constitutions provide for its hierarchical organization, and the Macedonian and Slovak Constitutions establish the its parliamentary election. In other cases, constitutions provided for the list of competences exercised by the general prosecutor and demand to the legislation the detailed discipline.[130]

5.8 Illiberal Turn and the Fate of Constitutional Justice and Judicial Power

The recent illiberal turn which has marked some CEBBE countries, in particular Hungary and Poland, has seriously impacted on the rules regulating constitutional adjudication bodies and the judicial power by undermining their independence.

In Hungary, the Orbán government – which since 2010 political elections has managed to secure a two-thirds majority in parliament – has repeatedly claimed its intention to build an illiberal democracy in the country. The term illiberal democracy was originally coined to describe negatively some hybrid regimes that combine authoritarian and democratic elements,[131] but today the same concept is invoked by Hungary with positive connotations. In fact, it is presented as a valid alternative to what is defined as a failed model of liberal democracy.

The Hungarian illiberal turn started even before the adoption of the 2011 Fundamental Law, and the Constitutional Court was the first constitutional body that immediately suffered that consequences. In 2010, the parliament approved a series of changes to the rules on the selection of constitutional judges. This resulted in an alteration of the number of judges, which was increased from 11 to 15 as well as in an extension of the term of office from 9 to 12 years, and in the erasure of the age limit applicable to the term of office, previously set at seventy years. These changes have allowed the government to designate eleven out of fifteen constitutional judges. Moreover, with the entry into force of the 2011 Fundamental Law and its numerous amendments, the powers of the Constitutional Court

129 *See* Bulgaria (Arts. 129, 130, and 133 Constitution); Croatia (Art. 121 Constitution); Lithuania (Art. 112 Constitution); Macedonia (Arts. 104-105 Constitution); Poland (Art. 60 Constitution); Romania (Arts. 124, 132-133 Constitution), and Slovenia (Art. 131 Constitution).

130 *See* Romania (Art. 131 Constitution); Bulgaria (Art. 126 Constitution); Macedonia (Art. 106 Constitution); Slovakia (Art. 150 Constitution); Estonia (Art. 151 Constitution); Lithuania (Arts. 135-136 Constitution), *etc.*

131 *See* F. Zakaria, 'The Rise of Illiberal Democracy, Foreign Affairs', *Foreign Affairs*, No. 6, 1997, p. 22.

were subjected to several limitations. In particular, the Hungarian Court lost its power to review the constitutionality of tax and financial measures until the state debt exceeds half of GDP; to decide on the *actio popularis* (although the constitutional complaint was introduced to compensate for this limit); to use as a basis for interpreting the new constitutional text the case law adopted before the entry into force of 2011 Fundamental Law, thus eliminating all previous case law adopted from 1990 to 2011, and to review the content of constitutional amendments. Following these limitations, the Hungarian Court, once defined as the most powerful constitutional court of the world,[132] did not adopt any decision that has seriously challenged government policies. By now all of its members are judges loyal to the government.[133]

Once ensuring the political control over the Constitutional Court, the reform of the judicial system has been put forward. It has been enclosed in the 2011 Fundamental Law; the law CLXI on the organization and administration of courts, and the law CLXII on the legal status and remuneration of judges both adopted on 28 November 2011. The new constitutional text is quite laconic in regulating the judiciary system, deferring the additional discipline to the adoption of cardinal acts. In particular, the Article 26, para. 1 of the Fundamental Law proclaims the independence of judges (which are subjected only to the law) and the prohibition for judges to carry out political activities. In addition, the Supreme Court has been replaced with a new body, called Curia, which exercises the same competences previously attributed to the Supreme Court. The Fundamental Law also establishes that, with the sole exception of the president of the Curia, judges cannot maintain their posts if they reach the retirement age. Such provision should be read together with the law CLXII of 2011, which reduced the retirement age of judges and established that it should be immediate and retroactive, and the Article 12, para. 1 of Transitional and Final Provisions to the Fundamental Law (adopted separately from the constitutional text), which introduced deadlines for reaching the retirement age. This meant in practice that the judicial retirement age has been reduced from 70 to 62 years, thus forcing around 274 judges into early retirement.[134] Although the Constitutional Court proclaimed the unconstitutionality of the measure (Constitutional Court of Hungary, sent. N. 33/2012 (VII. 17.) of 16 July 2012), and the ECJ considered it not in line with the European law as it violated EU equal treatment rules (Court of Justice of the European Union, case C-286/12, *European Commission v. Hungary*, judgment of 6 November 2012), none of these decisions were really able to reinstate the fired judges into their original position.

132 *See* K.L. Scheppele, 'The New Hungarian Constitutional Court', *East European Constitutional Review*, No. 4, 1999, p. 34.

133 *See* G. Halmai, 'Abuse of Constitutional Identity. The Hungarian Constitutional Court on Interpretation of Art. E) (2) of the Fundamental Law', *Review of Central and Eastern European Law*, No. 1, 2018, p. 23.

134 *See* G. Halmai, 'The Early Retirement Age of the Hungarian Judges', *in* F. Nicola & B. Davies (Eds.), *EU Law Stories*, Cambridge, Cambridge University Press, 2017, p. 471.

On the contrary, in order to fill the vacancies created by the forced early retirement of judges the government has introduced a new system of selection of judges. The Article 11 of the Transitional and Final Provisions to the Fundamental Law empowers the National Office for Judiciary to perform, starting from 1 January 2012, several competences previously attributed to the National Judicial Council, while the latter has been relegated to a purely advisory body. More particularly, the selection of new judges has been attributed to the head of the National Office for the Judiciary, who exercises over fifty competences, including: the power to propose to the President of the Republic the appointment and dismissal of judges; the power to appoint presidents, vice-presidents and heads of divisions of courts and appellate courts; the power to decide on the assignments and transfer of judges in case of reorganization of courts (who in case of refusal can be removed); the power to decide on the assignment of cases and the transfer of cases from one court to another. Following the opinion No. 663/2012 of the Venice Commission, according to which the reform of the judicial system reduced the guarantees of an independent selection of candidates, the Hungarian parliament has introduced a series of surface changes, continuing at the same time to fill the vacant posts with new judges. In addition, the early retirement has affected the president of the Supreme Court as it was expressly established by Transitional and Final Provisions to the Fundamental Law. In this case, it was the European Court of Human Rights that intervened by condemning Hungary (European Court of Human Rights, *Baka v. Hungary*, decision of 27 May 2014).[135]

Finally, the Seventh Amendment to the Fundamental Law of June 2018 has further altered the judicial system by providing for a new system of administrative courts with a

135 On Hungarian illiberal turn and its impact on constitutional justice and the judicial system *see* K.L. Scheppele, 'Hungary's Unconstitutional Constitution', 2 January 2012, https://krugman.blogs.nytimes.com/2012/01/02/the-unconstitutional-constitution/ (last accessed April 2019); G. Halmai, 'Towards an Illiberal Democracy. Hungary's New Constitution', *Eurozine*, 25 January 2012; 'Opinion on Hungary's New Constitutional Order, Amicus Brief for the Venice Commission on the Transitional Provisions of the Fundamental Law and the Key Cardinal Laws', February 2012, https://lapa.princeton.edu/hosteddocs/hungary/Amicus_Cardinal_Laws_final.pdf (last accessed April 2019); G. Halmai, 'The Early Retirement Age of the Hungarian Judges', *in* F. Nicola & B. Davies (Eds.), *EU Law Stories*, cit.; K.L. Scheppele, 'How to Evade the Constitution: The Case of the Hungarian Constitutional Court's Decision on the Judicial Retirement Age', *VerfBlog*, 9 August 2012; K.L. Scheppele, 'EU Commission v. Hungary: The Case for the Systemic Infringement Action', *VerfBlog*, 22 November 2013; K.L. Scheppele, 'Hungary's Attacks on the Rule of Law and Why They Matter for Business', *Financial Times*, 5 February 2014; K.L. Scheppele, 'Hungary and the End of Politics', 26 May 2014, www.thenation.com/article/hungary-and-end-politics/ (last accessed April 2019); G. Halmai, 'The Rise and Fall of Constitutionalism in Hungary', *in* P. Blokker (Ed.), *Constitutional Acceleration within the European Union and Beyond*, London, Routledge, 2017; G. Halmai, 'Second-Grade Constitutionalism: the Cases of Hungary and Poland', *in* I. Motoc & P. de Pinto de Albuquerque & K. Wojtyczek (Eds.), *New Developments in Constitutional Law, Essays in honour of András Sajó*, The Hague, Eleven International Publishing, 2017; G. Halmai, 'Illiberal Constitutionalism? The Hungarian Constitution in European Perspective', *in* S. Kadelbach (Ed.), *Verfassungskrisen in der EU*, Baden-Baden, Nomos, 2018; G. Halmai, 'The Coup Against Constitutional Democracy. The Case of Hungary', *in* M. Graber, S. Levinson & M. Tushnet (Eds.), *Constitutional Democracy in Crisis?*, Oxford, Oxford University Press, 2018.

new High Administrative Court at the top. The reform, which will be implemented on 1 January 2020, has been criticized especially for the competence of minister of justice to appoint judges of the new High Administrative Court. In addition, the minister of justice can designate presidents of administrative courts, decide on their promotions, and decide on the budget of administrative courts. According to the Hungarian Helsinki Committee, the reform when fully implemented will further weaken the independence of the national judicial system, with the minister of justice that will exercise even more powers than the head of the National Office for the Judiciary.[136] More recently, the Venice Commission also criticized the new system of administrative courts by denouncing the absence of checks and balances.[137]

In Poland, illiberal trends emerged following the 2015 parliamentary and presidential elections, which led to the victory of Law and Justice (PiS). The latter obtained an absolute majority in the parliament, and its candidate was also elected to the presidency of the Republic. As in the Hungarian case, the first constitutional body that suffered the consequences of the illiberal turn has been the Constitutional Tribunal. The tug-of-war between the new government and the constitutional adjudication body started due to the misconduct of the previous legislature which adopted the new Constitutional Tribunal Act on 25 June 2015 and designated five new constitutional judges on 8 October 2015 (*see supra*, para. 4.1). The President of the Republic refused the oaths of the newly elected constitutional judges, while on 25 November 2015 the new legislature erased the five appointments and elected five new constitutional judges on 2 December 2015.

The Constitutional Tribunal then intervened in the crisis: with the decision K 34/15 of 3 December 2015 it annulled the appointment of two out of five judges elected on 8 October 2015, while with the decision K 35/15 of 9 December 2015 it annulled the appointment of three out of five judges elected on 2 December 2015. However, the refusal of the President of the Republic to accept the oath of the three constitutional judges legitimately elected on 8 October 2015, as established by decision K 34/15, led the Constitutional Tribunal to exercise its activities in a restricted composition of twelve out of fifteen judges. Finally, on 22 December 2015 new amendments to the Constitutional Tribunal Act were adopted; this completely paralysed the functioning of the constitutional adjudication body since it was required that decisions on unconstitutionality of legislation should be adopted by a qualified majority of thirteen out of fifteen judges. In the decision K 47/15 of 9 March

136 Hungarian Helsinki Committee, *Independence of the Judiciary under attack in Hungary*, 12 September 2018, in www.osce.org/odihr/393824?download=true (last accessed April 2019).

137 Opinion of the Venice Commission of 19 March 2019, *Hungary. Opinion on the law on Administrative Courts and on the law on the entry into force of the law on Administrative Courts and certain transitional rules. Adopted by the Venice Commission at its 118th Plenary Session* (Venice, 15-16 March 2019), www.venice.coe.int/webforms/documents/default.aspx?pdffile=CDL-AD(2019)004-e (last accessed April 2019).

2016 the Constitutional Tribunal declared the unconstitutionality of the amendments, but the government refused once again to publish the decision in the Official Gazette. Following Venice Commission criticism (opinion No. 833/2015) a new Constitutional Tribunal Act was adopted on 22 July 2016 (which incorporated some indications provided by the Venice Commission).

Later, the Constitutional Tribunal Act of 22 July 2016 has been replaced by three entirely new laws: the law on the status of judges of the Constitutional Tribunal of 30 November 2016; the law on the organization and proceedings before the Constitutional Tribunal of 30 November 2016, and the law on introductory provisions to the law on organization and proceedings before the Constitutional Tribunal of 13 December 2016. Following the adoption of the new legislation, the Constitutional Tribunal was altered in its composition: first, Julia Przyłębska, a person close to the government, has been elected as a new president; second, the vice-president Stanisław Biernat (a person not close to the government) has been forced to early retirement; finally, the three constitutional judges appointed before the electoral victory of PiS were ousted from office. This means that by now the majority of constitutional judges are persons loyal to the government.

The establishment of the political control over the Constitutional Tribunal has been followed by the judiciary reform, which includes: the law amending the law on the National School of the Judiciary of 11 May 2017; the law amending the law on the system of ordinary courts and other laws of 12 July 2017; the law amending the law on the National Council of the Judiciary and other laws, and the law on the Supreme Court of 8 December 2017.

The reform of the judicial system has significantly impacted on the independence of the National Council of the Judiciary, the Supreme Court and ordinary courts. The innovations introduced in relation to the National Council of the Judiciary concern in particular the selection of its members. According to the Article 187 of the Polish Constitution, the National Council of the Judiciary is composed of the first president of the Supreme Court, the president of the High Administrative Court and the minister of justice; a member appointed by the President of the Republic, four members chosen by the *Sejm* from among its deputies and two members chosen by the Senate from among its senators, and fifteen judges chosen from among the judges of the Supreme Court, ordinary courts, administrative courts and military courts. The law of 20 December 2017 established the complete renewal of the National Council of the Judiciary within three months of its entry into force, and introduced new rules on the selection of fifteen judges sitting in the National Council of the Judiciary. Traditionally, they were selected by courts, but the new law established their designation by the *Sejm*, with the result that the National Council of the Judiciary has been transformed into a body almost completely dependent on the legislative power.[138]

---

138 As noted by G. Ragone, 'La Polonia sotto accusa. Brevi note sulle circostanze che hanno indotto l'Unione Europea ad avviare la c.d. opzione nucleare', *Osservatorio costituzionale AIC*, No. 1, 2018, p. 4, since the

Similarly, the law of 20 December 2017 changed the composition of the Supreme Court. On the one hand, it has reduced the retirement age of judges from 70 to 65 years, which led to the renewal of about 40 percent of judges. There is the possibility to extend judges' term of office after the request to the President of the Republic, who decides on the issue in discretionary manner. The appointment of new judges rests within presidential competences; it should be proposed by the National Council of the Judiciary – a body which weak independence from the political power has been already mentioned. On the other hand, the reform introduced two new Supreme Court's sections; the first has the competence to verify the regularity of elections, while the second is responsible for deciding on disciplinary appeals against judges. The members of the new Supreme Court's sections are also appointed by the President of the Republic.

Finally, in relation to ordinary courts the reform establishes that judges, upon reaching the retirement age, may request an extension of the term of office to the minister of justice, who decides on the issue in discretionary manner. Moreover, the minister of justice has the competence to appoint presidents of appellate and district courts (without any prior opinion of the respective general assembly, requested previously), while the reasons which allow the dismissal of presidents and vice-presidents of courts have been expanded. The removal of judges by the ministry of justice is subjected to the opinion of the National Council of the Judiciary, and can take place now due to poor efficiency in supervising and organizing the work of lower level courts.[139]

The illiberal turn of Poland and especially the reform of judicial system has created serious tensions between Poland and the European Union, thus leading the European Commission in December 2017 to launch the procedure established by the Article 7, para.

---

government and the presidency of the Republic belong to the same political party that maintains parliamentary majority, in addition of having its own minister of justice within the National Council of the Judiciary, the PiS can influence the appointment of other twenty-two members (fifteen judges and seven other members) out of a total of twenty-five members.

139 On Polish illiberal turn and its impact on constitutional justice and the judicial system *see* W. Sadurski, 'How Democracy Dies (in Poland): A Case Study of Anti-Constitutional Populist Backsliding', *Sydney Law School Research Paper*, No. 18/01, 2018; J. Sawicki, 'Democrazie illiberali? L'Europa centro-orientale tra continuità apparente della forma di governo e mutazione possibile della forma di Stato', cit.; Id., 'Portata a compimento la riforma governativa della Corte suprema e dell'ordinamento giudiziario. La separazione del terzo potere appare ormai memoria del passato', cit.; A. Angeli, 'Polonia. Le derive di una democrazia (quasi) maggioritaria: tra rischio di paralisi dell'organo di giustizia costituzionale e dualismo giuridico', cit.; A. Di Gregorio, J. Sawicki & A. Angeli, 'La controversa approvazione del "pacchetto giustizia" nella Polonia di "Diritto e Giustizia": ulteriori riflessioni sulla crisi del costituzionalismo polacco alla luce del contesto europeo', *DPCE Online*, No. 3, 2017; S. Bartole, 'I casi di Ungheria e Polonia. L'organizzazione del potere giudiziario tra Consiglio d'Europa e Unione europea', *Quaderni costituzionali*, No. 1, 2018; A. Sanders & L. von Danwitz, 'The Polish Judiciary Reform: Problematic under European Standards and a Challenge for Germany', *VerfBlog*, 28 March 2017; R. Coman, 'Quo Vadis Judicial Reforms? The Quest for Judicial Independence in Central and Eastern Europe', *Europe-Asia Studies*, No. 6, 2014; T.T. Koncewicz, 'The Court Is Dead, Long Live the Courts? On Judicial Review in Poland in 2017 and "Judicial Space" Beyond', *VerfBlog*, 8 March 2018.

1 of the Treaty on European Union, on the grounds that there is a clear risk of a serious breach of rule of law in Poland.[140]

5.9 Concluding Remarks

Today, almost thirty years since the beginning of democratic transition, constitutional courts have become a permanent part of political and legal landscapes of CEBBE countries. The features which have contributed in shaping the current systems of constitutional justice are essentially three: the transplantation of foreign models, national historical precedents of constitutional review and (some) innovations. These three features led to the establishment of complex systems of constitutional review, especially if compared to the systems of constitutional justice established in Western Europe. In particular, constitutional courts of CEBBE countries have been equipped with a wide range of powers, which usually vary from powers with which courts can condition political choices to powers susceptible to influence the structure and the articulation of political power, as well as powers aimed at protecting human rights and fundamental freedoms, and powers which can influence the relationship between national and supranational legal orders. The active use by constitutional courts of this wide range of powers had a strong impact on the evolution of their case law, showing in almost all cases a 'chameleonic nature' of constitutional courts, that is the ability to transform and retransformed themselves, assuming new multiple roles in accordance with the development of their constitutional orders. In fact, in the initial phase of democratic transition, when their political and legal systems were characterized by uncertainty and instability, and their political institutions by fragility, courts turned into active political players and arbiters of political conflicts; when their national systems became more mature and stable, courts transformed themselves into 'protectors' of human rights; when, finally, their countries experienced the challenge of EU integration, constitutional courts became both the engine and the brake on the process of Europeanization.

However, the most recent illiberal trends that have spread across several CEBBE countries and, in particular, in Hungary and Poland have undermined the role and the powers of constitutional courts and the judiciary. In fact, today in the Hungarian and Polish legal systems both are subjected to political control. This has also transformed the very nature of constitutional courts which are transforming themselves from bodies aimed at protecting democracy to bodies loyal to the government. In both countries such devel-

140 *See* Press release of the European Commission, *Rule of Law: European Commission Acts to Defend Judicial Independence in Poland*, 20 December 2017, http://europa.eu/rapid/press-release_IP-17-5367_en.htm (last accessed April 2019); M.A. Orlandi, 'La Polonia di Kaczyński: l'approvazione del "pacchetto giustizia" e l'avvio della procedura dell'art. 7 TUE', *DPCE Online*, No. 4, 2017.

opments are threatening the fundamental principles of the rule of law and the separation of powers, which represent the basis of every democratic state.

Epilogue: The 'Wounded' Constitutionalism in Hungary and Poland

Angela Di Gregorio with the collaboration of Jan Sawicki and Arianna Angeli

The drafting of this volume required years of work, during which the constitutional degenerations in Hungary and Poland progressively intensified. Since the economy of this work does not allow thoroughly discussing this topic – which is, in any case, the subject of many other studies – we chose to dedicate to it our final words, in addition to the references already contained in the entire volume. Those latter show a broader constitutional development of the two countries both from the historical point of view and from the regional dynamics, to consent a more complete evaluation of the developments in progress, which are in continuous evolution.[1]

The cases of Hungary and Poland show – starting from the general elections respectively of 2010 and 2015,[2] which delivered self-sufficient majorities to conservative right-wing parties – a divergent constitutional trajectory with respect to the general framework outlined in this volume. Although in other countries weaknesses, regressions or immaturity may be found in the liberal-democratic fabric that was imported and/or reconstructed in the aftermath of the transition from communism, what happened in recent years in Hungary and Poland is particularly striking in terms of speed, hardness and sometimes for the ruthlessness which characterized the constitutional 'inversion'. The astonishment is all the greater, since this regression takes place in countries, which, as widely illustrated in this volume, were the pioneers in the 'happy' importation of European constitutional standards. The degenerations seem more serious because they occur in the 'new' heart of European integration, with EU financial support, despite protests in various forums and

1 And that will be therefore have to be taken into account up to a certain point, considering that the Volume was presented to the publisher in its final version at the end of April 2019.

2 In Hungary, the legislative elections of 11 and 25 April 2010 (in two rounds), of 6 April 2014 and 8 April 2018, confirmed, with a majority higher than two-thirds of the seats of the National Assembly, the Fidesz-KDNP coalition, which is composed by the Fidesz and the small Christian-Democratic Popular party since 2006 (in 2010 the coalition achieved the 68.1 percent of seats with 52.7 percent of votes, in 2014 66.8 percent of seats with 44.9 percent of votes, in 2018 66.8 percent of seats with 49.3 percent of votes). After the by-elections called to fill two seats that had become vacant in February and in April 2015, the Fidesz-KDNP had lost its constitutional majority, which was subsequently reconquered with the 2018 elections. In Poland, these are the presidential elections of 24 May 2015 and those of 25 October 2015 for the parliament, which gave the party Law and Justice or PiS a total of 235 seats out of 460 (with 37.6 percent of the votes) to the *Sejm* and of 61 seats out of 100 in the Senate. The renewal of the Polish parliament is scheduled for October 2019.

institutions at an European Union and Council of Europe level, and because they represent a failure of the pre-entry conditionality path as well as of the post-entry control mechanisms.

The Hungarian constitutional regression began after the parliamentary elections of 2010, when the coalition dominated by the conservative party Fidesz (Fidesz-KDNP) obtained a broad enough majority to allow it to modify the constitution then in force[3] and subsequently to adopt a new Fundamental Law. From the constitutional point of view, the Hungarian measures expressing the constitutional involution are innumerable, beginning with the new constitution. In fact, in addition to its conservative contents, highlighted above, the modalities in which it was adopted have been contested, as they were scarcely participative.[4]

The Hungarian conservative party, as will be later the case for the Polish one, took advantage of some defects of the previous constitutional and legislative framework, which it managed to exploit, before proceeding to distort it. In the Hungarian case, the defects were first a 'contained' constitutional rigidity – two-thirds of the members of the unicameral parliament are sufficient to approve a new constitution. The initiative to do so can come even from a single member of the parliament. This has allowed setting up a permanent framing process, as can be proved by the seven constitutional revisions that took place after 2011, the last approved on 20 June 2018.[5] Another defect which has been exploited

3 Between 2010 and 2011, twelve revision laws have been adopted to modify the constitution then in force, which dated back to 1949, but was completely rewritten after 1989, especially in the two-year period 1989-1990.

4 M. Bánkuti, G. Halmai & K.L. Scheppele, 'Hungary's Illiberal Turn: Disabling the Constitution', *Journal of Democracy*, Vol. 23, No. 3, 2012; N. Chronowski, 'The New Hungarian Fundamental Law in the Light of the European Union's Normative Values', *Revue Est Europa*, No. 1, 2012; G.F. Ferrari (Ed.), *La nuova legge fondamentale ungherese*, cit.; G.A. Toth (Ed.), *Constitution for a Disunited Nation: On Hungary's 2011 Fundamental Law*, New York, Budapest, CEU Press, 2012; I. Pogány, 'The Crisis of Democracy in East Central Europe: The 'New Constitutionalism' in Hungary', *European Public Law*, Vol. 19, No. 2, 2013; F. Vecchio, *Teorie costituzionali alla prova. La nuova Costituzione ungherese come metafora della crisi del costituzionalismo europeo*, Padova, Cedam, 2013; G. Halmai, 'An Illiberal Constitutional System in the Middle of Europe', *in* W. Benedek, F. Benoît-Rohmer, W. Karl, C. Kettemann & M. Nowak (Eds.), *European Yearbook of Human Rights*, Cambridge, Intersentia, 2014; A. Arato, *Post Sovereign Constitutional Making: Learning and Legitimacy*, Oxford, Oxford University Press, 2016; A.L. Pap, *Democratic Decline in Hungary: Law and Society in an Illiberal Democracy*, London, Routledge, 2018.

5 The first amendment, dated 4 June 2012, among other things, incorporated the disputed transitional provisions in the text of the Fundamental Law, making them even more controversial (this decision was then invalidated by the Constitutional Court on 28 December 2012, with decision 45/2012. (XII. 29) to be in turn superseded by the fourth amendment). The second amendment, dated 29 October 2012, introduced a preliminary registration as a requirement to participate in national elections. It was later declared unconstitutional by the Constitutional Court, on 4 January 2013, with decision 1/2013 (I.7) AB). The third amendment, dated 17 December 2012, reserved for cardinal laws – to be adopted by a two-thirds majority of Members of Parliament present – the legislation concerning the sale and purchase of agricultural land or forests. The fourth amendment, of 11 March 2013, is the largest and the most organic: it brings back into force the transitional provisions whose incorporation into the Fundamental Law had been declared illegitimate. With the occasion, it states that the constitutionality control on constitutional laws can only be carried out due to procedural defects, and no longer for substantive aspects. It also states that the Con-

was an electoral law highly rewarding for the first political party, which Fidesz proceeded to manipulate to art.

In the reform plan designed to achieve the goals pursued by Prime Minister Orbán, that is to say the construction of a nationalist, homogeneous and self-referential society – Orbán also theorized 'illiberal' democracy[6] – we may find a rather simple scheme, which was then imitated by the Polish PiS. This scheme provided for the neutralization/control and downsizing of the Constitutional Court, which was – thanks to the broad possibility to access it and its authority –[7] the main obstacle in the process of adopting 'reformist' legislative packages. Then, it foresaw the replacement of the majority of judges in office through early retirements, as well as the reformulation of the rules to access top-level

stitutional Court can no longer refer to its own jurisprudence adopted between 1990 and the date of entry into force of the Fundamental Law; that political parties taking part in national and European elections will be able to issue propaganda announcements only on public media, in accordance with to criteria established by cardinal law; that the freedom of expression guaranteed in the Fundamental Law cannot be used to damage human dignity, the dignity of the Hungarian nation or of any national, ethnic or religious minority group; that those who have benefited from university scholarships will have to work for an indefinite period in Hungarian companies or institutions. With the fifth amendment, adopted on 16 September 2013, for the first time critical remarks made by the European Union and the Council of Europe were partially taken into account. Hence, the faculty for the president of the National Judicial Office of transferring judicial proceedings from one court to another was suppressed. Privileges that were attributed on the basis of cardinal laws to 'recognized churches' have been limited. The prohibition made to the parties to issue propaganda or press releases on commercial media is eliminated, provided, however, that such forms of communication are allowed, free of charge, to all political subjects, in accordance with the criteria of equality. On the other hand, the possibility of abolishing the Financial Supervisory Authority, through its incorporation into the National Bank of Hungary – immediately implemented by ordinary law – is restored. Moreover, with the sixth amendment of 7 June 2016 – that was also approved with the votes of the opposition of ultra-nationalist right-wing party Jobbik – the National Assembly is authorized to declare a 'state of terroristic emergency', on the initiative of the government, in case of 'attack or significant and direct danger of terrorist attack'. The amendment gives the government the power to suspend the laws in force and to take extraordinary measures during the period of validity of this state of emergency. However, the declaration, and any extension thereof, requires the vote of two-thirds of the members of the Assembly. Finally, the seventh amendment, of 20 June 2018, declares the obligation for all state organs to protect the 'Hungarian constitutional identity' and the 'Christian culture'. It prevents 'alien populations' from settling in Hungary, and makes the condition of homelessness illegal, prohibiting to live in a public place. Lastly, it establishes an order and a body of administrative justice separate from the civil and criminal one. All the details of the revisions may be found on https://theorangefiles.hu/amendments-to-the-fundamental-law/ (last accessed April 2019).

6 Speech of 26 July 2014, made in Tusnádfürdő, in 'Hungarian' Romania, at the Bálványos Summer Free University and Student Camp, an annual intellectual forum established in 1990 with the aim of promoting cross-border cooperation. On the subject, A. Di Gregorio, 'L'Ungheria e i valori europei. Un matrimonio difficile', *Rassegna Parlamentare*, No. 2, 2018, pp. 445-451

7 The Court's competences were indeed very broad, above all due to the possibility it had to rule abstractly through the mechanism of the *actio popularis*, a possibility substituted by the individual appeal of the citizens, which was, however, perceived as a downscaling, as it is not suitable to face 'systemic issues'. With regard to its authority, the Court had demonstrated its independence both in terms of protection of fundamental rights and enforcement of checks and balances, often opposing the political majority of the moment.

positions in the courts and in the self-governing body of the judiciary[8] – this in order to block the corruption investigations on political figures of the majority, and to avoid a *de facto* transfer before the ordinary judges of the constitutionality control. The scheme also provided for the increase of control over the power of attorney (for similar reasons). It implied to control access to representation – by reforming the electoral law in a way useful to favour even more the majority party, intervening on party financing rules, electoral propaganda, control over elections and adopting gerrymandering[9] techniques. Lastly, it foresaw the exploitation of other forms of expression of popular consensus – by organizing various types of extremely populist consultations, other than referendums, not regulated by the Constitution. Moreover, a series of fundamental freedoms, as well as minority/immigrant rights were limited, as it is accurately recalled in the Sargentini Report[10] and in those

8 The alignment of the retirement age for judges, with the exception of the president of the *Kúria*, to the general retirement age (and therefore the decrease from 70 to 62 years), starting from the entry into force of the new FL (Art. 26 of Fundamental Law and Art. 15 of the Transitional Provisions) was officially justified by the need to make the judicial system more efficient through the inclusion of younger judges. It was, instead, an actual purge that involved a relevant number of judges (274 out of 2,900) and in particular the high positions of the judiciary (about a quarter of the judges of the Supreme Court and half of the presidents of the regional and provincial courts). Furthermore, a substantial reform of the body corresponded to the change of the name of the Supreme Court, with the reintroduction of the name prior to the communist period, namely *Kúria*. The appointment of a new president of the *Kúria* was provided for (Art. 14 of Transitional Provisions) as well as new rules for the election of that office (Art. 114 law 61/2011), which have prevented the re-election of the previous president. Finally, in the new FL, there was no explicit mention of the National Judicial Council – one of the first judicial self-governing bodies established in the countries that were part of the socialist bloc, introduced in Hungary in 1997 – whose competences were mostly transferred to the National Judicial Office, and in particular to the president of the NJO. The NJC was not abolished, but became an essentially advisory body (*see also* Chapter 5 of this Volume). In this regard, *see* the opinions of the Venice Commission of 19 March 2012, 28 August 2012 and 15 October 2012. *See also* S. Benvenuti, 'La riforma del sistema giudiziario ungherese tra recrudescenze autoritarie e governance europea', *Nomos*, No. 3, 2012; G. Halmai, 'The Early Retirement Age of the Hungarian Judges', *in* F. Nicola & B. Davis (Eds.), *EU Law Stories: Contextual and Critical Histories of European Jurisprudence*, Cambridge University Press, 2017 and W. Brzozowski, 'The Removal of Judges and the Rule of Law', *in* M. Belov (Ed.), *Rule of Law at the Beginning of the Twenty-First Century*, The Hague, Eleven International Publishing, 2018.

9 In this regard, please refer to the OSCE periodic reports adopted at the time of the main electoral rounds.

10 The European Parliament voted on 12 September 2018 with a large majority (448 votes in favor, 197 against and 48 abstentions) a Resolution on the so-called Sargentini Report (from the name of the Dutch member of the Green Group) which asked the Council for the activation of the Art. 7.1 of the TUE. The Resolution analytically lists the various stages of Hungarian illiberal degeneration that justify the danger of a systematic violation of the values of the Union as summarized in Art. 2 of the TUE. Please refer to C. Curti Gialdino, 'Il Parlamento europeo attiva l'art. 7, par. 1 TUE nei confronti dell'Ungheria: quando, per tutelare lo "Stato di diritto", si viola la regola di diritto', *federalismi.it*, 19 September 2018. In addition to this, several infringement procedures raised by the European Commission before the European Court of Justice produced a series of decisions unfavourable to the Hungarian government (still pending at the time of delivery of this Volume are the appeals concerning the so-called stop-Soros package and the anti-Central European University legislation). For example, in the decision of 6 November 2012, the Court ruled that the decrease in retirement age for judges, notaries and prosecutors from 70 to 62 years constitutes an unjustified discrimination based on age. In the decision of 8 April 2014 the European Court ruled that with the early termination of the mandate of the Commissioner for the protection of personal data, Hungary violated the obligations

that preceded it (in particular: freedom of association,[11] of the media,[12] of religion,[13] academic freedom,[14] freedom of expression, the rights of women, of minorities,[15] of the homeless, of privacy, etc.). Faithfully following the program, a transformation is being carried out, not only for what concerns institutions or the form of state, but also of the Hungarian civil society itself, tamed by the pounding nationalist rhetoric of the external enemy.

---

assumed under the directive 95/46. For what concerns the Strasbourg Court, with the decision of 27 May 2014 on the Baka case (the president of the Supreme Court was ordered to resign from office three and a half years before the expiry of his mandate) this Court recognized the violation of both Art. 6 of the ECHR, for lack of remedies for the protection of the right to judicial protection, and Art. 10, since in the actions of the government there had been the clear intention of persecution against those who had expressed criticism against the reforms of the judiciary in progress. The decision of the Court of Justice of November 2012 was implemented through the Law XX of March 2013, in which the pension age for judges, notaries and prosecutors was gradually lowered from 70 to 65 with the final transition at the new threshold since 1 January 2023. The law provides for a plan for the reintegration of judges previously retired with three possibilities (effective reintegration, placement in 'expectation' lists, compensation for damage). With the decision of 6 September 2017, the Court of Justice rejected the appeal of Hungary and Slovakia against the decision of the European Council of September 2015 'establishing temporary measures in the field of international protection for the benefit of Italy and Greece', on the relocation, in a two-year period, of 120,000 people in clear need of international protection. The European Commission – which had launched an infringement procedure against Hungary in December 2015 in connection with the law on asylum – in July 2018 referred Hungary to the Court of Justice for violating, with the laws of the so called 'stop-Soros' package, the directives on the procedures for granting/withdrawing international protection (directive 2013/32/EU), on reception (directive 2013/33/EU) and on repatriation (2008/115/EC) of the asylum seekers.

11 *See* the opinion of the Venice Commission of 20 June 2017 on the draft law on transparency of NGOs receiving support from abroad. In this regard also *see* P. Kruzslicz, 'L'acte récent d'un dialogue constitutionnel exigeant et intensif: la loi hongroise sur la transparence des organisations soutenues par l'étranger devant la Commission de Venice', *Lettre de l'Est*, No. 9/10, 2017.

12 On which the Venice Commission issued an opinion on 22 June 2015, CDL-AD(2015)015 *Opinion on Media Legislation (ACT CLXXXV on Media Services and on the Mass Media, Act CIV on the Freedom of the Press, and the Legislation on Taxation of Advertisement Revenues of Mass Media) of Hungary*, adopted by the Venice Commission at its 103rd Plenary Session (Venice, 19-20 June 2015). *See also* the opinion of 18 October 2012 on legislative amendments referring to freedom of information CDL-AD(2012)023-e, *Opinion on Act CXII of 2011 on informational Self-determination and Freedom of Information of Hungary*, adopted by the Venice Commission at its 92nd Plenary Session (Venice, 12-13 October 2012).

13 CDL-AD(2012)004-e *Opinion on Act CCVI of 2011 on the right to freedom of conscience and religion and the legal status of churches, denominations and religious communities of Hungary* adopted by the Venice Commission at its 90th Plenary Session (Venice, 16-17 March 2012) of 19 March 2012.

14 In this respect, in addition to reforming the law on national higher education, penalizing, among others, the Central European University, the governmental majority has also launched a new reformist campaign that involves the Academy of Sciences. Moreover, it infringed in various ways academic freedom and scientific research. *See* T.D. Ziegler, *'It's Not Just About CEU: Understanding the Systemic Limitation of Academic Freedom in Hungary'*, *VerfBlog*, 26 March 2019. On the reform of the universities, *see* the opinion of the Venice Commission of 9 October 2017 CDL-AD(2017)022 *Opinion on Article XXV of 4 April 2017 on the Amendment of Act CCIV of 2011 on National Tertiary Education*, endorsed by the Venice Commission at its 112th Plenary Session (Venice, 6-7 October 2017).

15 CDL-AD(2012)011-e *Opinion on the Act on the Rights of Nationalities of Hungary* adopted by the Venice Commission at its 91st Plenary Session (Venice, 15-16 June 2012) of 19 June 2012.

Hence, the transformation of the Constitutional Court began even before the adoption of the new 2011 Fundamental Law, and touched both the methods of election of judges and their number and competences. Since June 2010, the methods for selecting candidates have changed. A special parliamentary commission, as before, choses the candidates, but within it political forces are represented in proportion to the number of parliamentary seats (previously, in the commission each parliamentary group had one member). The National Assembly then elects the judges, with a majority of two-thirds of its members – the same needed to elect the chair of the Court, from among the judges, according to the FL. Since September 2011, the number of judges has increased from 11 to 15. Since January 2012, the judges' mandate has increased from 9 to 12 years. Since December 2013, the age limit before retirement, which was set at 70, has been removed: this is typical of countries that have already secured the 'loyalty' of the judges.

The Court has tried to 'resist', but the constitutional legislator has gradually changed its competences or has constitutionalized legislative provisions that had been declared unconstitutional – in this way, there is no explicit violation of the Constitution, but certainly the disavowal of a decision of unconstitutionality does not appear opportune immediately after it. The final step was to nullify the jurisprudence prior to the new constitution, with the IV constitutional amendment approved on 11 March 2013.[16]

For what concerns the Fundamental Law of 2011, it can be reasonably defined a 'winner's' constitution. Even if the reduction of the powers of the Constitutional Court is not in itself significant – objectively, before 2010, it appeared to be excessively powerful – other changes, such as the selection methods of the judges and of the president, the nullifying of the jurisprudence preceding the entry into force of the LF and some other negative innovations that have generated its 'normalization' are noteworthy. These measures show an evident desire to punish a Court that had been particularly active and of great prestige in the phase subsequent to the transition from the communist system.

As for the Court's conduct following its 'neutralization', in addition to the decisions supporting the 'identity' vision of the government majority (especially that of 30 November 2016),[17] the tendency is to avoid politically relevant cases (through different gimmicks) or

16 CDL-AD(2013)012-e *Opinion on the Fourth Amendment to the Fundamental Law of Hungary* adopted by the Venice Commission at its 95th Plenary Session (Venice, 14-15 June 2013).

17 Immediately after the failed referendum on migrant quotas of 2 October 2016, the Hungarian government hastily drafted and submitted to parliament's approval the VII revision of the Fundamental Law. This last amendment would have explicitly introduced, among other things, the protection of the 'constitutional identity', emphasizing even more the nationalist profile of the constitution and erecting rather relevant counter-limits towards the sources of EU law. However, since two votes were missing for the approval of the amendment, the Constitutional Court came to the rescue of the Government, and with its decision of 30 November 2016 22/2016 (XII. 5) AB on the interpretation of Art. E), c. 2 of the Fundamental Law unequivocally asserted that the protection of constitutional identity, deriving from the Hungarian historical constitution, cannot be challenged by the requirements of European integration. Subsequently, on 20 June 2018, the National Assembly elected in spring, in which the Fidesz-KDNP government alliance held a

to decide in favour of the said majority.[18] Decision on sensitive issues is postponed as much as possible: the two most important examples are those of the petition against the law on foreign NGOs (the so-called stop-Soros)[19] and the one on the reform of the university system.

Furthermore, the Court focuses on individual petitions (since this type of appeal was introduced, it has become the most frequently used) even though some judges express their dissent through dissenting or concurrent opinions.[20] In general, as aforementioned,

---

majority of more than two-thirds (133 out of 199 deputies) approved the VII constitutional revision which contains an explicit provision according to which 'The protection of the Hungarian constitutional self-identity and Christian culture is the obligation of all organs [szerv] of the State'. As for decision 22/2016, it is a rather ambiguous one. While affirming that it reserves the right to carry out two types of control, regarding the joint exercise of the competences of the EU and Hungary (control of sovereignty and identity control) the Court has not clarified what is meant by 'constitutional identity', referring to vague principles and to the concept of 'historical constitution'. The appeal was based on the constitutional prohibition of 'collective' expulsion from Hungary (Art. XIV, c. 1) but the connection of this sentence with the relocation of migrants (asylum seekers) from other European countries has not been clarified. For further details, *see* T. Drinóczi, '*The Hungarian Constitutional Court on the Limits of EU Law in the Hungarian Legal System', Int'l J. Const. L. Blog*, 29 December 2016; G. Halmai, '*The Hungarian Constitutional Court and Constitutional Identity', VerfBlog, 10 January 2017;* R. Uitz, 'National Constitutional Identity in the European Constitutional Project: A Recipe for Exposing Cover Ups and Masquerades', *VerfBlog*, 11 November 2016. Also G. Poggeschi, 'Il cosiddetto pacchetto legislativo "stop-Soros" e la nuova revisione costituzionale ungherese: un altro passo (xenofobo) verso il consolidamento di una "democrazia illiberale"', *DPCEonline*, No. 2, 2018.

18 *See* E. Bodnár & F. Gárdos-Orosz, 'Hungary', *Global Review of Constitutional Law*, 2017, p. 130. Also Z. Szende, 'The Political Orientation of the Members of the Hungarian Constitutional Court between 2010 and 2014', *Constitutional Studies*, Vol. 1, No. 1, 2016, pp. 123-149, https://muse.jhu.edu/article/640098/pdf (last accessed April 2019).

19 The Court ruled on 28 February 2019 (while a European Commission infringement procedure was still pending before the Court against the stop-Soros legislative package) with a decision (IV/1565/2018) which, while acknowledging the constitutional legitimacy of the amendment of the penal code – after all, the FL had been integrated with the VII constitutional revision especially to allow the adoption of the legislative package in question – however introduces some distinctions that could open glimpses for a more permissive interpretation of the restrictions in question. In particular, while the criminal sanction for facilitating illegal immigration remains firm, the Court asks the courts to accurately verify the explicit knowledge of the concept of clandestinity by those who commit the crime, as well as the intention to commit it, and it does not consider humanitarian aid to refugees punishable as a criminal offence. For comments, *see* V.Z. Kazai, 'Stop Soros Law Left on the Books- The Return of the "Red Tail"?', *VerfBlog*, 5 March 2019. *See also* the opinion of the Venice Commission on the legislative package of 25 June 2018: CDL-AD(2018)013-ev *Joint Opinion on the Provisions of the so-called "Stop Soros" draft Legislative Package which directly affect NGOs (in particular Draft Article 353A of the Criminal Code on Facilitating Illegal Migration),* adopted by the Venice Commission at its 115th Plenary Session (Venice, 22-23 June 2018).

20 There were some decisions in favour of freedom of expression in response to individual petitions: 3001/2018, 34/2017. In any case, both decisions were adopted with eight votes against seven and this suggests that this case law could easily change. *See* E. Bodnár & F. Gárdos-Orosz, 'Hungary', cited above. *See also* Z. Tóth, 'Changes which Occurred in the Role of the Hungarian Constitutional Court in Protecting the Constitutional System', *Acta Univ. Sapientiae, Legal Studies*, Vol. 7, No. 1, 2018, pp. 95-107. The author reports that many decisions of the Court in recent years have considered the FL violated only for procedural and non-substantive reasons. Furthermore, it should be noted that after 2012 individual appeals constituted around 90 percent of all appeals.

the Court adopts a minimalist attitude and often focuses on procedural issues avoiding to go into details, in order not to contradict the government's political will.[21] For what concerns the question of (political) posters, the Court has ruled only on 18 December 2018 on the act which was challenged in 2017 that, as it was pointed out in the petition, risked severely limiting the freedom of electoral propaganda in view of the spring elections of 2018. The Court, among other things, rejected the appeal as the act would have been adopted with minor violations of parliament's standing orders and would not have violated the freedom of expression.[22] Finally, the lack of enforcement of the Strasbourg Court's decisions has also grown in recent years.[23]

However, it must be acknowledged that some recent rulings seem to show a willingness to accommodate some of the European institutions' remarks, or at least to smooth the heated tones typical of the members of the government majority. This happens both in the decision on the aforementioned stop-Soros package of 28 February 2019 and in the other connected decision of 25 February 2019, which concerns the broader question of the relationship between the Hungarian constitution and European law, again on the matter of accepting migrants. Having taken into account the European Commission note which considered a series of European acts violated by the package approved by the Hungarian parliament in June 2018 (including the VII constitutional revision)[24] the Constitu-

21 *See, e.g.*, with its decision 1/2017 on the act concerning the administrative process, which introduced a new type of courts, the Court limited to say that it was not possible to introduce new judicial bodies without amending the cardinal law on the judiciary, with two-thirds of the votes (*see also* the July 2017 decision on freedom of religion).

22 In the summer of 2017, the parliament was examining an amendment to the act on the functioning and economic activities of political parties. Among the proposals there were new requirements for the publication of political posters outside of electoral campaigns, with limitations for parties and advertising companies. The amendment, hastily redacted to allow the removal of posters wanted by Jobbik, that depicted Fidesz politicians, including Orbán, as criminals, would have made it much more difficult to finance this type of political propaganda by greatly increasing the costs. The amendments were not approved due to the absence of the required two-thirds majority (the act in question was a cardinal one). Subsequently, the content of this act had been transferred as an amendment to another act, this time an ordinary one, namely the law on the protection of urban decor (Act on Townscape Protection), regularly approved. This act had been challenged by fifty-two deputies. According to the Court, 'the requirement of regulating the subject matter in a cardinal Act may not be extended to an indirect connection to the economic management of political parties'. The Court also points out that 'the aim of the provisions is to make poster campaigns more transparent and to decrease the risk of corruption that may result from non-transparent pricing practice'.

23 Among the best known are the cases of the *Hungarian Christian Mennonite Church and Others v. Hungary* of 2014 and *Ilias and Ahmed v. Hungary* of 2017. In this last case the Strasbourg Court had established that the forced detention of asylum seekers is incompatible with Art. 3 of the ECHR, on the prohibition of inhuman and degrading treatment. In response to this condemnation, some prominent public figures close to the Hungarian government had even considered Hungary's withdrawal from the ECHR.

24 2/2019 (III. 5) AB of interpretation of Arts. E), c. 2, R), c. 1, XIV, c. 4 and 24, c. 1 of FL. As stated in the introductory part of the decision: "The background of this concrete constitutional issue is the official notice sent by the European Commission regarding the compliance with the Union law of the Act VI of 2018 on amending certain Acts relating to measures to combat illegal immigration and of the seventh amendment of the Fundamental Law. As explained by the European Commission in the notice, according to the Com-

tional Court shows a certain deference towards European law, despite the distinctions. The Court indeed provided an interpretation of the constitutional provision, for which a clarification was requested, favourable to the reception of migrants in need of assistance, even though it made clear that they do not enjoy a constitutional or subjective right to asylum (unless they enter Hungary coming from a country where they are at risk of persecution) but the ways of exercising this right must be established by the Hungarian parliament with a cardinal law. However, the Court accepts the principle of non-refoulement contained in the international law commitments signed by Hungary, it admits the humanitarian exception and reiterates the willingness to dialogue with the European institutions.[25] Within this decision, many things are encompassed among the contents of the historical constitution, including the commitment to join the EU, which should not be considered, however, as a preferential element but one that has to be balanced with the other components.

Despite the prosecution against judges and other control institutions, including a series of authorities, what emerges in the Hungarian case, is not only the violation of the rule of law but also of the other two components of the Copenhagen criteria, required for access to the EU, that is to say democracy and human rights (plus minority rights), even though the doctrinal and political discourse focused mainly on the first aspect, in addition to the question of accepting migrants. As can be seen from the aforementioned Sargentini Report, these are broad-based interventions that go in a direction that is not even that of a conservative democracy, as Orbán claims, but barely of an electoral democracy. In fact, the Fidesz has been governing without interruptions since 2010 (for Orbán, though, it is the fourth mandate, between 1998 and 2002 he was already head of a more composite and inhomo-

---

mission's interpretation, the amended Art. XIV of the Fundamental Law on asylum violates certain Articles of the Directive 2011/95/EU of the European Parliament and of the Council of 13 December 2011 on standards for the qualification of third-country nationals or stateless persons as beneficiaries of international protection, for a uniform status for refugees or for persons eligible for subsidiary protection, and for the content of the protection granted."

25 The Court establishes that "following from the second sentence of Art. XIV (4), which is interpretable with regard to the international obligations undertaken by Hungary, granting asylum for a non-Hungarian citizen who arrived to the territory of Hungary through a country where he or she was not subject to persecution or imminent risk of persecution, shall not be regarded as a constitutional obligation of the Hungarian State, however the Parliament may also grant asylum to such persons according to the substantive and procedural regulations it specifies". In the last part of its decision, the Court states that "in the course of the above interpretation it has taken into account the principle of constitutional dialogue within the European Union {C.p. Decision 22/2016 (XII. 5) AB, Reasoning [33]}], as well as its commitment to the accomplishment of European unity (*Europafreundlichkeit*), which originates in Art. E) (1) of the Fundamental Law. With regard to the above, the Constitutional Court interpreted the second sentence of Art. XIV (4) of the Fundamental Law on the one hand for the purpose of reaching a conclusion, which is in line with the overall spirit of the Fundamental Law and on the other hand to take into account the compatibility with the relevant provisions of the Directive interpreted in the light of the Charter of Fundamental Rights, in the spirit of contributing to the development of European unity in the interest of the constitutional dialogue and of expanding the freedom, prosperity and security of the nations of Europe".

geneous coalition) wounding the democratic value of changeovers of power. Inter alia, the media manipulations and the restrictions of a series of political freedoms such as those of association, press, meeting, propaganda, have clearly favoured Fidesz's success.

For what concerns Poland, the current post-communist Constitution is an expression of the compromises between former communist and former Solidarność parties, and was adopted at the end of a legislature dominated by centre-leftist parties. At the base of the current Polish political course there seems to be precisely the refusal of the consensual, negotiated and traded-off system resulting from the long Polish constituent season, which began in October 1989 and ended, through incremental stages, in October 1997. The precursors of PiS – that was back then a minority branch of the Solidarność movement that had undermined the communist orthodoxy – dissented and for years disdainfully refused to feel part of the constituent pact. This self-exclusion, the political failure of the short-lived PiS-led government between 2005 and 2007, and the tragic death in 2010 of President Lech Kaczyński and about 100 other high public functionaries, marked irreversibly both psyche and political behaviour of the current leader of PiS Jarosław Kaczyński.[26]

Closely following the Hungarian precedent, the new Polish leadership, that won the parliamentary elections on 25 October 2015 (and the previous presidential election on 24 May),[27] has gradually and systematically begun to bring under control of the government's all main counter-majority powers, starting with the Constitutional Tribunal and continuing with the media, the Public Prosecutor's Office and the other components of the judiciary (the body of self-government of the judiciary, the common courts, the Supreme Court).

The Polish Constitutional Tribunal had played an important role since 1986 (it had been introduced in the last phase of the communist system as an important signal of liberalization) but there had been ambiguities in the appointment of constitutional judges for the whole post-communist period (balance was obtained only thanks to the political changeovers in the different legislatures) because of the not so strict mechanism of selection (simple majority of the *Sejm*). Things changed with the 2015 elections, that gave the absolute majority in the two chambers to the PiS, which initially exploited some errors of

26 A. Angeli, A. Di Gregorio & J. Sawicki, 'La controversa approvazione del "pacchetto giustizia" nella Polonia di "Diritto e Giustizia": ulteriori riflessioni sulla crisi del costituzionalismo polacco alla luce del contesto europeo', cit.

27 Moreover both victories have been unexpected and due, especially in the second case, to a very low electoral participation, as well as to strategic mistakes of the major centre-left party 'Alliance of Left-winged Democrats'. In fact, it allied with another small left party, 'Your Movement', and therefore had to pass the higher minimum threshold envisaged for alliances, 8 percent, while running alone it would easily have passed the 5 percent threshold. To be precise, voter turnout was 50.9 percent in the legislative elections and 48.9 percent in the first round of the presidential elections (increased however to 55.3 percent in the second round, as per the official website of the Commission National Electoral PKW, www.pkw.gov.pl).

the previous ruling party, 'Civic Platform'.[28] There was the de-legitimization of the CT's composition through the replacement of three judges lawfully elected in October 2015[29] with three others elected at the beginning of the subsequent legislature, the following December. Subsequently, thanks to the termination of office of others judges (including chair Rzepliński) it was possible to almost completely renew the organ.[30]

In relation to the functioning of the constitutional justice body, the involution path provided for the adoption in the first place of acts amending the act of June 2015 (19 November 2015 and 22 December 2015) that impacted not only on the composition but also on the methods and order of adoption of the decisions,[31] and secondly of a completely new act in July 2016, as well as the denial to publish politically unwelcome judgments

28 Who had elected five new constitutional judges at the end of the legislature, despite having the right to elect only three. For further details, *see* J. Sawicki, 'Prove tecniche di dissoluzione della democrazia liberale: Polonia 2016', *Nomos*, No. 1, 2016, pp. 2-7.

29 It should be remembered that the failure to take office of the three judges – whose election was declared compliant with the Constitution by the Constitutional Tribunal with the decision K 34/15, dated 3 December 2015 – is due to the fact that they could not take the oath because the President of the Republic refused to accept it (although in the same ruling cited, it was clearly stated that the qualifying element of the selection of such judges, as per constitutional text, is the election by the *Sejm*, while the oath ceremony is foreseen only by the implementing law, evidently as a due and formal act: or at least it is not an integrative and discretionary element of the formation of a will). Moreover, the aforementioned decision, like other subsequent ones, has never been recognized and published by the current Government.

30 *See* A. Angeli, 'Polonia. Le derive di una democrazia (quasi) maggioritaria', *federalismi.it*, No. 17, 2016; J. Sawicki, 'La conquista della Corte costituzionale ad opera della maggioranza che non si riconosce nella Costituzione', *Nomos*, No. 3, 2016. For a less critical position towards the PiS reforms *see* A. Młynarska-Sobaczewska, 'Polish Constitutional Tribunal Crisis: Political Dispute or Falling Kelsenian Dogma of Constitutional Review', *European Public Law*, Vol. 23, No. 3, 2017.

31 The act of 22 December 2015, which entered into force without *vacatio legis*, introduced a structural quorum to deliberate in full format of thirteen members, instead of the nine required by the previous version, which had the consequence of paralysing the activity of the Constitutional Tribunal, that at the time consisted of only twelve judges. It also established a functional quorum of two-thirds to deliberate on the constitutionality of a law in the majority of cases (through the incorrect direct application of Art. 190.5 cost., which provides that 'the decisions of the Constitutional Court [are] adopted by majority of the votes', that is to say by a relative majority of votes). It provided that public or closed-door hearings would be held according to the chronological order in which the individual cases had been registered; imposed a period of not less than three months, or – depending on the case – not less than six months between the notification of the hearing to the parties to the proceedings and the hearing itself. J. Sawicki, 'Prove tecniche di dissoluzione della democrazia liberale', cit.

(in particular decisions K47/15 of 9 March 2016,[32] K39/16 of 11 August 2016,[33] K 44/16 of 7 November 2016).[34] All legislative initiatives were accompanied by negative opinions from the Venice Commission which were only partially taken into consideration.[35]

32 This is a very relevant and long decision (over 200 pages), in which the act of 22 December 2015 (also called by its authors *ustawa naprawcza*, or 'reorganization act') *en bloc*, is declared unconstitutional. It provided for amendments to the act of the previous June on the Constitutional Tribunal, in particular with regard to raising the constitutive quorum – which at that moment would have determined a partial inoperativeness of the body – as well as the deliberative one in some circumstances – up to two-thirds of judges. It also provided for the obligation to examine the cases according to the strict chronological order of their presentation – up to void the examination of the amendment act itself – and established draconian disciplinary measures against the constitutional judges, up to the possibility for the *Sejm* to revoke a judge at the request of the President of the Republic. It is to be noted that some of these provisions had to be 'non applied' by the Constitutional Tribunal before being declared illegitimate, as the act of 22 December itself was put into force, deliberately, without *vacatio legis*, and the Tribunal recognized to have had to implement such a measure for reasons of *force majeure*, providing moreover a disputed direct application of the Constitution – Art. 8, para. 2 – which has never been recognized by the Government, the President of the Republic and the majority party.

33 It concerns the act of 22 July 2016 on the Constitutional Tribunal, partly flawed, *inter alia*, due to the fact that it provided for the possibility of forming countless blocking minorities, against decisions taken by majority vote, by a minority of dissenting judges (the same Tribunal, in the decision's reasoning, with the help of mathematicians has calculated up to 1365 combinations); the act was then censured as it consented the executive to condition the functioning of the body, both with regard to the conduct of the hearings and of the final publication of the decisions. It also provided for the obligation for the outgoing chair of the Tribunal to call in service the three judges who had already been proved improperly elected by the aforementioned decision K 34/15, as the vacancies had already been filled. The act also perpetrated an interference with the competences of the Constitutional Tribunal, due to the fact that it ordered the official publication of the decisions adopted 'before 20 July 2016', but subsequently to the aforementioned decision K 47/15 of 9 March 2016, included: this because, according to the same act, it would have been 'decisions taken in violation of the act of 25 June 2015 on the Constitutional Tribunal' (of course, in the version containing the amendments introduced on 22 December 2015). The publication of these decisions, by the admission of the majority itself, would have had a mere historical value, aimed at soothing the conflict that had already arisen with the EU.

34 Also unrecognized and unpublished, despite the fact that it considered consistent with the Constitution some provisions of the act of 22 July 2016, concerning the criteria to allow the President of the Republic the choice between a list of three – and no longer two – candidates for president of the Constitutional Tribunal (it was a decisive detail because it would have allowed the head of state to nominate a candidate of what was at the time still a 'minority' of judges, that is to say those in favour of the ruling party). This decision was not published under the pretext that three of the 'new' judges had refused to take part in the related hearings, protesting against the failed admission to the college, by outgoing president Andrzej Rzepliński, of the other three illegitimately elected in December 2015 (situation solved with the end of Rzepliński's mandate and the election of new judges for part of the *Sejm*), and against the decision to deliberate, as was also permitted by the act, in a restricted panel of five judges (which would have allowed to deliberate without the three 'rebel' judges). In reality, it was an interpretative decision, which declared the constitutionality of the contested provisions on the condition that they were intended to allow each judge to express their preferences in order to prevent the head of state from appointing a judge not appreciated by the majority of the college – but welcome to the PiS – and that could have hypothetically collected only his/her own vote. The non-recognition by the executive of this decision is what allowed the presentation of the candidacy of Julia Przyłębska, then effectively appointed as chair of the Tribunal.

35 CDL-AD(2016)001-e *Opinion on amendments to the Act of 25 June 2015 on the Constitutional Tribunal of Poland*, adopted by the Venice Commission at its 106th Plenary Session (Venice, 11-12 March 2016), of

However, it is of great interest and significance that all this hostile legislation, that can be defined as restrictive and sometimes punitive, was just useful as long as the judges in favour of the majority party were the minority in the body, and it has ceased to be convenient, being replaced by other acts, as soon as the following renewals have brought to a new majority more in line with the political one. This happened in almost lightning-fast times, with the two distinct acts on the status of judges of the Constitutional Tribunal and on the organization and proceedings before the Constitutional Tribunal, both adopted on 30 November 2016.[36]

Other restrictive acts have concerned the subjugation of key institutions of the political system and the exercise of a series of fundamental freedoms. Only as an example, let us remember[37]: the act of 15 January 2016, amending the act on Police (more skills in online surveillance, excluding judicial controls),[38] the act of 28 January 2016 on the Office of the Public Prosecutor[39] (that, repealing a 2008 reform, has returned to merge the office of the Attorney General with that of minister of justice, thus subjugating the prosecutors to the executive), the act of 18 March 2016 on the ombudsman (it limited the guarantees of independence of this figure, above all by unsatisfactorily redefining its functional immunity),[40] the act of 10 June 2016 on anti-terrorism measures. All these measures,[41] together with the new act on the public service of 30 December 2015 and others on public media and freedom of assembly (such as the act of 22 June 2016 on National Media Council and the act of 18 March 2017 that modified the law on the right of assembly, considered legit-

11 March 2016, e CDL-AD(2016)026-e Poland – *Opinion on the Act on the Constitutional Tribunal*, adopted by the Venice Commission at its 108th Plenary Session, (Venice, 14-15 October 2016), of 14 October 2016.

36 *See* for a comment: W. Sadurski, *How Democracy Dies (in Poland): A Case Study of Anti-Constitutional Populist Backsliding*, cit. Please *see also* the contents of Chapter 5 of this Volume.

37 A complete list of measures can be found in the Recommendations on the rule of law of the European Commission and also in W. Sadurski, *How Democracy Dies*, cit. *See also* L. Pech & P. Wachowiec, '*1095 Days Later: From Bad to Worse Regarding the Rule of Law in Poland (Part I)*', *VerfBlog*, 13 January 2019 and '*(Part II)*', *VerfBlog*, 17 January 2019. A useful timeline of the events can be found in: P. Gambatesa, 'Timeline of EU-Poland Relations Dealing with the Rule of Law', https://free-group.eu/2019/01/26/%EF%BB%BFtimeline-of-eu-poland-relations-dealing-with-the-rule-of-law/ (last accessed April 2019).

38 On which the opinion of the Venice Commission of 13 June 2016, CDL-AD(2016)012-e Poland – *Opinion on the Act of 15 January 2016 amending the Police Act and certain other Acts*, adopted by the Venice Commission at its 107th Plenary Session (Venice, 10-11 June 2016).

39 Opinion of the Venice Commission of 11 December 2017CDL-AD(2017)028-e *Poland – Opinion on the Act on the Public Prosecutor's office*, as amended, adopted by the Venice Commission at its 113th Plenary Session (Venice, 8-9 December 2017).

40 As shown in the preliminary opinion issued by OSCE/ODIHR, which can also be consulted on the Ombudsman's website, www.rpo.gov.pl/sites/default/files/282_NHRI_POL_27Jan2016_en_Preliminary.pdf (last accessed April 2019).

41 On some of which see the OSCE assessments: www.legislationline.org/search/runSearch/1/country/10/rows/10/type/2/page/1 (last accessed April 2019).

imate by the 'new' Constitutional Tribunal),[42] have profoundly undermined a series of fundamental rights, thus eroding the rule of law, as highlighted by the European Commission in its four recommendations on the rule of law (2016/1374 of 27 July 2016, 2017/146 of 21 December 2016, 2017/1520 of 26 July 2017, 2018/103 of 20 December 2017).

Moreover, there is the so-called 'justice package' (already partially outlined in Chapter 5 of this volume).[43] It is essentially composed of three laws, the one on 'general' courts (civil and criminal courts), the one that amends the act on the National Council of the Judiciary (KRS) and the act on the Supreme Court (SN), adopted in a first version in July 2017. It can certainly be assumed that the direction previously set to constitutional justice was the one that led to proceed undisturbed on the path of these 'systematic' reforms, motivated by a pretext and goal-oriented. The pretext is that – almost thirty years after the democratic transformation of the country – the entire judicial system in Poland is extremely corrupt and inefficient (the first thing largely false, the second closer to the truth), as well as fully 'post-communist', in the literal sense of the term, that is to say polluted, also ideologically, by elements belonging to the previous totalitarian system or by those that were in any case compromised with it (even a simple 'generational' kind of argument would be in contrast with this interpretation). For these reasons the judges would resist to that national and conservative revolution that the country would need.[44] The aim, at least in in view of the results, seems to be to obtain a judicial system more pliable to the political one, in the broad sense, given that the general criterion that they have attempted to impose implies that the filling of offices and the permanence in the same is tied to the arbitrariness of parliamentary decisions. In any case, the first act mentioned above was signed by the President of the Republic on 26 July 2017 and entered into force on 9 August 2017, giving the Minister of Justice the power to appoint and dismiss, without any substantial limitation, the presidents of civil and criminal courts, within a period of six months from the entry into force of the act.

The process of adopting the two acts on the modification of the act on the KRS and on the Supreme Court was definitively more troubled. In fact, it provoked a conflict with President of the Republic Duda, besides contributing in a decisive way to the activation of Article 7.1 TEU against Poland, together with several infringement actions before the

42 With the decision Kp 1/17 of 16 March 2017, whose content is summarized in English, http://trybunal.gov.pl/en/news/press-releases/after-the-hearing/art/9622-prawo-o-zgromadzeniach/ (last accessed April 2019).

43 A. Angeli, A. Di Gregorio & J. Sawicki, 'La controversa approvazione del "pacchetto giustizia" nella Polonia di "Diritto e Giustizia"', cit.; P. Mikuli, 'The Declining State of the Judiciary in Poland', *Int'l J.Const. L. Blog*, 15 May 2018; P. Mikuli, 'Tug of War between the Judiciary and the Minister of Justice: On Court Administration in Poland', *in* P. Mikuli (Ed.), *Current Challenges in Court Administration*, The Hague Eleven, 2017.

44 These arguments, in addition to being widely present in the PiS election campaign in 2015, are also reported in a document prepared by the Government to 'defend' itself against European criticisms (and infringement procedures) – namely the White Paper (*see* below).

European Court of Justice.[45] On 24 July 2017, President Duda referred both acts to the *Sejm* (with no chance of adoption by the qualified majority) and on 24 September transmitted to the *Sejm* two new drafts on his own initiative. Following the rejection of the presidential projects, on 8 December the parliament approved the two new acts, on the Supreme Court and on the amendment of the KRS act – which indeed contained very little novelty with respect to the drafts presented in July 2017 – that entered into force on 3 April 2018 and 3 January 2018 respectively (except for some provisions in force since 17 January 2018) and were then amended following the request of the European Court of Justice (*see infra*).

In a nutshell, it is possible to detect two extremely critical aspects in these two acts. The first one is the dismissal of a great number of judges of the Supreme Court, including its first president, through the well-known pretext of anticipated (and retroactive) retirement age, which led to an actual 'purge'. This is the most striking aspect – that grabbed the attention of the international public opinion – but not the most worrisome one (considering that these same judges would have anyway retired in a few years). Indeed, the most deceitful aspect is the one related to the composition of the judicial self-government body, the National Council of the Judiciary, highly politicized. Through this institution, a complete renovation of the Supreme Court composition has been carried out, allowing the appointment of a great number of new judges, closer to PiS (*e.g.* seconded prosecutors to the Minister of Justice). These new judges have been appointed to the two newly created sections of the Supreme Court, *i.e.* the 'disciplinary' section and the 'supreme control of public affairs' one. The first one is a particularly coveted section, because of the privileged economic treatment of its members, and a greatly feared body in the judicial environment. The second one is endowed with the competence of reviewing a wide range of final judgments and of checking electoral processes. A relevant number of requests for preliminary ruling, referred by Polish judges on these issues, are currently pending before the CJEU.

Further critical aspects related to the PiS 'power takeover' concern several new appointments in public institutions and public companies, as well as the reform of school programs in a more conservative and patriotic direction.[46]

As highlighted by some Polish constitutionalists,[47] PiS 'reform' project has been planned a long time in advance, and then accurately perpetrated. It is no coincidence that the

45 J. Sawicki, 'La via giudiziaria come possibile soluzione alle minacce per lo stato di diritto: la Polonia dinanzi alla Corte di giustizia dell'Unione europea', *Osservatorio AIC*, 2019.

46 Including an ultra-Catholic one: following a failed PiS initiative in 2006, in April 2016 the parliament approved the symbolic coronation of Jesus Christ as King of Poland. The ceremony solemnly took place on 19 November 2016, in Krakow, at the presence of the highest state institutions, included the President of the Republic.

47 T.T. Koncewicz, 'Farewell to the Separation of Powers – On the Judicial Purge and the Capture in the Heart of Europe', *VerfBlog*, 19 July 2017; A. Śledzińska-Simon, 'The Polish Revolution: 2015-2017', *Int'l J. Const. L. Blog*, 25 July 2017. This latter author considers also the indirect consequences of the judicial reform.

Constitutional Tribunal has been initially 'paralysed' and then made harmless, in order to prevent acts introduced by the new government from being declared not in conformity to the constitution.[48] This confirms that the PiS did not simply emulate the Hungarian 'model', but followed a precise and independent political and ideological path, as it had already unsuccessfully tried to do between 2005 and 2007.[49] It should also be considered that the attack on judicial power followed a number of 'unpleasant' judgments – and of public inquiries that involved important political leaders – issued by judges that consequently 'had to be silenced' (see the well-known *affaire* Kamiński). The launch of the judicial reform was preceded by a defamatory campaign towards judges, portrayed as a self-referential and corrupt élite. In March 2018, in order to justify the reforms, the Prime Minister's chancellery published a white paper, in which the legislative 'package' on the judiciary was presented as necessary to comply with European standards regulating judicial independence and efficiency, as well as to ensure the respect of the rule of law principle.[50]

Different antibodies, both internal and external, were activated in order to fight against the constitutional devolution of these last years. Among the internal ones, we should mention public demonstrations (both spontaneous and organized by opposition parties) in which public readings of the constitution took place, the role of independent media, law faculties (even though some constitutional lawyers have supported the reforms, being in exchange elected as constitutional judges).[51] We should also consider the activities of several NGOs, of a spontaneous movement which was originally created on Facebook, *i.e.* KOD *Komitet Obrony Demokracji* (Committee for the Defence of Democracy), followed by the movement *Obywatele RP* (Citizens of Poland), and of a recent academic initiative for the rule of law.[52] Further antibodies have been activated up to now by ordinary judges

---

Among them, the management of control activities on elections and referendums, attributed to the Supreme Court; the control over the State Tribunal, which rules on the constitutional liability of people holding the highest offices of state and is headed by the first president of the Supreme Court, *etc.*

48 The CT opposed resistance through the set of judgements previously listed, before being 'paralysed'.

49 On PiS ideology *see* W. Bunikowski, 'The Crisis in Poland, and Schmittian Questions in "the Rule of Law" Debate', paper presented at the workshop 'The Erosion of the Rule of Law in East Central Europe', University of Helsinki, 15 February 2017. Some authors believe in an underestimation of the PiS political program in 2005: I. Krastev, 'The Strange Death of the Liberal Consensus', *Journal of Democracy*, Vol. 18, No. 4, 2007 and T. Daly, 'Diagnosing Democratic Decay, Comparative Constitutional Law Roundtable', Gilbert & Tobin Centre of Public Law, Sydney, UNSW, 07 August 2017, www.academia.edu/34052302/Diagnosing_Democratic_Decay (last accessed April 2019).

50 www.premier.gov.pl/mobile/en/news/news/the-government-presents-a-white-paper-on-the-reforms-of-the-polish-justice-system.html (last accessed April 2019).

51 As, *e.g.*, the present-day vice-president of the CT, Mariusz Muszyński.

52 https://ruleoflaw.pl/announcement-launching-new-resource-on-rule-of-law-in-poland (last accessed April 2019).

and local self-government bodies.[53] This is probably the reason that made it necessary to silence them, after the Constitutional Tribunal became a subservient body of the executive power.[54]

As for external pressures, they mainly consist in the mobilization of the international public opinion and in to a set of initiatives promoted by European Union's institutions (along with the behaviour of some Member States' courts, *e.g.* in relation to the denial to execute European Arrest Warrants issued by Polish authorities).[55] However, the only actual possibility to influence the Polish government would be a decision of the EU Commission to launch formal infringement procedures, according to Article 258 TFUE, by referring the issues to the Court of Justice. Such a countermeasure has already been experimented in the Hungarian case, with limited results (the Court of Justice found that Hungary failed to fulfil its EU obligations by lowering the retirement age of the judges; however most of them, with few exceptions, accepted a monetary compensation and were not reinstated in their own functions[56]; moreover, Hungary still refuses to comply with the CJEU judgment

53 *See* ordinary judges and regional councils repeated calls to comply with the judgements of the CT – despite the fact that the most intolerable for the government were not published – and the commitment of several judges not to recognize judgments adopted by three 'false' constitutional judges.

54 As testified by a set of decisions adopted since 2017, which legitimized judicial reforms or supported the position of governing majority in several ways. On this topic *see* W. Brzozowski, 'Can the constitutional court accelerate democratic backsliding? Lessons from the Polish experience', *in* M. Belov (Ed.), *Courts and Politics. Judicialization of Politics and Politicization of Judiciary*, Oxford, Routledge, *forthcoming*, 2019. The author identifies three different phases in the PiS takeover of the CT ('origins': duplicate constitutional judges; 'neutralization' stage: attempts at disabling the TC; 'absorption' stage: hostile takeover). As for the attitude of the CT since 2017, the author distinguishes decisions in which CT has shown a 'militant populism' (Judgment K 1/17 of 2017, in which CT stated that 'duplicate' judges were legitimate; K 10/17 of 2017 where CT ruled that ordinary courts were not entitled to ascertain the validity of the president of the CT); 'abetted' the government (K 5/17 of 2017: the National Council of the Judiciary in its previous composition was not legitimate and the parliament was endowed with full discretion in designing a new one; K 12/18 of 2019: the new NCJ is consistent with the Constitution); or has acted as a 'silent' supporter (Kp 1/17 of 2017, in which it approved the controversial amendment of the act on cyclic public gatherings; K 9/17 of 2018: the President of the Republic can grant pardon, in whatever moment, even prior to the final judgment).

55 The Irish High Court presented a request for a preliminary ruling before the Court of Justice, that accepted the request for an urgent procedure (Case C-216/18 PPU, Judgment of the Court (Grand Chamber) of 25 July 2018, ECLI:EU:C:2018:586). According to the CJUE, even if it is possible to rely on the EU Commission reports on the systemic violation of the rule of law in Poland, it is still necessary for the national court – called to decide whether a person in respect of whom a EAW has been issued is to be surrendered – to determine, specifically and precisely, whether there are substantial grounds to believe that that person will run such a risk. As stressed by S. Bartole, 'La crisi della giustizia polacca davanti alla Corte di giustizia: il caso Celmer', *Quaderni costituzionali*, No. 4, 2018, the only body in charge of rendering a final decision on the violation of the rule of law is the European Council. Up to that moment, MS are compelled to the general obligation of cooperation and mutual respect. *See also* M. Krajewski, 'Who is Afraid of the European Council? The Court of Justice's Cautious Approach to the Independence of Domestic Judges: ECJ 25 July 2018, Case C-216/18 PPU, The Minister for Justice and Equality v LM', *European Constitutional Law Review*, Vol. 14, No. 4, December 2018; C. Pinelli, 'Violazioni sistemiche dei diritti fondamentali e crisi di fiducia fra Stati membri in un rinvio pregiudiziale della High Court d'Irlanda', *Quaderni costituzionali*, No. 4, 2018.

56 For further details *see* A. Di Gregorio, 'The Fundamental Law of Hungary in the European context', cit.

on mandatory relocation of asylum seekers of 6 September 2017).[57] Furthermore, the infringement procedure takes a long time and has a set of limitations, given that it was not originally designed for 'systemic' violations of EU fundamental values. Following the first one of 29 July 2017,[58] a number of infringement initiatives have been launched by the Commission in the following months,[59] which led Poland to revise some of the most controversial acts.[60] On the other hand, the rule of law framework, activated for the first time against Poland, has already failed in achieving concrete results in October 2016. Poland was given a three months period to amend specific provisions considered to be in breach of the rule of law, but the deadline expired without any tangible result, and the same can be said of the two further months provided with the new Recommendation of 21 December

57 A. Circolo, 'Il principio di solidarietà tra impegno volontario e obbligo giuridico. La pronuncia della Corte di Giustizia (GS) nel caso Slovacchia e Ungheria c. Consiglio', *DPCE on line*, No. 1, 2018.

58 Sending a letter of formal notice to the Polish Government. Unfortunately, only limited aspects of the wide judicial package, which consists of four acts, can be contested, *i.e.* gender discrimination in judges' retirement age, which breaches Art. 157 TFUE and Directive 2006/54. In the letter of formal notice, however, the Commission condemned the wide discretionary powers conferred to the Minister of Justice, which was found inconsistent with the principle of judicial independence, as set out in Art. 19(1)TEU and Art. 47 of the Charter of Fundamental Rights.

59 In December 2017, the Commission officially referred Poland to the Court of Justice for the act on ordinary courts (Case C-192/18, *Commission v. Poland*). In particular, the Commission censored both the difference in retirement age of male and female judges, and the discretionary power of the minister of justice in extending the period of active service for judges who attained the retirement age. Following the already mentioned Judgment in Case Celmer, on 2 October 2018 the Commission referred Poland to the Court of Justice, based on Art. 258 TFUE, for the act on the Supreme Court (*Commission v. Poland*, Case C-619/18). The application concerns the lowering of judges retirement age from 70 to 65 years (which would have led to the retirement of 38 percent of judges in office, including the first president of SC) and, in this case also, the discretionary power of the head of state in extending the period of active service of the judges, upon request of a given judge and upon proposal of the National Council of the Judiciary (recently transformed into a politically subservient body). Following this second application, the vice-president of the Court of Justice ordered to suspend the entry into force of the act (*see* the next footnote) pending the decision of the Court (expected for end of May 2019). On 3 April 2019, the Commission launched a further infringement procedure, with reference to the new disciplinary regime for judges http://europa.eu/rapid/press-release_IP-19-1957_en.htm (last accessed April 2019). References on these events are extremely wide, both in constitutional and EU law. *See, among others*, M. Granat, 'Political and Legal Enforcement of the Rule of Law in Poland', *Quaderni costituzionali*, No. 4, 2018; A. Sledzinska-Simon, 'The Rise and Fall of Judicial Self-Government in Poland: On Judicial Reform Reversing Democratic Transition', *German Law Journal*, No. 7, 2018; A. Pertici, 'Il rispetto dei valori fondanti dell'Unione e l'attivazione della procedura di controllo alla luce delle recenti vicende di Polonia e Ungheria', *DPCEonline*, No. 1, 2019; M.A. Orlandi, 'La "democrazia illiberale". Ungheria e Polonia a confronto', *Diritto pubblico comparato ed europeo*, No. 1, 2019. *See also*, 'Editorial Comments', *Common Market Law Review*, Vol. 54, 2017.

60 On 17 December 2018, the President of the Republic signed Act of 21 November 2018 'that amends the Act on the Supreme Court', which entered into force on 1st January 2019. The new Act repeals Art. 37, paras. 1-4 and Art. 111, paras. 1 and 1a of the Act on the Supreme Court and reinstates judges of the Supreme Court, including its first president, who underwent anticipated retirement. Act of 21 November 2018 followed the Order of 19 October 2019 of the vice-president of the Court of Justice – adopted upon request of the Commission of 2 October 2018 – in which Polish authorities were required to temporary suspend the implementation of some provisions of the Act on the Supreme Court. The request of the Commission has finally been accepted with the Order of the Grand Chamber of the Court of Justice of 17 December 2018.

2016.[61] On 26 July 2017, the European Commission adopted a new Rule of Law Recommendation threatening to trigger Article 7 TUE against Poland, and so it did in December 2017.[62] The Commission's proposal of 2 May 2018 of a new mechanism to protect the EU budget from financial risks linked to generalized deficiencies regarding the rule of law in the Member States should also be mentioned. The new proposed tools would allow the Union to suspend, reduce or restrict access to EU funding in a manner proportionate to the nature, gravity and scope of the rule of law's deficiencies. Such a decision would be proposed by the Commission and adopted by the Council through reverse qualified majority voting (the proposal was amended by the European Parliament on 17 January 2019).[63]

Poland is only apparently following the Hungarian path. Not having a 'constitutional' majority in parliament (the one that in Hungary supported a more linear process), the PiS was obliged to introduce its reforms through ordinary laws – emptying and delegitimizing the Constitution – in breach of a consolidated constitutional jurisprudence.[64] At the beginning of the constitutional crisis, the Constitutional Tribunal has strenuously attempted to resist thanks to the international support and the backing of other judges. Nowadays, it can no longer be considered independent, and it is almost entirely composed by 'loyalist'[65] judges. Indeed, it has stopped issuing constitutionally meaningful decisions, and it is now

61 Even if the Polish parliament repealed some of the most controversial provisions of the Act on the Constitutional Tribunal of 22 July 2016, this latter has been negatively evaluated in the opinion of the Venice Commission of 15 October 2018.

62 COM (2017) 835: 'Proposal for a Council Decision on the determination of a clear risk of a serious breach by the Republic of Poland of the rule of law', www.europarl.europa.eu/RegData/docs_autres_institutions/commission_europeenne/com/2017/0835/COM_COM(2017)0835_EN.pdf (last accessed April 2019). For an update on the ongoing proceedings, *see* https://oeil.secure.europarl.europa.eu/oeil/popups/ficheprocedure.do?lang=en&reference=2017/0360(OLP) (last accessed April 2019). M.A: Orlandi, 'La Polonia di Kaczyński: l'approvazione del "pacchetto giustizia" e l'avvio della procedura dell'art. 7 TUE', *DPCEonline*, No. 4, 2017; M. Taborowski, 'The European Commission Launches Art. 7 TEU Proceedings against Poland for Breach of Rule of Law', *Quaderni costituzionali*, No. 1, 2018.

63 On this issue, *see* A. Somma, 'L'Europa difende lo Stato di diritto per affossare il welfare', *Sbilanciamoci.info*, 29 January 2019.

64 To be considered together with original shortcomings of the Constitution, *i.e.* the election of constitutional judges by the lower chamber with a simple majority, the absence of stricter requirements for the selection of constitutional judges and the reference made by the Constitution to an ordinary and non a constitutional act to regulate the activity of the CT.

65 Thanks not only to the appointment of three 'unconstitutional' judges – who are holding the office in place of the three judges legitimately elected in October 2015, who were prevented from taking their oath before the head of State – and to new vacancies occurred in the CT. Except for the three so-called 'anti-judges', only six among the remaining twelve judges have not been elected by the PiS (Kieres, Pyziak-Szafnicka, Rymar, Tuleja, Wronkowska-Jaśkiewicz, Zubik). Moreover, the term of office of judge Wronkowska-Jaśkiewicz will end in May 2019, and that of Rymar, Tuleja and Zubik in December 2019.

supporting the governing majority in its case law.[66] We witness a complete derogation of the Constitution, similarly to what had happened during the communist rule.[67]

Anyway, being the constitutional regression in Poland closest in time if compared to the Hungarian one, the development of a sort of 'parallel' legal and judicial system can be witnessed (as it happened, in a milder way, in Hungary).[68] In Poland, in fact, there is an ongoing confrontation between the political majority, on one side (government, head of State, parliament, National Council of the Judiciary and Constitutional Tribunal already transformed), and subjects and institutions that are resisting on the other (the Supreme Court, especially its first chair Gersdorf, almost all other judges, academia, opposition, and street protests movements).[69] Among other things, attempts to introduce a diffused

66 Among the decisions in which the Court, in the aftermath of its 'packing', took a politically stance in line with ruling majority, it is worth mentioning judgment of 16 March 2017 Kp 1/17 on holding periodic assemblies. In it, the CT privileged scheduled meetings, instead of spontaneous or short-noticed ones, thus limiting the freedom of expression and protest. Four dissenting opinions were attached to the final judgment: judges Wronkowska-Jaśkiewicz, Pyziak-Szafnicka and Kieres addressed the issue on the merit and judge Pszczółkowski (appointed in December 2015) expressed his dissent on the decision of the CT not to admit one of the questions asked by the President of the Republic, https://ipo.trybunal.gov.pl/ipo/view/sprawa.xhtml?&pokaz=dokumenty&sygnatura=Kp%201/17 (last accessed April 2019). In the judgment, the CT answered the requests of the President of the Republic related to the act of 13 December 2016, that amended the Act on Peaceful Assembly of 24 July 2015. The amendment act introduced a new category of public assembly, *i.e.* cyclic assembly: an event organized at least four times a year in the last three years. The act pursued the goal to commemorate the most relevant events of the Polish history. In the authorization process, therefore, such events should be privileged compared to other gatherings scheduled for that same date and place. The CT ruled that such provision is in conformity with the principle of equality before law. According to the CT, the possibility to hold an event in a specific date/location should be ensured with certainty to the promoters of the cyclic assemblies, *i.e.* events organized well in advance and with a certain frequency, considering that "at other times or places it would be irrelevant for their purpose which is to commemorate events of major importance to the history of the Republic". For an update on case-law refer, in Italian, to the quarterly chronicles Sawicki in *Nomos. Le attualità nel diritto*; in English, please refer to surveys published annually by *Global Review of Constitutional Law.* Among the most recent ones, *see* T.T. Koncewicz & A. Podolska, 'Poland', *2018 Global Review of Constitutional Law.*

67 J. Sawicki, *Prove tecniche di dissoluzione della democrazia liberale*, cit.

68 Considering that common courts in Hungary retain a certain degree of independence, Fidesz proposed the establishment of administrative courts. Two acts on the administrative courts system and on a new separated self-government body have been adopted on 12 December 2018. The new courts will start to operate in 2020. Thanks to this reform, Fidesz will have the opportunity to appoint 'loyalist' judges, which will be required to address controversies with a highly political impact (taxation, public procurement, asylum, electoral appeals, freedom of information, *etc.*). The Venice Commission has been rather critical in the opinion on the new Act on administrative tribunals of 19 March 2019, CDL-AD(2019)004-e Hungary – *Opinion on the law on administrative courts and the law on the entry into force of the law on administrative courts and certain transitional rules*, adopted by the Venice Commission at its 118th Plenary Session (Venice, 15-16 March 2019). Addressing some of the concerns expressed by the Venice Commission – even if showing as always, a truly ambiguous attitude towards European institutions – the Hungarian government decided to amend the acts adopted in December 2018. On 1st April 2019, the parliament approved a set of amendments, which only partially took into account the remarks of the Venice Commission. On this issue, *see* R. Uitz, 'What Does the Spring Bring for the Rule of Law in Europe?', *VerfBlog*, 6 April 2019.

69 Sawicki, *La via giudiziaria come possibile soluzione alle minacce per lo stato di diritto*, cit.

judicial review of legislation have been carried out, as it can be noticed in some decisions of the Supreme Court or of the Supreme Administrative Court. This is justified by the doctrine referring to the principles of necessity and direct application of the Constitution (as set out in Art. 8, para. 2 const.).[70]

This internal confrontation is accompanied by a dialogue between national judges and the EU Court of Justice. The large number of requests for preliminary rulings presented in these last months – in order to defend the principle of judicial independence (undermined by the violation of judges immovability, the full discretion of the head of State in the prorogation of the term of office, *etc.*) – was followed by 'retaliation' of the already manipulated judicial self-government body, which started disciplinary proceedings against these judges. Waiting for the results of European elections, but above all of the next parliamentary ones, a hope for change comes from the division present within the ruling élite, that unlike the Hungarian one, does not seem united.[71]

The neutralization of institutional checks and balances in these two countries shows both differences and similarities. Firstly, considering the different political majorities of conservative parties in the two countries (more than two-thirds majority in Hungary and absolute majority in Poland), constitutional regression had a different impact on the constitutions. In Hungary, the political majority had the chance to rewrite constitutional rules 'in his own image and likeness'. In Poland, on the other hand, the constitution has been disregarded, and openly violated (starting from the very beginning of the political takeover). Another relevant difference concerns the nature of the ruling party and its leadership. If in the Hungarian case the leadership is evident and undisputed, in Poland the effective political leader is a 'simple' Member of Parliament. Moreover, the longer permanence in power of Orbán makes any positive evolution in the short time improbable, also considering the massive institutional transformation taking place and that the electoral legislation in force is an obstacle to political turnovers. Despite this sad picture, examining the constitutional jurisprudence subsequent to the neutralization of the Constitutional Court, it can be said that it demonstrates a more articulated and sophisticated legal reasoning, if com-

70 Among the others *see* A. Gołębiewski, 'Review of the Constitutionality of Law in the Direct Application of the Constitution', *Annuals of the Administration and Law*, Vol. 17, No. 1, 2017.

71 Some conflicts between the President and the parliament (maybe artificially orchestrated?) have occurred. For example, the Senate, which is dominated by the PiS, blocked the presidential proposal to hold a consultative constitutional referendum, which would have strengthened the role of the head of state (26 July 2018). This latter in turn vetoed the reform of the European electoral law, that would have significantly heightened the quorum (17 August 2018). J. Sawicki, 'L'esecutivo si prepara a conquistare l'ordine giudiziario, che resiste appellandosi a una debole Europa', *Nomos*, No. 2, 2018, pp. 5-6.

pared to that of the Polish CT.[72] The attitude towards constitutional values of the current Polish leadership should be considered as 'rough and brutal'.[73]

The role of international organizations, mainly the Council of Europe and the European Union, has been ambivalent. On one side, as already said, such institutions favoured, up to a certain moment, important reforms. On the other, the failure of democratic conditionality in the aftermath of the accession to the European Union is blatant, as is the inadequacy of the integration model privileged by the EU. This latter neglected social profiles which were vital for countries who had experienced the communist 'solidarity', and which were not ready for a pure liberalist model.[74]

What is happening in Hungary and Poland represents a real danger for European constitutionalism. It is not a coincidence that Poland and Hungary are the most examined cases (through a multidisciplinary approach).[75] They not only present a concrete risk of imitation, but they also pose a real threat to the credibility of the entire European Union. Both the ability of the EU to defend itself from attacks on its core values, and the complex mechanisms set out for the enlargement process and the integration of 'young' democracies have been questioned. The paradigm of 'successful' transition from socialist system to constitutional democracy is undermined, even though it is not correct to assert that a democratic system failed to be consolidated in the twenty years after 1989.

A consideration on values – if they are really shared among European countries – is essential and must be complemented by a reflection on procedures and measures (on which the literature is constantly focused) aiming at stopping or slowing down these systemic transformations. Great attention should also be paid to the narrative on 'constitutional identity',[76] particularly misused in Hungary. This narrative tends to manipulate the TEU clause which protects national identities (Art. 4, para. 2) not considering the duty of solidarity[77] and the long and difficult path that led to the current European Union. Polish and

72 In the legal reasoning of the Hungarian Court a higher degree of maturity is detectable, even when it supports the governing majority.

73 It clearly emerges from the manipulation of fundamental principles such as the rule of law, in order to justify the reforms in Poland, as well as from documents such as the already mentioned *White Paper*, and the *Report of the Team of Experts on the Issues Related to the Constitutional Tribunal* of 15 July 2016, available at: www.sejm.gov.pl/media8.nsf/files/ASEA-ADRKC8/%24File/Report%20of%20the%20Team%20of%20Experts%20on%20the%20Issues%20Related%20to%20the%20Constitutional%20Tribunal.pdf (last accessed April 2019).

74 It is not a coincidence that both Fidesz and PiS resorted to public subsidies (especially for families) in order to strengthen their electoral support.

75 Among the others, *see* special issues dedicated to this topic on *Hague Journal on the Rule of Law*, Vol. 10, No. 1, April 2018 (Special Issue on the Crisis of Constitutional Democracy in Central and Eastern Europe); *Journal of Democracy*, Vol. 29, No. 3, July 2018 (Explaining Eastern Europe).

76 On this topic, *see* the dedicated section in the *German Law Journal*, Vol. 18, No. 7, 2017.

77 On this topic, *see* D. Keleman & L. Pech, 'Why autocrats love constitutional identity and constitutional pluralism. Lesson from Hungary and Poland', *Working Paper No. 2*, September 2018, www.reconnect-

Hungarian conservative rulers failed to concur with a vision of a European 'community' that is not opposed to the national one, and does not envisage to destroy it, but on the contrary to harmoniously interact with it.

europe.eu (last accessed April 2019). *See also* the special section on Constitutional Identity in Europe of the *German Law Journal*, Vol. 18, No. 7, 2017.

Comparative Public Law Treatise

Founded and directed by Giuseppe Franco Ferrari

Vincenzo De Falco, Administrative Action and Procedures in Comparative Law, 2018, ISBN 978-94-6236-842-2

Silvio Gambino, Jorge Lozano Miralles, Fernando Puzzo, Juan José Ruiz Ruiz, The Spanish Constitutional System, 2018, ISBN 978-94-6236-843-9

Eloy Garcia, Elisabetta Palici di Suni, Martin Rogoff, Direct Democracy in Comparative Law, 2018, ISBN 978-94-6236-844-6

Mauro Mazza (Ed.), The Constitutional Systems of East Asia, 2019, ISBN 978-94-6236-898-9

Angela di Gregorio (Ed.), The Constitutional Systems of Central-Eastern, Baltic and Balkan Europe, 2019, ISBN 978-94-6236-965-8

9 789462 369658

Printed by Libri Plureos GmbH in Hamburg,
Germany